THEORIES OF KNOWLEDGE:
A Critical Introduction

THEORIES OF KNOWLEDGE:
A Critical Introduction

ROBERT ACKERMANN
Associate Professor of Philosophy
Washington University

McGRAW-HILL BOOK COMPANY
New York   St. Louis   San Francisco   Toronto   London   Sydney

THEORIES OF KNOWLEDGE:
A Critical Introduction

Library of Congress Catalog Card Number 64 -8725

6789 DODO 79876543

For Inge

PREFACE

This book is an introductory study of the epistemological thought of seven major philosophers. Some passages from the philosophical writings of these philosophers have been reprinted as source material to which the study is directed. These passages have been chosen as representative of important arguments that are pertinent to the contemporary construction of a satisfactory theory of knowledge. Each philosopher is introduced by three chapters which attempt to exposit the important epistemological problems which the philosopher deals with in the reprinted passages and to give some characterization of the answers to them that he took to be most satisfactory. The passages have been augmented by critical footnotes explaining unusual terms or locutions and occasionally pointing to difficulties in interpretation which the student should want to consider. All this material is designed to aid the instructor of philosophy courses by raising certain philosophical issues in the course of a student's assigned reading. My hope is that this will free classroom time for careful discussion of the topics that the instructor considers to be most important.

Because of the focus on epistemological passages, the book can be considered as a text for courses in epistemology. At the same time, the introductory chapters and critical footnotes presuppose no previous philosophical training, so that the book may be suitable for use in any first course in philosophy that deals with epistemological issues. An attempt has been made to keep the book economical enough to permit the combination of this book with some appropriate paperbound editions in the planning of a semester's course.

Italics have been used to note mention of single words. They have also been used to note any occurrence of a symbol which is used as a naming expression as in the locution 'Let A be a group of human beings.' These usages should not be confused with italics of emphasis, and I believe that context is sufficient to mark these distinctions. Double quotes are used for the quotation of sentences, with only the punctuation of the sentence being quoted appearing within the double quotes. Single quotes are used to note the mention of phrases which are parts of sentences, in many cases to note the mention of phrases which would be turned into sentences by the substitution of appropriate terms for symbols which occur in the phrases. While such discrimination may seem excessive, it is necessary to maintain some of the distinctions that philosophers find it useful to draw.

The bibliographies which accompany the readings for each philosopher are not intended to be complete: they are meant to provide some suggestions for a student's further reading. It is assumed that an instructor using this book may wish to supplement these bibliographies by consideration of the topics he treats in class as well as by consideration of the library services available to his students. In particular, an evaluation of the various translations and editions of the philosophers studied is left to the discretion of the instructor. Bibliography entries for works that were available in paperbound editions as this manuscript was being completed have been marked with an asterisk.

I should like to express my gratitude to the publishing houses that have granted the reprint rights necessary for the source material which appears in the book. I am also grateful to Lewis White Beck, Arthur Danto, and D. J. O'Connor for helpful comments on various drafts of the manuscript.

ROBERT ACKERMANN

CONTENTS

Introduction

The issues that surround the general problem of investigating the nature and extent of human knowledge are known collectively by philosophers as the problems of epistemology. It is very important to realize from the beginning that epistemology is never undertaken from a completely naïve position. By the time any philosopher comes to reflect on the problem of what human beings can be said to know, he has already acquired a reasonably formidable education and some degree of sophistication. It is impossible for a philosopher to discover what he knows by simply thinking back to the time when nothing was known to him (if there was such a time) and then slowly tracing the acquisition of his knowledge. Indeed, another question must be answered first: what is described when one speaks of human knowledge? Unless this question is answered, a study of epistemology is totally useless, since it would not be possible to distinguish those moments which represented the acquisition of knowledge from those moments which represented, for example, the acquisition of nonsense.

The philosopher who is interested in epistemology is thus forced to begin in the middle of things by examining the results of what would normally be called his education. He will surely say a variety of things which might be cast into the general grammatical form 'I know that ———— .', where the blank space is filled with a phrase describing some item of information. Among these statements the following examples, or claims of a similar nature, may well occur:

1. I know that $3 + 5 = 8$.
2. I know that it will rain this afternoon.
3. I know that something caused the water to stop running.
4. I know that the Dodgers will win the pennant.
5. I know that I left the back door unlatched.

The grammatical similarity of form which the statements of this list exhibit

1

is not taken by any important philosopher to represent a single sense of the word *know*, since we feel quite differently on reflection about the certainty of the various things that are said to be known on any complete list which would be an extension of the list of statements just given. In some intuitive sense, we surely feel less secure about some of the items than about others.

One question often asked of someone who says 'I know that ——— .' is 'Are you sure (that ———)?'. With reference to the list, someone uttering all of the examples at various times might feel that 1–3 are all true, but that 4 and 5 are open to doubt and may in fact not be true if some check were to be made. In this case, he may say that he *knows* (in some stronger sense) only the items of information referred to in the first three sentences. The point is that when we are asked what we know in a situation where we must defend against possibly hostile criticism, we are likely to be more cautious in our claims to information than we would be at other times. And in the face of sustained criticism, we may often want to retreat to the position that we *know* only those things which are not open to any reasonable objection.

A great deal of technical philosophical epistemology has been developed by philosophers who have subjected the results of their own formal education or official schooling to severe and hostile criticism in an effort to winnow out those claims which will stand against any reasonable doubt. A philosopher may suddenly discover that he says that he knows many things of palpably differing certainty, or even that some of his information is contradictory. An obvious way of proceeding at this point to answer the question of the extent of his knowledge is to pick from it some examples he is certain are most defensible in some intuitive sense. Studying these examples, he can then look for some qualities that distinguish them from examples that he feels can be or should be questioned, if not dropped outright from the information that he wishes to take as defensible knowledge. On the basis of this investigation, a philosopher usually ends by giving a definition of *knowledge,* as distinct from *opinion* or *belief.* *Knowledge* then constitutes those claims that he thinks are ultimately defensible, while *opinion* or *belief* constitutes those claims for which *some* justification is possible, but not a complete defense. This way of looking at the start of epistemological investigations stresses the investigator's *feeling* of certainty about some of his knowledge claims. Because of this, it would not be surprising that different investigators should select different examples of knowledge as the basis of their definitions. Indeed the notion of *reasonable* objection is subjective to the point that we would expect major philosophers to disagree over the examples that may be accepted as paradigm or model instances of human knowledge. We will look at the basic epistemological problem not as that of discovering the *true* extent of human knowledge, but as that of *deciding* which of our ordinary knowledge claims can properly be called examples of human knowledge, and then of investigating the difference between these examples and examples of opinion in an effort to *justify* the decision. We will consider seven major philosophers who have chosen differently the paradigm cases of knowledge, and we will do this in an effort to determine how epistemology may enable us to make a consistent theory of knowledge out of the confusing class of purported claims to knowledge that accrue when we listen to those who profess to know something. In epistemology one does not try to build a system of knowledge from nothing, but one tries to *select* some relatively clear examples of knowledge in order to discover what else may reasonably be considered knowledge. On such a basis it is possible to create a consistent and useful account of all human information.

It should be immediately clear that the epistemological problem is one of the most basic problems of philosophy. An answer to it must be either found or presupposed before one can answer the more specific questions "What can I know about the world? (science)" or "What can I know about behaving in a moral fashion? (ethics)" or "What can I know about beauty? (aesthetics)" or any of the other questions that occupy philosophers with specialized interests.

Our survey of different positions with respect to some of the basic problems of epistemology will be made by considering seven major philosophers of the Western philosophical tradition. We shall do this by considering these seven philosophers in the order of their historical appearance, although biographical information about these philosophers will be almost totally suppressed. For our purposes they will be treated as contemporaries, that is, as though their basic positions could still be maintained by present-day philosophers. As a matter of fact, variations of these seven positions are taken by present-day philosophers (as well as other positions which we will not consider), although a present-day Platonist, for example, would have to defend against more subtle criticisms raised by other philosophers than Plato had to defend against. This has resulted in modifications of some of the positions which major historical figures seem to have argued for.

Of the seven philosophers, the first two, Plato and Aristotle, are distinguished by their appearance in Greek culture over two thousand years ago. In broad outlines, they established the problems that have occupied epistemologists to the present day, subject only to the more sophisticated problems that some recent discoveries in the natural sciences have raised. For this reason, they occupy a particularly important place in the history of Western philosophy. Plato and Aristotle, along with some other Greek philosophers, may be looked on as the beginning of epistemology as we have characterized it, and this appearance of epistemological problems in Greek thought unpreceded by any other epistemological reflection is worth some detailed consideration.

Perhaps the most important characteristic of Greek philosophy, that which may ultimately be judged to be the most important reason for its continuing influence, is its dependence upon human reason for the solution of problems. This statement raises a tangle of problems that are difficult to deal with. The first of these is the question of what is meant by human reason. Rather than attempting an answer to this question here, in view of the immense problems which the question of the nature of human reason has raised in philosophy and psychology, we can make useful progress without controversy by simply identifying it with what many people refer to when they speak of the human mind as an instrument for evaluating and organizing human experience. Exactly what this suggests is a matter of dispute, but it may make enough initial sense for us to say that the Greeks *thought as we do in many important respects,* and that they considered thought to be a process associated with the *human individual.*

The significance of the latter remark may not be clear without some reference to history. Prior to Greek philosophy, if thought was discussed at all, it was evidently supposed that the ideas in the mind and thought associated with them were explicable, not in terms of the individual thinking, but in terms of some god (or some sort of being beyond the influence of direct human control) who *caused* the human to have the ideas and the thought processes in order to direct his activity. This view of man as being in the control of higher agencies seems to predominate in cultures earlier than Greek culture whenever anything like thought is referred to. It is even in the early view of the Greeks, exhibited in Homer's *Iliad* and *Odyssey,* where we find instances of thoughts being implanted in the minds of the heroes of those epics by gods desirous of influencing the outcome of events. Between 600 and 300 B.C., however, which is the period that produced the important Greek philosophy which is still studied, many Greek philosophers and scientists (the distinction was not explicitly made by the Greeks) adopted the view that reason was something under individual control. This view, that reason is a process associated with human individuals, and in important respects a process under their control, has had important consequences for philosophy. For example, in ordinary moral judgments we do not consider the person who has made a bad moral choice in quite the same way as a person who has acted similarly but who cannot be said to have made a choice because he was compelled to act as he did. A psychotic is simply not morally culpable (he is *compelled* by insanity to do the act in question) as is a sane individual who deliberately chooses his action from among moral alternatives. This distinction is reflected in the way that the two cases are treated separately in courts of law. Morality, or ethics, in the contemporary sense, can only exist for individuals who have control, or choice, over their decision. Thus, the problem of which choice from among a range of choices is the best one is an ethical question only in the context of the view that human beings have control over their own actions. It is first formulated in the modern sense by the Greek philosophers, perhaps as a direct result of their views about human individualism.

Notice that it would not be correct to suppose that human individualism in the sense that each human being has control over his own thinking and action is to be necessarily equated with individualism in another sense, that of supposing that each human being is totally unlike every other and that any individual's choice is as good as any other individual's choice. On the contrary, and as we shall see in Plato and Aristotle, many Greeks supposed that the sustained use of reason would have the result that human beings could eventually hope to have a common standard of judgment, so that properly educated individuals, although each would do his thinking for himself, would have a common standard of truth in ethics and aesthetics as well as in the more obvious cases of mathematics and science. For Plato and Aristotle, individualism of the second kind is the result of lives based upon sensual pleasure rather than upon reason as a basis of choice. Not all Greek philosophers, however, would agree with Plato and Aristotle, and this point is raised here only to suggest that the mere adoption of the view that reason is under the control of the individual does not dictate the answers to the problems of philosophy, at least not until reason receives further clarification, and the philosophers have not agreed upon such a clarification, as we shall see.

Perhaps the similarity between what we call reason and what the Greek philosophers called reason (in contrast to earlier views) can best be brought out by an example, rather than by a straightforward definition or a pronouncement about intellectual history. Even the example about to be given cannot be defended as necessarily historical, but at the very least it is a charming story compatible with history that illustrates the difference that has here been claimed. Consider the so-called Pythagorean theorem from plane geometry as it is traditionally taught in school. The name of the theorem refers to Pythagoras, a Greek philosopher, although one of the historical problems is whether Pythagoras or a student of his first established it by a proof like that given below. The theorem, of course, is that the sum of the squares of the legs of a right-angled triangle is identical with the square of its hypotenuse. (The Greek influence is everywhere, as a check of the etymology of *hypotenuse* in the dictionary will confirm.) We may summarize that information by the expression '$a^2 + b^2 = c^2$', where a and b stand for the legs of some arbitrary right triangle, and c for its hypotenuse. Strictly speaking, a, b, and c stand for the *length* of the respective sides as represented by some number, although the Greeks gave this length a purely geometrical significance, as we will see in the proof given below.

The theorem of Pythagoras is not a piece of mathematical knowledge which just suddenly appeared in Greek history. Scattered mathematical information can be found in the remains of civilizations which long antedate Pythagoras, for example, in Babylonian and Egyptian documents. What is instructive in this case is to compare what the Egyptians did with mathematics with the approach that Pythagoras took, as an illustration of how strikingly modern Pythagoras's approach appears when we contrast it with what had gone before. Apparently some Egyptian, or perhaps several, had come across the following useful piece of information, perhaps entirely by accident; that is, they discovered it without consciously looking for a solution to the problem that it solves. By tying two knots in a long piece of cord or rope at some arbitrary distance apart (a relatively small distance with respect to the total length of the cord), it is possible to produce a series of equal lengths in the cord by tying more knots at the same distance from one another as the first two using the length marked by the first two as a standard. Suppose that thirteen such knots are tied, resulting in twelve equal lengths marked off on the cord or rope. Now suppose that the thirteenth knot and the first are held together, and the rope staked out on the ground by fixing the first and thirteenth knots together under one stake, and then stretching out three lengths in one direction, staking that down, and then stretching out the remainder of the rope by dividing it into lengths of four and five by seizing it at the proper point, stretching it out, and staking it down. The result would be a figure like this:

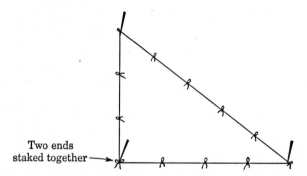

Two ends staked together →

The Egyptians discovered that this device, as well as other devices somewhat like it, proved useful in surveying and building measurement, since it could be used to determine the corners of rectangular fields or buildings. Although the Egyptians were able to use these rather isolated discoveries, they do not seem to have been tormented by the problem of explaining their success. At any rate no clear and distinct record of work on problems explaining the success of these devices exists, and no systematic treatment of geometry along the lines of Euclid's *Elements* is found until the Greeks worked on the problem. In a sense, the Egyptian discoveries may be looked on as *practical* devices for solving particular problems, in contrast to the Greek penchant for theoretical knowledge and solutions to general problems as represented by the Greek philosophical tradition.

By way of contrast to the Egyptian device just mentioned, let us consider what may have been the Pythagorean proof of the theorem that the sum of the squares of the legs of a right-angled triangle is identical with the square of the hypotenuse. Consider the following two drawings:

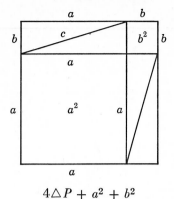
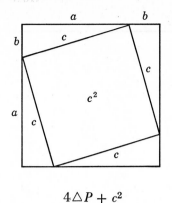

$$4\triangle P + a^2 + b^2 \qquad\qquad 4\triangle P + c^2$$

Let two legs of an arbitrary right-angled triangle be represented by a and b, and the hypotenuse by c. Each of the drawings is constructed by placing the arbitrary triangle in the upper left-hand corner, extending the legs, and building up the figure by placing replicas of the triangle in various positions with respect to the original triangle and its extended legs. A brief examination of the drawings will show how this can be done without going through the tedious detail of describing it step by step here. The result of performing these constructions consists of two squares, each of side $a + b$. The area of either of these squares is identical with that of the other, namely, $(a + b)^2$. Examining what is inside these two squares is somewhat interesting. In each of the squares four of the original triangles have been used. The one square contains an area equal to c^2, and the other square contains two areas equal to a^2 and b^2, in addition to the four triangles which appear in each square. If we call the triangle with which the construction was started triangle P, then the contents of each of the squares is summarized in an obvious way by the expression under each of the squares. But we know that the area of each of the squares is equal to that of the other, so that their areas are identical, a fact which we may state by means of the expression

$$4\triangle P + a^2 + b^2 = 4\triangle P + c^2$$

where the equality sign stands for the identity of the two areas. At this point the solution is plain to anyone, but we do need some kind of justification for canceling out the expression $4\triangle P$ on each side of our identity. The Greeks took a rule like "Equals subtracted from equals produce equals." to justify this cancellation. Although this rule is not obviously true, as the Greeks thought, it does justify this cancellation and the resultant proof of the expression $a^2 + b^2 = c^2$, which is interpreted according to our previous stipulations as a statement of the Pythagorean theorem.

A present day geometer would not be entirely happy with what has just transpired, and he would insist that a number of turns in the argument be clarified, as well as that the assumptions of the argument be made explicit. We assumed, for example, that the triangle we started with was a right-angled triangle, so that one would have to understand what is meant by a right-angled triangle before he could follow this proof. Further, the dependence of the proof on the drawings which we exhibited would be dropped. Drawings are not always reliable, for they may smuggle in extra assumptions as in the classic "proof" that all triangles are isosceles, which is reproduced in many elementary geometry texts. Nevertheless, the feeling that we have in following the argument just exhibited is a comfortable one: it is just like a great many arguments that we meet with every intellectual day. As a matter of fact, it can very easily be brought up to date, and the very fact that the proof is so intuitively convincing makes it the kind of knowledge that one can build on, in contrast to the rope figure, which is just an interesting curiosity, no matter how useful it might be, as it stands. The Pythagorean theorem suggests that other theorems might be proved in a similar way, so to speak, so that it is *stimulating* in a way that the discovery of accidental matters of fact can never be.

One aspect of the Pythagorean theorem deserves special attention in this context. Notice that the theorem does not mention any *particular* triangle, but affirms that a certain relationship will hold in any right-angled triangle whatsoever. In our statement of the theorem this is handled by allowing a, b, and c to be variables which stand for the legs and hypotenuse of any right-angled triangle that one might care to start with. In using variables in this fashion, our statement really summarizes what might otherwise have to be stated by a long series of statements, each one of which would mention the legs and hypotenuse of a particular triangle. Thus, we may look at the Pythagorean theorem as an explanation of a great many particular facts in terms of some simple concepts and variables which reason manipulates to convince us that the great number of facts is true without the necessity of our checking each one individually. No matter how sophisticated this basic claim may become, and it will become a great deal more sophisticated when made by a contemporary philosopher, it is nevertheless true that without some method of explaining a wide variety of particular facts by means of general concepts and some tactical aids like variables, science and mathematics as we know them would be impossible. It is not surprising that epistemologists since the Greeks have been concerned with finding an explanation for the existence of *general* human knowledge in this sense.

Another aspect of the Pythagorean theorem is important for the history of philosophical epistemology. The Pythagorean theorem is the kind of statement which may be defended against any reasonable doubt, and hence it furnishes along with other examples of provable mathematical truths, an example of knowledge which virtually every philosopher since the Greeks has included in his paradigm cases of human knowledge. In rebuttal of criticism, a sufficiently educated geometer can defend the steps of reasoning involved by reference to principles which it is unreasonable to doubt if anything is unreasonable to doubt. As a consequence, philosophers have generally supposed that at least *some* of the properties of mathematical knowledge would have to be properties of knowledge in general. The remaining sections of this book will exhibit the profound impact of this point of view on Western philosophers.

The general epistemological problem of separating purported information into the categories of knowledge and opinion has already been introduced. It is clear that the problem of drawing such an epistemological distinction might be undertaken with respect to a very limited field of interest. One might, for example, be interested in separating knowledge from opinion about some restricted problem, such as finding the best strategy for winning at checkers. Any person undertaking epistemological clarification of any problem, no matter how restricted, can be considered as thinking along philosophical lines, provided that he makes a reasonable effort to be impartial in conducting his analysis. The major philosophers of the Western philosophical tradition, including the seven that are considered in this book, have earned their importance partly because they have attempted epistemological clarification of a very wide range of purported beliefs which are associated with various human interests. In most cases, the major philosophers have attempted to sketch out some method of distinguishing knowledge and opinion in all sustained areas of human inquiry.

PART 1

Plato

(427–347 B.C.)

The Theory of Ideas

Plato's importance for the history of philosophy is grounded in the fact that he attempted to provide a theory of knowledge which would separate knowledge from opinion in all the major intellectual controversies of his time. His continuing importance is due to the fact that the intellectual controversies of his time were in many cases concerned with problems that are still the subject of intellectual dispute, and to the fact that his solution of the epistemological problems posed by these disputes is still thought by many people to provide a justifiable and logically consistent position for present-day philosophers.

There are interesting historical reasons for the important disagreements among the Greeks that Plato considered, but exploring the historical background adequately is not a necessary prerequisite for understanding the important positions that Plato reached as a result of his philosophical activity. For our purposes we may merely note that Greek civilization had beaten off Persian invaders of overwhelming numerical superiority about a hundred years before Plato wrote his philosophical works, an event which seems to have raised for the Greeks the question of accounting for their obvious qualitative superiority. But soon after this victory over the Persians, the Greeks, who lived in small groups called city-states, which were largely autonomous in their military, political, economic, and cultural organization, found themselves fighting internal civil wars. The important Greek city-states on opposite sides of the biggest of these civil wars, Athens and Sparta, were quite distinct in terms of traditions associated with the various aspects of city-state life that have just been mentioned. Sparta defeated Athens in the war, but did not completely crush Athens. In the years after the war, Athenians raised the issue of the causes of their defeat, an issue which developed into an examination of what was best in Greek life. Part of this examination was devoted explicitly to the question of which form of city-state government was most desirable.

Plato was confronted with a welter of opinions on the matter, ranging from traditional religious answers to skeptical views expressed by itinerant lecturers who were known as sophists. The religious tradition, like many religious traditions, supposed that there was divine guidance of human affairs and that wars were lost through failure to obey divine instructions. The sophists, on the other hand, who were cosmopolitan travelers and lecturers, pointed out that this kind of religious view was taken on both sides of any war and might consequently be ruled out as worthless with increasing sophistication. Sophists also urged skepticism against those philosophers who contended that some *form* of government was the secret to city-state success, arguing that human failure would corrupt any constitutional imposition of democratic or autocratic forms of government on a society. In addition to the political controversies of his time, Plato dealt with controversies over what was beautiful and what was morally good. Plato attempted to find philosophical solutions to these problems, even though it may be said that he seems to have exhibited aristocratic bias in some of his attitudes. We do not have to be concerned with this bias in discussing whether or not the solutions that he proposed were adequate.

In order to answer these special problems, Plato dealt with the more general epistemological question "What can we know?". In other words, Plato was interested in establishing what constituted human knowledge in any area, on the grounds that this would enable a careful investigator to decide which problems connected with some particular political, aesthetic, or ethical debate were definitely soluble and which were merely confusions based on conflicting opinion.

It is impossible to avoid assumptions in philosophy, but this does not vitiate philosophical investigation, since it would be unreasonable to demand that everything be proved. What is interesting to the philosopher is the question of which assumptions it would be best to adopt for some given purpose. One of Plato's assumptions seems to have been that human beings do have some knowledge. It is pretty easy to argue that this is a reasonable assumption, and Plato was given to exhibiting his assumption as true by pointing out examples of human knowledge. Some of his examples, and these are crucial examples for all of subsequent philosophy, are taken from familiar areas of mathematics. Consider two simple examples: the Pythagorean theorem of elementary geometry, which was proved earlier, and the arithmetic sum "$2+2=4$.". It is important to keep these examples in mind, since Plato uses mathematical examples to make an extremely important point: that truths of arithmetic and geometry seem to be examples of unquestionable truths, the certainty of which is sufficient to prove complete skepticism false. Plato also used other examples from ordinary skills, and he pointed out that crafts like piloting vessels and making shoes involve *knowledge*, in the sense that successful practitioners of these crafts might be said to know some things that others do not know. The pilot, for example, knows that certain areas of a harbor are too shallow for certain ships to pass over. Argument about claims made in these areas could be settled by appeal to someone with the appropriate knowledge. A skilled mathematician, for example, could settle any reasonable argument over whether the Pythagorean theorem was true by constructing a proof of the theorem. Plato's problem was whether or not all genuine human disagreements might be resolved by appeal to human knowledge, and in order to answer this special problem he had to consider the problems that we have previously characterized as epistemological.

The first clarification proposed by Plato was that something could be considered knowledge only if it could be said to be *certain*. This would rule out all guesses about the future as knowledge, on the grounds that no one can be *certain* what will happen in the future. At the same time it would preserve the examples given earlier, since it has been, is, and always will be the case, presumably, that "$2+2=4$." as well as that particular ships cannot pass over areas which are only of such and such a depth. There may be some doubt about the latter assertion, since we might argue that there might be developed a new system of propulsion which could enable a ship to pass over areas that it could not formerly pass. But then one might argue that the new system of propulsion changed the nature of the ship and that the statement of the pilot would still hold true of the particular ships that it talked about. Examples from piloting and shoemaking, however, do seem more troublesome than the examples from mathematics with respect to their certainty, and Plato had a tendency to fall back on the mathematical examples when he was pressed, since they seem to be the strongest examples in support of his contentions. We shall consider mathematical examples almost exclusively on the grounds that bona fide examples that support Plato's philosophy as strongly as possible are to be looked for if any accurate assessment of its final worth is to be made. In short, Plato's claim against skepticism that there is certain knowledge is *true* if mathematical examples *are* examples of certain knowledge. In Plato's philosophy, then, the word *knowledge* will be applied only to a claim that is certain, a claim which could not be said to be true today but false tomorrow, or even possibly false tomorrow. Mathematical statements of a sufficiently simple kind are obvious candidates for knowledge in this strong sense.

If we take it as established that human beings do have at least some certain knowledge, then in order to ask how much they might have, that is, how many questions might be capable of determinate resolution like simple mathematical claims are, we could proceed by inquiring how we came to have what certain knowledge we do have. Then, by extrapolation, we might be able to determine how much knowledge it would be possible for us to obtain by following the same process of acquisition that has worked for mathematical knowledge. This is one line of investigation that Plato probed.

The most influential theory to account for human knowledge in Plato's time was that it was acquired through the senses or by experience. This seems, of course, quite natural, on the grounds that human babies do not seem to know very much, yet learn more and more as they gradually acquire a greater range of experiences. But Plato was able to show that his test case of mathematical knowledge could not have been acquired as a result of experience. There are two arguments which show this convincingly: the first is that experience can never yield certain knowledge, and the second is that the knowledge expressed by mathematical statements is not about experienced objects.

To demonstrate the first point it is only necessary to show that sense experience often leads to unreliable impressions. It seems to follow from the frequent unreliability of sense experience that we can never be certain that sense experience has led to certain knowledge in any particular case. Many examples of mistaken sense impressions were known to the Greeks. A visual illusion such as the following will illustrate the point:

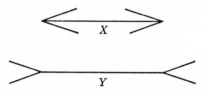

Line *X* appears to be shorter than line *Y* in the drawing. But it can be argued that they are of the same length, since measurement with a ruler indicates this to be the case. Now one might ask how the conclusion is drawn that they are of the same length, if all sense experience is taken to be potentially misleading. The point is that we ordinarily take measurement with a ruler as more reliable than sight alone in cases like the preceding, but we need not. As long as we notice that one way of determining length gives a different result than the other, it follows that sense experience alone cannot be taken as a reliable guide to knowledge. How do we know when to trust our sense impressions? The answer, in Platonic terms, is that we can never be certain when it is that they can be trusted. To express the unreliability of the senses in another way, and a way that has proved influential for the history of philosophy, it can be said that the senses yield only the *appearances* of things, but not their *reality*, so that in order to have *knowledge* about anything, we must know it through some other means than the senses. In the visual illusion, one sense experience makes it appear that *Y* is longer than *X*, the other makes it appear that *Y* is the same in length as *X*. But we know that both of these claims cannot really be true because they conflict. The existence of illusion, or conflicting reports from the senses, proves to Platonists that the senses cannot be trusted to provide knowledge in their sense.

This conclusion does not quite follow logically, since it might be the case that some sense impressions are accurate and others misleading, but Plato seems to be right that no way of distinguishing accurate from inaccurate sense experiences is readily available, and surely no way that is itself dependent upon sense experiences. If there were some sign associated with every accurate sense experience, like a funny pain in the brain, but this sign was never associated with inaccurate sense experiences, then sense experience might be a reliable guide, yielding knowledge when the pain was felt. But it is a convincing argument that no such sensed criterion of an accurate sense experience can be found when we analyze the quality of our sense experiences.

The other point in support of the claim that mathematical knowledge is not derived from sense experience is that the subject matter of the mathematical examples appears unaccessible to sense experience. Although we see a *2* quite often, we never see the number two. It is clear that *2* is not the number two since the expression '$2+2$' would show that there are at least two number twos, but we know from elementary arithmetic that there is only one number two. *2* somehow refers to the number two, and it is considered by many to be a *name* for the number two which we use to refer to the number two in the process of constructing mathematical proofs. From arguments like this, it is easy to show that neither numbers nor geometrical figures are the objects of any sense experience. As against objections that a jelly-jar lid is a circle, one can note that a jelly-jar lid does not have all of its radii equal, as a circle does. Thus, although we experience *circular* objects, we cannot be said to *experience* circles. It follows from these considerations that mathematical knowledge, being about nonexperienced objects, could hardly have been acquired from sense experiences of mathematical objects.

From the two established points that human beings have certain knowledge and that this is not acquired through the senses, Plato developed an idea that was already present in Greek culture in various religious traditions. This idea, quite simply, is that human beings remember or recollect knowledge from a past life, rather than acquire it in their current lives through experience.

You may be familiar with an idea like this in connection with the term *transmigration*, and Plato's ideas are like some of those which are normally associated with transmigration. Transmigrationists hold that souls are immortal and pass from human body to human body as these bodies die or wear out. Notice that this view holds at least implicity that human beings are made from two completely different entities, their bodies (which are mortal) and their souls (which are immortal). Now if we read *mind* for *soul*, we begin to get an impression of what Platonism is like. Historically, it is not entirely accurate to translate the appropriate Greek work as *mind*, but it seems even more misleading in view of Christian associations to translate it as *soul*. Plato's view is then that the human mind is the locus of human knowledge, and that the human body, through experience, can only provide the kind of misleading sense impressions that we spoke of earlier. We explain the fact that the human baby becomes more and more sophisticated not by the gradual acquisition of knowledge through experience, but by the mind's gradual remembrance of knowledge due to the prodding of sense experience.

It is important to realize that the Platonic explanation is compatible with the observed facts of child development. The fact that a child's knowledge increases as his experience increases does not prove that the two are causally correlated, and it certainly does not show that increasing experience is the *cause* of increasing knowledge. In fact, when human beings grow senile, their knowledge decreases at the same time that they continue to have more and more sense experiences.

An explanation of the origin of the knowledge that the mind recollects is now clearly required, since denying that knowledge originates in sense experience does not explain the origin of knowledge very satisfactorily. Plato's explanation will be presented as an analogy to begin with, since more exacting treatments of it require a great deal of detailed study of the relevant Platonic texts. The basic idea is this: just as there are objects which the senses experience, so there are objects which the mind experiences; only these objects are quite different, and they will be called *ideas* or *forms*. The mind may be said to *experience* these ideas or forms through a process which has subsequently been called *Intuition*. *Intuition* will be used as a proper name to refer to this special faculty of the mind invoked by Plato to explain knowledge of ideas, although the word *intuition* will occasionally be used to refer to our ordinary, unreflective beliefs. The notion is then this: just as the senses experience objects in the (ordinary) world, so the mind Intuits ideas or forms in the world of ideas or forms. The experiencing of objects is subject to uncertainty. In contrast, Intuition may produce *certain* information about the forms it scrutinizes, since it is concerned with forms that are (assumed) clear and unchanging. The ordinary world is called the world of becoming to emphasize the changing nature of it as it is revealed by sense experience, and the world of ideas is called the world of being, or the *real* world, which means here that it is the one that we are concerned about if we wish to have knowledge.

The structure of Plato's position is rather interesting. It is based on the powerful arguments that he can bring to bear to show that we do have knowledge and that it cannot be acquired through sense experience if it is to be certain like the mathematical knowledge exhibited in his examples. His theory of ideas (a name given to the whole conception that the mind's Intuition of the ideas is the source of human knowledge) is offered as the theory of knowledge that will save knowledge from skepticism or an inadequate grounding in sense experience. Plato's theory seems to fit the facts that he adduces to support it. But for the discerning reader there will be a number of crucial problems: what is the relationship between the body and the soul; if ideas or forms do not exist in the ordinary world of experience, then where do they exist; how can one who has never felt that he was intuiting an idea be convinced that this is what he has in fact done when he has learned mathematical theorems; and so on. The acceptability of Plato's philosophy will have to hinge on whether or not these questions can be satisfactorily answered, to say nothing of whether or not it is possible to prove that Plato's position is the only one that will explain how human beings can have certain knowledge without acquiring it through the senses.

Standards for Judgment

We have seen that Plato takes a human being to be composed of two fundamentally different kinds of entities, the body and the mind (or soul). When knowledge is taken to be certain or indubitable, and it is shown that the objects in the universe are too changing to be objects of knowledge (what is true of them today may be false of them tomorrow), it follows that for knowledge to be possible, unchanging objects like Plato's forms must be the objects of knowledge. This position is supported by the evidence that mathematics is about objects which are not found in the universe but is about ideas or forms. Plato thus proposes a view which is compatible with our commonsense observations about mathematical knowledge, and he extends his view in proposing that knowledge is only possible where there are forms. Mathematics does not exhaust the possible knowledge of forms, but only of certain mathematical forms, among which is the form of the number two. If ethical and aesthetic knowledge is to be obtained, it must be founded on the intuited existence of ethical and aesthetic forms. Our immediate problem, then, is to determine the totality of forms in an effort to discover whether ethical, aesthetic, or any kind of forms can be shown to exist, in order to justify the existence of knowledge in traditional areas of human interest other than mathematics.

Although Plato held that knowledge is to be limited to certain or indubitable statements among those which we might ordinarily say that we know to be true, he did not hold also, as he is sometimes misrepresented as holding, that complete skepticism is the only position with respect to the world of becoming. Plato did suppose that some estimates about future events in the universe, or evaluations of current events, were better than others. But he gave claims about the world of becoming the status of opinion or belief, as opposed to knowledge, because statements of opinion cannot be said to be certain. Some opinions may be better than others, but none is certain. Better opinions will be formed by those who compare their mental knowledge of the forms with their sensual knowledge of the

20

universe, for the world of becoming and the world of being are related, somewhat like an image of an object as seen in a distorted mirror may be related to the object itself. Thus, a distorted image of a teapot may enable one to form an opinion about the qualities of the actual teapot that is more reliable than a guess based on no information at all, but it can hardly compare with the knowledge that examining the teapot itself can yield. We may now take Plato to be effecting a definition of knowledge and opinion in the following sense: he maintains that all the occasions of someone's uttering 'I know that X' are to be divided into two large groups. Those utterances which are based on sense experience and constitute an expression of opinion would go into one group, and those utterances based on intuitions of the forms or ideas would go into the other group. In this way, knowledge and opinion become *defined* terms for Platonic philosophy, and they are not used in that philosophy in quite the same way that many persons are likely to use them.

We have seen that one powerful argument for the existence of the forms or ideas is the fact of the apparent certainty of the truths of elementary arithmetic and geometry. The fact that the world of being and the world of becoming are related, however, gives some additional support to the theory of forms. Suppose, for example, that I draw the following figures:

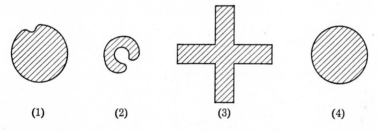

| (1) | (2) | (3) | (4) |

Anyone asked to arrange these figures in order of increasing circularity would no doubt order them in the following way: 3, 2, 1, 4. The Platonist might now make the following point. In order for comparisons of circularity to be made, it seems reasonable to suppose that the comparisons are made by examing each figure against some standard of circularity, and saying that that figure which most nearly matches the standard is the most circular, and so on. The standard of circularity involved is undoubtedly the circle mentioned in geometry. But geometrical circles are not to be met with in experience, as we have seen. No circular object can be said to have all its radii *identical* in length within the limits of some measuring instrument that is available. That this claim is true can be seen from the fact that only a finite number of radii could even in principle be checked by measurement, while a circle has an infinite number of radii that might be measured. But waiving such difficulties, suppose that there were a manhole cover or some other circular object, all of whose radii are equal in length so far as anyone can tell. If this manhole cover were taken as the standard of circularity, we still could not effect a comparison of the drawn figures with the cover, for they are of different sizes. We must imagine some of the figures to change size, but not shape, in order to make the comparison. This shows that the comparisons of the figures to any standard must be mental comparisons, and it shows that the drawn figures are not compared to a mental picture of a circle of any size, since the problem of comparing sizes would still remain. Platonists argue that only the idea of circularity can be a suitable standard to explain the comparisons of circularity that we are able to make. They further argue that an ordering in terms of circularity is to be explained by saying that those objects which rank higher in the ordering than others *participate* more in the form of circularity. The notion of participation, of course, needs some further clarification, but it expresses the idea that objects in the world of becoming are what they are because of their relationships to the forms or ideas.

Let us consider one more example. Suppose that several people were asked (in turn) to collect all the green objects in some room into one place, and that the possible complication of borderline objects is not present because every object in the room is clearly black, or green, or yellow, or red, and no other color, in terms of our everyday use of such words. It seems to follow from our everyday experiences that a variety of people might well select the same objects as green in such an experiment. Platonists would insist on some epistemological explanation of this uniformity. It is a simple fact of language usage that people of diverse backgrounds can understand one another by using their common vocabularies in a uniform way when they wish to describe to each other some new experiences. In reply to a request for *his* explanation of the uniform usage of *green* exhibited when a variety of people pick the same objects to be green when they are confronted with a collection they have not see before, a Platonist would reply that the uniformity could be explained because people have remembered the same form, to which each of them assigns the name *green* in conformity with linguistic practice. (We shall assume that they are all English speakers.) Confronted with the roomful of objects, they simply observe which objects participate in the form, and then they can name those objects green. Other uniformities in practice could be similarly explained.

Now suppose that someone objects to the Platonist that his argument shows only that the ideas might exist, since if they did they would account for this kind of sorting behavior, but that in fact the ideas do not exist, so that Platonism is not a tenable theory of knowledge. A Platonist can reasonably demand to know what criterion for separation of kinds could be invoked by his critic. It might be claimed by his opponent, for example, that the separation is effected by a learned verbal response, in the following sense. Perhaps objects similar or identical to those in the room have previously been labeled *green, blue,* etc., by someone who had taught us the language. The separations are then effected by applying the labels in the way that they had been previously learned. But this explanation fails to do justice to the way in which we are able to employ the word *green*. After being shown a relatively small number of objects that are called *green*, normal human beings who are developing in a culture using English as a means of communication are quickly able to extend this word in a correct fashion (by ordinary standards) to objects completely unlike the ones to which the word *green* has been applied except for the common color. To say that *green* is used to apply to any object *like* those which have been called *green* in the past encounters the difficulty that any two objects are alike in an infinite number of ways. This remark is trivially true. Two objects may be said to be alike because they are both *not* on Mt. Everest. When such likenesses are taken into account, we can see that it will be trivial to find a great number of likenesses between any group of green objects and some new object. This great number of likenesses makes it difficult to explain why people should choose likenesses in a way that would account for linguistic uniformities of usage. To say simply that we apply a word to new objects which are like those to which the word has been applied in the past must be supplemented by some account which explains the relatively uniform way in which speakers of some given language learn to use certain words. It is not true, and Platonists know that it is not, that words are always used in a uniform way by good speakers of a language. There are situations in which considerable argument may arise between speakers of a language as to which words are appropriately used. But there are simple situations in which uniformity seems to be observed, and an adequate theory of knowledge will have to account for them. Platonists would argue that the use of words in uniform fashion is explained by the ideas; application of some word to a group of objects gradually causes the mind to take that word as the linguistic name for the form which it intuits that all the objects participate in. Any suggestion that objects may be similar in an infinite number of ways along the lines just suggested would be met by the Platonist with the claim that only certain forms exist, but that it is possible to string together words to which we can assign some meaning but which do not correspond to a form. With reference to the example given above, it would be said that there is a form of greenness but not a form of not-being-on-Mt.-Everest. This explains the commonsense observation that people see green things as being green but they do not say that they see them as not being on Mt. Everest.

From these considerations it follows that the existence of the forms seems to be proved both by consideration of elementary mathematical truths and from consideration of the judgments or opinions that we can express about the world. Against this background of arguments, a question like "What is beautiful?" is ambiguous. It can be taken as a question about the world of becoming, equivalent to the question "What things are beautiful?", or it may be taken as a question about the world of being, equivalent to the question "What makes things beautiful?". The answer to the former question is a list of beautiful objects, or a description of the beautiful objects which would go on such a list. The latter question is a request for information about the form of beauty, and Plato sometimes reformulates this questions as "What is *the* beautiful?". It is the answer to this latter question that determines whether or not any answer to the first question is justifiable.

Two points that have been discussed in connection with Plato represent enduring philosophical positions that may more or less be said to begin in the Western tradition with his speculations. One of these points is the definition of knowledge that restricts knowledge to judgments or statements that can be said to be certain or indubitable. The other point is the belief, accompanied by telling examples, that sense experience cannot lead to knowledge in this defined sense because it results in judgments or statements which are not certain. Many philosophers of the Western tradition have held these positions in common with Plato. In fact, these two fundamental positions occur so frequently that it is useful to call any philosopher who adopts them a *rationalist*. It follows from acceptance of these two positions that the occurrence of human knowledge has to be explained by some means other than an origin in sense experience, and rationalistic philosophers after Plato have entities in their theories of knowledge corresponding to Platonic forms or ideas, as well as a non-sensual faculty corresponding to what has here been called Intuition that enables these entities to be known. Some rationalists have called the faculty that knows the ideas or forms in their theory of knowledge *Reason* rather than *Intuition,* which is a natural extension of the role which reasonable doubt is called upon to play in constructing answers to epistemological problems.

It will be interesting later to compare Descartes with Plato, in that both of them are rationalists, but Descartes's method of explaining the origin of certain human knowledge is different from Plato's. Philosophers who take the position that sense experience is the source of knowledge are conveniently called *empiricists*. Empiricists usually deny that there is any faculty corresponding to Platonic Intuition, and many of them have claimed that sense experience *can* lead to certain knowledge. It is clear from Plato's arguments that any empiricist who makes this claim must find some way of distinguishing veridical sense experiences that can lead to certain knowledge from sense experiences which are illusory, in that they suggest false beliefs.

Problems in Participation

Certainly the theory of ideas can provide an explanation for human knowledge, where human knowledge is defined according to Plato's technical usage. Although the theory may therefore be true, or at least adequate in some sense, the crucial question is whether or not it can be said to be superior to any alternative, and this gives rise to problems. The most important of these is whether or not the forms or ideas may be described more directly than by simply describing them as entities which must be postulated in order to account for human knowledge.

Plato ruled out the answer to the question of the form 'What is Y?' (This is different from the question of the form 'What is a Y?' as quite different linguistic terms fill the two blank spaces represented by Y.) that would be given by pointing to something and saying 'That is Y.'. Clearly an instance of Y, or an object which is Y, is not identical with Y. Things are red, for example, but we cannot point to any thing which *is* red (all of redness). Still, Plato was influenced by the implicit theory of his time that words have meaning because they refer to or name some object. Since the Y in 'X is Y' judgments names no sense object, the theory of ideas may be looked at in another way as the generation of entities that Y in such judgments can refer to, and this would in turn explain how we could understand Y. If we say "Tom is tall." and "Harry is tall.", Platonists and non-Platonists alike may agree that there is something which Tom and Harry both *are*, i.e., *tall*, but Platonists are distinguished by arguing further that there is something (some thing—a single entity) which Tom and Harry both have, or which they are both related to, in this case the form of *tallness*. Now the difficulties with the theory of ideas may in many cases be reduced to difficulties about how a single thing (tallness) may be related to many things (Tom and Harry) and to difficulties about the description or knowledge of what tallness (the form) is like. For example, tallness cannot be related to Tom and Harry by virtue of the fact that some *part* of tallness occurs in both Tom and Harry, for then tallness would not

25

be a single entity by which the participation of things could be judged. On the other hand, if tallness as an idea or form exists in a world of being completely separate from Tom and Harry who exist in the world of becoming, the relationship between tallness and Tom or Harry is something that Plato's theory of knowledge should describe in some detail. Calling it participation does not solve the problem of the relationship, since such a relationship is not *explained* by giving it a name, unless it is also specified how it can be determined that the relationship does or does not obtain in particular cases. For example, to decide whether the relationship described by 'heavier than' holds between two objects *a* and *b*, we can proceed by techniques of measuring weight that we know to be related to the problem of determining whether one object is heavier than another. Faced with the question whether *a* participates in the form *X*, no procedure for determining the answer is as yet available.

An interesting study of the possible relationship between particular red objects and the idea of redness may be made by studying the relationship between particular pound weights and the standard pound. The pound, under traditional methods of setting standards, was some fixed object kept under relatively invariant conditions in a bureau of standards. An ordinary pound weight was then defined to be any ordinary weight which would balance the standard pound. Of course, these comparisons would have to be made indirectly, but we may treat all of them as involving the weight of the standard pound. For two arbitrary objects, it would be easy to define a sense in which one would be said to be 'closer to a pound' than the other, using well-known techniques of measurement. Consequently, the status of the standard pound for determining the *poundness* of other objects has an analogy to the relation between a form and the particular sense objects which are said to participate in it.

Interesting as this comparison may seem on first consideration, it does not suffice to indicate completely what the relationship of the forms or the ideas are to particular objects in the world of becoming. To begin with, the standard pound is still something that we can see, feel, smell, etc., at least in principle, so that it is an object of the world of becoming. A form or idea, however, is not an object of sense experience. Further, because the standard pound is a sense object, we can imagine it changing over a period of time, even though it is chosen and kept in such a fashion that it changes very slowly, or remains unchanged for a long time, by comparison to other sense objects. A form, however, is defined in part to be something which is eternal, that is, something which never changes.

At this point, we can preview an argument between Platonists and non-Platonists. A Platonist takes the following question to be a sensible one: "Does the standard pound weigh the same today as it did yesterday?". In other words, the Platonist can imagine that some object whose weight remained constant might be said to become heavier (*appear* to become heavier) because the standard pound became lighter. Real weight, then, cannot be arbitrarily identified with physical standards. An empiricist, however, might argue that the question "Does the standard pound weigh the same today as it did yesterday?" is in fact nonsense, since to be a pound is to be equivalent in weight to the standard. Now if *A* is the standard pound, and *B* and *C* are two other objects equivalent in weight to *A*, and suddenly *A* was found to be lighter than *B* and *C*, which remained equivalent in weight, we would be faced with a question about which of the objects had changed in weight. But this is the question as to which object is to be taken as the standard. If, for example, we saw someone cut *A* into two pieces, we would switch to some other object (possibly *B* or *C*) as the standard. The point is that some *object* is the standard, apart from which talk of weight is nonsense to the empiricist. The perennial problem of the significance of everything doubling weight might be mentioned in this context. Suppose that all objects simultaneously doubled in weight (*pretend* that all objects are decomposable into atoms, each of which, by fiat of divinity, doubles in weight). For the Platonist, this is a legitimate possibility, so that the question "Has everything doubled in weight in the last five minutes?" is meaningful, even though it may not be answerable. On the other hand, because it is not answerable in terms of the standard weight (whose weight relationships with other objects remain unchanged), the question is nonsense to most empiricists, or at least it is a question not worth asking.

A slightly different question, namely, the question of whether the standard pound is a pound may also be asked. The question seems odd, but the oddness is difficult to trace down. Since the standard pound cannot be balanced with itself, it does not follow that it is a pound by application of the usual techniques of measurement invoked in defining a pound. Yet the standard pound must have some weight, and assigning it any weight but a pound would seem ridiculous. It surely has the same weight as it has itself, and that is the weight which we call a pound. If these considerations are transferred to forms or ideas, some difficult problems ensue. Consider the idea of Justice, which Plato explicitly mentions as an idea existing in the world of being. We may ask whether (the idea of) Justice is just. This, in effect, is to raise consideration of what we may say about the forms. If *no* properties or relations between forms may be described by philosophers, the theory of ideas reduces to the kind of visionary scheme that describes the goal for a program without giving evidence that the goal is attainable or any suggestions for a program that will enable attainment of the goal. In this case, the theory of ideas would be of little help, being at best an ex post facto justification for what knowledge we think that we have. On the other hand, if properties may be legitimately ascribed to the forms, and relations between them affirmed by philosophers, some very awkward consequences follow unless extreme care is taken in the statement of a theory of forms. Although it may seem awkward to say that the standard pound is a pound, it may seem even more awkward to deny that the standard pound is a pound. Similarly, injustice cannot be attributed to Justice (the form), since it is the standard by which examples of justice are judged. Therefore, if any properties can belong to the form of justice, *just* would seem to be among them. Any judgment like "Justice is just.", in which some property is ascribed to a form such that the form is taken to be the cause of objects in the world of becoming having a property with a similar name, may be said to be an instance of self-predication.

Examples of self-predication lead to the following problem. Suppose we take the collection of all acts, etc., which may be said to participate in Justice. These things are all said to be just because of their participation in Justice. But we cannot say, as the theory of forms seems to suggest, that a thing can be just only if it participates in some form of justice. For now, in addition to the class, call it *J*, of things which are just by their participation in Justice, there is the form of justice, Justice itself. We may call this form *F*. If self-predication be allowed along the lines suggested above, we can imagine *F* to be just. Consider the class *J'* which consists of every member of *J* plus the form *F*. Everything in *J'* is just. But if all these things are just, by the theory of forms there must be a form, call it *F'*, which accounts for their being just. Continuing in this manner, an infinite series *J, J', J''*, *J'''*, ... of classes and an infinite series *F, F', F'', F'''*, ... of forms may be constructed. These infinite sequences conflict with the Platonic description of the world of being, particularly the Platonic description of the unity and uniqueness of the forms. This example was recognized as a criticism of the theory of forms by Plato in the dialogue *Parmenides,* and the problem of rebutting it successfully is one of the interesting features of Platonic scholarship. Apparently paradox is to be avoided by some restriction on forming any class of the kind *J'*, or else self-predication is to be construed in some more sophisticated way, but Plato himself does not provide a clear answer to this difficulty.

The world of being is as yet unanalyzed in any fruitful way. Yet Plato did provide a partial criterion for determining whether or not particular claims made about the world of being were tenable. There are elements of mysticism in Plato's writings suggesting that a philosopher might have insight into the structure of the world of being. Accepting the possibility of these individual insights, a general epistemological problem is raised when different philosophers claim to have insights into the world of being, but their insights are different. The general criterion introduced by Plato and accepted by subsequent rationalists for resolving these disputes is that any inconsistent description of the world of being will be an incorrect description. Rationalists have held in addition that any incorrect description of the world of being will be inconsistent. Since it is not always possible to prove that something is inconsistent, this criterion is used in practice to *reject* any inconsistent description as a description of the world of being, but it does not compel the adoption of a description not known to be inconsistent as a description of the world of being. The Platonic attack on the problem of discovering true claims about the world of being is to examine rival descriptions of the world of being in order to find inconsistencies in them. The process of letting rival views clash until some consequence of one is found inconsistent with another consequence of it is reflected in the arguments occurring in Plato's dialogues and is sometimes called *dialectic*.

Claims about the structure of the world of being have important consequences for particular examples of participation. Participation is extremely important in this respect because an object may participate in more than one form. In ordinary terms, an object can be both spherical and red and hence participate in two forms. Structure in the world of being is considered to be hierarchical in that one form may be said, for example, to be higher than another. Thus Goodness may be said to be higher than Justice, which means that anything which participates in Justice will also participate in Goodness, or that anything which is just is also good. Any way in which the properties of objects are invariably related would be a result of some association between the relevant forms that they participate in. Attempts to locate structure in the world of being of this kind have been very frequent in rationalistic philosophy since Plato.

Readings from Plato

The selections which follow have been chosen for the purpose of exhibiting Plato's epistemological thought in his own writings. Identification of the selections is made by the name of the dialogue from which the selection is taken and by the initial Greek line in which the translation starts. '*Phaedo* 64+' means that selection *A* begins in Greek line 64 of Plato's *Phaedo*. Greek manuscript line numbers are accepted by convention among scholars, and they will be reprinted in the margins of most good editions. There are four selections, labeled *A*, *B*, *C*, and *D* on the pages where they begin below, and they are as follows:

A. *Phaedo* 64+
B. *Phaedo* 72+
C. *Phaedo* 100+
D. *Republic* 506+

All selections are reprinted from *The Dialogues of Plato*, 4th edition, translated by Benjamin Jowett, 1953. They are reprinted here by kind permission of The Clarendon Press, Oxford.

Both the *Phaedo* and the *Republic* are dialogues, as are most of Plato's extant writings. Philosophical dialogues are literary compositions in which two or more persons discuss a philosophical topic. In the *Phaedo*, the discussants are principally Socrates, Simmias, and Cebes. In the *Republic*, they are Socrates, Adeimantus, and Glaucon. It is the discussant called *Socrates* who expresses the views which are attributed to Plato in the preceding chapters.

The figure called *Socrates* is obviously a sketch of the historical philosopher Socrates, who had a major influence in turning Plato to philosophical speculation. Since there is no philosophical literature which can be attributed to Socrates, possibly because his social status as the son of an artisan prevented him from receiving the formal education necessary for writing literary Greek, a major problem in interpreting the Platonic dialogues is that of distinguishing the views of Plato from the views of the

30

historical Socrates. Other accounts of Socrates than Plato's exist, but they are much less flattering. This has led some commentators to suppose that Plato's account is *idealized,* but it may only reflect the fact that Plato *understood* what Socrates was saying while the others did not. A close study of the texts is sufficient to prove that both Plato and Socrates were original and important philosophers. The crucial theory of ideas as it has been presented seems to have been an insight of Socrates that Plato shaped into a comprehensive and impressive theory of knowledge. It is assumed, consequently, that Plato can be taken as the author of the theory of ideas which is discussed in the book and exhibited in the following selections. With this issue brought into the open, we are not concealing anything by taking the *Socrates* of the dialogue to represent the historical Socrates's most sophisticated epistemological reflection as interpreted by an outstanding student.

Other dialogues which the student may wish to read after reading the *Phaedo* and the *Republic* more fully are the *Meno,* the *Protagoras,* the *Euthyphro,* the *Symposium,* and the *Gorgias.* Like the *Phaedo,* these dialogues are lively discussions of philosophical topics by Socrates and other participants.

Plato's later philosophical speculation seems to have become much more technical and sophisticated. Issues in epistemology are discussed in the *Parmenides,* the *Theaetetus,* the *Sophist,* the *Statesman,* and the *Philebus.* The *Theaetetus,* in particular, may represent Plato's most sophisticated epistemological speculation. A student of Plato will have to study these dialogues closely, but they are much more difficult than the dialogues which are cited above. It is well known to Platonic scholars that the theory of ideas is somewhat differently handled in these later dialogues. For example, the argument for the theory which is presented in the *Phaedo* as depending on the notion of *recollection* becomes considerably less important, while difficulties in the notion of *participation* come to dominate many of the discussions. These differences raise the important problem (an instance of a general problem for the consideration of any historical philosopher) of whether the theory of ideas is a single theory that Plato always adopted or whether Plato started with a Socratic theory that he had to modify considerably as various objections were raised against it. This question is the question of whether all the dialogues can be taken to propose a consistent theory of knowledge or whether the dialogues propose several theories of knowledge that Plato adopted serially during his lifetime.

One must not make the mistake of supposing that if a major philosopher gives up one position for another, the newer view is necessarily the better or more defensible one. In fact, it is clear that the last view that a philosopher holds may be worse than the first one, if for no reason other than that he has become senile. This introduction to Plato tries to present some of the basic problems and insights that led Plato to suppose that some theory of ideas was a necessary part of any adequate theory of knowledge. The difficult interpretive questions which have been raised above are normally dealt with in specialized studies of Plato. Many of the books cited below can provide the student with a detailed consideration of them.

There are many editions of Plato's dialogues and a great many translators of particular dialogues. As with any translations, there are legitimate arguments about which of the translations most accurately conveys what Plato said. The *Library of Liberal Arts*, published by the Bobbs-Merrill Company, is a paperbound series that has some excellent commentaries on particular Platonic dialogues. For those who can read classical Greek, *The Loeb Classical Library* publishes editions with facing English and Greek texts. The entries in the following bibliography are those of important secondary sources and recent books for the study of Plato's philosophy.

Allen, R. E.: "Forms and Standards," *The Philosophical Quarterly*, vol. 9, pp. 163–167, 1959.

Cherniss, Harold: *The Riddle of the Early Academy*, New York, 1962.

Cornford, Francis M.: *Plato's Theory of Knowledge*, New York, 1957.

Crombie, I. M.: *An Examination of Plato's Doctrines*, New York, 1962.

Cushman, R. E.: *Therapeia, Plato's Conception of Philosophy*, Chapel Hill, 1958.

During, I., and G. E. L. Owen (eds.): *Aristotle and Plato in the Mid-fourth Century*, Göteborg, 1960.

*Friedlander, Paul: *Plato: An Introduction*, New York, 1963. (Harper Paperbound.)

*Grube, G. M. A.: *Plato's Thought*, London, 1935. (Beacon Paperbound.)

Gulley, N.: *Plato's Theory of Knowledge*, Cambridge, 1962.

Havelock, E. A.: *A Preface to Plato*, Oxford, 1962.

Levinson, R. B.: *In Defense of Plato*, Cambridge, 1953.

Lodge, R. C.: *Philosophy of Plato*, London, 1956.

Mills, K. W.: "Plato's *Phaedo* 74 b7–c6," *Phronesis*, vol. 2, pp. 128–147, 1957; vol. 3, pp. 40–58, 1958.

Ross, W. D.: *Plato's Theory of Ideas*, Oxford, 1953.

Runciman, W. G.: *Plato's Later Epistemology*, Cambridge, 1962.

Sprague, R. K.: *Plato's Use of Fallacy*, London, 1962.

*Taylor, A. E.: *Plato: The Man and His Work*, London, 1955. (Meridian Paperbound.)

Wedberg, Anders: *Plato's Philosophy of Mathematics*, Stockholm, 1955.

*Winspear, A. D.: *The Genesis of Plato's Thought*, New York, 1940.

Zeller, E.: *Plato and the Older Academy*, New York, 1962.

A   PHAEDO 64+

There is another question, which will probably throw light on our present inquiry if you and I can agree about it:—Ought the philosopher to care about such pleasures—if they are to be called pleasures—as those of eating and drinking?

Certainly not, answered Simmias.

And what about the pleasures of love—should he care for them?

By no means.

And will he think much of the other ways of indulging the body, for example, the acquisition of costly raiment or sandals, or other adornments of the body? Instead of caring about them, does he not rather despise anything more than nature needs? What do you say?   e

I should say that the true philosopher would despise them.

Would you not say that he is entirely concerned with the soul and not with the body? He would like, as far as he can, to get away from the body and to turn to the soul.

Quite true.

First, therefore, in matters of this sort philosophers, above all other men, may be observed in every sort of way to dissever the soul from the   65
communion of the body.

Very true.

Whereas, Simmias, the rest of the world are of opinion that to him who has no taste for bodily pleasures and no part in them, life is not worth having; and that he who is indifferent about them is as good as dead.

Perfectly true.

What again shall we say of the actual acquirement of knowledge?— is the body, if invited to share in the inquiry, a hindrance or a help? I mean   b
to say, have sight and hearing, as found in man, any truth in them? Are they not, as the poets are always repeating, inaccurate witnesses? and yet, if even they are inaccurate and indistinct, what is to be said of the other senses?—for you will allow that they are the best of them?

Certainly, he replied.

Then when does the soul attain truth?—for in attempting to consider anything in company with the body she is obviously deceived by it.

True.   c

Then must not true reality be revealed to her in thought, if at all?

Yes.

And thought is best when the mind is gathered into herself and none of these things trouble her—neither sounds nor sights nor pain, nor again any pleasure,—when she takes leave of the body, and has as little as possible to do with it, when she has no bodily sense or desire, but is aspiring after true being?

Certainly.

And here again it is characteristic of the philosopher to despise the body; his soul runs away from his body and desires to be alone and by   d
herself?

That is true.

Well, but there is another thing, Simmias: Is there or is there not an absolute justice?

Assuredly there is.

And an absolute beauty and absolute good?

Of course.

But did you ever behold any of them with your eyes?

Certainly not.

Or did you ever reach them with any other bodily sense?—and I speak not of these alone, but of absolute greatness, and health, and e strength, and, in short, of the reality or true nature of everything. Is the truth of them ever perceived through the bodily organs? or rather, is not the nearest approach to the knowledge of their several natures made by him who so orders his intellectual vision as to have the most exact conception of the essence of each thing which he considers?

Certainly.

And he attains to the purest knowledge of them who goes to each with the intellect alone, not introducing or intruding in the act of thought 66 sight or any other sense together with reason, but with the intellect in its own purity searches into the truth of each thing in its purity; he who has got rid, as far as he can, of eyes and ears and, so to speak, of the whole body, these being in his opinion distracting elements which when they associate with the soul hinder her from acquiring truth and knowledge—who, if not he, is likely to attain to the knowledge of true being?

What you say has a wonderful truth in it, Socrates, replied Simmias.

B   PHAEDO 72+

Yes, said Cebes interposing, your favourite doctrine, Socrates, that our learning is simply recollection, if true, also necessarily implies a previous time in which we have learned that which we now recollect. But this would be impossible unless our soul had been somewhere before existing in this 73 form of man; here then is another proof of the soul's immortality.

But tell me, Cebes, interrupted Simmias, what arguments are urged in favor of this doctrine of recollection. I am not very sure at the moment that I remember them.

One excellent proof, said Cebes, is afforded by questions. If you put a question to a person properly, he will give a true answer of himself, but how could he do this unless there were knowledge and a right account of the matter already in him? Again, this is most clearly shown when he is b taken to a diagram or to anything of that sort.[2]

But if, said Socrates, you are still incredulous, Simmias, I would ask you whether you may not agree with me when you look at the matter in another way;—I mean, if you are still incredulous as to whether what is called learning is recollection?

Incredulous I am not, said Simmias; but I want to have this doctrine of recollection brought to my own recollection, and, from what Cebes has started to say, I am beginning to recollect and be convinced: but I should still like to hear you develop your own argument.

This is what I would say, he replied:—We should agree, if I am not   c
mistaken, that <u>what a man is to recollect he must have known at some
previous time.</u>

Very true.[3]

And do we also agree that knowledge obtained in the way I am about to describe is recollection? I mean to ask, Whether a person who, having seen or heard or in any way perceived anything, knows not only that, but also thinks of something else which is the subject not of the same but of some other kind of knowledge, may not be fairly said to recollect that of which he thinks?[4]   d

How do you mean?

I mean what I may illustrate by the following instance:—The knowledge of a lyre is not the same as the knowledge of a man?

Of course not.

And yet what is the feeling of lovers when they recognize a lyre, or a cloak, or anything else which the beloved has been in the habit of using? Do not they, from knowing the lyre, form in the mind's eye an image of the youth to whom the lyre belongs? And this is recollection. In like manner anyone who sees Simmias may often remember Cebes; and there are endless examples of the same thing.

Endless, indeed, replied Simmias.

And is not this sort of thing a kind of recollection—though the word   e
is most commonly applied to a process of recovering that which has been already forgotten through time and inattention?

Very true, he said.

Well; and may you not also from seeing the picture of a horse or a lyre recollect a man? and from the picture of Simmias, you may be led to recollect Cebes?

True.

Or you may be led to the recollection of Simmias himself?

Quite so.   74

And in all these cases, the recollection may be derived from things either like or unlike?

It may be.

And when the recollection is derived from like things, then another consideration is sure to arise, which is—whether the likeness in any degree falls short or not of that which is recollected?

Certainly, he said.

Now consider this question. We affirm, do we not, that there is such a thing as equality, not of one piece of wood or stone or similar material thing with another, but that, over and above this, there is absolute equality? Shall we say so?[5]

b   Say so, yes, replied Simmias, and swear to it, with all the confidence in life.

And do we know the nature of this absolute existence?

To be sure, he said.

And whence did we obtain our knowledge? Did we not see equalities of material things, such as pieces of wood and stones, and conceive from them the idea of an equality which is different from them? For you will acknowledge that there is a difference? Or look at the matter in another way:—Do not the same pieces of wood or stone appear to one man equal, and to another unequal?[6]

That is certain.

c   But did pure equals ever appear to you unequal? or equality the same as inequality?

Never, Socrates.

[Then these equal objects are not the same with the idea of equality?]

I should say, clearly not, Socrates.

And yet from these equals, although differing from the idea of equality, you obtained the knowledge of that idea?

Very true, he said.

Which might be like, or might be unlike them?

Yes.

But that makes no difference: so long as from seeing one thing you

d   conceive another, whether like or unlike, there must surely have been an act of recollection?

Very true.

But what would you say of equal portions of wood or other material equals? and what is the impression produced by them? Are they equals in the same sense in which absolute equality is equal? or do they fall short of this perfect equality in a measure?

Yes, he said, in a very great measure too.

And must we not allow, that when a man, looking at any object, reflects 'the thing which I see aims at being like some other thing, but falls

e   short of and cannot be like that other thing, and is inferior', he who so reflects must have had a previous knowledge of that to which the other, although similar, was inferior?

Certainly.

And has not this been our own case in the matter of equals and of absolute equality?

Precisely.

Then we must have known equality previously to the time when we

75   first saw the material equals, and reflected that they all strive to attain absolute equality, but fall short of it?

Very true.

And we recognize also that we have only derived this conception of absolute equality, and can only derive it, from sight or touch, or from some other of the senses, which are all alike in this respect?

Yes, Socrates, for the purposes of the present argument, one of them is the same as the other.

[From the senses then is derived the conception that all sensible equals aim at an absolute equality of which they fall short?]   b

Yes.

Then before we began to see or hear or perceive in any way, we must have had a knowledge of absolute equality, or we could not have referred to that standard the equals which are derived from the senses?— for to that they all aspire, and of that they fall short.

No other inference can be drawn from the previous statements.

And did we not begin to see and hear and have the use of our other senses as soon as we were born?[7]

Certainly.

Then we must have acquired the knowledge of equality at some   c previous time?

Yes.

That is to say, before we were born, I suppose?

It seems so.

And if we acquired this knowledge before we were born, and were born having the use of it, then we also knew before we were born and at the instant of birth not only the equal or the greater or the less, but all other such ideas; for we are not speaking only of equality, but of beauty,   d goodness, justice, holiness, and of all which we stamp with the name of absolute being in the dialectical process, both when we ask and when we answer questions. Of all this we affirm with certainty that we acquired the knowledge before birth?

We do.

But if, after having acquired, we have not on each occasion forgotten what we acquired, then we must always come into life having this knowledge, and shall have it always as long as life lasts—for knowing is the acquiring and retaining knowledge and not losing it. Is not the loss of knowledge, Simmias, just what we call forgetting?

Quite true, Socrates.   e

But if this knowledge which we acquired before birth was lost by us at birth, and if afterwards by the use of the senses we recovered what we previously knew, will not the process which we call learning be a recovering of knowledge which is natural to us, and may not this be rightly termed recollection?

Very true.

So much is clear—that when we perceive something, either by the   76 help of sight, or hearing, or some other sense, that perception can lead us to think of some other thing like or unlike which is associated with it but has been forgotten. Whence, as I was saying, one of two alternatives follows:—either we all have this knowledge at birth, and continue to know through life; or, after birth, those who are said to learn only recollect, and learning is simply recollection.

Yes, that is quite true, Socrates.

b And which alternative, Simmias, do you prefer? Have we the knowledge at our birth, or do we recollect afterwards things which we knew previously to our birth?

I cannot decide at the moment.

At any rate you can decide whether he who has knowledge will or will not be able to render an account of his knowledge? What do you say?

Certainly, he will.[8]

But do you think that every man is able to give an account of the matters about which we were speaking a moment ago?

Would that they could, Socrates, but I much rather fear that to-morrow, at this time, there will no longer be anyone alive who is able to give an account of them such as ought to be given.

c Then you are not of opinion, Simmias, that all men know these things?

Certainly not.

They are in process of recollecting that which they learned before?

Certainly.

But when did our souls acquire this knowledge?—clearly not since we were born as men?

Certainly not.

And therefore, previously?

Yes.

Then, Simmias, our souls must also have existed without bodies before they were in the form of man, and must have had intelligence.

Unless indeed you suppose, Socrates, that all such knowledge is given us at the very moment of birth; for this is the only time which remains.

d Yes, my friend, but if so, when, pray, do we lose it? for it is not in us when we are born—that is admitted. Do we lose it at the moment of receiving it, or if not at what other time?

No, Socrates, I perceive that I was unconsciously talking nonsense.

Then may we not say, Simmias, that if there do exist these things of which we are always talking, absolute beauty and goodness, and all that class of realities; and if to this we refer all our sensations and with

e this compare them, finding the realities to be pre-existent and our own possession—then just as surely as these exist, so surely must our souls have existed before our birth? Otherwise our whole argument would be worthless. By an equal compulsion we must believe both that these realities exist, and that our souls existed before our birth; and if not the realities, then not the souls.

C   *PHAEDO* 100+

... I should like to know whether you agree with me in the next step; for I cannot help thinking, if there be anything beautiful other than absolute beauty it is beautiful only in so far as it partakes of absolute beauty—and I should say the same of everything. Do you agree in this notion of the cause? [9]

Yes, he said, I agree.

He proceeded: I no longer look for, nor can I understand, those other ingenious causes which are alleged; and if a person says to me that the bloom of colour, or form, or any such thing is a source of beauty,   d I dismiss all that, which is only confusing to me, and simply and singly, and perhaps foolishly, hold and am assured in my own mind that nothing makes a thing beautiful but the presence or participation of beauty in whatever way or manner obtained; for as to the manner I am uncertain, but I stoutly contend that by beauty all beautiful things become beautiful.[10] This appears to me to be the safest answer which I can give, either to myself or to another, and to this I cling, in the persuasion that this principle will never be overthrown, and that to myself or to anyone who   e asks the question, I may safely reply, That by beauty beautiful things become beautiful. Do you not agree with me?

I do.

And that by greatness great things become great and greater greater, and by smallness the less become less?

True.

Then if a person were to remark that A is taller by a head than B, and B less by a head than A, you would refuse to admit his statement, and   101 would stoutly contend that what you mean is only that the greater is greater by, and by reason of, greatness, and the less is less only by, and by reason of, smallness. I imagine you would be afraid of a counter-argument that if the greater is greater and the less less by the head, then, first, the greater is greater and the less less by the same thing; and, secondly, the greater man is greater by the head which is itself small, and so you get the monstrous absurdity that a man is great by something   b small. You would be afraid of this, would you not? [11]

Indeed I should, said Cebes, laughing.

In like manner you would think it dangerous to say that ten exceeded eight by, and by reason of, two; but would say by, and by reason of, number; or you would say that two cubits exceed one cubit not by a half, but by magnitude?—for there is the same danger in all these cases.

Very true, he said.

Again, would you not be cautious of affirming that the addition of one to one, or the division of one, is the cause of two? And you would   c loudly asseverate that you know of no way in which anything comes into existence except by participation in the distinctive reality of that in which it participates, and consequently, as far as you know, the only cause of two is the participation in duality—this is the way to make two, and the participation in unity is the way to make one. You would say: 'I will let alone all subtleties like these of division and addition—wiser heads than mine may answer them; inexperienced as I am, and ready to start, as the proverb says, at my own shadow, I cannot afford to give up the sure ground of the original postulate. And if anyone fastens on you there, you would not mind him, or answer him until you could see whether the consequences which follow agree with one another or not, and when you are further required to give an account of this postulate, you would give it in the same way, assuming some higher postulate which seemed to you to be the best founded, until you arrived at a satisfactory resting-place; but you would not jumble together the fundamental principle and the consequences in your reasoning, like the eristics—at least if you wanted to discover real existence. Not that this confusion signifies to them, who probably never care or think about the matter at all, for they have the wit to be well pleased with themselves however thorough may be the muddle of their ideas. But you, if you are a philosopher, will certainly do as I say.

D   REPUBLIC 506 +

Evidently, then, there are many great differences of opinion about the good.

    Undoubtedly.

    Is it not likewise evident that many are content to do or to have, or to seem to be, what is just and beautiful without the reality; but no one is satisfied with the appearance of good—the reality is what they seek; in the case of the good, appearance is despised by every one.[12]

    Very true, he said.

    Of this then, which every soul of man pursues and makes the end of all his actions, having a presentiment that there is such an end, and yet hesitating because neither knowing the nature nor having the same assurance of this as of other things, and therefore losing whatever good there is in other things,—of a principle such and so great as this ought the best men in our State, to whom everything is entrusted, to be in the darkness of ignorance?

    Certainly not, he said.

    I am sure, I said, that he who does not know how the noble and the just are likewise good will be but a sorry guardian of them; and I suspect that no one who is ignorant of the good will have a true knowledge of them.

    That, he said, is a shrewd suspicion of yours.

    And if only we have a guardian who has this knowledge our State will be perfectly ordered?

Of course, he replied; but I wish that you would tell me whether you conceive this supreme principle of the good to be knowledge or pleasure, or different from either?

Sir, I said, I could see quite well all along that you would not be contented with the thoughts of other people about these matters.

True, Socrates; but I must say that one who like you has passed a lifetime in the study of philosophy should not be always repeating the opinions of others, and never telling his own.

Well, but has anyone a right to say positively what he does not   c
know?

Not, he said, with the assurance of positive certainty; he has no right to do that: but he may say what he thinks, as a matter of opinion.

And have you not observed, I said, that all mere opinions are bad, and the best of them blind? You would not deny that those who have any true notion without intelligence are only like blind men who feel their way along the right road?

Very true.

And do you wish to behold what is blind and crooked and base,   d
when others will tell you of brightness and beauty?

Still, I must implore you, Socrates, said Glaucon, not to turn away just as you are reaching the goal; if you will only give such an explanation of the good as you have already given of justice and temperance and the other virtues, we shall be satisfied.

Yes, my friend, and I shall be at least equally satisfied, but I cannot help fearing that I shall fail, and that my indiscreet zeal will bring ridicule upon me. No, sirs, let us not at present ask what is the actual   e
nature of the good, for to reach what is now in my thoughts would be an effort too great for me. But of the child of the good who is likest him, I am ready to speak, if I could be sure that you wished to hear—otherwise, not.

By all means, he said, tell us about the child, and you shall remain in our debt for the account of the parent.

I do indeed wish, I replied, that I could pay, and you receive, the   507
account of the parent, and not, as now, of the offspring only; take, however, this latter by way of interest, and at the same time have a care that I do not pay you in spurious coin, although I have no intention of deceiving you.

Yes, we will take all the care that we can: proceed.

Yes, I said, but I must first come to an understanding with you, and remind you of what I have mentioned in the course of this discussion,   b
and at many other times.

What?

The old story, that there are many beautiful things and many good. And again there is a true beauty, a true good; and all other things to which the term *many* has been applied, are now brought under a single idea, and, assuming this unity, we speak of it in every case as *that which really is.*[13]

Very true.

The many, as we say, are seen but not known, and the Ideas are known but not seen.

c   Exactly.

And what is the organ with which we see the visible things?

The sight, he said.

And with the hearing, I said, we hear, and with the other senses perceive the other objects of sense?

True.

But have you remarked that sight is by far the most costly and complex piece of workmanship which the artificer of the senses ever contrived?

Not exactly, he said.

Then reflect: have the ear and voice need of any third or additional
d   nature in order that the one may be able to hear and the other to be heard?

Nothing of the sort.

No, indeed, I replied; and the same is true of most, if not all, the other senses—you would not say that any of them requires such an addition?

Certainly not.

But you see that without the addition of some other nature there is no seeing or being seen?

How do you mean?

Sight being, as I conceive, in the eyes, and he who has eyes wanting to see; colour being also present in the objects, still unless there be a third
e   nature specially adapted to the purpose, sight, as you know, will see nothing and the colours will be invisible.

Of what nature are you speaking?

Of that which you term light, I replied.

True, he said.

508   Then the bond which links together the sense of sight and the power of being seen, is of an evidently nobler nature than other such bonds—unless sight is an ignoble thing?

Nay, he said, the reverse of ignoble.

And which, I said, of the gods in heaven would you say was the lord of this element? Whose is that light which makes the eye to see perfectly and the visible to appear?

I should answer, as all men would, and as you plainly expect—the sun.

May not the relation of sight to this deity be described as follows?

How?

Neither sight nor the organ in which it resides, which we call the eye, is the sun?

No.   b

Yet of all the organs of sense the eye is the most like the sun?

By far the most like.

And the power which the eye possesses is a sort of effluence which is dispensed from the sun?

Exactly.

Then the sun is not sight, but the author of sight who is recognized by sight?

True, he said.

And this, you must understand, is he whom I call the child of the good, whom the good begat in his own likeness, to be in the visible world, in relation to sight and the things of sight, what the good is in the   c
intellectual world in relation to mind and the things of mind:

Will you be a little more explicit? he said.

Why, you know, I said that the eyes, when a person directs them towards objects on which the light of day is no longer shining, but the moon and stars only, see dimly, and are nearly blind; they seem to have no clearness of vision in them?   d

Very true.

But when they are directed towards objects on which the sun shines, they see clearly and there is sight in them?

Certainly.

And the soul is like the eye: when resting upon that on which truth and being shine, the soul perceives and understands, and is radiant with intelligence; but when turned towards the twilight and to those things which come into being and perish, then she has opinion only, and goes blinking about, and is first of one opinion and then of another, and seems to have no intelligence?

Just so.

Now, that which imparts truth to the known and the power of knowing to the knower is, as I would have you say, the Idea of good, and this   e
Idea, which is the cause of science and of truth, you are to conceive as being apprehended by knowledge, and yet, fair as both truth and knowledge are, you will be right to esteem it as different from these and even   509
fairer; and as in the previous instance light and sight may be truly said to be like the sun and yet not to be the sun, so in this other sphere science and truth may be deemed to be like the good, but it is wrong to think that they are the good; the good has a place of honour yet higher.

What a wonder of beauty that must be, he said, which is the author of science and truth, and yet surpasses them in beauty; for you surely cannot mean to say that pleasure is the good?

God forbid, I replied; but may I ask you to consider the image in another point of view?

b   In what point of view?

You would say, would you not, that the sun is not only the author of visibility in all visible things, but of generation and nourishment and growth, though he himself is not generation?

Certainly.

In like manner you must say that the good not only infuses the power of being known into all things known, but also bestows upon them their being and existence, and yet the good is not existence, but lies far beyond it in dignity and power.

c   Glaucon said, with a ludicrous earnestness: By the light of heaven, that is far beyond indeed!

Yes, I said, and the exaggeration may be set down to you; for you made me utter my fancies.

And pray continue to utter them; at any rate let us hear if there is anything more to be said about the similitude of the sun.

Yes, I said, there is a great deal more.

Then omit nothing, however slight.

I expect that I shall omit a great deal, I said, but shall not do so deliberately, as far as present circumstances permit.

I hope not, he said.

d   You have to imagine, then, that there are two ruling powers, and that one of them is set over the intellectual world, the other over the visible. I do not say heaven, lest you should fancy that I am playing upon the name (οὐρανός, ὁρατός).[14] May I suppose that you have this distinction of the visible and intelligible fixed in your mind?

I have.

Now take a line which has been cut into two unequal parts, and divide each of them again in the same proportion, and suppose the two main divisions to answer, one to the visible and the other to the intel-
e   ligible, and then compare the subdivisions in respect of their clearness and want of clearness, and you will find that the first section in the sphere
510   of the visible consists of images.[15] And by images I mean, in the first place, shadows, and in the second place, reflections in water and in solid, smooth and polished bodies and the like: Do you understand?

Yes, I understand.

Imagine, now, the other section, of which this is only the resemblance, to include the animals which we see, and every thing that grows or is made.

Very good.

Would you not admit that both the sections of this division have different degrees of truth, and that the copy is to the original as the sphere of opinion is to the sphere of knowledge?

b   Most undoubtedly.

Next proceed to consider the manner in which the sphere of the intellectual is to be divided.

In what manner?

Thus:—There are two subdivisions, in the lower of which the soul, using as images those things which themselves were reflected in the former division, is forced to base its enquiry upon hypotheses, proceeding not towards a principle but towards a conclusion; in the higher of the two, the soul proceeds *from hypotheses*, and goes up to a principle which is above hypotheses, making no use of images as in the former case, but proceeding only in and through the Ideas themselves.

I do not quite understand your meaning, he said.

Then I will try again; you will understand me better when I have c made some preliminary remarks. You are aware that students of geometry, arithmetic, and the kindred sciences assume the odd and the even and the figures and three kinds of angles and the like in their several branches of science; these are their hypotheses, which they and everybody are supposed to know, and therefore they do not deign to give any account of them either to themselves or others; but they begin with them, and go on until they arrive at last, and in a consistent manner, at the d solution which they set out to find?

Yes, he said, I know.

And do you not know also that although they make use of the visible forms and reason about them, they are thinking not of these, but of the ideals which they resemble; not of the figures which they draw, but of the absolute square and the absolute diameter, and so on—the forms which they draw or make, and which themselves have shadows and re- e flections in water, are in turn converted by them into images; for they are really seeking to behold the things themselves, which can only be seen with the eye of the mind?

That is true.   511

And this was what I meant by a subdivision of the intelligible, in the search after which the soul is compelled to use hypotheses; not ascending to a first principle, because she is unable to rise above the region of hypothesis, but employing now as images those objects from which the shadows below were derived, even these being deemed clear and distinct by comparison with the shadows.

I understand, he said, that you are speaking of the province of b geometry and the sister arts.

And when I speak of the other division of the intelligible, you will understand me to speak of that other sort of knowledge which reason herself attains by the power of dialectic, using the hypotheses not as first principles, but literally as hypotheses—that is to say, as steps and points of departure into a world which is above hypotheses, in order that she may soar beyond them to the first principle of the whole; and clinging to this and then to that which depends on this, by successive steps she de- scends again without the aid of any sensible object, from ideas, through c Ideas, and in Ideas she ends.

I understand you, he replied; not perfectly, for you seem to me to be describing a task which is really tremendous; but, at any rate, I understand you to say that that part of intelligible Being, which the science of dialectic contemplates, is clearer than that which falls under the arts, as they are termed, which take hypotheses as their principles; and though the objects are of such a kind that they must be viewed by the under-

d   standing, and not by the senses, yet, because they start from hypotheses and do not ascend to a principle, those who contemplate them appear to you not to exercise the higher reason upon them, although when a first principle is added to them they are cognizable by the higher reason. And the habit which is concerned with geometry and the cognate sciences I suppose that you would term understanding and not reason, as being intermediate between opinion and reason.

You have quite conceived my meaning, I said; and now, corresponding to these four divisions, let there be four faculties in the soul—reason

e   answering to the highest, understanding to the second, faith (or conviction) to the third, and perception of shadows to the last—and let there be a scale of them, and let us suppose that the several faculties have clearness in the same degree that their objects have truth.

I understand, he replied, and give my assent, and accept your arrangement.

BOOK VII

514   And now, I said, let me show in a figure how far our nature is enlightened or unenlightened:—Behold! human beings housed in an underground cave, which has a long entrance open towards the light and as wide as the interior of the cave; here they have been from their childhood, and

b   have their legs and necks chained, so that they cannot move and can only see before them, being prevented by the chains from turning round their heads. Above and behind them a fire is blazing at a distance, and between the fire and the prisoners there is a raised way; and you will see, if you look, a low wall built along the way, like the screen which marionette players have in front of them, over which they show the puppets.

I see.

And do you see, I said, men passing along the wall carrying all

c   sorts of vessels, and statues and figures of animals made of wood and

515   stone and various materials, which appear over the wall? While carrying their burdens, some of them, as you would expect, are talking, others silent.

You have shown me a strange image, and they are strange prisoners.

Like ourselves, I replied; for in the first place do you think they have seen anything of themselves, and of one another, except the shadows which the fire throws on the opposite wall of the cave?

How could they do so, he asked, if throughout their lives they were   b
never allowed to move their heads?

And of the objects which are being carried in like manner they
would only see the shadows?

Yes, he said.

And if they were able to converse with one another, would they not
suppose that the things they saw were the real things?

Very true.

And suppose further that the prison had an echo which came from
the other side, would they not be sure to fancy when one of the passers-by
spoke that the voice which they heard came from the passing shadow?

No question, he replied.

To them, I said, the truth would be literally nothing but the shadows   c
of the images.

That is certain.

And now look again, and see in what manner they would be released from their bonds, and cured of their error, whether the process
would naturally be as follows. At first, when any of them is liberated and
compelled suddenly to stand up and turn his neck round and walk and
look towards the light, he will suffer sharp pains; the glare will distress
him, and he will be unable to see the realities of which in his former state
he had seen the shadows; and then conceive someone saying to him that
what he saw before was an illusion, but that now, when he is approaching   d
nearer to being and his eye is turned towards more real existence, he has
a clearer vision,—what will be his reply? And you may further imagine
that his instructor is pointing to the objects as they pass and requiring
him to name them,—will he not be perplexed? Will he not fancy that
the shadows which he formerly saw are truer than the objects which are
now shown to him?

Far truer.

And if he is compelled to look straight at the light, will he not have   e
a pain in his eyes which will make him turn away to take refuge in the
objects of vision which he can see, and which he will conceive to be in
reality clearer than the things which are now being shown to him?

True, he said.

And suppose once more, that he is reluctantly dragged up that
steep and rugged ascent, and held fast until he is forced into the presence
of the sun himself, is he not likely to be pained and irritated? When he
approaches the light his eyes will be dazzled, and he will not be able to   516
see anything at all of what are now called realities.

Not all in a moment, he said.

He will require to grow accustomed to the sight of the upper world.
And first he will see the shadows best, next the reflections of men and
other objects in the water, and then the objects themselves; and, when he
turned to the heavenly bodies and the heaven itself, he would find it easier

b   to gaze upon the light of the moon and the stars at night than to see the sun or the light of the sun by day?

Certainly.

Last of all he will be able to see the sun, not turning aside to the illusory reflections of him in the water, but gazing directly at him in his own proper place, and contemplating him as he is.[16]

Certainly.

He will then proceed to argue that this is he who gives the seasons and the years, and is the guardian of all that is in the visible world, and in a

c   certain way the cause of all things which he and his fellows have been accustomed to behold?

Clearly, he said, he would arrive at this conclusion after what he had seen.

And when he remembered his old habitation, and the wisdom of the cave and his fellow-prisoners, do you not suppose that he would felicitate himself on the change, and pity them?

Certainly, he would.

And if they were in the habit of conferring honours among themselves on those who were quickest to observe the passing shadows and to remark which of them went before and which followed after and which were

d   together, and who were best able from these observations to divine the future, do you think that he would be eager for such honours and glories, or envy those who attained honour and sovereignty among those men? Would he not say with Homer,

'Better to be a serf, labouring for a landless master',[17]

and to endure anything, rather than think as they do and live after their manner?

e   Yes, he said, I think that he would consent to suffer anything rather than live in this miserable manner.

Imagine once more, I said, such a one coming down suddenly out of the sunlight, and being replaced in his old seat; would he not be certain to have his eyes full of darkness?

To be sure, he said.

And if there were a contest, and he had to compete in measuring the

517   shadows with the prisoners who had never moved out of the cave, while his sight was still weak, and before his eyes had become steady (and the time which would be needed to acquire this new habit of sight might be very considerable), would he not make himself ridiculous? Men would say of him that he had returned from the place above with his eyes ruined; and that it was better not even to think of ascending; and if anyone tried to loose another and lead him up the light, let them only catch the offender, and they would put him to death.

No question, he said.

b   This entire allegory, I said, you may now append, dear Glaucon, to the previous argument; the prison-house is the world of sight, the light of the fire is the power of the sun, and you will not misapprehend me if you interpret the journey upwards to be the ascent of the soul into the intellectual world according to my surmise, which, at your desire, I have expressed —whether rightly or wrongly God knows. But, whether true or false, my opinion is that in the world of knowledge the Idea of good appears last of all, and is seen only with an effort; although, when seen, it is inferred to be   c the universal author of all things beautiful and right, parent of light and of the lord of light in the visible world, and the immediate and supreme source of reason and truth in the intellectual; and that this is the power upon which he who would act rationally either in public or private life must have his eye fixed.

I agree, he said, as far as I am able to understand you.

Moreover, I said, you must agree once more, and not wonder that those who attain to this vision are unwilling to take any part in human affairs; for their souls are ever hastening into the upper world where they desire to dwell; which desire of theirs is very natural, if our allegory may   d be trusted.[18]

Yes, very natural.

And is there anything surprising in one who passes from divine contemplations to the evil state of man, appearing grotesque and ridiculous; if, while his eyes are blinking and before he has become accustomed to the surrounding darkness, he is compelled to fight in courts of law, or in other places, about the images or the shadows of images of justice, and must strive against some rival about opinions of these things which are   e entertained by men who have never yet seen the true justice?

Anything but surprising, he replied.

Anyone who has common sense will remember that the bewilderments   ¡518 of the eyes are of two kinds and arise from two causes, either from coming out of the light or from going into the light, and, judging that the soul may be affected in the same way, will not give way to foolish laughter when he sees anyone whose vision is perplexed and weak; he will first ask whether that soul of man has come out of the brighter life and is unable to see because unaccustomed to the dark, or having turned from darkness to the day is dazzled by excess of light. And he will count the one happy in his   b condition and state of being, and he will pity the other; or, if he have a mind to laugh at the soul which comes from below into the light, this laughter will not be quite so laughable as that which greets the soul which returns from above out of the light into the cave.   c

That, he said, is a very just distinction.

But then, if I am right, certain professors of education must be wrong when they say that they can put a knowledge into the soul which was not there before, like sight into blind eyes.

They undoubtedly say this, he replied.

Whereas our argument shows that the power and capacity of learning

exists in the soul already; and that just as if it were not possible to turn the eye from darkness to light without the whole body, so too the instrument of knowledge can only by the movement of the whole soul be turned from the the world of becoming to that of being, and learn by degrees to endure the sight of being, and of the brightest and best of being, or in other words, of
d   the good.

Very true.

And must there not be some art which will show how the conversion can be effected in the easiest and quickest manner; an art which will not implant the faculty of sight, for that exists already, but will set it straight when it has been turned in the wrong direction, and is looking away from the truth?

Yes, he said, such an art may be presumed.

And whereas the other so-called virtues of the soul seem to be akin to
e   bodily qualities, for even when they are not originally innate they can be implanted later by habit and exercise, the virtue of wisdom more than anything else contains a divine element which never loses its power, and by this conversion is rendered useful and profitable; or, by conversion of
519   another sort, hurtful and useless. Did you never observe the narrow intelligence flashing from the keen eye of a clever rogue—how eager he is, how clearly his paltry soul sees the way to his end; he is the reverse of blind, but his keen eye-sight is forced into the service of evil, and he is mischievous in proportion to his cleverness?

Very true, he said.

But what if such natures had been gradually stripped, beginning in childhood, of the leaden weights which sink them in the sea of Becoming,
b   and which, fastened upon the soul through gluttonous indulgence in eating and other such pleasures, forcibly turn its vision downwards—if, I say, they had been released from these impediments and turned in the opposite direction, the very same faculty in them would have seen the truth as keenly as they see what their eyes are turned to now.

NOTES

1   Is this argument valid? Knowledge might have been *given* to the mind at birth in some fashion: this is discussed and dismissed below. The dismissal of this, and other possibilities, follows from the Platonic view of the soul. A full discussion of this argument requires that the properties of the soul be made explicit.

2   The mention of diagrams is in reference to drawings used in finding geometrical truths. In the *Meno*, another Platonic dialogue, a slave *proves* a geometrical theorem by answering questions put to him by Socrates. Notice that this passage explicitly acknowledges that the questioner's way of putting questions is important, but that in spite of this necessary skill on the questioner's part, the right answers are still possible only if the soul has had previous knowledge.

3   No other answer seems possible because of the meaning which is being given to *recollection*. This is an example of the important way in which definitions function in philosophical argument.

4   This is a difficult passage, and Plato proceeds to discuss it at great length. It seems to be a compact way of announcing his view that sense experience may prod the soul to remember true knowledge, even though the soul's knowledge does not *depend* on sense experience.

5   The following passage is extremely difficult for Platonic expositors. You can find extended discussions of it in the articles "Forms and Standards," by R. E. Allen, and "Plato's *Phaedo* 74 b7–c6," by K. W. Mills, which are cited above in the bibliography for this part. What is translated here as 'absolute equality' ($\alpha\dot{v}\tau\grave{\alpha}$ $\tau\grave{\alpha}$ $\dot{\iota}\sigma\alpha$) is normally taken to refer to the form of equality and the term *equals* occurring in later lines ($\tau\alpha\hat{v}\tau\alpha$ $\tau\grave{\alpha}$ $\dot{\iota}\sigma\alpha$) to actual objects which are judged to be equal. The total passage then suggests that absolute equality is equal, that is, has the property of equality. This kind of passage supports a crucial premise of the infinite regress argument against the theory of forms discussed in "Problems in Participation," namely, the premise asserting self-predication of the forms. Now the key problem of interpretation becomes that of explaining how equality, which is a relation between two or more things, can be known by a form of equality, which by the nature of forms can have no parts.

6   A familiar Platonic point! Equal things are not always equal or are not equal in every respect. On the other hand, the idea of equality remains the same. Thus our knowledge of equality cannot be reduced to knowledge of actual pairs of things, since our idea of equality has a property (invariance) which pairs of experienced equal things do not have.

7   The ambiguity of the word *see* must be considered in evaluating this argument. Although babies *see* when they are born (those that are not born blind), babies do not seem to *see* mother, *see* father, *see* danger, and so forth. Exactly what they see is extremely problematic. In terms of Plato's argument, if babies see when they are born, why do they not seem to recollect knowledge until they are older?

8   Remembrance or recollection is invoked to explain obvious differences in human knowledge. Plato rules out the possibility that these differences are due to relative *abilities* or to differing biographies. Does the claim that anyone who has knowledge will be able to render an account of it seem as obviously true as Simmias takes it to be? Or can someone know something that he cannot explain to others?

9   The *cause* of something's beauty is said to be the form of beauty. This notion of causation must be distinguished from causation as it might be understood in science. By the cause of what is beautiful Plato refers to what enables us to know or to recognize what is beautiful.

10   Natural causation is here excluded. Plato is claiming that explaining one sense experience (a beautiful flower) by other sense experiences is to explain the inexplicable by means of the inexplicable, as we do not have knowledge of *any* sense experiences. *Ingenious* is used sardonically.

11   Passages like this are indicative of Platonic difficulties in handling relations.

Let Tom, Dick, and Harry be arranged in order of relative height, with Tom as the tallest. If Tom's height relative to Dick's is explained by Tom's participation in the form of tallness, and Dick's participation in the form of smallness, how is Dick's relative tallness to Harry to be explained? Dick cannot presumably participate in both smallness and tallness. It should be pointed out that the theory of ideas has difficulty in accounting for complex relationships among a number of objects.

12   The point is that although one may wish to appear just in order, for example, to pursue political power, no one considers himself evil. This is a curiosity of moral theory. With the exception of some religious saints, most people seem to feel that they are good people (or mostly good) in terms of their own standards. Plato uses this point in support of the claim that to know the good is to do the good, by virtue of the fact that he took it to be obvious that one would not willingly fail to do what he knew to be the good thing to do.

13   Here is a succinct formulation of the Platonic point that anytime we may separate some class of objects from the rest of things in some nonarbitrary way, this separation may be accounted for by an Idea in which these things participate.

14   It is not clear what pun Plato may have had in mind. There is some suspicion that he may have been avoiding an argument from words which would support his position on the accidental etymology of the words used crucially in the argument.

15   There are some subtle difficulties in Plato's account of the divided line. See, for example, Robert S. Brumbaugh's "Plato's Divided Line," *Review of Metaphysics,* June, 1952, pp. 529–534, which shows that the figure as described by Plato cannot be constructed. Suppose a line to be divided into segments with the ratio $m:n$. Let m be divided into segments a and b, and n into segments c and d. Now by the construction, $m/n = a/b = c/d$. If r is the length of the original line, one can show $b = (m/r)n$, and $c = (n/r)m$. Consequently, b and c have the same length. But in context, the significance of the length of the segments (the clearness of the knowledge in the nontechnical sense that is represented by the segment) indicates that the segments should get increasingly longer in one direction. The problem then becomes one of deciding whether or not this discrepancy is a slip on Plato's part, or of some other significance.

16   An interesting problem is that of relating the Allegory of the Cave (which is what this section of the *Republic* is called) to the fourfold division of the line described above. Richard Robinson (in *Plato's Earlier Dialectic,* 2d ed., Oxford, 1953, p. 182), among others, has argued that there is no exact correspondence indicated in the text. In "The Line and the Cave," *Phronesis,* vol. 7, pp. 38–45, 1962, John Malcolm argues that a correspondence is intended by Plato. If the Allegory of the Cave is taken as a description of the philosopher's acquisition of knowledge, Malcolm correlates watching the shadows on the wall of the cave with the uneducated state of the common man, seeing the objects in the cave with true belief about material objects, seeing the reflections of objects in the world above with the study of mathematics, and contemplating the objects in the world above with knowledge of the forms. Most of the relevant bibliography associated with the problem of correlating the Allegory of the Cave and the divided line is cited in Malcolm's article. In view of Malcolm's conjecture, is the allegory helpful? Are the fire and the sun identical? Why should those

released from the cave look at the shadows of the world above before looking at the objects themselves?

17   The shade of Achilles in Hades said this when he was asked what he thought of life after death (Greek style). See Homer's *Odyssey*, 11: 489–491.

18   A justification for the impracticality of the philosopher in the eyes of the ordinary man and citizen.

PART 2

Aristotle

(384–322 B.C.)

Plato and Aristotle

Aristotle discerned a difference between knowledge and opinion in human thought, but he drew the boundaries of knowledge more liberally than Plato, extending the range of examples of human knowledge to cases that Plato would have rejected. Where Plato had a tendency to conflate opinion and ignorance, making uncertain information almost as inconsequential as complete ignorance, Aristotle developed analyses of subject matter where certainty was, by his own admission, impossible, but where he took the discovery of statements *true in most instances* to have important consequences for guiding human action. For Aristotle, informed opinion is a kind of knowledge. All cases of knowledge exhibited in human claims to knowledge are considered by Aristotle under two classifications, dependent on whether or not the knowledge considered represents what is always true or what is merely true in many cases, yet of value for practical action. Knowledge which represents what is necessarily true independently of human desires and hopes is called theoretical science. True statements of theoretical science are always true, and hence the range of theoretical science is quite similar to the range of *knowledge* in Plato's defined sense. On the other hand, practical science is the result of studying what is quite often true (perhaps even true in every observed case), but which need not be true if human beings should desire to bring about some change.

Practical science is the result of collecting and speculating upon observed regularities among things, taking into account information accumulated by other human beings as relevant data. Aristotle's contributions to what he called practical science range over analyses of what would now be called biology, psychology, ethics, political science, and literary criticism. His development of techniques of analysis for these areas and the acuteness of many of his conclusions constitute one of the great single contributions to human knowledge. For example, his analysis of drama into plot, character, etc., and his definition of tragedy have become staples of literary criticism in all intellectual traditions which may be traced back to Greek origins. Still, Aristotle's practical science is largely to be tested by later observations of a factual kind, and its content is not as important for philosophy as what he considered to lie within the domain of theoretical science.

Theoretical science, to repeat, is the study of what is necessarily true independently of human desires. The truths of theoretical science are thus certain, and they may be taken to be those universal truths which may be deduced from what Aristotle called *self-evident* principles. Self-evident principles are defined to be those principles which no properly disciplined mind could deny. This does not mean that everyone understands them and knows them to be true, or even that anyone whose attention has been drawn to them sees them immediately to be true and universal, but it means that those who give the matter sufficient attention and take time to learn the techniques of inquiry will come to see their truth. Aristotle concludes that some knowledge of this kind is available to human beings as certain truth. This has the consequence that Aristotle is as impatient with complete skepticism as Plato is.

Two remarks about Aristotle's method might well be made before we consider the content of theoretical science. The point of these remarks may be summarized by saying that Aristotle's approach to philosophical questions is considerably more analytical than Plato's. To begin with, Aristotle often takes comparatively minor problems and examines them carefully, without particular regard in each case for consistency with what he says elsewhere. Thus, although certain points appear in a number of places in Aristotle's writings, there are likely to be discrepancies between the treatments in these places which are not always easy to resolve. This may be due to the fact that there is no dominant insight in Aristotle's writings that plays quite the same role as the theory of ideas does in Platonic philosophy. Instead, Aristotle often uses his philosophical concepts (form, matter, substance, cause, potentiality, actuality, substratum, etc.) as *tools*, to be used in any way that advances the solution of a particular problem. Tools are used at different times in different ways, and perhaps this is why it appears that some of Aristotle's tools are described differently in different contexts. Dealing with the problem of whether these varied accounts are actually consistent with one another is one of the major challenges of Aristotelian scholarship. A consequence of the differences of approach of Aristotle and Plato is that although Platonic philosophy seems to stand or fall with the acceptability of the theory of ideas, Aristotle's analyses can often be accepted or rejected independently of one another. In particular, many philosophers accept much of Aristotle's logical speculation and large amounts of his contributions to practical science, while rejecting many conclusions of his discussions of topics in theoretical science.

The other remark about Aristotle's method is that he introduced to philosophy and science an important technique that is now commonplace. Confronted with some problem, Aristotle often surveyed the answers that had already been given to the problem, as well as possible answers that had not been explicitly given but which could be given. In this way, he was often able to discuss all of the answers to some question in a general way, since it could be shown that any possible answer would be equivalent to one of the answers discussed in the survey. A good classification of the possible answers and an efficient method of working through such a classification often reveals some of the characteristics of any good answer to the problem being considered. The usefulness of this technique is enormous, as is immediately apparent from the fact that an infinite number of incorrect solutions which it is possible to formulate for some problem may be eliminated from consideration if they are all shown to be equivalent to some kind of answer that can be shown to be unacceptable. Classification of possible answers may also be used to answer the question of how many different kinds of something there are, as in the syllogism, where classification into figures, moods, etc., enables one to discover how many valid arguments of syllogistic form there are by working through a finite classification of possible forms of syllogistic argument and checking them for validity.

Consider any two classes of things, say the class of men and the class of animals. To keep the discussion conveniently abstract, we may call these classes A and B. The A's (that is, the members of the class A) and the B's may be related in a number of ways, but Aristotle proposed that they could all be analyzed in terms of four relationships which we may express in the following four *categorical* statements: All A's are B's, No A's are B's, Some A's are B's, and Some A's are not B's. Traditionally, a syllogism is any argument in which three categorical statements appear, one as conclusion and the other two as premises, such that the categorical statements are about three classes, each of which is mentioned in two of the categorical statements of the syllogistic argument. The following two arguments are syllogisms:

All men are animals.
All animals are mortal beings.
Therefore, All men are mortal beings.

and

All petunias are plants.
All plants are living things.
Therefore, All petunias are living things.

To begin with, it might be said that these arguments are obviously *different*, in that one argument is about men, animals, and mortal beings, and the other argument is about petunias, plants, and living things. We might express this difference by saying that the two arguments have different subject *matter.* At the same time, we might take these arguments as having the same *form,* and hence as belonging to the same classification. For example, consider the following *form* of an argument:

All *X*'s are *Y*'s.
All *Y*'s are *Z*'s.
Therefore, All *X*'s are *Z*'s.

This form is not an *argument* because it does not have sentences as parts, but expressions which may be turned into sentences when appropriate substitutions are made for *X*'s, *Y*'s, and *Z*'s. Both of our previous *arguments* can be taken to have this *form,* since substitution of *men* for *X*'s, *animals* for *Y*'s, and *mortal beings* for *Z*'s results in the first argument, while substitution of *petunias* for *X*'s, *plants* for *Y*'s, and *living things* for *Z*'s results in the second argument. Since *X*'s, *Y*'s, and *Z*'s could be substituted for by the names of any collections of things, it is clear that an *infinite* number of possible actual arguments might have this form.

There will be only a finite number of *forms* of syllogistic argument, since each argument has three categorical statements and three classes mentioned in it. One can make a list of these possible *forms* and work through the list checking those forms which are valid. Then when one wants to know if a syllogistic argument is valid, he can determine the form of the argument and then check the list of forms that he has constructed. This is what Aristotle attempted, and it shows the power of the analytic method. An *infinite* number of possible syllogistic arguments is analyzed by constructing a finite *classification* of such arguments such that any actual syllogistic arguments must belong to one of the classifications. Studying the classification, in turn, enables us to have *knowledge* about *all* the possible particular syllogistic arguments that we might encounter in philosophical practice.

An exhaustive classification of possible answers may also be applied to questions of theoretical science, which, as we have seen, deals with truths not affected by human desires. One question is: what kinds of entities is theoretical science about? If Platonic antecedents are taken into account, two properties of entities may be considered which, taken together, provide a fourfold classification of the possible objects dealt with by theoretical science. Plato considers objects which are sensible (known to sense experience), like tables and chairs, and objects which are not sensible, the ideas or forms. Further, we find in Plato reference to changing objects and to objects which do not change. Now in Plato's discussion, sensible objects and changing objects are correlated, as are the non-sensible and eternal objects, in that any object belonging to one of the correlated classes also belongs to the other. The possible fourfold classification suggested by the four terms (sensible changing objects, sensible eternal objects, non-sensible eternal objects, and non-sensible changing objects) is discussed by Aristotle. He finds objects in all these classes except the class of non-sensible changing objects. Physics is the theoretical science of sensible changing objects, mathematics the study of sensible eternal objects (Aristotle notes that some mathematical statements appear to speak of non-sensible eternal objects), and metaphysics or theology is the study of non-sensible eternal objects.

A comparison of this classification of Aristotle's range of certain knowledge with Plato's range of certain knowledge is sufficient to point up a marked difference between Plato and Aristotle. Whereas Plato felt that the objects of certain knowledge must be unchanging, Aristotle held that we might have certain knowledge about changing objects. Thus, a crucial difference between Plato and Aristotle is that the latter felt that an adequate philosophy would have to explain knowledge of changing things. Is there such knowledge? Evidently Aristotle felt that one could know just as certainly that some arbitrary acorn would grow, in proper circumstances, into an oak tree, as that one could know that the arithmetical sum of two and two is four. We shall see in succeeding chapters how Aristotle justified the claim that theoretical science could be about changing objects. It is worth noticing, however, that Plato's Theory of Ideas cannot provide a ready justification for physics in the Aristotelian sense, although it can provide a justification for mathematical knowledge without difficulty. The structure of the world of being, as Plato described it, has remarkable similarities to the structure of many branches of mathematics. For example, just as the relationships between the ideas never change, so the relationships between the integers can be taken never to change. An integer is eternally odd or even, prime or not prime, divisible or not divisible by some other integer. If the world of being is used in an attempt to justify knowledge about changing objects, difficulties arise. Suppose an object of sense experience to be red. As long as it stays red, one might explain its redness by saying that it participates in the idea of redness. But suppose that it turns blue, as some objects do, over a period of time. At the end of the time, this can be explained by saying that it now participates in the idea of blueness. But what of the time between? Does it participate less and less in one form, and more and more in the other? Is there a time at which it participates in neither? Problems of this kind prove difficult for Platonic philosophy. Plato seems to have considered them, but perhaps it was the difficulty in answering them which led him to deny certain knowledge of changing objects.

Since Plato and Aristotle disagree, we might inquire which of them is right and which of them is wrong. The point at issue between Platonic and Aristotelian philosophy is that of the definition of *knowledge*. It is not generally thought that definitions are true or false. Whether one definition is better than another is a question of which definition preserves certain accepted usages of the word being defined, and which definition makes it possible to communicate in the most convenient fashion. Such questions are not settled by any simple appeal to commonly agreed-upon facts. As our characterization of epistemology has shown, a basic problem of epistemology is to decide which of the knowledge claims that we make are philosophically deserving of the honorific term *knowledge*. Is it as certain that an acorn cannot grow into a lion as it is that four is the sum of two and two? The choice between philosophies which assert and deny, respectively, that the one claim is as certain as the other is somewhat difficult. While one can say that to accept *both* the Platonic and Aristotelian philosophies is to contradict oneself, to say that one of them must be false is to make a mistake. The strongest claim it is reasonable to make is that one or both of them does not define *knowledge* in a way compatible with what we consider a fruitful way of explaining human experience.

There are difficulties in completing the philosophical program suggested by either Plato or Aristotle. Attacks on the difficulties of completing one program by someone who accepts another philosopher's viewpoint do not constitute a *proof* that the attacker occupies a superior philosophical position, since the attack does not *prove* in turn that the attacker's position is satisfactory. An uncommitted person attempts to evaluate the epistemological claims of philosophers by a study of human experience in an effort to determine which definition of *knowledge* seems to fit human experience best. In such a study, there seems to be room for legitimate disagreement. In comparing Plato and Aristotle, for example, it is necessary to decide whether certainty ought to be a property of what we wish to call knowledge. This decision is not to be made simply on commonly accepted facts but is in part a decision as to how we wish to use our language.

Categories and Classification

The philosophies of both Plato and Aristotle are at least partly based on the supposition that every sentence expressing a knowledge claim can be analyzed as having two essential *parts*, which may be called the subject and the predicate. The *subject*, in this sense, is the expression designating what is talked about in the sentence, and the *predicate* is the expression which attributes some characteristic to the subject. Not every sentence has an obvious predicate expression and an obvious subject expression, for example, "John plays tennis.". The theory of analysis referred to, however, argues that any sentence which is a knowledge claim is equivalent in meaning to some sentence which does consist of a subject expression and a predicate expression between which occurs some form of the verb *to be*, normally, an occurrence of *is* or *are*. "John plays tennis." may thus be transformed into "John is a tennis player.". "John is playing tennis." would not be the appropriate equivalent sentence since "John plays tennis." may be true when it is said (because John *is* a tennis player) even though "John is playing tennis." is false at that time. With care in application, the position that all knowledge may be analyzed as being of the form 'X is Y.', where X is a subject expression and Y is a predicate expression, it true of many claims to knowledge. As we have seen, the distinctive feature of Platonic epistemology is the argument that a knowledge claim 'X is Y.' is true if X is some object in the world of becoming and Y is a form in which the object participates. The Platonic theory of knowledge implicitly assumes that 'X is Y.' is the general structure of knowledge claims.

Aristotle employed his method of classification to answer two kinds of questions about knowledge expressed in the general form 'X is Y.'. One question asks how many different kinds of Y there might be in such sentences, and the other question asks in what way X and Y might be related. The first question is answered by Aristotle in a list of ten *categories*, the Y of any particular 'X is Y.' statement belonging to one of the ten cate-

63

gories. The second question is answered by Aristotle in a discussion of the _predicables_, which for any particular statement of 'X is Y.' form explains the relationship between the X and the Y of the statement.

In both of these cases, Aristotle discusses distinctions made _in the language_ of the statement 'X is Y.', so that the categories may be taken partly as a grammatical division of all possible expressions which may take the place of Y in some 'X is Y.' statement; and he also takes the distinctions as reflecting distinctions in being, or what exists, so that the categories may be taken to explain _what_ may be distinctly predicated of some object. The categories are ten in number:

1. Substance   (what X is, what kind of a thing X is)
2. Quantity   (some measure of X)
3. Quality   (some qualitative property of X)
4. Relation   (some relationship of X to other things)
5. Place   (some place where X is)
6. Time   (some time at which X is referred to)
7. Situation   (some environment in which X is found)
8. State   (some condition in which X is found)
9. Action   (something X does or is doing)
10. Passion   (something done to X)

The following example may indicate how the categories are to be interpreted, since for each of the ten examples, the predicate belongs to the appropriate category in the list of categories:

1. Socrates is a man.
2. Socrates is 5 feet 7 inches (tall).
3. Socrates is wise.
4. Socrates is the husband of Xanthippe.
5. Socrates is in Athens.
6. Socrates is alive in 321 B.C.
7. Socrates is surrounded by his students.
8. Socrates is barefoot.
9. Socrates is running.
10. Socrates is defeated.

It is clear that the categories involve some problems, in that it may prove difficult to place the Y of some particular 'X is Y.' statement into a definite category, but it is equally clear that the categories represent prima facie an interesting and fruitful classification into which we might try to place particular Y's. For reasons that will be discussed shortly, the most important distinction for Aristotle is that between the category _substance_ and all the other categories. Consequently, difficulties with placing a Y into a category are serious only if the Y in question seems to belong both to the category _substance_ and some other category. Aristotle's theory of knowledge supposes that this difficulty will not arise, although one may have the minor difficulty of deciding between, for example, the categories *place* and *situation* in a particular analysis.

Given some particular 'X is Y.' statement and knowledge of the appropriate category of Y, the problem is still to be raised as to how X and Y are related. For example, suppose of two such statements 'X is Y.' and 'X is Z.' that X is the same in both, but that Y and Z are two predicates belonging to some one category. Could these predicates, both belonging to the same category, express differing kinds of information about X? The Aristotelian answer is that they can and indeed that there are five possible relationships between the X and Y of any 'X is Y.' statement:

1. Definition
2. Genus
3. Differentia
4. Attribute
5. Accident

Because these notions have become common intellectual coin, they are easy to understand in one sense but difficult to reconstruct in exactly the way that Aristotle meant them. 'X is Y.' is a definition if Y defines X, but in Aristotle's philosophy there is only one way of accomplishing this correctly. Y must be what X is essentially.

To see what this means, an example may prove helpful. Suppose we ask "What is a man?", anticipating a definition of the form 'A man is W.'. What will take the place of W? To answer this question, the properties of three *normal* men, say Tom, Dick, and Harry, will be compared. Any property not shared by all men would be ruled out as a possible defining property of *man*. This, for Aristotle, will not include examination of those properties of some men which have been taken from them as the result of accident, for example, the losing of a leg. To consider the definition of man, we consider the properties common to those specimens that we would pick out without reservation as men. Suppose that Tom is 5 feet 10 inches tall, but Dick and Harry are of some other height. If we put '5 feet 10 inches tall' for W in the definition, we get "A man is 5 feet 10 inches tall.". This statement, construed as "Some man is 5 feet 10 inches tall." is true, but false if construed as "All men are 5 feet 10 inches tall." Being-5-feet-10-inches-tall is apparently a property that a man may or may not have. It is consequently, an *accidental* property of any man of whom it is true. Relationship (5) above, accident, holds between an X and Y when Y is an accidental property of X, that is, a property which some X's may have, while others may not have.

It is thus necessary to restrict attention to properties shared by *all* X's. A possibility is that Y is some property shared by all X's as well as by some non-X's. For example, if we substitute 'an animal' for W, we get the statement "A man is an animal.", which is true, but which is similar to the true statements "A goat is an animal.", "A horse is an animal.", etc.

Thus *Y* may be predicable of each *X*, but also of *A*'s, *B*'s, etc. In this case, *X* and *Y*, if *Y* is predicable of each member of classes other than *X*, like *A*, *B*, etc., are such that *Y* is said to be a genus of *X*, and expresses the existence of some large class of things of which *X* is a subclass. Now, in some other '*X* is *Y*.' statement, *Y* may describe the property of some genus of *X* which singles out the class of *X*'s as a subclass or species of that genus. Aristotelians usually consider the class of animal to be a genus of the class of men, which is distinguished in the genus of animals by the property of rationality. Thus "A man is a rational animal." is taken to express the fact that *rational* is the *differentia* of the species man within the genus animal, since all men are rational and no animals who are not men are rational.

To this point we have considered properties which a man might or might not have, as well as properties which all men have, but other beings might have as well. (There may be other beings than man which possess the property of rationality in Aristotelian systems, God being an obvious non-animal candidate.) This has enabled us to consider briefly *accident, genus,* and *differentia.*

What is left is apparently the class of those properties which *all* men have, and only men have. It is at this point that the *crucial* notion of Aristotle's scheme becomes apparent. Of those properties of men, or of any arbitrary class *X*, Aristotle distinguishes between those which are considered necessary for the members of the class and those which are merely contingent. This distinction, of utmost importance to Aristotelian thought, might be considered in the following way. In the case of man, suppose that we are faced with two properties compounded of simple properties, namely, *laughing animal* and *rational animal*, which all men and only men exhibit. Aristotelians would consider the latter property an *essential* or *necessary* property of man, because it is the meaning of *man* which is defined in its terms, while the former is only an attribute, because it is conceivable that all men and only men may have laughed as animals because of historical accident. In this case, the contingent property of being a laughing animal is an attribute of man (we say that all men and only men laugh but not that this property is essential to man), while the necessary property of being a rational animal is the defining property of man. Thus "A man is a rational animal." ends the search for a definition of man, yielding a property which all men and only men have in some necessary sense. The property that defines man, or any *X*, is also called the essence or form of *X*, so that being a rational animal is the form or essence of man.

The discussion of the predicables, generalized from our discussion of 'A man is a *W*.', is extremely important to an understanding of Aristotle. Further, a great deal of the acceptability or unacceptability of Aristotelian philosophy may be traced to the acceptability or unacceptability of the notion of a necessary property used in describing the essence of anything. What is involved in the notion of a necessary property? It seems to rest on *two* important considerations: one of them is that there are *natural* groupings of clearly separated objects of sense experience in the world which may be called *natural kinds*, such as men, horses, etc., and secondly that these groupings are to be accounted for in some nonarbitrary fashion, that is, that there is only one correct way of dividing up the properties of members of a natural kind into contingent and necessary properties, so as to discover the essence of a natural kind. Without such an essence, as will be shown, there is no *knowledge* of natural kinds for Aristotelians. In a way, Aristotelians transfer the basis for certainty from the unchanging structure of a world of being to an unchanging structure of natural kinds defined in terms of essences or forms. These natural kinds are groupings in the Platonic world of becoming, and hence could not be objects of knowledge for Platonists.

This unchanging structure is clearly related to the difference between what is called essential and accidental predication. To see why a distinction between these two kinds of predication is called for, the following examples are useful:

A. Socrates is a man. A man is an animal.

B. Socrates is 5 feet 7 inches. 5 feet 7 inches is a height.

From (A) we may legitimately conclude "Socrates is an animal.", but (B) yields "Socrates is a height.", which is absurd. What has gone wrong? It might be claimed that the first sentence in (B) is not grammatically well formed: one wants to ask of this sentence "5 feet 7 inches *what?*" In many contexts, we know that this means 5 feet 7 inches tall. But it *may* mean 5 feet 7 inches from the door, or almost anything. Now, if this sentence and the other one are made explicit, something like (B′) can be obtained:

B′. Socrates is 5 feet 7 inches tall. 5 feet 7 inches tall is a height.

It is clear that (A) and (B′) are not exactly grammatical parallels in several ways. To see this, note that the paraphrase "Any entity which is a man is also an entity which is an animal.", which is suitable for the second sentence of (A), results in nonsense of the following kind for (B′): "Any entity which is 5 feet 7 inches tall is an entity which is a height.". A more Aristotelian way of marking the difference is to note that in the examples given above for Socrates, sentences 2–10 are of the kind that are true at some time for Socrates but not necessarily true at all times. On the other hand the first sentence is true at all times for Socrates and is consequentially an essential predication since we could not imagine it otherwise, while 2–10 are accidental predications. In terms of traditional English grammar, sentences like the first are completed with a common noun in the place of *Y*, and the rest of the sentences are completed with different kinds of predicate expressions.

Reflection indicates that any '*X* is *Y*.' statement in which *Y* is related to *X* as genus, or as differentia, or as definition, is an example of an essential predication of Y to X. Where essential predication obtains, the rule 'If Y is predicated of X (essentially), and X is predicated of Z (essentially), then Y is predicated of Z.' may be used to make inferences, but not where accidental predication is involved. From these considerations, it is clear that theoretical science will be based upon essential predications and predicates which belong to the category *substance*.

Essential Predication

Restricting consideration of predication to essential predication makes it clear that predications can be arranged in a kind of hierarchy. To begin with, the following diagram might be chosen to represent the example of predications about Socrates given earlier. In this diagram, an arrow will signify that what stands at the point of the arrow is what is predicated of what stands at the nock: *tip/edge*

Animal

↑

Man

↑

Socrates

Ways of expanding this hierarchy are obvious. It might be rapidly expanded to the following:

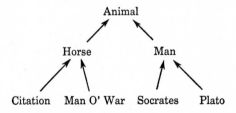

This is reminiscent of the way in which classification of living things is undertaken in biology, and it well might be so reminiscent, since the classificatory scheme of biology is derived from biologists who were familiar with Aristotelian notions of classification. Problems of biological classification may be thought of as problems for this kind of classification in general. One problem is whether or not everything can be brought into the classification. For Aristotelians, the answer is affirmative, since each individual belongs to a natural kind, and the structure may be developed from the necessary properties associated with each natural kind. Acceptance of the Aristotelian outlook may be traced to this problem: Is the lack of a completely suitable biological classification a proof that the Aristotelian notion of natural kinds and an associated hierarchy is mistaken? Not necessarily. To an Aristotelian, it may indicate that the necessary properties of individuals have not all been isolated yet.

Adopting the Aristotelian viewpoint that a complete hierarchy is possible, there are still problems to be faced:

1. What will be at the bottom places in the hierarchy? *primary sub,*
2. What will be at the top places in the hierarchy? *substance*
3. Are there levels in the hierarchy such as those assumed in our fragment? *yes*
4. If (3) is answered in the affirmative, will the bottom places in the hierarchy be at the same level? *yes*
5. If (3) is answered in the affirmative, will the top places in the hierarchy be at the same level? *yes*
6. Will there be a finite or infinite number of places in the hierarchy?
7. Can anything occur in more than one place in the hierarchy? *no*

Although this is obviously not a complete listing of such problems, the questions raised here represent the kind of problem that Aristotle and Aristotelians must deal with. Actually, the Aristotelian position that the hierarchy is possible means that (6) must be answered by saying that there are only a finite number of places in the hierarchy. Aristotle argues that an infinite number of places is impossible because then knowledge of the hierarchy would be impossible. This argument is not conclusive since it shows only that philosophy and science may not attain complete understanding of the hierarchy if there are an infinite number of places in it, but that in some sense may be the case. However, it can be shown (although Aristotle probably did not know this) that a finite hierarchy follows from the assumption that no individual has more than a finite number of properties that are necessary, as well as the assumption that the hierarchy can be consistently described.

The answer to (1) is that *primary* substances stand in the bottom places of the hierarchy. Because a primary substance is defined to be anything of which things may be predicated, but which are predicated of nothing, this follows from the characterization of a primary substance. From examples which are given by Aristotle, the answers to both (3) and (4) appear to be affirmative. On the other hand, the answers to (2) and (5) prove difficult. There is some evidence that the answer to (2) is *substance*, in which case (5) is trivially answered in the affirmative, since there will be only one top place in the hierarchy. *Substance*, of course, was also the first category, so that some discussion of *substance* is required to distinguish this kind of substance from primary substance. Further, we may ask whether what is at any place in the hierarchy exists, and if so in what sense.

Primary substances are the only things which can be said to exist in a fundamental sense, precisely in the sense that nothing could be said to exist if they did not. This marks an important distinction between Plato and Aristotle. Where the ideas are said to *exist,* they are also conceived in a fashion which apparently makes their existence independent of the existence of objects of sense experience. The idea of red refers to an entity which exists independently of any object in the world of becoming. In Aristotelian philosophy, however, the possible truth of any sentence of the form 'X is red.' is not dependent on a relationship between X and objects in a world of being. Thus, a universal like *red* is defined to be *that which is common* to a number of objects, with no suggestion that the universal is a separately existing thing. The reason that a universal may be predicated of any of a number of things is that it may be predicated of any of the things which have that universal in common. A universal is simply a predicate that might be applied to any arbitrary object. For Aristotle, only the individuals of sense experience *exist,* which means that all other affirmations of an 'X is Y.' kind and all human knowledge is dependent on primary substances which are objects of sense experience.

What may prove initially surprising is that knowledge (theoretical science) is not knowledge *of* primary substances but of something else which is developed from an analysis of primary substances. If primary substances are the objects of sense experience, Aristotle's point can be gathered from his observations that sense experience is not knowledge. On this point, although not on its significance, Aristotle and Plato agree. In an interesting argument which occurs at the beginning of the *Metaphysics,* Aristotle notes that all men have the power of sense experience and that indeed they may share this with other animals. Yet knowledge is so unevenly distributed among human beings that it cannot be equivalent to sense experience. Memory must be added to sense experience, as well as *experience* in a broader sense, which enables man (unlike the other animals) to profit by noting similarities between remembered sense experiences and present sense experiences, in effect making present sense experience more sophisticated than it would otherwise be. This point is supported by the generally superior judgments of humans compared with the judgments that we may impute to animals. Even this kind of human experience, however, is not equivalent to knowledge, for the ability of men to perform effective action is more evenly distributed than the ability to assimilate theoretical knowledge. The point here is that two men may be equally good artisans of some kind but quite unequal in the degree in which they can explain their art. Knowledge is really the ability to understand and explain why things are as they are, and knowledge must be knowledge, not of the things themselves, but of the causes, principles, etc., which account for the way things are. Knowledge is thus knowledge of the difference, say, between the accidental and essential properties of something. Clearly two men may be able to deal with Socrates's actions with roughly equal practical success, while only one of them can explain Socrates and his actions in terms of Socrates's accidental and essential properties, as well as in terms of the relations of these properties to the properties of other individuals. Thus it is not surprising in Aristotle that the individual is not the subject of knowledge, even though only individuals are said to exist. The individual can be known only by comparing its properties with the properties of other things. But this is knowing essential properties, since it is through essential properties that things are compared.

The result of this Aristotelian scheme is that what exists is dependent on individuals, or primary substances, at the bottom of the hierarchy described earlier. Knowledge, however, is not knowledge of these primary substances, but knowledge is about the hierarchy, that is, the essential properties that link individuals to other individuals. Aristotelianism, if successful, avoids one difficulty, that of explaining how Red (as a unique idea or form) can be shared by many particulars because it *defines* red to be what is shared by a certain class of particulars. But Aristotelianism has its own problems, among them that of explaining how similarities are noted and of presenting a methodology to ensure that the similarities that are used to construct the hierarchy are in fact based on essential properties.

Further, there is the problem that not all '*X* is *Y*.' statements true of the hierarchy are such that *X* refers to a primary substance. Some '*X* is *Y*.' statements are true of higher levels of the hierarchy; for example, our repeated fragment contains the statement "A man is an animal.". The subject of this statement is not an individual (What man could be referred to?). Aristotelians call the subjects of these higher level statements 'secondary substances', but the question is how is it possible to explain knowledge about secondary substances in terms of the fundamental primary substances.

Finally, it should be clear that the answer to (7) must be negative. We do not want to have both '*X* is *Y*.' and '*Y* is *X*.' true of the *hierarchy* unless *X* and *Y* are identical. The appearance of such statements would destroy the levels structure of the hierarchy, and Aristotle takes time to demonstrate that no essential predication could occur along with its converse predication within the structure of human knowledge.

From what has been said about Aristotle it may be possible to obtain some clues about the Aristotelian treatment of change. Where Plato had taken all change to be without the realm of knowledge, Aristotle argued that objects in the world of sense experience changed but that there was an invariant, nonchanging aspect of these objects which might be the object of knowledge about them. Thus, any object of sense experience could be considered the member of a natural kind, in so far as it is intelligible, whose essence or form could be known and could serve as the basis of knowledge about the object. Apparent change in an object, where one accidental property of it became replaced by another accidental property, is as far from being known through theoretical science as it is through the theory of ideas.

Readings from Aristotle

The relationship between Socrates, Plato, and Aristotle is easy to remember. Plato was a student of Socrates's and Aristotle was a student of Plato's. *Student*, however, does not mean the same thing in each case. Plato, as a young man, heard Socrates discoursing on the streets of Athens and learned from him by absorbing what must have been the substance of a group of speeches delivered on haphazard topics as they were raised to Socrates for consideration. Aristotle was a student in Plato's *Academy* and as a result was no doubt exposed to a systematic treatment of Plato's philosophical positions. In turn, Alexander the Great was tutored in King Philip of Macedonia's court by Aristotle. This sequence of three teacher-student relationships is contemporaneous with the last one hundred years of the Greek intellectual achievements that proved influential for the Western philosophical tradition.

For Aristotle, the problem of textual interpretation is particularly acute. Not all of Aristotle's writings are consistent, and they are usually made coherent by putting them into a sequence which is supposed to represent his early acceptance of the theory of ideas which he learned in the Academy and his gradual achievement of a distinctively Aristotelian epistemology which is inconsistent with the theory of ideas. This hypothesis is developed in *Aristotle: Fundamentals of the History of His Development* by Werner Jaeger. The chapters on Aristotle, as well as the selections which are here included, are taken from Aristotelian writings which represent more or less mature Aristotelian thought in that they explicitly argue against the theory of ideas and in favor of those doctrines that are thought to be the basis of Aristotle's developed philosophical position.

Aristotle's writings do not have the polish and literary elegance ascribed to the Platonic dialogues. Some commentators have felt that Aristotle wrote some literary works which could match Plato's in terms of elegance, but that they have not survived the vagaries of manuscript history. Certainly the manuscripts that are available represent compilations of what may have been lecture notes as well as rough manuscript which contains internal evidence that Aristotle intended to revise it. Some of the manuscript material is almost certainly lecture-note material not written by Aristotle, but taken down by one of his students. Out of all this montage, it is difficult to settle on particular statements that are *Aristotle's*, as opposed to being *Aristotelian*.

It is not obvious that sound philosophy must be elegantly written, as many scholars who compare Aristotle invidiously with Plato on this account seem to have assumed. Where Plato and Berkeley seem to have written important philosophy with a literary flair, Aristotle and Kant seem to have produced rather dull copy for their exciting philosophical ideas. It would take an extremely partisan historian to argue that philosophical importance lies primarily with those who can write elegant prose. There may, in fact, be a rather easily grasped relationship between the analytical approach of Aristotle to philosophy that is discussed in earlier chapters and the choppy construction of the manuscripts available to us that no editing could entirely remove. In fact, one might make an invidious comparison in the other direction by arguing that a literary style makes it easier to camouflage weakness of argument under a stylistic cover. It is important for the purposes of philosophical evaluation to keep considerations of style from influencing one's judgment of the cogency of the argument.

Three selections from Aristotle's epistemological writings have been reprinted here:

A. *Categories*   Chapters 1–5:33, Greek 1–2^b.
B. *Posterior Analytics* Books 1–6:10, Greek 71^a–74^b.
C. *Metaphysics*   Book 7:1–7:7, Greek 1028^a–1032^a.

These selections are reprinted from the Oxford translation of *The Works of Aristotle*, edited by J. A. Smith and Sir W. D. Ross. Selections *A* and *B* are from volume I, and selection *C* is from volume VIII. They are reprinted here by kind permission of The Clarendon Press, Oxford. For those who can read classical Greek, *The Loeb Classical Library* editions have a facing English and Greek text.

The following bibliography consists of some secondary sources for the study of Aristotle:

Aaron, R. I.: *The Theory of Universals*, Oxford, 1952.

Allan, D. J.: *The Philosophy of Aristotle*, London, 1952.

Anton, J. P.: *Aristotle's Theory of Contrariety*, New York, 1957.

During, I., and G. E. L. Owen (eds.): *Aristotle and Plato in the Mid-fourth Century*, Göteborg, 1960.

Hamlyn, D. W.: "Aristotle on Predication," *Phronesis*, vol. 6, pp. 110–127, 1961.

*Jaeger, W.: *Aristotle: Fundamentals of the History of His Development*, Oxford, 1960. (Oxford Paperbound.)

Joseph, H. W. B.: *An Introduction to Logic*, Oxford, 1916.

Lukasiewicz, J.: *Aristotle's Syllogistic from the Standpoint of Modern Formal Logic*, Oxford, 1957.

*Mure, G. R. G.: *Aristotle*, Oxford, 1935. (Oxford Paperbound.)

Owens, J.: *The Doctrine of Being in the Aristotelian* Metaphysics, Toronto, 1957.

*Randall, J. H. Jr.: *Aristotle*, New York, 1960. (Columbia Paperbound.)

*Ross, W. D.: *Aristotle*, New York, 1956. (Meridian Paperbound.)

Sellars, Wilfrid: "Substance and Form in Aristotle," *The Journal of Philosophy*, vol. 54, pp. 688–699, 1957.

*Taylor, A. E.: *Aristotle*, New York, 1955. (Dover Paperbound.)

Zeller, E.: *Aristotle and the Earlier Peripatetics*, New York, 1962.

A   From the CATEGORIES

1°   Things are said to be named 'equivocally' when, though they have a   1
common name, the definition corresponding with the name differs for each.
Thus, a real man and a figure in a picture can both lay claim to the name
'animal'; yet these are equivocally so named, for, though they have a
common name, the definition corresponding with the name differs for each.
5   For should any one define in what sense each is an animal, his definition in
the one case will be appropriate to that case only.

On the other hand, things are said to be named 'univocally' which
have both the name and the definition answering to the name in common.
A man and an ox are both 'animal', and these are univocally so named,
inasmuch as not only the name, but also the definition, is the same in both
10   cases: for if a man should state in what sense each is an animal, the
statement in the one case would be identical with that in the other.

Things are said to be named 'derivatively', which derive their name
from some other name, but differ from it in termination. Thus the gram-
15   marian derives his name from the word 'grammar', and the courageous
man from the word 'courage'.

Forms of speech are either simple or composite. Examples of the   2
latter are such expressions as 'the man runs', 'the man wins'; of the former
'man', 'ox', 'runs', 'wins'.

20   Of things themselves some are predicable of a subject, and are never
present in a subject. Thus 'man' is predicable of the individual man, and is
never present in a subject.

By being 'present in a subject' I do not mean present as parts are
present in a whole, but being incapable of existence apart from the said
subject.[1] *see notes—*

25   Some things, again, are present in a subject, but are never predicable
of a subject. For instance, a certain point of grammatical knowledge is
present in the mind, but is not predicable of any subject; or again, a certain

whiteness may be present in the body (for colour requires a material basis), yet it is never predicable of anything.[2]

Other things, again, are both predicable of a subject and present in a subject. Thus while knowledge is present in the human mind, it is predicable   1ᵇ
of grammar.[3]

There is, lastly, a class of things which are neither present in a subject nor predicable of a subject, such as the individual man or the individual horse. But, to speak more generally, that which is individual and has the   5
character of a unit is never predicable of a subject. Yet in some cases there is nothing to prevent such being present in a subject. Thus a certain point of grammatical knowledge is present in a subject.[4]

3   When one thing is predicated of another, all that which is predicable   10
of the predicate will be predicable also of the subject. Thus, 'man' is predicated of the individual man; but 'animal' is predicated of 'man'; it will, therefore, be predicable of the individual man also: for the individual   15
man is both 'man' and 'animal'.

If genera are different and co-ordinate, their differentiae are themselves different in kind.[5] Take as an instance the genus 'animal' and the genus 'knowledge'. 'With feet', 'two-footed', 'winged', 'aquatic', are differentiae of 'animal'; the species of knowledge are not distinguished by the same differentiae. One species of knowledge does not differ from another in being 'two-footed'.

But where one genus is subordinate to another, there is nothing to   20
prevent their having the same differentiae: for the greater class is predicated of the lesser, so that all the differentiae of the predicate will be differentiae also of the subject.

4   Expressions which are in no way composite signify substance,   25
quantity, quality, relation, place, time, position, state, action, or affection. To sketch my meaning roughly, examples of substance are 'man' or 'the horse', of quantity, such terms as 'two cubits long' or 'three cubits long', of quality, such attributes as 'white', 'grammatical'. 'Double', 'half', 'greater', fall under the category of relation; 'in the market place', 'in the Lyceum',   2ᵃ
under that of place; 'yesterday', 'last year', under that of time. 'Lying', 'sitting', are terms indicating 'position'; 'shod', 'armed', state; 'to lance', 'to cauterize', action; 'to be lanced', 'to be cauterized', affection.

No one of these terms, in and by itself, involves an affirmation; it is by the combination of such terms that positive or negative statements arise.   5
For every assertion must, as is admitted, be either true or false, whereas expressions which are not in any way composite, such as 'man', 'white', 'runs', 'wins', cannot be either true or false.   10

5   Substance, in the truest and primary and most definite sense of the word, is that which is neither predicable of a subject nor present in a subject; for instance, the individual man or horse. But in a secondary sense those things are called substances within which, as species, the primary

15 substances are included; also those which, as genera, include the species. For instance, the individual man is included in the species 'man', and the genus to which the species belongs is 'animal'; these, therefore—that is to say, the species 'man' and the genus 'animal'—are termed secondary substances.

It is plain from what has been said that both the name and the
20 definition of the predicate must be predicable of the subject. For instance, 'man' is predicated of the individual man. Now in this case the name of the species 'man' is applied to the individual, for we use the term 'man' in describing the individual; and the definition of 'man' will also be predicated of the individual man, for the individual man is both man and
25 animal. Thus, both the name and the definition of the species are predicable of the individual.

With regard, on the other hand, to those things which are present in a subject, it is generally the case that neither their name nor their definition is predicable of that in which they are present. Though, however, the
30 definition is never predicable, there is nothing in certain cases to prevent the name being used. For instance, 'white' being present in a body is predicated of that in which it is present, for a body is called white: the definition, however, of the colour 'white' is never predicable of the body.[6]

Everything except primary substances is either predicable of a primary substance or present in a primary substance. This becomes evident
35 by reference to particular instances which occur. 'Animal' is predicated of the species 'man', therefore of the individual man, for if there were no individual man of whom it could be predicated, it could not be predicated
2ᵇ of the species 'man' at all. Again, colour is present in body, therefore in individual bodies, for if there were no individual body in which it was present, it could not be present in body at all. Thus everything except primary substances is either predicated of primary substances, or is present
5 in them, and if these last did not exist, it would be impossible for anything else to exist.

Of secondary substances, the species is more truly substance than the genus, being more nearly related to primary substance. For if any one should render an account of what a primary substance is, he would render a more instructive account, and one more proper to the subject, by stating
10 the species than by stating the genus. Thus, he would give a more instructive account of an individual man by stating that he was man than by stating that he was animal, for the former description is peculiar to the individual in a greater degree, while the latter is too general. Again, the man who gives an account of the nature of an individual tree will give a more instructive account by mentioning the species 'tree' than by mentioning the genus 'plant'.

15 Moreover, primary substances are most properly called substances in virtue of the fact that they are the entities which underlie everything else, and that everything else is either predicated of them or present in them.

Now the same relation which subsists between primary substance and everything else subsists also between the species and the genus: for the species is to the genus as subject is to predicate, since the genus is predi- 20 cated of the species, whereas the species cannot be predicated of the genus. Thus we have a second ground for asserting that the species is more truly substance than the genus.

Of species themselves, except in the case of such as are genera, no one is more truly substance than another. We should not give a more appropriate account of the individual man by stating the species to which 25 he belonged, than we should of an individual horse by adopting the same method of definition. In the same way, of primary substances, no one is more truly substance than another; an individual man is not more truly substance than an individual ox.

It is, then, with good reason that of all that remains, when we exclude primary substances, we concede to species and genera alone the name 'secondary substance', for these alone of all the predicates convey a 30 knowledge of primary substance. For it is by stating the species or the genus that we appropriately define any individual man; and we shall make our definition more exact by stating the former than by stating the latter. All other things that we state, such as that he is white, that he runs, and so 35 on, are irrelevant to the definition. Thus it is just that these alone, apart from primary substances, should be called substances.

B   From the *POSTERIOR ANALYTICS*

BOOK I

1 All instruction given or received by way of argument proceeds from 71ᵃ pre-existent knowledge. This becomes evident upon a survey of all the species of such instruction. The mathematical sciences and all other speculative disciplines are acquired in this way, and so are the two forms of dialectical reasoning, syllogistic and inductive; for each of these latter 5 makes use of old knowledge to impart new, the syllogism assuming an audience that accepts its premisses, induction exhibiting the universal as implicit in the clearly known particular. Again, the persuasion exerted by rhetorical arguments is in principle the same, since they use either example, a kind of induction, or enthymeme, a form of syllogism.[7] 10

The pre-existent knowledge required is of two kinds. In some cases admission of the fact must be assumed, in others comprehension of the meaning of the term used, and sometimes both assumptions are essential. Thus, we assume that every predicate can be either truly affirmed or truly denied of any subject, and that 'triangle' means so and so; as regards 'unit' we have to make the double assumption of the meaning of the word and the existence of the thing. The reason is that these several objects are not 15 equally obvious to us. [Recognition of a truth may in some cases contain as factors both previous knowledge and also knowledge acquired simultaneously with that recognition]—knowledge, this latter, of the particulars actually falling under the universal and therein already virtually known. For example, the student knew beforehand that the angles of every trian-

20   gle are equal to two right angles; but it was only at the actual moment at which he was being led on to recognize this as true in the instance before him that he came to know this figure inscribed in the semicircle to be a triangle. For some things (viz. the singulars finally reached which are not predicable of anything else as subject) are only learnt in this way, i.e. there is here no recognition through a middle of a minor term as subject to a major. Before he was led on to recognition or before he actually drew a conclu-

25   sion, we should perhaps say that in a manner he knew, in a manner not.[8]

If he did not in an unqualified sense of the term *know* the existence of this triangle, how could he *know* without qualification that its angles were equal to two right angles? No: clearly he *knows* not without qualification but only in the sense that he *knows* universally. If this distinction is not drawn, we are faced with the dilemma in the *Meno*: either a man will <u>learn</u>

30   <u>nothing or what he already knows;</u> for we cannot accept the solution which some people offer. A man is asked, 'Do you, or do you not, know that every pair is even?' He says he does know it. The questioner then produces a particular pair, of the existence, and so *a fortiori* of the evenness, of which he was unaware. The solution which some people offer is to assert that they do not know that every pair is even, but only that

71   everything which they know to be a pair is even: yet what they know to be even is that of which they have demonstrated evenness, i.e. what they made the subject of their premiss, viz. not merely every triangle or number which they know to be such, but any and every number or triangle without reservation. For no premiss is ever couched in the form 'every number which you know to be such', or 'every rectilinear figure which you know to

5   be such': the predicate is always construed as applicable to any and every instance of the thing. On the other hand, [I imagine there is nothing to prevent a man in one sense knowing what he is learning, in another not knowing it. The strange thing would be, not if in some sense he knew what he was learning, but if he were to know it in that precise sense and manner in which he was learning it.]

[We suppose ourselves to possess unqualified scientific knowledge of   2

10   a thing, as opposed to knowing it in the accidental way in which the sophist knows, when we think that we know the cause on which the fact depends, as the cause of that fact and of no other, and, further, that the fact could not be other than it is. Now that scientific knowing is something of this sort is evident—witness both those who falsely claim it and those who actually possess it, since the former merely imagine themselves to be, while the latter are also actually, in the condition described. Consequently

the proper object of unqualified scientific knowledge is something which cannot be other than it is.[9]

There may be another manner of knowing as well—that will be discussed later. What I now assert is that at all events we do know by demonstration. By demonstration I mean a syllogism productive of scientific knowledge, a syllogism, that is, the grasp of which is eo *ipso* such knowledge. Assuming then that my thesis as to the nature of scientific knowing is correct, the premisses of demonstrated knowledge must be true, primary, immediate, better known than and prior to the conclusion, which is further related to them as effect to cause. Unless these conditions are satisfied, the basic truths will not be 'appropriate' to the conclusion. Syllogism there may indeed be without these conditions, but such syllogism, not being productive of scientific knowledge, will not be demonstration. The premisses must be true: for that which is non-existent cannot be known—we cannot know, e.g., that the diagonal of a square is commensurate with its side. The premisses must be primary and indemonstrable; otherwise they will require demonstration in order to be known, since to have knowledge, if it be not accidental knowledge, of things which are demonstrable, means precisely to have a demonstration of them. The premisses must be the causes of the conclusion, better known than it, and prior to it; its causes, since we possess scientific knowledge of a thing only when we know its cause, prior, in order to be causes; antecedently known, this antecedent knowledge being not our mere understanding of the meaning, but knowledge of the fact as well. Now 'prior' and 'better known' are ambiguous terms, for there is a difference between what is prior and better known in the order of being and what is prior and better known to man. I mean that objects nearer to sense are prior and better known to man; objects without qualification prior and better known are those further from sense.[10] Now the most universal causes are furthest from sense and particular causes are nearest to sense, and they are thus exactly opposed to one another. In saying that the premisses of demonstrated knowledge must be primary, I mean that they must be the 'appropriate' basic truths, for I identify primary premiss and basic truth. A 'basic truth' in a demonstration is an immediate proposition. An immediate proposition is one which has no other proposition prior to it. A proposition is either part of an enunciation, i.e. it predicates a single attribute of a single subject. If a proposition is dialectical, it assumes either part indifferently; if it is demonstrative, it lays down one part to the definite exclusion of the other because that part is true. The term 'enunciation' denotes either part of a contradiction indifferently. A contradiction is an opposition which of its own nature excludes a middle. The part of a contradiction which conjoins a predicate with a subject is an affirmation; the part disjoining them is a negation.[11] I call an immediate basic truth of syllogism a 'thesis' when, though it is not susceptible of proof by the teacher, yet ignorance of it does not constitute a total bar to progress on the part of the pupil: one which the pupil must know if he is to learn anything whatever is an axiom. I call it an axiom because there are such truths and we give them the name of axioms *par excellence*. If a thesis assumes one part or the other of an enunciation, i.e. asserts either the existence or the non-existence of a subject, it is a hypothesis; if it does not so assert, it is a definition. Definition *is* a 'thesis' or a 'laying something down', since the arithmetician lays it down that to be a unit is to be quantitatively indivisible; but it is not a hypothesis, for to define what a unit is is not the same as to affirm its existence.

Now since the required ground of our knowledge—i.e. of our conviction—of a fact is the possession of such a syllogism as we call demonstration, and the ground of the syllogism is the facts constituting its premisses, we must not only know the primary premisses—some if not all of them—beforehand, but know them better than the conclusion: for the cause of an attribute's inherence in a subject always itself inheres in the subject more firmly than that attribute; e.g. the cause of our loving anything is dearer to us than the object of our love. So since the primary premisses are the cause of our knowledge—i.e. of our conviction—it follows that we know them better—that is, are more convinced of them— than their consequences, precisely because our knowledge of the latter is the effect of our knowledge of the premisses.[12] Now a man cannot believe in anything more than in the things he knows, unless he has either actual knowledge of it or something better than actual knowledge. But we are faced with this paradox if a student whose belief rests on demonstration has not prior knowledge; a man must believe in some, if not in all, of the basic truths more than in the conclusion. Moreover, if a man sets out to acquire the scientific knowledge that comes through demonstration, he must not only have a better knowledge of the basic truths and a firmer conviction of them than of the connexion which is being demonstrated: more than this, nothing must be more certain or better known to him than these basic truths in their character as contradicting the fundamental premisses which lead to the opposed and erroneous conclusion. For indeed the conviction of pure science must be unshakable.

Some hold that, owing to the necessity of knowing the primary premisses, there is no scientific knowledge. Others think there is, but that all truths are demonstrable. Neither doctrine is either true or a necessary deduction from the premisses. The first school, assuming that there is no way of knowing other than by demonstration, maintain that an infinite regress is involved, on the ground that if behind the prior stands no primary, we could not know the posterior through the prior (wherein they are right, for one cannot traverse an infinite series): if on the other hand— they say—the series terminates and there are primary premisses, yet these are unknowable because incapable of demonstration, which accord- ing to them is the only form of knowledge. And since thus one cannot know

the primary premisses, knowledge of the conclusions which follow from them is not pure scientific knowledge nor properly knowing at all, but rests on the mere supposition that the premisses are true. The other party agree with them as regards knowing, holding that it is only possible by demon-   15
station, but they see no difficulty in holding that all truths are demonstrated, on the ground that demonstration may be circular and reciprocal.

[Our own doctrine is that not all knowledge is demonstrative: on the contrary, knowledge of the immediate premisses is independent of demonstration.[13] (The necessity of this is obvious; for since we must know   20
the prior premisses from which the demonstration is drawn, and since the regress must end in immediate truths, those truths must be indemonstrable.) Such, then, is our doctrine, and in addition we maintain that besides scientific knowledge there is its originative source which enables us to recognize the definitions.

[Now demonstration must be based on premisses prior to and better   25
known than the conclusion; and the same things cannot simultaneously be both prior and posterior to one another:] so circular demonstration is clearly not possible in the unqualified sense of 'demonstration', but only possible if 'demonstration' be extended to include that other method of argument which rests on a distinction between truths prior to us and truths without qualification prior, i.e. the method by which induction produces   30
knowledge. But if we accept this extension of its meaning, our definition of unqualified knowledge will prove faulty; for there seem to be two kinds of it. Perhaps, however, the second form of demonstration, that which proceeds from truths better known to us, is not demonstration in the unqualified sense of the term.

The advocates of circular demonstration are not only faced with the difficulty we have just stated: in addition their theory reduces to the mere statement that if a thing exists, then it does exist—an easy way of proving anything. That this is so can be clearly shown by taking three terms, for to   35
constitute the circle it makes no difference whether many terms or few or even only two are taken. Thus by direct proof, if A is, B must be; if B is, C must be; therefore if A is, C must be. Since then—by the circular proof—if A is, B must be, and if B is, A must be, A may be substituted for C above.   73°
Then 'if B is, A must be' = 'if B is, C must be', which above gave the conclusion 'if A is, C must be': but C and A have been identified. Consequently the upholders of circular demonstration are in the position of saying that if A is, A must be—a simple way of proving anything. More-   5
over, even such circular demonstration is impossible except in the case of attributes that imply one another, viz. 'peculiar' properties.

Now, it has been shown that the positing of one thing—be it one term or one premiss—never involves a necessary consequent: two premisses constitute the first and smallest foundation for drawing a conclusion at all   10
and therefore a *fortiori* for the demonstrative syllogism of science. If, then, A is implied in B and C, and B and C are reciprocally implied in one

another and in A, it is possible, as has been shown in my writings on the syllogism, to prove all the assumptions on which the original conclusion

15   rested, by circular demonstration in the first figure. But it has also been shown that in the other figures either no conclusion is possible, or at least none which proves both the original premisses. Propositions the terms of which are not convertible cannot be circularly demonstrated at all, and since convertible terms occur rarely in actual demonstrations, it is clearly frivolous and impossible to say that demonstration is reciprocal and that

20   therefore everything can be demonstrated.

Since the object of pure scientific knowledge cannot be other than it   4 is, the truth obtained by demonstrative knowledge will be necessary. And since demonstrative knowledge is only present when we have a demonstration, it follows that demonstration is an inference from necessary premisses. So we must consider what are the premisses of demonstration—

25   i.e. what is their character: and as a preliminary, let us define what we mean by an attribute 'true in every instance of its subject', an 'essential' attribute, and a 'commensurate and universal' attribute. I call 'true in every instance' what is truly predicable of all instances—not of one to the exclusion of others—and at all times, not at this or that time only; e.g. if

30   animal is truly predicable of every instance of man, then if it be true to say 'this is a man', 'this is an animal' is also true, and if the one be true now the other is true now. A corresponding account holds if point is in every instance predicable as contained in line. There is evidence for this in the fact that the objection we raise against a proposition put to us as true in every instance is either an instance in which, or an occasion on which, it is not true. Essential attributes are (1) such as belong to their subject as ele-

35   ments in its essential nature (e.g. line thus belongs to triangle, point to line; for the very being or 'substance' of triangle and line is composed of these elements, which are contained in the formulae defining triangle and line): (2) such that, while they belong to certain subjects, the subjects to which they belong are contained in the attribute's own defining formula. Thus

40   straight and curved belong to line, odd and even, prime and compound,
73ᵇ   square and oblong, to number; and also the formula defining any one of these attributes contains its subject—e.g. line or number as the case may be.

Extending this classification to all other attributes, I distinguish those that answer the above description as belonging essentially to their respective subjects; whereas attributes related in neither of these two ways to their subjects I call accidents or 'coincidents'; e.g. musical or white is a 'coincident' of animal.

5   Further (a) that is essential which is not predicated of a subject other than itself: e.g. 'the walking [thing]' walks and is white in virtue of being something else besides; whereas substance, in the sense of whatever signifies a 'this somewhat', is not what it is in virtue of being something else

besides. Things, then, not predicated of a subject I call essential; things predicated of a subject I call accidental or 'coincidental'.[14]

In another sense again (b) a thing consequentially connected with   10 anything is essential; one not so connected is 'coincidental' An example of the latter is 'While he was walking it lightened': the lightning was not due to his walking; it was, we should say, a coincidence. If, on the other hand, there is a consequential connexion, the predication is essential; e.g. if a beast dies when its throat is being cut, then its death is also essentially connected with the cutting, because the cutting was the cause of death, not   15 death a 'coincident' of the cutting.

So far then as concerns the sphere of connexions scientifically known in the unqualified sense of that term, all attributes which (within that sphere) are essential either in the sense that their subjects are contained in them, or in the sense that they are contained in their subjects, are necessary as well as consequentially connected with their subjects. For it is impossible for them not to inhere in their subjects—either simply or in the qualified sense that one or other of a pair of opposites must inhere in the subject; e.g. in line must be either straightness or curvature, in number either   20 oddness or evenness. For within a single identical genus the contrary of a given attribute is either its privative or its contradictory; e.g. within number what is not odd is even, inasmuch as within this sphere even is a necessary consequent of not-odd. So, since any given predicate must be either affirmed or denied of any subject, essential attributes must inhere in their subjects of necessity.

Thus, then, we have established the distinction between the attribute   25 which is 'true in every instance' and the 'essential' attribute.

I term 'commensurately universal' an attribute which belongs to every instance of its subject, and to every instance essentially and as such; from which it clearly follows that all commensurate universals inhere necessarily in their subjects. The essential attribute, and the attribute that belongs to its subject as such, are identical. E.g. point and straight belong to line essentially, for they belong to line as such; and triangle as such has   30 two right angles, for it is *essentially* equal to two right angles.

An attribute belongs commensurately and universally to a subject when it can be shown to belong to any random instance of that subject and when the subject is the first thing to which it can be shown to belong. Thus, e.g., (1) the equality of its angles to two right angles is not a commensurately universal attribute of figure. For though it is possible to show that a   35 figure has its angles equal to two right angles, this attribute cannot be demonstrated of any figure selected at haphazard, nor in demonstrating does one take a figure at random—a square is a figure but its angles are not equal to two right angles. On the other hand, any isosceles triangle has its angles equal to two right angles yet isosceles triangle is not the primary subject of this attribute but triangle is prior. So whatever can be shown to

40 have its angles equal to two right angles, or to possess any other attribute, in any random instance of itself and primarily—that is the first subject to which the predicate in question belongs commensurately and universally, and the demonstration, in the essential sense, of any predicate is the proof

74ᵇ of it as belonging to this first subject commensurately and universally: while the proof of it as belonging to the other subjects to which it attaches is demonstration only in a secondary and unessential sense. Nor again (2) is equality to two right angles a commensurately universal attribute of isosceles; it is of wider application.

We must not fail to observe that we often fall into error because our   5
5 conclusion is not in fact primary and commensurately universal in the sense in which we think we prove it so. We make this mistake (1) when the subject is an individual or individuals above which there is no universal to be found: (2) when the subjects belong to different species and there is a higher universal, but it has no name: (3) when the subject which the demonstrator takes as a whole is really only a part of a larger whole; for
10 then the demonstration will be true of the individual instances within the part and will hold in every instance of it, yet the demonstration will not be true of this subject primarily and commensurately and universally. When a demonstration is true of a subject primarily and commensurately and universally, that is to be taken to mean that it is true of a given subject primarily and as such. Case (3) may be thus exemplified. If a proof were given that perpendiculars to the same line are parallel, it might be supposed that *lines thus perpendicular* were the proper subject of the demonstration because being parallel is true of every instance of them.
15 But it is not so, for the parallelism depends not on these angles being equal to one another because each is a right angle, but simply on their being equal to one another. An example of (1) would be as follows: if isosceles were the only triangle, it would be thought to have its angles equal to two right angles *qua* isosceles. An instance of (2) would be the law that proportionals alternate.[15] Alternation used to be demonstrated separately of numbers, lines, solids and durations, though it could have been proved
20 of them all by a single demonstration. Because there was no single name to denote that in which numbers, lengths, durations, and solids are identical, and because they differed specifically from one another, this property was proved of each of them separately. To-day, however, the proof is commensurately universal, for they do not possess this attribute *qua* lines or *qua* numbers, but *qua* manifesting this generic character which they are
25 postulated as possessing universally. Hence, even if one prove of each kind of triangle that its angles are equal to two right angles, whether by means of the same or different proofs; still, as long as one treats separately equilateral, scalene, and isosceles, one does not yet know, except sophistically, that triangle has its angles equal to two right angles, nor does one yet know that triangle has this property commensurately and universally,
30 even if there is no other species of triangle but these. For one does not

know that triangle as such has this property, nor even that 'all' triangles have it—unless 'all' means 'each taken singly': if 'all' means 'as a whole class', then, though there be none in which one does not recognize this property, one does not know it of 'all triangles'.

When, then, does our knowledge fail of commensurate universality, and when is it unqualified knowledge? If triangle be identical in essence with equilateral, i.e. with each or all equilaterals, then clearly we have unqualified knowledge: if on the other hand it be not, and the attribute belongs to equilateral *qua* triangle; then our knowledge fails of commen-   35
surate universality. 'But', it will be asked, 'does this attribute belong to the subject of which it has been demonstrated *qua* triangle or *qua* isosceles? What is the point at which the subject to which it belongs is primary? (i.e. to what subject can it be demonstrated as belonging commensurately and universally?)' Clearly this point is the first term in which it is found to inhere as the elimination of inferior *differentiae* proceeds. Thus the angles of a brazen isosceles triangle are equal to two right angles: but eliminate brazen and isosceles and the attribute remains.[16] 'But'—you may say—   **74ᵇ**
'eliminate figure or limit, and the attribute vanishes.' True, but figure and limit are not the first *differentiae* whose elimination destroys the attribute. 'Then what is the first?' If it is triangle, it will be in virtue of triangle that the attribute belongs to all the other subjects of which it is predicable, and triangle is the subject to which it can be demonstrated as belonging commensurately and universally.

6   Demonstrative knowledge must rest on necessary basic truths; for the   5
object of scientific knowledge cannot be other than it is. Now attributes attaching essentially to their subjects attach necessarily to them: for essential attributes are either elements in the essential nature of their subjects, or contain their subjects as elements in their own essential nature. (The pairs of opposites which the latter class includes are necessary because one member or the other necessarily inheres.) It follows from this   10
that premisses of the demonstrative syllogism must be connexions essential in the sense explained: for all attributes must inhere essentially or else be accidental, and accidental attributes are not necessary to their subjects.

C   *From the* METAPHYSICS

BOOK Z

1   There are several senses in which a thing may be said to 'be', as we   10
pointed out previously in our book on the various senses of words; for in one sense the 'being' meant is 'what a thing is' or a 'this', and in another sense it means a quality or quantity or one of the other things that are predicated as these are.[17] While 'being' has all these senses, obviously that which 'is' primarily is the 'what', which indicates the substance of the thing.   15

For when we say of what quality a thing is, we say that it is good or bad, not that it is three cubits long or that it is a man; but when we say *what* it is, we do not say 'white' or 'hot' or 'three cubits long', but 'a man' or 'a god'. And all other things are said to be because they are, some of them, quantities of that which *is* in this primary sense, others qualities of it, others

20   affections of it, and others some other determination of it.[18] And so one might even raise the question whether the words 'to walk', 'to be healthy', 'to sit' imply that each of these things is existent, and similarly in any other case of this sort; for none of them is either self-subsistent or capable of being separated from substance, but rather, if anything, it is that which

25   walks or sits or is healthy that is an existent thing. Now these are seen to be more real because there is something definite which underlies them (i.e. the substance or individual), which is implied in such a predicate; for we never use the word 'good' or 'sitting' without implying this. Clearly then it is in virtue of this category that each of the others also *is*. Therefore that which is primarily, i.e. not in a qualified sense but without qualification,

30   must be substance.

Now there are several senses in which a thing is said to be first; yet substance is first in every sense—(1) in definition, (2) in order of knowledge, (3) in time. For (3) of the other categories none can exist independently, but

35   only substance. And (1) in definition also this is first; for in the definition of each term the definition of its substance must be present. And (2) we think we know each thing most fully, when we know what it is, e.g. what man is

1028ᵇ or what fire is, rather than when we know its quality, its quantity, or its place; since we know each of these predicates also, only when we know *what* the quantity or the quality *is*.[19]

And indeed the question which was raised of old and is raised now and always, and is always the subject of doubt, viz. what being is, is just the question, what is substance? For it is this that some assert to be one,

5   others more than one, and that some assert to be limited in number, others unlimited.[20] And so we also must consider chiefly and primarily and almost exclusively what that is which *is* in *this* sense.

Substance is thought to belong most obviously to bodies; and so we   2

10   say that not only animals and plants and their parts are substances, but also natural bodies such as fire and water and earth and everything of the sort, and all things that are either parts of these or composed of these (either of parts or of the whole bodies), e.g. the physical universe and its parts, stars and moon and sun. But whether these alone are substances, or

15   there are also others, or only some of these, or others as well, or none of these but only some other things, are substances, must be considered. Some think the limits of body, i.e. surface, line, point, and unit, are substances, and more so than body or the solid.[21]

Further, some do not think there is anything substantial besides sensible things, but others think there are eternal substances which are more in number and more real; e.g. Plato posited two kinds of substance—

the Forms and the objects of mathematics—as well as a third kind, viz. the   20
substance of sensible bodies.[22] And Speusippus made still more kinds of
substance, beginning with the One, and assuming principles for each kind
of substance, one for numbers, another for spatial magnitudes, and then
another for the soul; and by going on in this way he multiplies the kinds of
substance.[23] And some say Forms and numbers have the same nature, and   25
the other things come after them—lines and planes—until we come to the
substance of the material universe and to sensible bodies.[24]

Regarding these mattters, then, we must inquire which of the common
statements are right and which are not right, and what substances there
are, and whether there are or are not any besides sensible substances, and
how sensible substances exist, and whether there is a substance capable of   30
separate existence (and if so why and how) or no such substance, apart
from sensible substances; and we must first sketch the nature of substance.

3   The word 'substance' is applied, if not in more senses, still at least to
four main objects; for both the essence and the universal and the genus are
thought to be the substance of each thing, and fourthly the substratum.   35
Now the substratum is that of which everything else is predicated, while it
is itself not predicated of anything else. And so we must first determine the
nature of this; for that which underlies a thing primarily is thought to be in   1029°
the truest sense its substance. And in one sense matter is said to be of the
nature of substratum, in another, shape, and in a third, the compound of
these. (By the matter I mean, for instance, the bronze, by the shape the
pattern of its form, and by the compound of these the statue, the concrete   5
whole.) Therefore if the form is prior to the matter and more real, it will be
prior also to the compound of both, for the same reason.

We have now outlined the nature of substance, showing that it is that
which is not predicated of a stratum, but of which all else is predicated.
But we must not merely state the matter thus; for this not enough. The
statement itself is obscure, and further, on this view, *matter* becomes
substance. For if this is not substance, it baffles us to say what else is. When   10
all else is stripped off evidently nothing but matter remains. For while the
rest are affections, products, and potencies of bodies, length, breadth, and
depth are quantities and not substances (for a quantity is not a substance),
but the substance is rather that to which these belong primarily. But when   15
length and breadth and depth are taken away we see nothing left unless
there is something that is bounded by these; so that to those who consider
the question thus matter alone must seem to be substance. By matter I mean   20
that which in itself is neither a particular thing nor of a certain quantity nor
assigned to any other of the categories by which being is determined. For
there is something of which each of these is predicated, whose being is
different from that of each of the predicates (for the predicates other than
substance are predicated of substance, while substance is predicated of
matter). Therefore the ultimate substratum is of itself neither a particular
thing nor of a particular quantity nor otherwise positively characterized;

25   nor yet is it the negations of these, for negations also will belong to it only by accident.

If we adopt this point of view, then, it follows that matter is substance. But this is impossible; for both separability and 'thisness' are thought to belong chiefly to substance. And so form and the compound of form and

30   matter would be thought to be substance, rather than matter. The substance compounded of both, i.e. of matter and shape, may be dismissed; for it is posterior and its nature is obvious. And matter also is in a sense manifest. But we must inquire into the third kind of substance; for this is the most perplexing.[25]

Some of the sensible substances are generally admitted to be sub-

1029ᵇ stances, so that we must look first among these. For it is an advantage to advance to that which is more knowable. For learning proceeds for all in this way—through that which is less knowable by nature to that which is

5   more knowable; and just as in conduct our task is to start from what is good for each and make what is without qualification good good for each, so it is our task to start from what is more knowable to oneself and make what is knowable by nature knowable to oneself. Now what is knowable and primary for particular sets of people is often knowable to a very small

10   extent, and has little or nothing of reality. But yet one must start from that which is barely knowable but knowable to oneself, and try to know what is knowable without qualification, passing, as has been said, by way of those very things which one does know.

1   Since at the start we distinguished the various marks by which we   4
determine substance, and one of these was thought to be the essence, we

13   must investigate this.[26] And first let us make some linguistic remarks about it. The essence of each thing is what it is said to be *propter se*. For being you is not being musical, since you are not by your very nature musical.

15   What, then, you are by your very nature is your essence.

Nor yet is the whole of this the essence of a thing; not that which is *propter se* as white is to a surface, because being a surface is not *identical* with being white. But again the combination of both—'being a white surface'—is not the essence of surface, because 'surface' itself is added. The formula, therefore, in which the term itself is not present but its

20   meaning is expressed, this is the formula of the essence of each thing. Therefore if to be a white surface is to be a smooth surface, to be white and to be smooth are one and the same.[27]

But since there are also compounds answering to the other categories

25   (for there is a substratum for each category, e.g. for quality, quantity, time, place, and motion), we must inquire whether there is a formula of the essence of each of them, i.e. whether to these compounds also there belongs an essence, e.g. to 'white man'. Let the compound be denoted by cloak.[28] What is the essence of cloak? But, it may be said, this also is not a *propter se* expression. We reply that there are just two ways in which a

predicate may fail to be true of a subject *propter se,* and one of these   30
results from the addition, and the other from the omission, of a determinant. One kind of predicate is not *propter se* because the term that is
being defined is combined with another determinant, e.g. if in defining
the essence of white one were to state the formula of white *man*; the *other*
because in the subject another determinant is combined with that which
is expressed in the formula, e.g. if 'cloak' meant 'white man', and one
were to define cloak as white; white man is white indeed, but its essence
is not to be white.

But is being-a-cloak an essence at all? Probably not. For the essence   1030ᵉ
is precisely what something *is*; but when an attribute is asserted of a subject other than itself, the complex is not precisely what some 'this' *is*, e.g.
white man is not precisely what some 'this' *is*, since thisness belongs only   5
to substances. Therefore there is an essence only of those things whose
formula is a definition. But we have a definition not where we have a
word and a formula identical in meaning (for in that case all formulae or
sets of words would be definitions; for there will be some name for any
set of words whatever, so that even the *Iliad* will be a definition), but
where there is a formula of something primary; and primary things are   10
those which do not imply the predication of one element in them of another element. Nothing, then, which is not a species of a genus will have
an *essence*—only species will have it, for these are thought to imply not
merely that the subject participates in the attribute and has it as an affection, or has it by accident; but for everything else as well, if it has a name,
there will be a *formula of its meaning*—viz. that this attribute belongs to   15
this subject; or instead of a simple formula we shall be able to give a
more accurate one; but there will be no definition nor essence.

Or has 'definition', like 'what a thing is', several meanings? 'What
a thing is' in one sense means substance and the 'this', in another one or   20
other of the predicates, quantity, quality, and the like. For as 'is' belongs
to all things, not however in the same sense, but to one sort of thing
primarily and to others in a secondary way, so too 'what a thing is' belongs in the simple sense to substance, but in a limited sense to the other
categories. For even of a quality we might ask what it is, so that quality
also is a 'what a thing is',—not in the simple sense, however, but just as,   25
in the case of that which is not, some say, emphasizing the linguistic form,
that that which is not *is*—not *is* simply, but *is* non-existent; so too with
quality.

We must no doubt inquire how we should express ourselves on each
point, but certainly not more than how the facts actually stand. And so
now also, since it is evident what language we use, essence will belong,
just as 'what a thing is' does, primarily and in the simple sense to substance, and in a secondary way to the other categories also,—not essence   30
in the simple sense, but the essence of a quality or of a quantity. For it

must be either by an equivocation that we say these *are*, or by adding to and taking from the meaning of 'are' (in the way in which that which is not known may be said to be known),—the truth being that we use the
35   word neither ambiguously nor in the same sense, but just as we apply the word 'medical' by virtue of a *reference* to one and the same thing, not
1030ᵇ   *meaning* one and the same thing, nor yet speaking ambiguously; for a patient and an operation and an instrument are called medical neither by an ambiguity nor with a single meaning, but with reference to a common end. But it does not matter at all in which of the two ways one likes
5   to describe the facts; this is evident, that definition and essence in the primary and simple sense belong to substances. Still they belong to other things as well, only not in the primary sense. For if we suppose this it does not follow that there is a definition of every word which means the same as any formula; it must mean the same as a particular kind of formula; and this condition is satisfied if it is a formula of something which
10   is one, not by continuity like the *Iliad* or the things that are one by being bound together, but in one of the main senses of 'one', which answer to the senses of 'is'; now 'that which is' in one sense denotes a 'this', in another a quantity, in another a quality. And so there can be a formula or definition even of white man, but not in the sense in which there is a definition either of white or of a substance.

It is a difficult question, if one denies that a formula with an added   5
15   determinant is a definition, whether any of the terms that are not simple but coupled will be definable. For we *must* explain them by adding a determinant. E.g. there is the nose, and concavity, and snubness, which is compounded out of the two by the presence of the one in the other, and it is not by *accident* that the nose has the attribute either of concavity or
20   of snubness, but in virtue of its nature; nor do they attach to it as whiteness does to Callias, or to man (because Callias, who happens to be a man, is white), but as 'male' attaches to animal and 'equal' to quantity, and as all so-called 'attributes *propter se*' attach to their subjects.²⁹ And such attributes are those in which is involved either the *formula* or the *name* of the subject of the particular attribute, and which cannot be explained
25   without this; e.g. white can be explained apart from man, but not female apart from animal. Therefore there is either no essence and definition of any of these things, or if there is, it is in another sense, as we have said.

But there is also a second difficulty about them. For if snub nose and
30   concave nose are the same thing, snub and concave will be the same thing; but if snub and concave are not the same (because it is impossible to speak of snubness apart from the thing of which it is an attribute *propter se*, for snubness is concavity-*in-a-nose*), either it is impossible to say 'snub nose' or the same thing will have been said twice, concave-nose nose; for snub nose will be concave-nose nose. And so it is absurd that such

things should have an essence; if they have, there will be an infinite re-   35
gress; for in snub-nose nose yet another 'nose' will be involved.

Clearly, then, only substance is definable. For if the other categories   1031ᵃ
also are definable, it must be by addition of a determinant, e.g. the
qualitative is defined thus, and so is the odd, for it cannot be defined apart
from number; nor can female be defined apart from animal. (When I say
'by addition' I mean the expressions in which it turns out that we are saying the same thing twice, as in these instances.) And if this is true, coupled   5
terms also, like 'odd number', will not be definable (but this escapes our
notice because our formulae are not accurate). But if these also are definable, either it is in some other way or, as we said, definition and
essence must be said to have more than one sense. Therefore in one sense   10
nothing will have a definition and nothing will have an essence, except
substances, but in another sense other things will have them. Clearly, then,
definition is the formula of the essence, and essence belongs to substances
either alone or chiefly and primarily and in the unqualified sense.

6   We must inquire whether each thing and its essence are the same   15
or different. This is of some use for the inquiry concerning substance; for
each thing is thought to be not different from its substance, and the essence
is said to be the substance of each thing.

Now in the case of accidental unities the two would be generally
thought to be different, e.g. white man would be thought to be different   20
from the essence of white man. For if they are the same, the essence of
man and that of white man are also the same; for a man and a white man
are the same thing, as people say, so that the essence of white man and
that of man would be also the same. But perhaps it does not follow that
the essence of accidental unities should be the same as that of the simple
terms. For the extreme terms are not in the same way identical with the
middle term.[30] But perhaps *this* might be thought to follow, that the ex-   25
treme terms, the accidents, should turn out to be the same, e.g. the
essence of white and that of musical; but this is not actually thought to be
the case.[31]

But in the case of so-called self-subsistent things, is a thing necessarily
the same as its essence? E.g. if there are some substances which have no
other substances nor entities prior to them—substances such as some assert   30
the Ideas to be?—If the essence of good is to be different from good-
itself, and the essence of animal from animal-itself, and the essence of
being from being-itself, there will, firstly, be other substances and entities   1031ᵇ
and Ideas besides those which are asserted, and, secondly, these others
will be prior substances, if essence is substance. And if the posterior substances and the prior are severed from each other, (α) there will be no
knowledge of the former, and (β) the latter will have no being. (By   5
'severed' I mean, if the good-itself has not the essence of good, and the
latter has not the property of being good.) For (α) there is knowledge of

each thing only when we know its essence. And (β) the case is the same for other things as for the good; so that if the essence of good is not good, neither is the essence of reality real, nor the essence of unity one. And all

10   essences alike exist or none of them does; so that if the essence of reality is not real, neither is any of the others. Again, that to which the essence of good does not belong is not good.—The good, then, must be one with the essence of good, and the beautiful with the essence of beauty, and so with all things which do not depend on something else but are self-subsistent and primary. For it is enough if they are this, even if they are not

15   Forms; or rather, perhaps, even if they *are* Forms. (At the same time it is clear that if there are Ideas such as some people say there are, it will not be substratum that is substance; for these must be substances, but not predicable of a substratum; for if they were they would exist only by being participated in.)[32]

Each thing itself, then, and its essence are one and the same in no

20   merely accidental way, as is evident both from the preceding arguments and because to *know* each thing, at least, is just to know its essence, so that even by the exhibition of instances it becomes clear that both must be one.[33]

(But of an accidental term, e.g. 'the musical' or 'the white', since it has two meanings, it is not true to say that it itself is identical with its essence; for both that to which the accidental quality belongs, and the acci-

25   dental quality, are white, so that in a sense the accident and its essence are the same, and in a sense they are not; for the essence of white is not the same as the man or the white man, but it is the same as the attribute white.)

The absurdity of the separation would appear also if one were to

30   assign a name to each of the essences; for there would be yet another essence besides the original one, e.g. to the essence of horse there will belong a second essence. Yet why should not some things be their essences from the start, since essence is substance? But indeed not only are a thing

1032ᵃ   and its essence one, but the formula of them is also the same, as is clear even from what has been said; for it is not by accident that the essence of one, and the one, are one. Further, if they are to be different, the process will go on to infinity; for we shall have (1) the essence of one, and (2) the one, so that to terms of the former kind the same argument will be applicable.[34]

5   Clearly, then, each primary and self-subsistent thing is one and the same as its essence. The sophistical objections to this position, and the question whether Socrates and to be Socrates are the same thing, are obviously answered by the same solution; for there is no difference either in the standpoint from which the question would be asked, or in that from which one could answer it successfully. We have explained, then, in what sense each thing is the same as its essence and in what sense it is not.

NOTES

1   The difficulties in reading Aristotle are amply illustrated by the preceding paragraphs. At first, Aristotle speaks about forms of speech, and then he seems to switch to consideration of things, rather than of words, in a somewhat confusing fashion. Perhaps Aristotle did not distinguish carefully between speaking about things and speaking about a language in which they are described. On the other hand, the word *thing* in this context may be taken as a neutral word like *entity*, since Aristotle clearly holds that a particular man exists in a different sense than the manhood which may be predicated of him. Note that while 'being present in an object' is explained somewhat by Aristotle, being 'predicable of a subject' is not. These two predicates, 'being present in a subject' and 'being predicable of a subject', allow a fourfold classification, depending on whether each of the predicates holds or does not hold. Aristotle proceeds to give examples of each possibility.

2   Why can a certain whiteness not be predicable of anything? Because it is not *common* to more than one object in terms of Aristotle's example.

3   Is this example puzzling? It could be that *knowledge* is used equivocally of the content of the mind and of one property of grammar.

4   Notice that the things belonging to this fourth division are apparently defined as primary substances in section 5 of the *Categories.*

5   To speak of them as coordinate, by reference to the notion of *subordinate* used below, seems to mean that one does not stand above the other in the hierarchy of predication discussed in chapter on Aristotle's hierarchy above.

6   Compare this remark with footnote 2. *White,* as a predicable, is not present in any subject. The particular color present in a subject, however, may be what we call *white,* so that *white* is predicable of the subject.

7   Induction will be considered later in the chapters on the philosophies of Hume and Peirce. Aristotle's notion of induction is quite different. In general, it is a way of proving a generalization like 'All *A*'s are *B*'s.' from an examination of cases of *A*. The premises of scientific syllogisms must be ultimately established by inductions, which are grounded in knowledge derived from particular objects. But Aristotle's treatment of induction seems contradictory and misleading. (See the discussion on pp. 24–37 of William Kneale's *Probability and Induction,* Oxford, 1949.) *Enthymeme* is now used by logicians to refer to an argument with suppressed premises, usually premises that are taken as obvious by the arguer. Aristotle meant a syllogism whose premises were either general truths (not true in every case) or particular facts. (See the discussion on pp. 350–351 of H. W. B. Joseph's *An Introduction to Logic,* Oxford, 1957.)

8   This discussion of knowledge in connection with a mathematical example is of interest in comparison to Plato's treatment. For Aristotle, prior knowledge is increased in learning some particular case which falls under it, while Plato would hold only that more was recollected. Aristotle's self-awareness of this difference is indicated by the reference immediately following to Plato's *Meno,* mentioned earlier in the footnotes to the Plato readings.

9   The necessity of what the possessor of scientific knowledge knows (theoretical science) is a rationalistic element that pervades Aristotle's thought.

10   Aristotle points out an essential ambiguity in *prior* and *better known.* Having explained this ambiguity, does he clarify his original formulation? Could *appropriate*, as used a few lines later, be used to indicate that either sense of the ambiguity may be correct in some specific demonstrations?

11   Given a predicate *P* and a subject *S,* an enunciation is of the form '*S* is *P* or *S* is not *P*.'. '*S* is *P*.' and '*S* is not *P*.' are propositions. A demonstrative proposition is simply the affirmation of the truth of one of these propositions. *S* is assumed to be single, which evidently indicates that *S* must have *P* or not *P*. Aristotle seems to assume here that *S* exists (otherwise neither demonstrative proposition obtained from the enunciation above need be true), which is an example of his tendency to talk about (existing) things, even where his philosophical point may appear to be about the language in which these things are described.

12   To many philosophers, this view would seem mistaken. It might at least be possible that we know the premises and conclusion of an argument equally well. And, in Peirce's abductive inference, which will be discussed later, a well-known conclusion, found to follow deductively from premises that we are not sure of, may increase our belief that these premises are true, but even this resulting belief may not be as strong as the belief that the conclusion is true.

13   Does this not suggest the self-evident principles of the first chapter in the text discussing Aristotle? If so, what are the consequences for the discussion referred to in footnote 10?

14   This paragraph requires close examination. Something predicated of a subject (see the discussion in the *Categories* in the first reading) must be common to that subject and other subjects. A definition of a subject *S* for Aristotle would be an attribute without which *S* would not be and which could not apply to anything other than *S*. If, however, a definition is a conjunction of more than one predicate, all the predicates are essentially predicated of *S,* since the absence of any. of them means that *S* does not occur. Consequently, this discussion of essential attributes must be an illustration of a particular kind of essential attribute if consistency with other remarks is to be maintained. Is this kind of essential attribute what Aristotle calls a 'commensurately universal' attribute below?

15   The law that proportionals alternate is apparently the law that if '$a/b = c/d$', then also '$a/c = b/d$'. Aristotle's point is not dependent on the exact statement of this law but on the fact that it need not be proved for every domain in which the appropriate arithmetic is used. See Sir Thomas Heath, *Mathematics in Aristotle*, Oxford, 1949, pp. 41–44, for an interesting comment on this passage.

16   The word translated here as *brazen* also means *bronze*. Notice that Plato would not make a statement like this about a metal triangle, which would not, strictly speaking, exist in terms of his epistemology.

17   The reference to previous work is probably to the *Metaphysics*, V, vii. Here the primary substances are said to *be* in some fundamental sense, all other things having existence because they belong to some category and may be predicated of some primary substance.

18   This reference to the *Categories* should occur to the reader.

19   Some study of the last phrase is required. Qualities, quantities, etc., can be considers *whats*, since they may be the subject of some attribute. Now this passage could mean that we know these instances of various categories where we predicate of them only when we know them as individuals. But since they are not individuals, this interpretation involves some obscurities. On the other hand, the passage could be read as saying that we know some quality (to take an example) only when we know what has that quality, so that 'the quality or the quantity' refers to whatever quality or quantity is being considered at some given time.

20   Aristotle was conscious of his philosophical predecessors, and he refers often to their views but not to their names. Evidently he used their views largely to establish a systematic way of exploring a problem, while arguing for his own solution. In this case, the three views referred to belong to the Milesians and Eleatics, the Pythagoreans and Empedocles, and the Atomists and Anaxagoras, respectively. For their detailed views, see G. S. Kirk and J. E. Raven, *The Presocratic Philosophers,* Cambridge, 1957.

21   This may refer to the Pythagoreans. See Kirk and Raven, *op. cit.*

22   The view that only sensible entities exist was held by some Sophists and pre-Socratics, certainly not by Plato.

23   Speusippus followed Plato as the head of the Platonic Academy. The Academy was a place for philosophers to study that Plato established in the town of Academe, near Athens. After Plato's death, the members of the Academy seem to have spent much of their time arguing over *the* correct interpretation of Plato's philosophy.

24   Xenocrates was the head of the Academy following Speusippus, and this mathematization of Platonic forms is often attributed to him.

25   To summarize the preceding argument is difficult. Bodies were first taken to be the most obvious candidates for primary substances. But Aristotelian analysis elsewhere has taken any body to be a composite of form and matter. The problem is to see whether primary substance can be identified with form alone, matter alone, or the composite of the two. It cannot be identified with matter since the properties of primary substance, among them separateness and individuality (thisness), are *not* properties of matter. The composite of form and matter is what is accidentally predicated of, since it is this intelligible object which has accidental attributes, and hence it is a kind of substrate. But, the form is prior to the composite, so that if the doctrine of priority is held here, the form must, in some sense, be the primary substance of sensible objects.

26   This introduces an apparent turning point in the argument. Essence will now be discussed, but as a way of understanding form. Any body will have a form, but *form* is somewhat ambiguous. The important part of the form of anything is its essence, as will be discussed. In this way, this change in topic carries out the conclusion of the preceding section. Compare the introduction of essence as a topic with the list—substratum, essence, genus, and universal—given earlier.

27   From the standpoint of contemporary philosophy, this passage is very interesting. The essence of something is said to be given in the formula which expresses

its meaning. Many modern philosophers would reject the assumption made here that there is exactly one such formula, and with the rejection of this assumption the Aristotelian notion of essence becomes even less clear. An apparently hypothetical suggestion in the text, that to be a white surface means to be a smooth object, may originate in the views of the pre-Socratic Democritus that the color of a surface was a function of its texture.

28   *Cloak* here may be replaced by *X*, since it is used as an arbitrary but simple expression standing for *white man*.

29   Snubness is a *propter se* attribute of noses, because *snub* is said correctly only of noses. Concavity, on the other hand, may be found in all kinds of objects.

30   Aristotle says that man and the essence of man, since man is a substance, may be regarded as identical, but white man and essence of white man may not be regarded as identical. Since white man and man, if it is regarded as an accidental unity that the class of men and the class of white men are coextensive (because all men are white), do not as a result have the same essence, we cannot use the identity of man and white man to conclude that the essence of man and the essence of white man are identical. This later identity is not the same as the first, and such inferences are invalid.

31   This is a little puzzling. Aristotle seems to suggest that accidental identities might be validly combined in syllogisms, but it is not clear that this could be of any use.

32   The preceding paragraph is an attack on the Platonic theory of ideas, successful in so far as it shows the Platonic theory is not compatible with Aristotle's own theory of essences.

33   At this point the basic answer to the question of what substance is can be given.

34   By identifying essence and substance, the question of the essence of an essence is avoided. In view of the preceding remarks about the theory of ideas, perhaps Aristotle is pointing out that the kind of paradox discussed in connection with the Platonic theory of ideas cannot arise for the Aristotelian system.

PART 3

Descartes

(1596–1650)

remarks to make about the painting in other contexts. They may, for example, both consider the painting beautiful in spite of these differences. This observation poses serious problems for the Platonic world of being, since the agreement that dialectic may force upon arguing philosophers is no guarantee that they do not differ from one another in the noncommunicable aspects of the forms. It thus appears that one human being may have knowledge that he cannot communicate to another human being, and it is this kind of observation that lies behind the problem of individualism in modern philosophy. Many modern philosophers are concerned to satisfy themselves of what they themselves know, leaving the problem (apparently more difficult) of what human beings may know in common as something to be solved after some sort of acceptable answer has been found to the former question.

Descartes's approach to the problem of what knowledge he could satisfy himself that he had has fascinated subsequent philosophers. Like many important arguments, it is essentially simple. In fact, it is of the form which mathematicians use quite frequently, and call the argument from *reductio ad absurdum*. The basic idea is this: if one wishes to prove that some proposition p is true, but can see no straightforward way of doing so, it is quite possible to prove p indirectly by assuming that p is false, and looking for an obviously false statement (preferably a contradiction) which follows from this assumption. By the definition of validity, if such a consequence can be found, it is equivalent to the assertion that 'p is false' is false, and this in turn is equivalent to the assertion that p is true. In such an argument, p or not-p (the latter being assumed as true if p is taken to be false) may be conjoined with other logically true statements. The fact that the other assumed statements are logically true means that if a contradiction is found, it may be blamed on either of p or not-p, whichever was assumed in addition. Descartes had observed, for reasons not much different from those that had convinced Plato and other earlier philosophers, that in many cases statements that had been thought to constitute knowledge would turn out to be uncertain or false under scrutiny. These examples were usually examples from sense-experience reports, but that is not crucial here. In order to show that human beings have some knowledge, so that they can obtain satisfactory axioms for a deductive system of human knowledge, it is necessary to show that not every case in which they believe themselves to possess knowledge is in fact uncertain or mistaken. The proof of the existence of one such piece of knowledge is sufficient to settle this question. Let p be "There is some human knowledge.". Its denial, not-p, is then "There is no human knowledge.". In both cases, *knowledge* is to be read in the technical sense of indubitable truth. To prove p, therefore, it is sufficient to show that not-p, if assumed, leads to an obvious falsehood. This, in effect, was the way that Descartes argued. It is clear that his argument is not *entirely* satisfactory, since in order to look for the consequences of some statement, according to the definition of deductive argument, one has to know how to look for consequences, and hence it is difficult to see how one might assume that he knows nothing, and then look for consequences which follow from that assumption. Nevertheless, it is of interest to see whether or not absurd consequences do follow from such an assumption as the one that there is no knowledge, using only logically valid steps of inference. We might suppose for the course of investigation that we are not human beings. Then, just as the natural scientist, who is not a fish, may think about fish, so we might imagine ourselves temporarily as higher beings who are scrutinizing human activity to see whether any of it might lead to knowledge. Descartes removes himself from the problem in such a manner by supposing that there is some evil power who has deceived him about everything. The question for Descartes is then whether or not the existence of such a power can be consistently held.

It turns out that if we question those beliefs which we have that we consider most secure by means of such a sweeping criticism, most of them seem *possibly* wrong or mistaken, which is sufficient to condemn them for any philosophy, like Descartes's or Plato's, that wishes to discover *certain* knowledge. We shall see that the empiricists will be different from the rationalists partly because they will question the propriety of considering *knowledge* to consist only of *certain* beliefs. But for the present, it would appear that Descartes could hold his view about the evil power without inconsistency.

There is no difficulty in showing that no knowledge obtained through the senses could be knowledge in Descartes's philosophical sense. An interesting argument that Descartes employed to indicate this is the argument from a seeming inability to determine whether or not we are awake. The distinction between being awake and being asleep, which may be clear enough to most of us most of the time, is open to potential confusion. Descartes, as well as most of us, occasionally mixed up some impressions from a dream with those from reality. Surely dreamers often experience terror and other emotions in their dreams, and it is clear that sometimes dreamers suppose that they are awake at the time of these experiences. If the dream state and the waking state are confused occasionally, how can it ever be known by someone with certainty that he is awake or dreaming at any given moment? It appears that he can never know for certain, since a sufficiently evil power might cause him to be confused about the distinction with great frequency. Descartes supposes that a distinction can be made, although perhaps he does so in a manner which is not entirely satisfactory. Empiricists will contend that even if one cannot know with certainty, there are ways of distinguishing the two states which are adequate for the purposes of scientific investigation, and hence derivatively adequate for philosophy.

But the results of assuming the existence of the evil power cut much deeper than obliterating the certain distinction between dreaming and being awake. The significance of being unable to make that distinction is largely that if sense experience is taken as the source of knowledge, and if sense experience does not occur during sleep and dreaming although one feels himself to be having sense experiences during dreams, then no feeling of having a sense experience can be taken as conclusive evidence that one is having a sense experience. The argument from the evil power is apparently sufficient to show that sense experience cannot be the origin of knowledge. But consider any statement of fact, that is, significant statement about the world, which is such that it seems to be certain. Clearly any such statement must refer to some past events, and its certainty must be related to some past observations, sense-experiential, or otherwise. To put this another way, a judgment of certainty rests upon previous knowledge that we have acquired, if for no other reason than that we need to have learned some language in order to express any judgment that we would like to make. But this view raises the question of the reliability of memory. If a present judgment or observation is to be certain, and it rests upon past judgments or observations, then there must be some *past* judgments which are certain if there are to be **any** present judgments or observations which are certainly true. But the conception of an evil power makes it clear at once that there can be no certain past. Whatever events we have memory of may be dream events which we have confused with reality. But even more importantly, it is possible, given everything that we think we know now, that there has been no past; in short, that the evil power created the world just yesterday or a few seconds ago. The objection to this is that we can think back to events which happened before yesterday or a few seconds ago. But how powerful is this objection? Suppose that we only dreamed about past events when we were created, and that we can dream about events in a couple of seconds which would stretch over long periods of time if they were memories of actual, experienced events. And, of course, we might have been created with full memories of past events which never happened. If memory, for example, is to be explained on the basis of some organic structure of the brain, then we might surely have been created with an organic structure which gives us the impression of past events which never happened. When memory is questioned, it would appear that most of our knowledge of sense-experienced events is of dubious quality. Note that if memory is questioned, the argument is not only against the view that sense experience is the origin of knowledge, since past intuitions have to be remembered to account for knowledge, but also against one view of any philosopher like Plato, whose view of the acquisition of knowledge depends upon the recollection of past intuitions.

The Cogito Argument

In spite of the apparent success of the argument from universal doubt in showing that most of the instances of purported knowledge that we might bring forward without reflection are dubious, that is, open to possible error under scrutiny, Descartes does find at least one proposition that he considers certain. This proposition is his specific counterexample to the argument that human beings may not possess any knowledge. It is the famous "Cogito, ergo sum.". We turn now to an analysis of this proposition to see whether Descartes's contention that it is indubitable is really satisfactory.

We shall consider this proposition in its English form, namely, "I think, therefore I am.". The occurrence of the word *therefore* is almost always a sign that some inference is being made. As a result, it is tempting to suppose that "I think, therefore I am." expresses a logical inference, and that Descartes takes the certainty of the logical inference in conjunction with the certainty that he is thinking to prove that he exists. Let us suppose that *a* stands for Descartes. '*Tx*' might stand for the expression '*x* thinks', which may be turned into a sentence by substituting someone's name for *x*. In this way, Descartes's proposition might be formulated in the expression '*Ta*', as it would be by many modern logicians. The problem of finding some formulation or symbolic expression for the statement "Descartes exists." is much more difficult.

There is, of course, a superficial grammatical similarity between the two sentences "Descartes thinks." and "Descartes exists.". In both cases, a subject noun is followed by a verb. But a serious problem for philosophical analysis is that grammatical similarities can prove to be misleading. Consider the following two sentences:

A. The wastepaper basket in this room is circular.
B. The wastepaper basket in this room exists.

Suppose, in the first case, that there is a wastepaper basket (and only one) in the room. In this case, the first sentence is quite clearly true or false, under an appropriate definition of *circular,* but the second sentence seems somehow to be redundant, or to convey very little information. Certainly it is the kind of thing that one would rarely say. At the same time, if there is no wastepaper basket in the room, the second sentence may seem to be either false or peculiar, while the first sentence seems to be quite peculiar, in that it seems neither true nor false. Philosophers have been perplexed by problems like these concerning existence since Plato, whose philosophy requires some explanation for the existence of the forms or ideas which do not exist in the ordinary sense that cats and dogs and people and Chevrolet cars exist.

Briefly, some philosophers have wanted to maintain that every grammatical, meaningful, indicative sentence should be true or false, but not both. For these philosophers, it is usually the case that, if the wastepaper basket exists, sentence B is true and sentence A is true or false depending on its construction, while if the wastepaper basket does not exist, sentence A is false along with sentence B. But this view, although it is very neat and simple in that it makes every grammatically well-formed sentence either true or false, does entail some revision of what common English usage seems to suggest. Since this is so, other revisions have been looked for. It will not be required here to survey these issues nor the various solutions to the difficulties inherent in them which have been proposed in the literature.

For our purpose, we merely note that the existence of a problem about existence is sufficient to cause us to refrain from putting down the sentence "Descartes exists." as something with the form 'Ea' with any assurance that we are doing something equivalent to what was done in the formulation of 'Ta'. The problem, then, is this: Is there any plausible way of writing down "Descartes exists." so as to make the inference from "Descartes thinks." to "Descartes exists." valid in some logical system? The general answer is that this is quite possible, but that in all known cases it results in an inference which is trivial in a way that Descartes clearly did not intend. Thus, many logicians write down 'a exists.' as '(Ex) $(x = a)$', which may be read 'There is at least one thing x such that x is identical with a.'. This seems to be a satisfactory way of expressing the claim that a exists for reasons that are too complicated to summarize quickly. If this reading is taken, then the inference 'If Ta, then $(Ex)(x=a)$.' may be proved in many logical systems as a consequence of the logically true statement 'If Ta, then (Ex) $(x = a$ and $Tx)$.', which is provable in very simple logical systems. Therefore, if 'Ta' symbolizes a sentence which is both true and asserts that Descartes thinks, we can also prove the truth of a statement which asserts that Descartes exists.

The importance of these observations is considerably diminished, however, by a closer look at the logical systems in which the inference 'If Ta, then $(Ex)(x=a)$.' can be proved. To begin with, these systems tacitly presuppose that the symbols which stand for nouns in their syntax, symbols into which *Descartes,* for example, would be translated, denote existing individuals. Consequently, at any time that one can assert '*Ta*' in such a system, one can also assert that *a* exists, since *a* cannot be used as a symbol in the system unless it refers to an existing individual. This makes the inference in question vacuous in the sense that we must know that the conclusion is true in order to formulate the premise correctly. Although the logical points that need to be made here are quite subtle, it is possible to demonstrate quite easily that the general form of an argument that goes like the following, '*Da,* therefore *a* exists.', is invalid, where '*Da*' in the sentence expressing the inference stands for any complete sentence that tells us about some property (other than existence) that *a* has. Consider the following argument: Hamlet thinks, therefore Hamlet exists. Here the transition is made from a sentence that most of us might consider true if we were asked casually about it to one that most of us would consider false, which means that the inference is not valid if the sentences are interpreted in this way. Hamlet does, of course, *exist* in some sense in the English language, but it is clear that Descartes does not mean to establish that he exists in the same sense that Hamlet exists. Therefore, if we treat the inference about Hamlet as invalid, Descartes's argument appears to be invalid. If we treat the inference about Hamlet as valid (proving that Hamlet exists), there remains the difficulty of distinguishing Hamlet's kind of existence from Descartes's existence, so that the inference does not do the job that Descartes seems to take it to do.

Descartes's notion of existence will be at least as complicated as Plato's. The sense of existence in which we say that Hamlet exists poses a number of philosophical problems. Those philosophers who have discussed fictional existence have generally tried to show how the existence of fictional characters could be analyzed in terms of the existence of other kinds of experienced objects. But Descartes cannot suppose that he exists in the same sense that experienced objects exist. The existence of the demon demonstrated to Descartes that the objects of sense experience might all be illusory, and that the whole notion of a world of sense experience can be doubted. Since Descartes felt that his own existence could not be doubted, it is clear that he did not identify himself with an object of sense experience. Descartes does not refer to the existence of his body when he says "I exist.". He is saying that thinking substances (souls) exist in a fashion quite different than material or corporeal bodies. Descartes, like Plato, uses *exist* in at least two ways, both of which must receive attention in his total theory of knowledge.

It might be argued that the logical framework which has been constructed thus far is misleading in that by means of it "I think, therefore I am." is subtly changed into "Descartes thinks, therefore he exists.", which is somewhat different. Suppose, therefore, that we try to construe the *cogito* argument as an argument which is **not** valid in general, since one cannot know about the thoughts of others, but which is valid only for the person who is proposing the argument, somewhat along the lines that Descartes intended. The notion of personal validity is not countenanced by most logicians, but Descartes may have implicitly believed that there were some arguments that I could not give an interpretation for myself in which the premises were true and the conclusion false, even though I might be able to imagine such an interpretation of the argument for others. In other words, Descartes may have intended that no one could prove the existence of another human being from the fact that the other human being seemed to think, while he intended that the *cogito* argument could be used by an individual to prove his own existence. "I think, therefore I am." in this case is not a valid argument to me if someone else utters it of himself, but it is a valid argument to me if I utter it of myself.

Suppose that I argue as follows:*

> If I am right in thinking that I exist, then I exist. If I err in thinking that I exist, then I exist, since I must exist in order to err. But either I am right in thinking that I exist or I err in thinking that I exist. Therefore, I exist.

The apparent plausibility of this argument to many people is a good reason for urging the study of logic. Suppose, for example, that someone in a fit of madness should suppose that everything in the Old Testament of the Bible was not literally true. In particular, suppose that he doubted the historical existence of Moses. Ordinarily, we might take the existence of any historical figure to be a matter of doubt. But an orthodox opponent might argue in the following fashion:

> If Moses was a Jew, then he existed, since no one could be a Jew without existing. If Moses was a Gentile (someone other than a Jew), then he existed, since no one could be a Gentile without existing. But Moses was either a Jew or a Gentile. Therefore, Moses existed.

It would be interesting to inform historical scholars that all problems of the existence of historical figures could be solved without doing any research. Apparently, restricting the argument to the case of someone asserting it for himself will not avoid the problem that arguments proving existence are either invalid or beg the question, in that the conclusion must be known to be true for the premises to be appropriately formulated. That Descartes could not have seriously intended the argument to rest on its logical merits alone is clear from the fact that he rejects the argument "I sweat, therefore I am." for his existence, even though it seems to be of the same logical form, and hence valid or invalid with the argument from the property of thinking.

Nevertheless the force of Descartes's argument is related to the fact

* This argument, as well as some of the other illustrations in the discussion of the *cogito* argument, is to be found in an excellent article by Jaakko Hintikka, "*Cogito, Ergo Sum:* Inference or Performance?" *The Philosophical Review,* vol. 71, pp. 3–33, January, 1962.

that it is an individual who is making it, and this requires some further study. Consider the following two sentences:

1. Samuel Richardson says that Tom Jones is dead.
2. Tom Jones says that Tom Jones is dead.

The first sentence may be taken both literally and metaphorically, but the second is peculiar in that it can make sense only metaphorically. Dead men tell no tales, least of all the one that they are dead. That seems unthinkable, apart from science fiction and spiritualism, which will not be taken into account here. Therefore, although anyone but Descartes may consistently argue that Descartes does not exist or is dead (as it was once argued that Hitler was dead in spite of apparent evidence to the contrary), Descartes himself cannot take this line of argument. Descartes, if he argues at all about the matter, must argue that he exists, or be considered mad. None of these reflections shows that Descartes's *cogito* argument is a piece of certain knowledge, indeed they argue to the contrary, but the difficulties raised by Descartes's argument have directly or indirectly stimulated a great deal of the discussions of the significance of individual experience that have taken place among philosophers since his time.

For Descartes, the *cogito* argument established one indubitable truth, the existence of his self, and from this Descartes thought that he could ultimately establish the existence of God, and from the nature of God the certainty that mathematics and science, properly pursued, could establish indubitable truth about the world in which we live.

The *cogito* argument is not an argument that one accepts like a demonstration in geometry; it must be taken rather as Descartes's report of what happened when he followed the hypothesis of doubt to some of its consequences. Presumably, others who follow the regimen of doubt will all come to the conclusion that they exist. Descartes himself did not devote much attention to whether this might be true. Later philosophers have been considerably perplexed by the problem of proving the existence of other selves, even if one can establish by the *cogito* argument the existence of one's own. What thinks, doubts, imagines, etc., is not a body, but a mind. Since one person cannot always see another thinking (unless one accepts a very strong version of behaviorist psychology), the *cogito* argument cannot be extended to prove that other beings exist, and hence by itself cannot prove the existence of human knowledge which is accessible to more than one person.

The *cogito* argument shows the existence of the philosopher's mind, which has the ideas that give him knowledge. These ideas, unlike those of Plato, exist in the mind of the philosopher, not as entities to which differ-ent philosophers have equal access through dialectic. Knowledge which is not based on sense experience is in effect the grasp of these ideas and the entities which they represent. Some of these ideas are related to objects of sense experience in such a way as to lead to science, but it is through tl ideas, and not through sense experiences, that these objects are known by scientists.

Although both Plato and Aristotle had drawn distinctions between bodies and souls, their more primary epistemological distinctions were drawn between the world of becoming and the world of being, or the difference between form and matter. Their problem had been the nature of things, with the account of human acquisition of knowledge of that nature somewhat secondary. In Descartes, mind and body, or mind and matter, is the fundamental epistemological distinction, and the acquisition of knowledge the fundamental epistemological problem. It has continued to be so for later philosophers.

Clearness and Distinctness

To come to an understanding of Descartes's full position, it would be necessary to examine his proofs of the existence of God, as well as his conclusions from the nature of God that certain statements are indubitably true. Still, day-to-day development of human knowledge is not dependent on constant examination of metaphysical foundations, and we may profitably look at Descartes's discussion of how ideas may be said to provide knowledge, independently of the connection between the origin of these ideas and God's nature in Descartes's full system.

It is true that there are innumerable difficulties in Descartes's conception of the mind as a kind of real, though immaterial, organ of perception. If we grant Descartes at least the possibility that the mind may exist as he describes it, we can find in Descartes a number of apparently convincing arguments that no explanation not involving such a mind could account for scientific information which is indubitable.

Descartes's most famous example is taken from information about a piece of wax, chosen because it might seem to be something which could be comprehended by the senses, if anything could be comprehended by them. The illustration involves a piece of wax all of whose sensed properties change over a short period of time. In spite of the change in *all* the sensed properties, it is still possible to know something about the wax, notably that it is the same piece of wax at both the beginning and end of the interval in which it is considered, in spite of the fact that there is no sensed property which it has both at the beginning and end of that period of time. This argument shows that if we can truly say that the wax is the same piece of wax at both times, we cannot explain this fact by appealing to our sense experiences of the wax. What we know in this case, and by extension in other cases like it, cannot be fully explained by an appeal to sense experience. It is important to notice that sense experience is not totally irrelevant, in that we may not be able to form the judgment that we are considering a piece of wax without some sense experiences, but it shows that what we can *know* about the piece of wax is not *reducible* to descriptions of sense experiences that we have. Thus, by an argument similar to those we considered earlier in connection with Plato's philosophy, Descartes seems to have established that *certain* knowledge cannot be satisfactorily justified or explained in terms of sense experience alone, although Descartes seems inclined to allow sense experience a more important role in leading us to this certain knowledge than Plato did.

In connection with the piece of wax, Descartes notes that when we *abstract* from the color, shape, etc., of the wax, we are left with the knowledge that the wax is something which is extended and movable. These properties, extension and motion, form the basic notions of Cartesian physics. It is the position of Descartes that the possible incorrectness of our attributions of particular sensed properties to objects, possibly incorrect because we observe that different sense properties may characterize the same object at different times, does not extend to extension and motion, which objects always have. For Descartes, extension and motion must be intuited of objects by the mind, but to show this it is necessary to show that they are not sensual properties.

Descartes takes it as clear that these properties are not *directly* sensed in an object, since we would sense both (if that were possible) by *comparison* of one object with another. But Descartes distinguishes a faculty that he calls imagination from the faculty of understanding, which is the result of the mind's comprehension of truth through ideas. Imagination is the result of combining parts of different particular sense experiences so as to frame a conception of something that it would be possible to experience. A mermaid, on this view, is a creature of imagination, since the conception of a mermaid results from combining parts of two or more particular sense experiences. In the case of the mermaid, the probability of experiencing this possible object of sense experience seems arbitrarily close to zero. Why cannot motion or extension in an object be the result of the operation of the imagination, that is, the combination in some fashion of a large number of particular sense experiences? Descartes's response that they cannot result from an exercise of imagination hinges on the fact that imagination can combine only a *finite* number of sense experiences (those that we have had), while an infinitude of motions and extensions seems possible. Knowledge of motion and extension, involving a conception of an infinite number of possibilities, cannot result solely from imagination. For Descartes, the more we know about wax, the more we know that our selves (minds) exist, and the more we know about our *selves*, since knowledge is not about sense-experienced objects.

Where Plato had provided arguments that seemed to show that mathematical knowledge could not be accounted for solely by sense experiences, Descartes provides arguments to show that this is true of scientific knowledge as well. This argument is one that cannot be lightly dismissed, even though one may wish to renounce the particular metaphysics that Descartes employs to prove it. The reason why the argument cannot be lightly dismissed is related to the growth of modern scientific *theory*, a phenomenon beginning to develop in Descartes's time, but almost totally unknown in Plato's time. The objects spoken of in fragments of scientific theory, such as ideal gases and frictionless surfaces, to take some examples, are often such that they could not be experienced. Almost any important subject of scientific theorizing in the last one hundred years, for example, *gene, electron, DNA,* etc., can hardly be construed as something which is sense-experienced.

The relationship of theoretical entities and sense experience is an extremely difficult one to interpret. To take a simple example, one which Descartes considered, the sun of astronomical theory has an average distance from the earth of some 93 million miles, although no one has experienced that distance. Further, the sun of astronomical theory is known to have a diameter of 865,000 miles, while the sun of sense experience is a small disk. Without multiplying examples unnecessarily, we can see that many, perhaps even all, of the things which science theorizes about are not to be confused with the objects of sense experience, for they have different properties. To say this is to raise the problem of the relationship between the objects of sense experience and the objects of scientific theorizing, a problem that neither Plato's nor Descartes's rationalism fully answers, although the arguments of Plato and Descartes for rationalism point up the difficulties which must be encountered in framing a satisfactory account of the relationship of theory to practice. What is important for Descartes is that *knowledge* is partly mathematical and scientific, and that sense experience cannot explain the certainty found in at least these areas of knowledge. It is assumed here that mathematical truths and truths of scientific theorizing are certain, a position which is obviously capable of a vigorous defense.

For Plato, the ideas constituting knowledge were those corresponding to the ideas or forms in the world of being. Descartes, not having a world of being, must depend on some other criterion for separating the sound ideas from unsound ideas which may occur to us. The Cartesian criterion is twofold: those ideas are sound, that is, capable of good use in developing knowledge, which are both *clear* and *distinct*. The impact of the notions of clearness and distinctness on subsequent philosophy calls for some closer attention to what Descartes meant.

Descartes notices that our thoughts (comprising everything that we may call an *idea* ordinarily) may be divided into ideas proper and judgments. The former are, simply, the images that appear in the mind without any reflection as to their significance. Judgments are decisions as to the significance of ideas proper, or perhaps as to the relationships between ideas. Ideas proper cannot be right or wrong; we simply have them. Judgments, on the other hand, may be right or wrong. Thus, we may experience some red, about which experience we cannot be mistaken, although we may be mistaken in judging that the red we experienced was part of a cardinal, for example, or that it was the particular red that we call scarlet. This kind of distinction occurs over and over in epistemology since Descartes, notoriously in the notion of sense data, which are like Cartesian ideas proper in that they are not capable of being false. Many philosophers have hoped that such sense data might be taken as a sound basis for the epistemological foundation of science.

The clear and distinct ideas involved in knowledge are not ideas proper, since they are things that we have reflected on. It may be less misleading to speak of clear and distinct thoughts. Here, a *clear* thought is one which may be the direct object of apprehension, and hence may be described as a thought which is not vague. This means that it may be considered by itself, without reference to other ideas or judgments.

On the other hand, a *distinct* thought is one which may be comprehended or understood by itself, that is, whose understanding does not depend on other thoughts. The clear and distinct thoughts that are useful for developing knowledge are such that the notion of distinctness conflates with the notion of simplicity. A simple thought is a thought which is pregnant or endlessly fruitful for the development of some line of thought. For example, the concepts of *group* and *limit* are simple in mathematics in this sense, for they may be used to understand and develop mathematical truth in seemingly endless particular contexts. *Simple* may contrast with *adventitious*, yet an adventitious idea may be clear, and in some sense distinct, without being fruitful. Adventitious ideas are chance ideas, or ideas forced upon us by the vagaries of sense experience. In contrast to group and limit, the concept of a chiliagon would be an adventitious idea in mathematics. A distinct thought is then a thought which may be comprehended by itself and which it is fruitful to contemplate. In thinking of clear and distinct ideas it may be helpful to note that distinct ideas are also necessarily clear ideas, but that an idea may be clear without being distinct.

The status of the thought "I think, therefore I am." is surely that of a clear and distinct idea for Descartes, which he finds fruitful in developing his later epistemological claims. This may explain why Descartes thought that so much could be based on it that cannot be *deduced* from it by the rules of formal logic. While clearness and distinctness are not themselves entirely clear and distinct, they have proved influential notions for the thinking of many later philosophers who were rationalists in epistemology, particularly with respect to the problem of distinguishing those ideas that might constitute human knowledge.

Readings from Descartes

The readings which are reprinted here consist of the first two meditations and part of the third from Descartes's *Meditations on the First Philosophy in Which the Existence of God and the Distinction between Mind and Body Are Demonstrated.* They are reprinted here from *The Philosophical Works of Descartes,* translated by E. S. Haldane and G. R. T. Ross. This reprinting is by kind permission of the Cambridge University Press. The Haldane and Ross translation has also been available as a Dover paperbound.

Descartes's *Discourse on Method* and his *Meditations* are usually regarded as his philosophical masterpieces. They should be studied along with the sets of *Objections* to the *Meditations* which are found in Descartes's complete works. A friend of Descartes, the Rev. Father Mersenne, circulated the *Meditations* among various theologians and philosophers who then sent their comments and criticisms to Descartes. Descartes replied to the objections and published the entire correspondence along with the *Meditations.* These so-called *Objections and Replies* constitute what is perhaps the most valuable commentary on the *Meditations.*

Descartes is one of the major philosophers who would be important in intellectual history even if his philosophical achievements had been entirely neglected. He deserves a place in mathematical history, for example, because of his contributions to geometry. A short biography and summary of his mathematical achievements may be found in E. T. Bell's *Men of Mathematics,* New York, 1937. His most important mathematical insight was the discovery of the method of coordinates which made analytic geometry possible. The method of coordinates proposed by Descartes is the familiar one of dividing the Euclidean mathematical plane into four quadrants by means of two intersecting straight lines called the ordinate and the abscissa. As is well known, any geometrical curve in the plane can then be defined as an *equation* which represents each point of the curve by means of its perpendicular distances to the ordinate and the abscissa. The

116

importance of analytic geometry, which is the study of geometrical problems expressed as algebraic equations, is that many difficult geometrical problems can be quickly solved when they are *translated* into algebraic equations whose solution is a matter of routine.

It is characteristic of the life of Descartes that the method of coordinates should have occurred to him while he was lying in bed watching a housefly walk on the ceiling of his room. Descartes saw that the position of the fly could always be represented by its perpendicular distances to any two walls forming a corner of the room, and this observation may quickly be abstracted into the notion of coordinates.

The following bibliography contains some secondary-source material in English. A vast literature on Descartes is available in French to those students who can read that language, and French sources may be obtained by consulting the bibliographies of the books which are listed here.

Balz, A. G. A.: *Descartes and the Modern Mind,* New Haven, 1952.

Beck, L. J.: *The Method of Descartes, a Study of the Regulae,* Oxford, 1952.

Carney, James D.: *"Cogito, Ergo Sum* and *Sum Res Cogitans," The Philosophical Review,* vol. 71, pp. 492–497, 1962.

Hintikka, Jaakko: *"Cogito, Ergo Sum:* Inference or Performance?" *The Philosophical Review,* vol. 71, pp. 3–33, 1962.

Smart, J. J. C.: "Descartes and the Wax," *Philosophical Quarterly,* vol. 1, pp. 50–57, 1950.

Smith, N. K.: *Studies in Cartesian Philosophy,* London, 1914.

————: *New Studies in the Philosophy of Descartes,* London, 1952.

Versfeld, M.: *An Essay on the Metaphysics of Descartes,* London, 1940.

Weinberg, J. R.: *"Cogito, Ergo Sum:* Some Reflections on Mr. Hintikka's Article," *The Philosophical Review,* vol. 71, pp. 483–492, 1962.

Wright, J. N.: "Descartes and the Wax," *Philosophical Quarterly,* vol. 1, pp. 352–355, 1950.

From Descartes's *MEDITATIONS*

MEDITATION I: OF THE THINGS WHICH MAY BE BROUGHT WITHIN THE SPHERE OF THE DOUBTFUL

It is now some years since I detected how many were the false beliefs that I had from my earliest youth admitted as true, and how doubtful was everything I had since constructed on this basis; and from that time I was convinced that I must once for all seriously undertake to rid myself of all the opinions which I had formerly accepted, and commence to build anew from the foundation, if I wanted to establish any firm and permanent structure in the sciences. But as this enterprise appeared to be a very great one, I waited until I had attained an age so mature that I could not hope that at any later date I should be better fitted to execute my design. This reason caused me to delay so long that I should feel that I was doing wrong were I to occupy in deliberation the time that yet remains to me for action. Today, then, since very opportunely for the plan I have in view I have delivered my mind from every care (and am happily agitated by no passions) and since I have procured for myself an assured leisure in a peaceable retirement, I shall at last seriously and freely address myself to the general upheaval of all my former opinions.

Now for this object it is not necessary that I should show that all of these are false—I shall perhaps never arrive at this end. But inasmuch as reason already persuades me that I ought no less carefully to withhold my assent from matters which are not entirely certain and indubitable than from those which appear to me manifestly to be false, if I am able to find in each one some reason to doubt, this will suffice to justify my rejecting the whole. And for that end it will not be requisite that I should examine each in particular, which would be an endless undertaking; for owing to the fact that destruction of the foundations of necessity brings with it the downfall of the rest of the edifice, I shall only in the first place attack those principles upon which all my former opinions rested.

All that up to the present time I have accepted as most certain and true I have learned either from the senses or through the senses; but it is sometimes proved to me that these senses are deceptive, and it is wiser not to trust entirely to any thing by which we have once been deceived. But it may be that although the senses sometimes deceive us concerning things which are hardly perceptible, or very far away, there are yet many others to be met with as to which we cannot reasonably have any doubt, although we recognize them by their means. For example, there is the fact that I am here, heated by the fire, attired in a dressing gown, having this paper in my hands and other similar matters. And how could I deny that these hands and this body were mine, were it not perhaps that I compare myself to certain persons, devoid of sense, whose cerebella are so troubled and clouded by the violent vapors of black bile, that they constantly assure us that they think they are kings when they are really quite poor, or that they are clothed in purple when they are really without covering, or who imagine that they have an earthenware head or are nothing but pumpkins or are made of glass.[1] But they are mad, and I should not be any the less insane were I to follow examples so extravagant.

At the same time I must remember that I am a man, and that consequently I am in the habit of sleeping, and in my dreams representing to myself the same things or sometimes even less probable things, than do those who are insane in their waking moments. How often has it happened to me that in the night I dreamt that I found myself in this particular place, that I was dressed and seated near the fire, whilst in reality I was lying undressed in bed?[2] At this moment it does indeed seem to me that it is with eyes awake that I am looking at this paper; that this head which I move is not asleep, that it is deliberately and of set purpose that I extend my hand

and perceive it; what happens in sleep does not appear so clear nor so distinct as does all this. But in thinking over this I remind myself that on many occasions I have in sleep been deceived by similar illusions, and in dwelling carefully on this reflection I see so manifestly that there are no certain indications by which we may clearly distinguish wakefulness from sleep that I am lost in astonishment. And my astonishment is such that it is almost capable of persuading me that I now dream.

Now let us assume that we are asleep and that all of these particulars, e.g. that we open our eyes, shake our head, extend our hands, and so on, are but false delusions; and let us reflect that possibly neither our hands nor our whole body are such as they appear to us to be. At the same time we must at least confess that the things which are represented to us in sleep are like painted representations which can only have been formed as the counterparts of something real and true, and that in this way those general things at least, *i.e.* eyes, a head, hands, and a whole body, are not imaginary things, but things really existent. For, as a matter of fact, painters, even when they study with the greatest skill to represent sirens and satyrs by forms the most strange and extraordinary, cannot give them natures which are entirely new, but merely make a certain medley of the members of different animals; or if their imagination is extravagant enough to invent something so novel that nothing similar has ever before been seen, and that then their work represents a thing purely fictitious and absolutely false, it is certain all the same that the colors of which this is composed are necessarily real. And for the same reason, although these general things, to wit, (a body), eyes, a head, and such like, may be imaginary, we are bound at the same time to confess that there are at least some other objects, yet more simple and more universal, which are real and true; and of these just in the same way as with certain real colors, all these images of things which dwell in our thoughts, whether true and real or false and fantastic, are formed.

To such a class of things pertains corporeal nature in general, and its extension, the figure of extended things, their quantity or magnitude and number, as also the place in which they are, the time which measures their duration, and so on.[3]

That is possibly why our reasoning is not unjust when we conclude from this that Physics, Astronomy, Medicine and all other sciences which have as their end the consideration of composite things, are very dubious and uncertain; but that Arithmetic, Geometry, and other sciences of that kind which only treat of things that are very simple and very general, without taking great trouble to ascertain whether they are actually existent or not, contain some measure of certainty and an element of the indubitable.[4] For whether I am awake or asleep, two and three together always form five, and the square can never have more than four sides, and it does not seem possible that truths so clear and apparent can be suspected of any falsity (or uncertainty).

Nevertheless I have long had fixed in my mind the belief that an all-powerful God existed by whom I have been created such as I am. But how do I know that He has not brought it to pass that there is no earth, no heaven, no extended body, no magnitude, no place, and that nevertheless (I possess the perceptions of all these things and that) they seem to me to exist just exactly as I now see them? And, besides, as I sometimes imagine that others deceive themselves in the things which they think they know best, how do I know that I am not deceived every time that I add two and three, or count the sides of a square, or judge of things yet simpler, if anything simpler can be imagined? But possibly God has not desired that I should be thus deceived, for He is said to be supremely good. If, however, it is contrary to His goodness to have made me such that I constantly deceive myself, it would also appear to be contrary to His goodness to permit me to be sometimes deceived, and nevertheless I cannot doubt that He does permit this.[5]

There may indeed be those who would prefer to deny the existence of a God so powerful, rather than believe that all other things are uncertain.[6] But let us not oppose them for the present, and grant that all that is said of God is a fable; nevertheless in whatever way they suppose that I have arrived at the state of being that I have reached—whether they attribute it to fate or to accident, or make out that it is by a continual succession of antecedents, or by some other method—since to err and deceive oneself is a defect, it is clear that the greater will be the probability of my being so imperfect as to deceive myself ever, as is the Author to whom they assign my origin the less powerful. To these reasons I have certainly nothing to reply, but at the end I feel constrained to confess that there is nothing in all that I formerly believed to be true, of which I cannot in some measure doubt, and that not merely through want of thought or through levity, but for reasons which are very powerful and maturely considered; so that henceforth I ought not the less carefully to refrain from giving credence to these opinions than to that which is manifestly false, if I desire to arrive at any certainty (in the sciences).

But it is not sufficient to have made these remarks, we must also be careful to keep them in mind. For these ancient and commonly held opinions still revert frequently to my mind, long and familiar custom having given them the right to occupy my mind against my inclination and rendered them almost masters of my belief; nor will I ever lose the habit of deferring to them or of placing my confidence in them, so long as I consider them as they really are, *i.e.* opinions in some measure doubtful, as I have just shown, and at the same time highly probable, so that there is much more reason to believe than to deny them. That is why I consider that I shall not be acting amiss, if, taking of set purpose a contrary belief, I allow myself to be deceived, and for a certain time pretend that all these opinions are entirely false and imaginary, until at last, having thus balanced my former prejudices with my latter (so that they cannot divert my opinions more to one side than to the other), my judgment will no longer be dominated by bad usage or turned away from the right knowledge of the truth. For I am assured that there can be neither peril nor error in this course, and that I cannot at present yield too much to distrust, since I am not considering the question of action, but only of knowledge.[7]

I shall then suppose, not that God who is supremely good and the fountain of truth, but some evil genius not less powerful than deceitful, has employed his whole energies in deceiving me; I shall consider that the heavens, the earth, colors, figures, sound, and all other external things are nought but the illusions and dreams of which this genius has availed himself in order to lay traps for my credulity; I shall consider myself as having no hands, no eyes, no flesh, no blood, nor any senses, yet falsely believing myself to possess all these things; I shall remain obstinately attached to this idea, and if by this means it is not in my power to arrive at the knowledge of any truth, I may at least do what is in my power (*i.e.* suspend my judgment), and with firm purpose avoid giving credence to any false thing, or being imposed upon by this arch deceiver, however powerful and deceptive he may be. But this task is a laborious one, and insensibly a certain lassitude leads me into the course of my ordinary life. And just as a captive who in sleep enjoys imaginary liberty, when he begins to suspect that his liberty is but a dream, fears to awaken, and conspires with these agreeable illusions that the deception may be prolonged, so insensibly of my own accord I fall back into my former opinions, and I dread awakening from this slumber, lest the laborious wakefulness which should follow the tranquillity of this repose should have to be spent not in daylight, but in the excessive darkness of the difficulties which have just been discussed.

MEDITATION II: OF THE NATURE OF THE HUMAN MIND; AND THAT IT IS MORE EASILY KNOWN THAN THE BODY

The Meditation of yesterday filled my mind with so many doubts that it is no longer in my power to forget them. And yet I do not see in what manner I can resolve them; and, just as if I had all of a sudden fallen into very deep water, I am so disconcerted that I can neither make certain of setting my feet on the bottom, nor can I swim and so support myself on the surface. I shall nevertheless make an effort and follow anew the same path as that on which I yesterday entered, *i.e.* I shall proceed by setting aside all that in which the least doubt could be supposed to exist, just as if I had discovered that it was absolutely false; and I shall ever follow in this road until I have met with something which is certain, or at least, if I can do nothing else, until I have learned for certain that there is nothing in the world which is certain. Archimedes, in order that he might draw the terrestrial globe out of its place, and transport it elsewhere, demanded only that one point should be fixed and immovable; in the same way I shall have the right to conceive high hopes if I am happy enough to discover one thing only which is certain and indubitable.[8]

I suppose, then, that all the things that I see are false; I persuade myself that nothing has ever existed of all that my fallacious memory represents to me. I consider that I possess no senses; I imagine that body, figure, extension, movement and place are but the fictions of my mind. What, then, can be esteemed as true? Perhaps nothing at all, unless that there is nothing in the world which is certain.[9]

But how can I know that there is not something different from those things which I have just considered, of which one cannot have the slightest doubt? Is there not some God, or some other being by whatever name we call it, who puts these reflections into my mind? That is not necessary, for is it not possible that I am capable of producing them myself? I myself, am I not at least something? But I have already denied that I had senses and body. Yet I hesitate, for what follows from that? Am I so dependent on body and senses that I cannot exist without these? But I was persuaded that there was nothing in all the world, that there was no heaven, no earth, that there were no minds, nor any bodies; was I not then likewise persuaded that I did not exist? Not at all; of a surety I myself did exist since I persuaded myself of something (or merely because I thought of something). But there is some deceiver or other, very powerful and very cunning, who ever employs his ingenuity in deceiving me. Then without doubt I exist also if he deceives me, and let him deceive me as much as he will, he can never cause me to be nothing so long as I think that I am something. So that after having reflected well and carefully examined all things, we must come to the definite conclusion that this proposition: I am, I exist, is necessarily true each time that I pronounce it, or that I mentally conceive it.[10]

But I do not yet know clearly enough what I am, I who am certain that I am; and hence I must be careful to see that I do not imprudently take some other object in place of myself, and thus that I do not go astray in respect of this knowledge that I hold to be the most certain and most evident of all that I have formerly learned. That is why I shall now consider anew what I believed myself to be before I embarked upon these last reflections; and of my former opinions I shall withdraw all that might even in a small degree be invalidated by the reasons which I have just brought forward, in order that there may be nothing at all left beyond what is absolutely certain and indubitable.

What then did I formerly believe myself to be? Undoubtedly I believed myself to be a man. But what is a man? Shall I say a reasonable animal? Certainly not; for then I should have to inquire what an animal is, and what is reasonable; and thus from a single question I should insensibly fall into an infinitude of others more difficult; and I should not wish to waste the little time and leisure remaining to me in trying to unravel subtleties like these.[11] But I shall rather stop here to consider the thoughts which of themselves spring up in my mind, and which were not inspired by anything beyond my own nature alone when I applied myself to the consideration of my being. In the first place, then, I considered myself as having a face, hands, arms, and all that system of members composed of bones and flesh as seen in a corpse which I designated by the name of body. In addition to this I considered that I was nourished, that I walked, that I felt, and that I thought, and I referred all these actions to the soul: but I did not stop to consider what the soul was, or if I did stop, I imagined that it was something extremely rare and subtle like a wind, a flame, or an ether, which was spread throughout my grosser parts. As to body I had no manner of doubt about its nature, but thought I had a very clear knowledge of it; and if I had desired to explain it according to the notions that I had then formed of it, I should have described it thus: By the body I understand all that which can be defined by a certain figure: something which can be confined in a certain place, and which can fill a given space in such a way that every other body will be excluded from it; which can be perceived either by touch, or by sight, or by hearing, or by taste, or by smell: which can be moved in many ways not, in truth, by itself, but by something which is foreign to it, by which it is touched (and from which it receives impressions): for to have the power of self-movement, as also of feeling or of thinking, I did not consider to appertain to the nature of body: on the contrary, I was rather astonished to find that faculties similar to them existed in some bodies.

But what am I, now that I suppose that there is a certain genius which is extremely powerful, and, if I may say so, malicious, who employs all his powers in deceiving me? Can I affirm that I possess the least of all those things which I have just said pertain to the nature of body? I pause to consider, I resolve all these things in my mind, and find none of which I can say that it pertains to me. It would be tedious to stop to enumerate them. Let us pass to the attributes of soul and see if there is any one which is in me? What of nutrition or walking (the first mentioned)? [12] But if it is so that I have no body it is also true that I can neither walk nor take nourishment. Another attribute is sensation. But one cannot feel without body, and besides I have thought I perceived many things during sleep that I recognized in my waking moments as not having been experienced at all. What of thinking? I find here that thought is an attribute that belongs to me; it alone cannot be separated from me. I am, I exist, that is certain. But how often? Just when I think; for it might possibly be the case if I ceased entirely to think, that I should likewise cease altogether to exist. I do not now admit anything which is not necessarily true: to speak accurately I am not more than a thing which thinks, that is to say a mind or soul, or an understanding, or a reason, which are terms whose significance was formerly unknown to me.[13] I am, however, a real thing and really exist; but what thing? I have answered: a thing which thinks.

And what more? I shall exercise my imagination (in order to see if I am not something more). I am not a collection of members which we call the human body: I am not a subtle air distributed through these members, I am not a wind, a fire, a vapor, a breath, nor anything at all which I can imagine or conceive; because I have assumed that all these were nothing. Without changing that supposition I find that I only leave myself certain of the fact that I am somewhat. But perhaps it is true that these same things which I supposed were non-existent because they are unknown to me, are really not different from the self which I know. I am not sure about this, I shall not dispute about it now; I can only give judgment on things that are known to me. I know that I exist, and I inquire what I am, I whom I know to exist. But it is very certain that the knowledge of my existence taken in its precise significance does not depend on things whose existence is not yet known to me; consequently it does not depend on those which I can feign in imagination. And indeed the very term *feign* in imagination proves to me my error, for I really do this if I imagine myself a something, since to imagine is nothing else than to contemplate the figure or image of a corporeal thing. But I already know for certain that I am, and that it may be that all these images, and, speaking generally, all things that relate to the nature of body are nothing but dreams (and chimeras). For this reason I see clearly that I have as little reason to say, "I shall stimulate my imagination in order to know more distinctly what I am," than if I were to say, "I am now awake, and I perceive somewhat that is real and true: but because I do not yet perceive it distinctly enough, I shall go to sleep of excess purpose, so that my dreams may represent the perception with greatest truth and evidence." And, thus, I know for certain that nothing of all that I can understand by means of my imagination belongs to this knowledge which I have of myself, and that it is necessary to recall the mind from this mode of thought with the utmost diligence in order that it may be able to show its own nature with perfect distinctness.

But what then am I? A thing which thinks. What is a thing which thinks? It is a thing which doubts, understands, (conceives), affirms, denies, wills, refuses, which also imagines and feels.[14]

Certainly it is no small matter if all these things pertain to my nature. But why should they not so pertain? Am I not that being who now doubts nearly everything, who nevertheless understands certain things, who affirms that one only is true, who denies all the others, who desires to know more, is averse from being deceived, who imagines many things, sometimes indeed despite his will, and who perceives many likewise, as by the intervention of the bodily organs? Is there nothing in all this which is as true as it is certain that I exist, even though I should always sleep and though he who has given me being employed all his ingenuity in deceiving me? Is there likewise any one of these attributes which can be distinguished from my thought, or which might be said to be separated from myself? For it is so evident of itself that it is I who doubts, who understands, and who desires, that there is no reason here to add anything to explain it. And

I have certainly the power of imagining likewise; for although it may happen (as I formerly supposed) that none of the things which I imagine are true, nevertheless this power of imagining does not cease to be really in use, and it forms part of my thought. Finally, I am the same who feels, that is to say, who perceives certain things, as by the organs of sense, since in truth I see light, I hear noise, I feel heat. But it will be said that these phenomena are false and that I am dreaming. Let it be so; still it is at least quite certain that it seems to me that I see light, that I hear noise and that I feel heat. That cannot be false; properly speaking it is what is in me called feeling; and used in this precise sense that is no other thing than thinking.

From this time I begin to know what I am with a little more clearness and distinction than before; but nevertheless it still seems to me, and I cannot prevent myself from thinking, that corporeal things, whose images are framed by thought, which are tested by the senses, are much more distinctly known than that obscure part of me which does not come under the imagination. Although really it is very strange to say that I know and understand more distinctly these things whose existence seems to me dubious, which are unknown to me, and which do not belong to me, than others of the truth of which I am convinced, which are known to me and which pertain to my real nature, in a word, than myself. But I see clearly how the case stands: my mind loves to wander, and cannot yet suffer itself to be retained within the just limits of truth. Very good, let us once more give it the freest rein, so that, when afterwards we seize the proper occasion for pulling up, it may the more easily be regulated and controlled.

Let us begin by considering the commonest matters, those which we believe to be the most distinctly comprehended, to wit, the bodies which we see and touch; not indeed bodies in general, for these general ideas are usually a little more confused, but let us consider one body in particular. Let us take for example, this piece of wax: it has been taken quite freshly from the hive, and it has not yet lost the sweetness of the honey which it contains; it still retains somewhat of the odor of the flowers from which it has been culled; its color, its figure, its size are apparent; it is hard, cold, easily handled, and if you strike it with the finger, it will emit a sound.[15] Finally all the things which are requisite to cause us distinctly to recognize a body, are met within it. But notice that while I speak and approach the fire what remained of the taste is exhaled, the smell evaporates, the color alters, the figure is destroyed, the size increases, it becomes liquid, it heats, scarcely can one handle it, and when one strikes it, no sound is emitted. Does the same wax remain after this change? We must confess that it remains; none would judge otherwise.[16] What then did I know so distinctly in this piece of wax? It could certainly be nothing of all that the senses brought to my notice, since all these things which fall under taste, smell, sight, touch, and hearing, are found to be changed, and yet the same wax remains.

Perhaps it was what I now think, viz. that this wax was not that sweetness of honey, nor that agreeable scent of flowers, nor that particular whiteness, nor that figure, nor that sound, but simply a body which a little before appeared to me as perceptible under these forms, and which is now perceptible under others. But what, precisely, is it that I imagine when I form such conceptions? Let us attentively consider this, and, abstracting from all that does not belong to the wax, let us see what remains. Certainly nothing remains excepting a certain extended thing which is flexible and movable. But what is the meaning of flexible and movable? Is it not that I imagine that this piece of wax being round is capable of becoming square and of passing from a square to a triangular figure? No, certainly it is not that, since I imagine that it admits of an infinitude of similar changes, and I nevertheless do not know how to compass the infinitude by my imagination, and consequently this conception which I have of the wax is not brought about by the faculty of imagination.[17] What now is this extension? Is it not also unknown? For it becomes greater when the wax is melted, greater when it is boiled, and greater still when the heat increases; and I should not conceive (clearly) according to truth what wax is, if I did not think that even this piece we are considering is capable of receiving more variations in extension than I have ever imagined. We must then grant that I could not even understand through the imagination what this piece of wax is, and that it is my mind alone which perceives it. I say this piece of wax in particular, for as to wax in general it is yet clearer. But what is this piece of wax which cannot be understood excepting by the (understanding or) mind? It is certainly the same that I see, touch, imagine, and finally it is the same which I have always believed it to be from the beginning. But what must be particularly observed is that its perception is neither an act of vision, nor of touch, nor of imagination, and has never been such although it may have appeared formerly to be so, but only an intuition of the mind, which may be imperfect and confused as it was formerly, or clear and distinct as it is at present, according as my attention is more or less directed to the elements which are found in it, and of which it is composed.

Yet in the meantime I am greatly astonished when I consider (the great feebleness of mind) and its proneness to fall (insensibly) into error; for although without giving expression to my thoughts I consider all this in my own mind, words often impede me and I am almost deceived by the terms of ordinary language. For we say that we see the same wax, if it is present, and not that we simply judge that it is the same from its having the same color and figure. From this I should conclude that I knew the wax by means of vision and not simply by the intuition of the mind; unless by chance I remember that, when looking from a window and saying that I see men who pass in the street, I really do not see them, but infer that what I see is men, just as I say that I see wax. And yet what do I see from the window but hats and coats which may cover automatic machines? Yet I judge these to be men. And similarly solely by the faculty of judgment which rests in my mind, I comprehend that which I believed I saw with my eyes.[18]

A man who makes it his aim to raise his knowledge above the common should be ashamed to derive the occasion for doubting from the forms of speech invented by the vulgar; I prefer to pass on and consider whether I had a more evident and perfect conception of what the wax was when I first perceived it, and when I believed I knew it by means of the external senses or at least by the common sense as it is called, that is to say by the imaginative faculty, or whether my present conception is clearer now that I have most carefully examined what it is, and in what way it can be known. It would certainly be absurd to doubt as to this. For what was there in this first perception which was distinct? What was there which might not as well have been perceived by any of the animals? But when I distinguish the wax from its external forms, and when, just as if I had taken from it its vestments, I consider it quite naked, it is certain that although some error may still be found in my judgment, I can nevertheless not perceive it without a human mind.[19]

But finally what shall I say of this mind, that is, of myself, for up to this point I do not admit in myself anything but mind? What then, I who seem to perceive this piece of wax distinctly, do I not know myself, not only with much more truth and certainty, but also with much more distinctness and clearness? For if I judge that the wax is or exists from the fact that I see it, it certainly follows much more clearly that I am or that I exist myself from the fact that I see it. For it may be that what I see is not really wax, it may also be that I do not possess eyes with which to see anything; but it cannot be that when I see, or (for I no longer take account of the distinction) when I think I see, that I myself who think am nought. So if I judge that the wax exists from the fact that I touch it, the same thing will follow, to wit, that I am; and if I judge that my imagination, or some other cause, whatever it is, persuades me that the wax exists, I shall still conclude the same. And what I have here remarked of wax may be applied to all other things which are external to me (and which are met with outside of me). And further, if the (notion or) perception of wax has seemed to me clearer and more distinct, not only after the sight or the touch, but also after many other causes have rendered it quite manifest to me, with how much more (evidence) and distinctness must it be said that I now know myself, since all the reasons which contribute to the knowledge of wax, or any other body whatever, are yet better proofs of the nature of my mind! And there are so many other things in the mind itself which may contribute to the elucidation of its nature, that those which depend on body such as these just mentioned, hardly merit being taken into account.

But finally here I am, having insensibly reverted to the point I desired, for, since it is now manifest to me that even bodies are not properly speaking known by the senses or by the faculty of imagination, but by the understanding only, and since they are not known from the fact that they are seen or touched, but only because they are understood, I see clearly that there is nothing which is easier for me to know than my mind. But because it is difficult to rid oneself so promptly of an opinion to which one was accustomed for so long, it will be well that I should halt a little at this point, so that by the length of my meditation I may more deeply imprint on my memory this new knowledge.

MEDITATION III: OF GOD: THAT HE EXISTS

I shall now close my eyes, I shall stop my ears, I shall call away all my senses, I shall efface even from my thoughts all the images of corporeal things, or at least (for that is hardly possible) I shall esteem them as vain and false; and thus holding converse only with myself and considering my own nature, I shall try little by little to reach a better knowledge of and a more familiar acquaintanceship with myself. I am a thing which thinks, that is to say, that doubts, affirms, denies, that knows a few things, that is ignorant of many (that loves, that hates), that wills, that desires, that also imagines and perceives; for as I remarked before, although the things which I perceive and imagine are perhaps nothing at all apart from me and in themselves, I am nevertheless assured that these modes of thoughts that I call perceptions and imaginations, inasmuch only as they are modes of thought, certainly reside (and are met with) in me.

And in the little that I have just said, I think that I have summed up all that I really know, or at least all that hitherto I was aware that I knew. In order to try to extend my knowledge further, I shall now look around more carefully and see whether I cannot still discover in myself some other things which I have not hitherto perceived. I am certain that I am a thing which thinks; but do I not then likewise know what is requisite to render me certain of a truth? Certainly in this first knowledge there is nothing that assures me of its truth, excepting the clear and distinct perception of that which I state, which would not indeed suffice to assure me that what I say is true, if it could ever happen that a thing which I conceived so clearly and distinctly could be false; and accordingly it seems to me that already I can establish as a general rule that all things which I perceive very clearly and distinctly are true.

At the same time I have before received and admitted many things to be very certain and manifest, which yet I afterwards recognized as being dubious. What then were these things? They were the earth, sky, stars and all other objects which I apprehended by means of the senses. But what did I clearly (and distinctly) perceive in them? Nothing more than that the ideas or thoughts of these things were presented to my mind. And not even now do I deny that these ideas are met with in me. But there was yet another thing which I affirmed, and which, owing to the habit which I had formed of believing it, I thought I perceived very clearly, although in truth I did not perceive it at all, to wit, that there were objects outside of me from which these ideas proceeded, and to which they were entirely similar. And it was in this that I erred, or, if perchance my judgment was correct, this was not due to any knowledge arising from my perception.

But when I took anything very simple and easy in the sphere of arithmetic or geometry into consideration, e.g. that two and three together made five, and other things of the sort, were not these present to my mind so clearly as to enable me to affirm that they were true? Certainly if I judged that since such matters could be doubted, this would not have been so for any other reason than that it came into my mind that perhaps a God might have endowed me with such a nature that I may have been deceived even concerning things which seemed to me most manifest. But every time that this preconceived opinion of the sovereign power of a God presents itself to my thought, I am constrained to confess that it is easy to Him, if He wishes it, to cause me to err, even in matters in which I believe myself to have the best evidence. And, on the other hand, always when I direct my attention to things which I believe myself to perceive very clearly, I am so persuaded of their truth that I let myself break out into words such as these: Let who will deceive me, He can never cause me to be nothing while I think that I am, or some day cause it to be true to say that I have never been, it being true now to say that I am, or that two and three make more or less than five, or any such thing in which I see a manifest contradiction. And certainly, since I have no reason to believe that there is a God who is a deceiver, and as I have not yet satisfied myself that there is a God at all, the reason for doubt which depends on this opinion alone is very slight, and so to speak metaphysical. But in order to be able altogether to remove it, I must inquire whether there is a God as soon as the occasion presents itself; and if I find that there is a God, I must also inquire whether He may be a deceiver; for without a knowledge of these two truths I do not see that I can ever be certain of anything.

And in order that I may have an opportunity of inquiring into this in an orderly way (without interrupting the order of meditation which I have proposed to myself, and which is little by little to pass from the notions which I find first of all in my mind to those which I shall later on discover in it) it is requisite that I should consider in which of these kinds there is, properly speaking, truth or error to be found. Of my thoughts some are, so to speak, images of the things, and to these alone is the title 'idea' properly applied; examples are my thought of a man or of a chimera, of heaven, of an angel, or (even) of God. But other thoughts possess other forms as well. For example in willing, fearing, approving, denying, though I always perceive something as the subject of the action of my mind, yet by this action I always add something else to the idea which I have of that thing; and of the thoughts of this kind some are called volitions or affections, and others judgments.[20]

Now as to what concerns ideas, if we consider them only in themselves and do not relate them to anything else beyond themselves, they cannot properly speaking be false; for whether I imagine a goat or a chimera, it is not the less true that I imagine the one than the other. We must not fear likewise that falsity can enter into will and into affections, for although I may desire evil things, or even things that never existed, it is not the less true that I desire them. Thus there remains no more than the judgments which we make, in which I must take the greatest care not to deceive myself. But the principal error and the commonest which we may meet with in them, consists in my judging that the ideas which are in me are similar or conformable to the things which are outside me; for without doubt if I considered the ideas only as certain modes of my thoughts, without trying to relate them to anything beyond, they could scarely give me material for error.

But among these ideas, some appear to me to be innate, some adventitious, and others to be formed (or invented) by myself; for, as I have the power of understanding what is called a thing, or a truth, or a thought, it appears to me that I hold this power from no other source than my own nature.[21] But if I now hear some sound, if I see the sun, or feel the heat, I have hitherto judged that these sensations proceeded from certain things that exist outside of me; and finally it appears to me that sirens, hippogryphs, and the like, are formed out of my own mind. But again I may possibly persuade myself that all these ideas are of the nature of those which I term adventitious, or else they are all innate, or all fictitious: for I have not yet clearly discovered their true origin.

And my principal task in this place is to consider, in respect to those ideas which appear to me to proceed from certain objects outside me, what are the reasons to think them similar to these objects. It seems indeed in the first place that I am taught this lesson by nature; and secondly, I experience in myself that these ideas do not depend on my will nor therefore on myself—for they often present themselves to my mind in spite of my will. Just now, for instance, whether I will or whether I do not will, I feel heat, and thus persuade myself that this feeling, or at least this idea of heat, is produced in me by something which is different from me, i.e., by the heat of the fire near which I sit. And nothing seems to me more obvious than to judge that this object imprints its likeness rather than anything else upon me.

Now I must discover whether these proofs are sufficiently strong and convincing. When I say that I am so instructed by nature, I merely mean a certain spontaneous inclination which impels me to believe in this connection, and not a natural light which makes me recognize that it is true.[22] But these two things are very different; for I cannot doubt that which the natural light causes me to believe to be true, as, for example, it has shown me that I am from the fact that I doubt, or other facts of the same kind. And I possess no other faculty whereby to distinguish truth from falsehood, which can teach me that what this light shows me to be true is not really true, and no other faculty that is equally trustworthy. But as far as (apparently) natural impulses are concerned, I have frequently remarked, when I had to make active choice between virtue and vice, that they often enough led me to the part that was worse; and this is why I do not see any reason for following them in what regards truth and error.

And as to the other reason, which is that these ideas must proceed from objects outside me, since they do not depend on my will, I do not find it any more convincing. For just as these impulses of which I have spoken are found in me, notwithstanding that they do not always concur with my will, so perhaps there is in me some faculty fitted to produce these ideas without the assistance of any external things, even though it is not yet known by me; just as, apparently, they have hitherto always been found in me during sleep without the aid of any external objects.

And finally, though they did proceed from objects different from myself, it is not a necessary consequence that they should resemble these. On the contrary, I have noticed that in many cases there was a great difference between the object and its idea. I find, for example, two completely diverse ideas of the sun in my mind; the one derives its origin from the senses, and should be placed in the category of adventitious ideas; according to this idea the sun seems to be extremely small; but the other is derived from astronomical reasonings, *i.e.*, is elicited from certain notions that are innate in me, or else it is formed by me in some other manner; in accordance with it the sun appears to be several times greater than the earth. These two ideas cannot, indeed, both resemble the same sun, and reason makes me believe that the one which seems to have originated directly from the sun itself, is the one which is most dissimilar to it.

All this causes me to believe that until the present time it has not been by a judgment that was certain (or premeditated), but only by a sort of blind impulse that I believed that things existed outside of, and different from me, which, by the organs of my senses, or by some other method whatever it might be, conveyed these ideas or images to me (and imprinted on me their similitudes).[23]

NOTES

1   The reference to black bile is an indication of the longevity of Greek ideas in Western culture. Greek physicians (notably Hippocrates and Galen) had developed a view due to the pre-Socratics, that all things were composed of some combination of four elements—earth, air, fire, and water. Further combinations of these four elements, taken two at a time, were supposed to produce the so-called four humours of human physiology. These were called blood, phlegm, black bile, and yellow bile. These liquids were balanced in quantity in a healthy individual. An excess of any of the four was thought to cause disease; an excess of black bile, for example, causing melancholy. These ancient speculations about the origins of certain human diseases were still widely accepted in Descartes's time.

2   Bertrand Russell points out in his *A History of Western Philosophy*, New York, 1945 that pyjamas and nightshirts had not been invented in Descartes's time.

3   What class of things is Descartes referring to? Is he saying that time and number with respect to corporeal things are manufactured by the imagination from parts of actual experiences? Apparently this is what he is saying, but confirmation of this requires development of his rather unusual views on these topics. With respect to time, for example, Descartes seems to have held that it is non-continuous, and composed of discrete instants. Descartes seemed to have thought that if a body existed continuously, it could be self-existent, but he wanted to hold that there must be some external cause for what we commonly call the continued existence of bodies. He imagined that in the absence of such a cause, bodies might pass inexplicably in and out of existence. Finally, he concluded that God causes existence, and causes the existence of any body at every instant when it exists. In this passage, then, he is literally saying that all of our knowledge of corporeal or experienced nature is the result of (possibly mistaken) amplification of our experiences by the imagination.

4   Physics, Astronomy, and Medicine are taken to be the study of composite things, but the objects of Arithmetic and Geometry can hardly be the simple things from which the subject matter of the former sciences is built up. This can be seen because the conclusions of mathematics are taken by Descartes to be indubitable. We might interpret this sentence by supposing that Descartes is here appealing to a commonsense recognition of the simplicity of Arithmetic, and intends his phrase "without taking . . . existent or not" to defer an examination of the exact nature of mathematical objects.

5   God permits us to be sometimes mistaken (we *are* sometimes mistaken, and Descartes's view of God is such that nothing can occur without his consent), which is contrary to what might be our initial view of his goodness, so that for the sake of argument we can suppose ourselves to be always deceived, without at this point compromising our view of God's goodness.

6   One way out of the coming difficulties is to deny the existence of such a God, since holding that some things are certain besides the existence of a God deceiving us at every turn implies that such a God does not exist. Descartes will want to hold that the existence of such a God is not possible, so that this doubt is merely hypothetical—consequently he defers argument on this point in the next sentence. The phrase 'a continual succession of antecedents' apparently refers to an error in reasoning which has no clear premises. The phrase itself is too obscure to be definitely explained otherwise. One argument Descartes suggests should be kept in mind for the time being is that the mere denial of the existence of the deceiving God may increase the possibility that I deceive myself. A full consideration of God's nature later indicates that this self-deception is not possible in the fully developed Cartesian philosophy.

7   The distinction between action and knowledge invoked at this point is apparently designed, as are some other passages, to quiet orthodox religious objections. Since a false hypothesis is being adopted only to test its intellectual consequences so that mistaken belief can be corrected, there is no danger of an evil act being performed on the false hypothesis, the consequences of which could be irrecoverable.

8   Archimedes was a Greek mathematician and scientist who, among other things,

is credited with discovering laws of the lever, and proving that an arbitrary weight might be lifted or moved by application of a lever whose length could be determined by mathematical calculation. This is the origin of his legendary claim to be able to move the earth if given a lever long enough, and a suitable fixed point for a fulcrum. Use of this analogy indicates how important Descartes took the discovery of a single indubitable truth to be.

9   Perhaps the statement that nothing is certain is the only true claim that we can make. This relates to an old philosophical problem. If I say "Everything is uncertain.", do I mean to say that this statement is also uncertain? If so, then something may be certain, contrary to what I intend to express. Consequently, it would seem that I must exempt the claim itself when I mean to say that everything is uncertain.

10   St. Augustine had used a similar line of reasoning in the fourth century. In his *The City of God*, XI, 26, translation by M. Dods, Edinburgh, 1872, he argues as follows:

> I am not at all afraid of the arguments of the Academicians, who say, What if you are deceived? For if I am deceived, I am. For he who is not, cannot be deceived; and if I am deceived, by this same token I am. And since if I am deceived, how am I deceived in believing that I am? for it is certain that I am if I am deceived. Since, therefore, I, the person deceived, should be, even if I were deceived, certainly I am not deceived in this knowledge that I am. And, consequently, neither am I deceived in knowing that I know. For, as I know that I am, so I know this also, that I know.

In spite of some apparent equivocation at the end of this passage, this argument by Augustine is very similar to Descartes's argument. Historical questions of precedence have been largely omitted from consideration in this book. Here, the passage in Augustine is incidental to Augustine's main argument, but Descartes's argument is crucial for his epistemology. The modern interest in the question is due almost entirely to Descartes's formulation.

11   Man was defined as *rational animal* in the Aristotelian tradition. Descartes rejects this definition as verbal and uninformative, since it then raises the question of the meaning of 'rational' and 'animal'. For Descartes, then, knowledge is not gained by verbal formulations, but by direct insight or intuition. In other words, some intuition must precede any meaningful verbal formulation, so that the verbal formulation is epistemologically unnecessary.

12   These are mentioned above, along with feeling and thought, as attributes of the soul. The soul *causes* change in the body, since the body cannot cause itself to change. Immediately following, sensation or feeling, along with nutrition and walking, are dismissed as part of Descartes (or anyone following the argument), since they involve the body which has been rejected for the purposes of this argument.

13   It may be hard to reconcile all Descartes's remarks on *reason, understanding, imagination, sense,* and *memory*. The soul is involved in all of these, depending on what type of object the *understanding* or *reason* is directed to. This explains why Descartes can go on to say that he is nothing that he can imagine, since imagination only analyzes and combines sense experiences, which are ruled out in this context by the fact that the deceiver renders the existence of my body a subject of doubt.

14   All of these things are ways in which thought can occur! At first, it might seem that feeling and imagination, in view of what has been said above, do not belong in this list. Yet Descartes includes a specific defense of their occurrence here in the next paragraph. In short, although what I imagine and feel may not correspond to anything, yet I cannot doubt that I do imagine and feel, or at least *seem* to, and hence their place is secure. Not every expression in this description of thought is argued for later. Willing, for example, is listed without later comment. Since the will is mentioned elsewhere as accounting for human error, perhaps its inclusion here is to be defended along similar lines as those which defend the inclusion of feeling. One might wish, however, for more extended treatment. Although 'I think' may seem proved, it is surprising to find Descartes including so many activities as sanctioned by this conclusion.

15   The translation *figure* here may prove misleading. It is helpful to read *shape* for *figure*, which approximates Descartes's meaning more closely.

16   This looks like an appeal to common sense, which seems out of place in Descartes. Surely the fact that we would all admit that it is the same piece of wax does not show that it is the same piece of wax. Descartes must mean that our intuitions will yield this knowledge, or he has slipped into using the notion of substance without arguing for it.

17   By the description of imagination, it can only combine previous sense experiences, or parts of them. But no one can experience infinitely many distinct objects, so that the infinite is beyond the grasp of the imagination. God's perfections, being infinite according to Descartes, are also beyond the grasp of the imagination, and must be known through the understanding.

18   It is interesting to notice how many passages in Descartes anticipate problems that later empiricists have to deal with. Here, Descartes notices that when I say "I see a man.", I cannot mean what the sentence may seem to suggest, but only that I see something which I take to be a man. Thus an inference seems to be involved in the simplest reports of observation, an inference which may be mistaken. Rationalists, accepting the conclusion, in some cases, of such inferences, must *know* the conclusion on some other basis than simply the sense experiences involved. Empiricists, on the other hand, must try to make do without such inferences. Clearly the rationalist comes closer to capturing what we intend to express in most observation reports.

19   Note Descartes's sharp distinction between human perception and the perception of animals. This is a reflection of his conception of soul, which he does not ascribe to animals (exclusive of man). Empiricists, who do not claim a special faculty peculiar to man as compared to animals for the acquisition of knowledge, will be more likely to suppose that the perception of some animals and that of men differs only in degree, and not in kind.

20   This is a good place to notice some differences between Plato's ideas and Descartes's ideas. An idea, for Plato, existed apart from any particular human mind, and common knowledge was explained by common intuition of the same ideas. Knowledge of ideas was the goal of human inquiry. In Descartes, ideas occur in individual minds, and are psychological entities. They represent, in important cases, some other kind of being, which we may come to know through the representing ideas. Thus God is known, not directly, but through the idea of God which exists in the mind. Ideas are not what is known in Descartes, but

they are what we use to acquire knowledge about what can be known. Although the use of *idea* in Berkeley's philosophy will be different from its use in either Plato or Descartes, it will be like Plato's usage in that it will be *ideas* that Berkeley says are known, and they will not be taken to represent something else, save possibly with the exception of the idea of God.

21   Adventitious ideas are those added to the mind, particularly those added as a result of sense experience.

22   The natural light may be taken to be the same as intuition or understanding. *Lumen naturale,* the expression here translated as *natural light,* was in common use among philosophers in Descartes's time. By its use, one might suggest how the mind was thought to illuminate truth. One might compare Plato's discussion of light in the Allegory of the Cave by way of indicating the antiquity of metaphors or analogies involving light in connection with knowledge.

23   Descartes goes on to establish God's existence, and the indubitable character of much of natural science. Ultimately, the existence of a benevolent God guarantees a correspondence between certain sense impressions and innate ideas which yield knowledge of the primary qualities of bodies, enabling Descartes to construct a rationalistic philosophy of science. (For primary qualities, see the first Berkeley chapter.) Descartes was one of the first to draw an epistemological distinction between various qualities of bodies, supposing that only some of them could be the source of knowledge of bodies, although the idea may have developed from the Aristotelian notion of essence.

PART 4

Berkeley

(1685–1753)

Science and Epistemology

It is not too surprising in retrospect that important philosophers before the seventeenth century, including all of the philosophers that we have so far considered, should have proposed epistemological systems which were largely rationalistic. Some qualification of this remark might be due Aristotle, who did study some beliefs that would now be considered scientific beliefs, as opposed to philosophical beliefs, and attempted a justification for them in his theory of knowledge. The point is this: if either mathematical systems or religious statements are taken as the test cases or paradigm cases of human knowledge that an adequate philosophy should have to explain, then it is a quite natural development that any philosopher working out an epistemological system should settle ultimately on some form of rationalism. Certainly there are good grounds for believing that mathematical objects are not experienced by the senses, as we have seen in connection with Plato. And it is quite obviously the case that objects of religious thought and study, such as God, are not known through sense experience; at least very few philosophers have thought them to be known through sense experience. If God and the square root of two, to take examples, are not known through sense experience, they must be known in some other way, and the faculty of intuition which rationalism introduces is an obvious candidate. Thus rationalism, if true, may provide an explanation of the way in which we acquire knowledge of mathematical and spiritual entities.

The seventeenth century is often cited as the century in which what is called modern science began to develop into a comprehensive, integrated system. Modern astronomy, for example, was largely shaped by Galileo and Newton, among others, who did their work in this one-hundred-year span. Before the seventeenth century, the only integrated systems of human thought were either mathematical or religious. After the seventeenth century, many philosophers began to take scientific knowledge as the test case for an adequate philosophical epistemology.

The publication of Sir Isaac Newton's *Principia* in 1686 made available to philosophers a complete scientific system which in its intuitive appeal was clearly the equal, if not the superior, of any mathematical or religious system of its time. An interesting feature of the *Principia* is that in it Newton completely ignores philosophical speculation, and simply supposes certain commonplace observations to be *facts* which he *explains* by appealing to certain other states of affairs which he assumes *must* be the case if the *facts* are to be explained in a convincing way. What is meant by saying that his system is the equal or superior of any system of its time may perhaps best be explained by noting that it is both *objective*, and that it deals with publicly observable objects. Numbered among these objects are the sun, the moon, and so forth, which are apparently sense-experienced objects, in that we check on the truth of some statement about them by making an observation, or a series of observations. The scientists who insisted that this was so had apparently not mastered Descartes, who, as we have seen, makes an observation a fairly different event than so-called common sense might suggest. Nevertheless, the report of scientists that sense observations constitute the test of a scientific statement (or at least of a wide class of testable scientific statements), has prejudiced many philosophers who have tried to justify scientific knowledge towards adopting an empiricistic epistemology.

What is meant by saying that scientific systems are objective is difficult to analyze. It is not enough for objectivity that the statements of some system be either true or false, but not both. Presumably the statements of religion, mathematics, or even astrology would all be objective in the sense that crucial sentences in these disciplines could not be both true and false, or neither true nor false. Objectivity is related primarily to the method for determining the truth or falsity of statements. Suppose that Newton's system predicts an eclipse of the sun at some place at some time. To test to see whether this statement is true, one goes to that place at that time and looks at the sun. (We assume that the weather permits.) The intuitive appeal of such observational tests is overwhelming. They seem conclusive in that almost universal agreement about what observation is to be made during the test can be obtained, and we can readily understand someone's report of his observations while making such a test. By comparison, religious statements are not nearly so objective, if they are objective at all. There are simply no commonly available observational tests for determining the truth or falsity of many religious statements. This remark may be justified by a comparative study of the history of the two kinds of systems.

While early scientists did their work without probing philosophical questions, philosophers were none the less interested in finding some explanation for the apparently objective results which scientists were able to reach in their practice. As science has become more and more comprehensive and useful, this justification has become almost imperative, so that most contemporary philosophers suppose that an adequate philosophy must *at least* justify scientific knowledge, and *then* religious knowledge, for example, depending on whether or not the philosopher wishes to give religious knowledge significance apart from science. Mathematical knowledge has by now been taken by empiricists as *part* of scientific knowledge, and it is not generally treated as a kind of knowledge distinct from scientific knowledge, in spite of sound rationalistic arguments to the contrary.

There are a number of fairly obvious problems which an empiricistic philosophy must face if it is to provide a justification for scientific knowledge. Some of these are philosophical problems that working scientists can often afford to ignore. One is the problem of making a transition from *personal* observations to the objective statements of science. The scientist may pretend that this problem does not exist, by treating observers as interchangeable, although it is clear that philosophers after Descartes cannot simply accept this move as a methodological principle which needs no justification. We might, however, suppose that these problems are separable, in that scientists may assume (not necessarily explicitly) that observers are interchangeable, while philosophers hunt for the justification of this assumption. The scientific discoveries based on such an assumption would then become epistemologically acceptable when such a justification was found.

A number of interesting philosophical problems occur as part of scientific inquiry. Two important questions will be mentioned here. One of them concerns the role of mathematics in science. If, as we have seen, mathematics seems to require a rationalistic justification, while scientific information distinct from mathematics is to be empirically justified, does this not require that a complete philosophy, justifying both, be neither a pure rationalistic system, nor an empiricistic system, but some compromise between the two? This point seems to hold against scientists who may wish to say that science can be justified by commonsense observations, in that the truth of the mathematics that they use cannot be so justified. Another question concerns the role of theoretical concepts in science. Early science, dealing with readily identifiable objects, raised this question only implicitly. In the twentieth century this question has caused a crisis for epistemology, since such concepts as that of *atom, gene, perfect gas*, etc., which abound in science, do not seem to be directly related to anything that is observed, at least in the sense that such terms do not seem to designate anything which is identifiable on the basis of ordinary sense experiences. Indeed, some of these entities seem as inaccessible to sense experience as the objects of mathematical inquiry. A serious problem for an empirical philosophy is that of showing how statements involving these terms can be related to observations in a way that will explain the objectivity reached by the application of scientific method.

The early attempts at an empirical philosophy which would justify modern science are well represented in the philosophy of John Locke, who preceded Berkeley. Locke's arguments against rationalism are not crushing refutations. He merely noted that there were strong common-sense grounds for doubting it, and then contended that since sense-experiential knowledge was necessary for scientific knowledge, and hence a necessary foundation for scientific knowledge in any adequate philosophical epistemology, and since all of the functions which innate ideas and intuition had performed in rationalistic philosophies could be handled in an empiricistic philosophy, that it was possible to demonstrate that rationalism was superfluous. Attention to Locke's position focuses on the question of whether or not he can demonstrate his claim that scientific knowledge may be satisfactorily justified on an empirical basis.

Locke's approach was to adopt a kind of commonsense theory of knowledge similar to that which many scientists of his time implicitly adopted. This commonsense theory is no doubt the commonsense theory of many people (including some scientists) at present, although it was not common sense in Locke's time. The fact that it has become something like the commonsense view is a result of the practical success of scientific inquiry. As an illustration, this theory finds three elements in any simple observation report, say the report of John that he sees a table: a thing, independent of John in some sense, transmission of light rays from the thing to John's retina where they form a pattern, and John's resulting idea or sensation or perception of the table. On this view there is a relationship between the table and John's seeing it, in that the table *causes* the seeing by virtue of the fact that it reflects light rays into John's eyes. Locke attempted to get from the unsatisfactory quality of private seeings, touchings, etc., to the objective domain of science, by supposing that our experiences were of two kinds of qualities, primary and secondary. The domain of science is concerned only with the former, and the vagaries of individual experience are to be explained by the presence of the latter. It is instructive to consider the differences between these two kinds of quality. Primary qualities include solidity, extension, motion, and number. Secondary qualities include colors, sounds, and tastes. It seems that we may be more easily mistaken about the presence of some particular secondary quality than about the presence of some primary quality. This is the point of the distinction which is explained by saying that primary qualities of things produce sensations in the mind which are in some sense accurate copies of themselves, while secondary qualities are *powers* of things to influence human perception which may vary with time or with respect to different observers. Thus Locke attempts to avoid the difficulties of earlier empirical philosophies which attempted to draw a distinction between false and veridical *experiences*, by drawing rather a distinction between false and veridical *parts* of any given experience. An experience of sensing a table is thus taken as a complex, rather than as a simple, in that the experience may be divided into false and veridical segments by philosophical analysis. These segments are not directly experienced but may be separated in any experience by a trained mind. An important consequence of this point of view is that we do not know the objects of experience directly but know their effects on us, which we call sensations, or ideas. Whether or not this foundation can justify science is not important here, since Berkeley successfully attacked the foundation, partly by claiming (as a close reader should suspect) that the distinction between primary and secondary qualities cannot itself be made on an empiricistic basis.

Perception in Empiricism

Berkeley took as one of his most important tasks that of refuting the theories of knowledge of ordinary people and of past philosophers and scientists. He contended that the refutation of these theories would result in the rejection of false views (those that he did not like, although this is irrelevant to our study of his philosophy) about various claims of religion and science.

The theory of knowledge that Berkeley imputed to ordinary people, and which might be called the commonsense view of his time in this connection, is difficult to formulate in a way that can lead to a direct refutation. This is due to the fact that ordinary people, whoever they are (philosophers have a tendency to impute views that they wish to reject to ordinary people, or 'the vulgar', in spite of a complete absence in most of their writings of any research into the matter of what a majority or plurality of people can reasonably be said to have as an implicit epistemological position), are not likely to hold self-conscious views about how they come to know what they profess to be aware of. In order to construct a commonsense view, it would be necessary to raise a theory about what theory of knowledge is implicit in ordinary behavior and ordinary conversation. There is the pitfall in this that if we could find an ordinary man and should start to ask him questions about epistemology and his implicit epistemological views, or even questions designed to reveal this information quite subtly, we might quickly turn him into a not-so-ordinary man, who would be responding from an increased sensitivity to problems that our questions had suggested.

We do want to say, however, that ordinary men know something, and that Berkeley was correct in pointing out that we must explain this knowledge in a manner compatible with what the ordinary man might reasonably be said to have at his command in the way of acquired knowledge. A good test case would be a young child who knows certain facts, but who could hardly be said to know anything about epistemology. Such a child may know that a book is red, for example, without being able to enunciate a theory as to what *red means* in sentences about the book's color. Berkeley's willingness to insist that such cases be discussed by philosophers is, in effect, construing knowledge much more broadly than Plato, Aristotle, or Descartes did. Plato, Aristotle, and Descartes might all say that the child does not *truly* know anything, and that the task of philosophy is to explicate the knowledge that the most informed people have, who do not consider themselves to know something until they understand why that something is what is to be known, and not something else. Berkeley argues that philosophy must explain the case of the knowledge of the young child, who typifies *common sense* in being unreflective. In this sense, Berkeley considered himself a *champion* of common sense.

An example may prove helpful. Suppose the question is asked how we may know that a given object A is further away than a given object B. One explanation is that the angle α shown in the diagram is greater than the angle β, which may be shown by investigation into the way in which the two eyes must converge in order to focus on the objects A and B. Although this is true, the size of the angles α and β cannot be the explanation of our seeing the object A as farther away than object B.

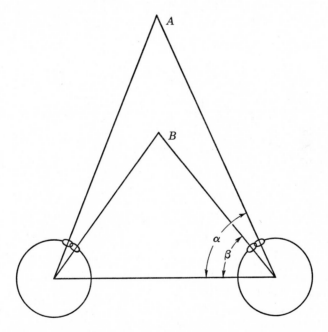

It is true that angle α is greater than angle β, but as we do not *see* the angles, we cannot compare them to make assessments of distance. Certainly the young child, who knows nothing of geometry or optics, is unaware of the angles α and β in any sense, but may still make distance judgments as accurately as the rest of us. To explain distance assessments in terms of α and β is to commit a fallacy of oversophistication. Berkeley, in an extremely important book (*The New Theory of Vision*), attempted to explain distance judgments in a manner compatible with the experiences of anyone who is in a position to make good distance judgments. Berkeleian objections to this pseudo-explanation are not a refutation of commonsense views, since he holds that an adequate philosophy must explain at least the more obvious and correct views of ordinary men in a manner compatible with their acquired knowledge and experiences.

The Berkeleian objection to commonsense views is largely that ordinary men confuse what they see with what they infer or judge to be true on the basis of what they see. Berkeley felt that this could easily be shown by analysis of ordinary experiences. Often two men, looking at the same object (what they would agree to be the same object), will say that they are looking at quite different things. Let us suppose that two men look at a painting in an art gallery, but that their past experiences with paintings are quite different. If we ask each of them "What are you looking at?", one might well say "Duchamp's *Nude Descending the Stairs*.", while the other would be at a loss to say what he was looking at, or could only describe it in terms of size, color, etc., as a painting on the wall. This situation repeats itself endlessly. What is a familiar object to one person may be mysterious or unrecognizable to another. Yet they still *see* the same object in another sense. In terms of our example, it might be awkward to deny that the two men are looking at the same painting.

The key to the resolution of the claim that the two men see and do not see the same thing is to be found in an ambiguity of the word *see*. Both men *see* the same thing in a primary sense which we may call *seeing*$_1$. Both men, that is, observe the same light and colors (or at least virtually identical light and colors—the differences are inessential at this point), or have the same *ideas* in Berkeley's sense. In our vocabulary they both *see*$_1$ the same thing, or have the same sensations, in the case of our example a rectangle of a certain size filled with colors that they might describe in common by means of a topological map. At the same time, one man sees that what he *sees*$_1$ is in fact Duchamp's *Nude Descending the Stairs*. In this sense he *sees*$_2$ that he sees *Nude Descending the Stairs*. Berkeley argues that this is an inference or judgment based on what he *sees*$_1$. There are two important aspects of this inference. The fact that one man makes it and the other does not is conveniently explained by the past experiences of the one. The man who sees the painting as *Nude Descending the Stairs* may be an art student, while the man who sees only colors in a rectangle may be someone unschooled in art history whose wife has commanded his presence in front of the painting. The inference that the painting is a Duchamp may obviously be mistaken, in that the painting may be misidentified through a mistake (in which case it may be quite unlike Duchamp's painting), or thought to be Duchamp's painting when in fact it is a sufficiently clever fake to fool him. We might say that the inference expresses the claim that what is *seen*$_1$ would yield certain other *ideas* in different circumstances. Sufficient repetition of a set of circumstances, or associated ideas, leads us to expect this repetition when some of the set of circumstances is repeated.

The distinction between $seeing_1$ and $seeing_2$ may also be drawn in the other senses. Then $seeing_1$, $touching_1$, $hearing_1$, $tasting_1$, etc., form the common foundation of human knowledge. Ordinary men often fail to observe this distinction. As a matter of fact, there is no proof that it must be made to explain their pronouncements about what they know, so that Berkeley has clearly lapsed into philosophy in his discussion. The proper objects of sight for Berkeley are what is $seen_1$. When a person sees something as outside his body, what he has done is *judged* or *inferred* that it is outside on the basis of what he $sees_1$, though he ambiguously reports that he *sees* it as outside his body. When one says "I see a red book on the table.", one really means that he $sees_1$ some red patch, etc., which he judges to be a book that is red which is on the table. In this analysis of seeing, the fact that one $sees_1$ red is relatively (perhaps completely) unassailable, although the fact that there is a red book on the table may be false because of illusion, the lighting of the table surface, one's emotional state at the time, and so on. For these reasons, Berkeley dismisses many commonsense knowledge reports as *inferences* from ideas, a fact which philosophers may discover by analysis. This, in effect, grounds Berkeley's epistemology in knowledge of ideas in this technical sense of $seeing_1$, $touching_1$, $hearing_1$, etc., experiences.

Berkeley's analysis, as well as others like it, runs into the problem that the inferences or judgments based on ideas are not always, indeed they are rarely, consciously performed. An empiricist may argue that these judgments or inferences become habitual, but this raises difficulties about whether or not the inference is to be taken as self-conscious at an early age, as well as the difficulty of explaining why certain habits are formed by human beings rather than other habits, solely in terms of an empiristic epistemology.

The view of philosophers concerning the proper objects of sight which Berkeley opposed was already developed by Locke, who explicitly bears the brunt of many Berkeleian attacks. This view, which we have already summarized, is that there are objects independent of our thinking of them which *cause* ideas in the mind as a result of the transmission of light waves (ideas of sight), sound waves (ideas of hearing), etc. Objects independent of our thinking are known collectively as *matter* and are taken to be the objects of scientific thinking and theorizing. Now a result of scientific theorizing is that the scientist and the ordinary man find themselves in a position similar to the two art-gallery patrons that were discussed earlier. The scientist and the ordinary man, both looking at the sun, see_1 a bright, yellowish disk. The scientist also sees a star, composed of gas at high temperatures, some 93 million miles away, etc., so that he $sees_2$ the sun as something else, namely, the astronomical body that is at one focus of the elliptical orbit of the earth. On the other hand, the ordinary man may *see*$_2$ no more than he *sees*$_1$ or may simply *see*$_2$ the sun as a hot sphere some distance away, depending on the amount of astronomical information that he has assimilated.

Berkeley's concern is that the scientist should not allow his scientific view to contradict his ideas, since on Berkeley's view, the whole purpose of science is to explain why we observe certain repeatable congeries of ideas (what we call objects) as well as successions of ideas in some definite patterns. Science must not do this at the expense of impugning the ideas that it is developed to explain.

It is clear that Berkeley's approach to the whole problem determines that the answer to the question "Does matter exist?", when matter is construed as referring to objects obeying scientific laws that we do not directly experience, must be in the negative. There is nothing to be known except our ideas, that is, perceptions of the *seeing*$_1$, *hearing*$_1$, etc., kind. Consequently, there can be no matter that we can know about, discourse intelligently about, and make the object of scientific theorizing. Berkeley felt that those who fell into the trap of speaking seriously about nonexperienced entities also fell into talking nonsense.

The program that Berkeley has left for other empirical philosophers, that of building up from ideas our commonsense view of the world, as well as the body of knowledge called science, is referred to as *phenomenalism*. A phenomenalist tries to complete the kind of program that Berkeley argues is possible; namely, to analyze objects into congeries of, and regular sequences of, *ideas* in Berkeley's technical sense. No such program has been completely successful, although it is clear that the successful completion of such a program would establish the basic empiricistic claim that human knowledge does not require more than human experience organized in some appropriate way.

The Problem of Abstraction

An interesting fact about the history of philosophy is that Berkeley has often been held to support doctrines that a careful reading of his writings shows that he explicitly condemns. We have noted that his purpose in identifying the foundation of knowledge with what he calls *ideas* is to save commonsense views against the oversophistication to be found in some scientific theorizing. In spite of this, the notion of matter which he attacked seems to have become so well entrenched that his views have often been taken as representative of a philosophy at wide variance with the judgments of common sense.

This may be a result of mistaken inferences from capsulated versions of Berkeley's statements about *ideas*. These capsulated versions usually quote the phrase "esse est percipi." as a summary of Berkeley's views, translating this as "To be is to be perceived.". It seems to follow that what is not perceived does not exist. Unfortunately, there are important ambiguities in this inference. Caricatures of Berkeley take this to mean 'If x is not perceived now, then x does not exist now.', which is perhaps at variance with what may be deduced from "esse est percipi.". For example, one might just as well conclude 'If x is not perceived *at some time,* then x does not exist.', which is quite different from the earlier statement.

From the earlier statement, it has been argued that when one turns his back on something, it no longer exists because he is not perceiving it. But this does not follow from Berkeley's philosophical position. What does follow is that if I turn my back on something, then *if no one is perceiving it,* it does not exist. If we understand that saying that it does not exist here means that no one has present knowledge of it, the remark is a truism, since any statement about its current properties is an inference or judgment based on *what was known* about it. On the other hand, the feeling of absurdity that may accompany contemplation of this view is no doubt a feature of the fact that it conflicts with an entrenched, but on the Berkeleian view false, theory about matter.

Berkeley, like Descartes, introduces God at important places in his philosophy. In Berkeley's philosophy, God may play the role of a perceiver whose perceptions of ideas keep the world of experience as orderly and stable as we think it to be. Nevertheless, as with Descartes, we shall be concerned to examine the consequences of the philosophy without resort to invoking a divine being to help support weak places in the argument. A difficulty, which might as well be mentioned, is that it is not easy to see how Berkeley's God can be *known* within the framework of his empiricism. Evidently there are no direct *ideas* of God, who is not *seen$_1$*, *touched$_1$*, etc. A consistent Berkeleian empiricism must then find some way of admitting God as the result of an inference or judgment based on *ideas*, but for empiricists this is equivalent to admitting that God's existence is not certain, *contra* the position of most traditional theologians.

Berkeley's argument about existence is more properly summarized in another way. The *esse* (of a sensible object) is *percipi* (to be perceived), and the *esse* (of a perceiver—particularly a human being) is *percipere* (to perceive). Berkeley's universe consists of perceivers and what they know, i.e., their ideas. What can neither be labeled an idea or a perceiver cannot be *known* to exist, and by a tacit use of simplicity (we do not affirm the existence of what we do not know to exist), is said not to exist. In order to preserve the distinction between hallucination and veridical perception, we cannot *identify* what we think we perceive with what exists, but only what we do perceive with what exists.

The Berkeleian idea is *not mental* in the sense that its being mental suggests that it is not real. We do not invent or compose the world in our minds since our minds have ideas independently of our desires and wishes. It is important to realize that Berkeley is opposed to *matter* but convinced that all our views about the permanence of various objects (congeries of certain *ideas* for Berkeley) and casual sequences may be kept intact in a philosophy which repudiates the notion of matter. Reflection on the claim that this must be so because we can know only ideas, and not unperceived, obscure causes of them, if such causes existed, is so persuasive that some view like Berkeley's must constitute the basis of a respectable empiricism. In order to reinforce this, two sections (8, 38) of Berkeley's *Of the Principles of Human Knowledge* will be quoted here. Any suitable interpretation of Berkeley must be consistent with these passages, which deserve careful scrutiny.

Section 8 argues the plausibility of ideas as the foundation of human knowledge:

> But, say you, though the ideas themselves do not exist without the mind, yet there may be things like them, whereof they are copies or resemblances, which things exist without the mind in an unthinking substance. I answer, an idea can be like nothing but an idea; a color or figure can be like nothing but another color or figure. If we look but ever so little into our thoughts, we shall find it impossible for us to conceive a likeness except only between our ideas. Again,

I ask whether those supposed originals or external things, of which our ideas are the pictures or representations, be themselves perceivable or no? If they are, then they are ideas and we have gained our point; but if you say they are not, I appeal to anyone whether it be sense to assert a color is like something which is invisible; hard or soft, like something which is intangible; and so of the rest.

Section 38 attempts to make clear the relation between what are ordinarily called *things*, and Berkeley's *ideas*.

But, after all, say you, it sounds very harsh to say we eat and drink ideas, and are clothed with ideas. I acknowledge it does so; the word 'idea' not being used in common discourse to signify the several combinations of sensible qualities which are called 'things'; and it is certain that any expression which varies from the familiar use of language will seem harsh and ridiculous. But this doth not concern the truth of the proposition, which in other words is no more than to say, we are fed and clothed with those things which we perceive immediately by our senses. The hardness or softness, the color, taste, warmth, figure, or such-like qualities, which combined together constitute the several sorts of victuals and apparel, have been shown to exist only in the mind that perceives them; and this is all that is meant by calling them 'ideas'; which word if it was as ordinarily used as 'things' would sound no more harsher nor more ridiculous than it. I am not for disputing about the propriety, but the truth of the expression. If therefore you agree with me that we eat and drink and are clad with the immediate objects of sense, which cannot exist unperceived or without the mind, I shall readily grant it is more proper or conformable to custom that they should be called things rather than ideas.

To this point we have emphasized Berkeley's program of replacing matter with *ideas* in his technical sense. Now given the fact that the foundation of human knowledge consists in ideas, one might well wonder why it is not possible to infer the existence of matter in some legitimate fashion from this foundation. Berkeley is not opposed in general to inferences or judgments based on ideas. He is, however, opposed to the inference that matter exists. To block this inference, he subsumes the inference that matter exists under the general heading of abstractive inference, all of which inferences to *abstract* ideas he condemns as contradictory or meaningless. In order to complete an introduction to Berkeley's philosophy, it is important to consider why Berkeley felt that *abstract* ideas were not possible. Although Berkeley's reasoning on this point contains difficulties, much of it embodies conceptions about language that are now thought to be quite sophisticated.

Berkeley does not deny that abstract *words* are used in communicating knowledge. But, where Plato and other philosophers had assumed that these words have meaning because they stand for abstract ideas (note that Plato's ideas are quite unlike Berkeley's), Berkeley argues that there are no abstract ideas for them to correspond to. Berkeley's program, consequently, has two parts: he must show that abstract ideas are not possible, and he must account for the significance of abstract words by some means other than by letting them correspond to abstract ideas. To understand Berkeley's points, the example of the abstract word *triangle* can be used, since, as we have seen, it is the kind of abstract word that would receive significance in Plato's philosophy, and in most rationalistic philosophies, through its correspondence to an idea or form. Now it is possible, according to Berkeley, to abstract or generalize somewhat from ideas. Looking at an automobile, we can consider just the fender of the automobile, since it is a part of our original idea. Further, we may be able to consider Chevrolets as a group, since they possess some distinguishing part, such as the Chevrolet ornament. But this kind of abstracting must stop at a very low level, because it is probably not possible to find an *idea* which is part of every idea of an automobile. In the case of triangles, we may be able to understand the notion of scalene triangle, equilateral triangle, and so forth, because of ideas which the members of such classes have in common (such as equal sides). This indicates that Berkeley felt that the primary sense of *triangle* is that of actual figures drawn on blackboards, etc., while the problem is to understand the general case. This is the reverse of Plato's problem. A problem analogous to Plato's problem of participation occurs in Berkeley's problem of abstraction. Participation proved a difficult notion because the diverse properties of actual objects made it difficult to understand how they might be said to all participate in the same idea. On Berkeley's view, the diverse properties of ideas means that an abstracted idea must have contradictory properties, which seems unintelligible. *Triangle*, for example, must include both scalene and equilateral triangles, but one cannot understand how there can be an idea which has and has not equal angles. An abstract idea on any very high level must have contradictory properties; and on Berkeley's construal of *idea* this must be absurd. He therefore concludes that abstract ideas are not possible.

It is interesting to observe that Berkeley's rejection of abstract ideas makes him a nominalist. In this connection, a nominalist may be defined as someone who rejects the idea that abstract words can have meaning by referring to some abstract idea, as in Plato.

Now we may ask if the Platonic objection that actual triangles cannot be judged triangles without a standard is not sufficiently crushing to eliminate Berkeley's epistemology from serious consideration. But Berkeley is not open to a direct refutation by means of this observation. The Platonic objection holds cogently against empiricist theories which take objects, or resemblances between objects, as their starting point. Berkeleian ideas fare somewhat differently. We may take some idea, better, a class of ideas, and give it a name that we will use whenever this idea or class of ideas is repeated. Whenever this method runs into trouble, it will be because an idea must be added or subtracted from an experienced class in order to make some distinction that we are interested in. When that happens, we may change names or add names to our language. This seems to avoid direct confrontation of Plato's objection, but at severe cost, since (apart from problems about the mental mechanism for identifying classes) our experiences are so limited that the number of such classes that we would be able to distinguish may well be much smaller than common sense indicates that it should be. Thus, we have not experienced any idea common to all the objects which we have called *triangle*. The problem is whether or not Berkeley can find some way of explaining our use of words like *triangle* and *automobile* in terms of the relatively limited congeries of ideas to which we give direct names.

Berkeley's answer to this is the position that abstract words stand for less abstract *words*, not for any idea which might be correlated to them. Admittedly, this notion is not entirely clear in Berkeley's writing, but it adumbrates (as suggested earlier) a view that is now widely received about the meaning of at least some words: that a word has meaning not because of what it refers to, but because of how it is used in a language. An abstract word is a kind of placeholder for any of a number of particular words whose meaning *is* grounded in reference to particular ideas. Thus, a sentence about *triangles*, for example, "Every triangle has the sum of its interior angles equal to 180°." is simply construed (Caution: philosophers before the twentieth century meant every plane Euclidean triangle was such that . . .) as a compendious way of saying "Every scalene triangle has the sum of its interior angles equal to 180° and every equilateral triangle has the sum of its interior angles equal to 180° and every . . .".

This suggestion, ingenious as it is, is only *programmatic* in the sense that Berkeley's contention can only be shown to be true by an exhibition of a satisfactory way of writing out every sentence involving an abstract word in terms of sentences involving only nonabstract words whose meanings are appropriately grounded in particular ideas. No empiricist has been able to provide a successful algorithm for writing out sentences involving abstract words in terms of sentences not involving such words, along the lines that Berkeley suggests, but the program has been so attractive that a great many have worked on the problem. There are a number of reasons why rationalists are convinced that the program cannot succeed. One reason is an interesting variant of Plato's objection, cited earlier, that seems to apply directly to this program. The objection is that there does not seem to be any hope for an empiricist criterion for deciding which particular words are to be subsumed under a given abstract word. For example, labeling things *scalene triangle* and *equilateral triangle* yields a common element (the word *triangle*) that provides a natural candidate for abstraction. But why are these particular triangles so universally abstracted into the same abstract class, and not into two abstract classes corresponding to some different classification? If the two classes were called *gubs* and *migs*, no prejudice would appear in the naming, but the abstractive process becomes correspondingly obscure. The empiricist can reply that our abstractive classifications are due to convenience or perhaps to the satisfaction of certain human purposes, but as yet no empiricist has made this completely plausible. Berkeley's significance is that he first provides an empiricistic program that, if completed, could avoid some of the more persuasive arguments of the rationalists that empiricism is *necessarily* defective.

Readings from Berkeley

Two selections are reprinted here from Berkeley's *Three Dialogues between Hylas and Philonous the Design of Which Is Plainly to Demonstrate the Reality and Perfection of Human Knowledge, the Incorporeal Nature of the Soul, and the Immediate Providence of a Deity in Opposition to Sceptics and Atheists:*

    A. From *The First Dialogue between Hylas and Philonous*
    B. From *The Third Dialogue between Hylas and Philonous*

The text is Fraser's edition, and it is reprinted here by kind permission of the Clarendon Press, Oxford.

As in Plato, these dialogues are a discussion between two philosophers, Hylas and Philonous, about the existence of material substance and the nature of the soul. Philonous represents the Berkeleian position, and Hylas the positions which are to be refuted. This is obvious from a consideration of Berkeley's philosophy and the fact that *Hylas* and *Philonous* are constructed from Greek roots and might be translated *Materialist* and *Lover of the Mind*, respectively. The positions discussed here in dialogue form are exposited in a more didactic fashion in Berkeley's *A Treatise concerning the Principles of Human Knowledge*, which should be studied after the *Dialogues. An Essay towards a New Theory of Vision* is also an important work for students of Berkeley to consider.

Berkeley has an interesting moment in American history. In January, 1729, he landed in Newport, Rhode Island, in order to buy land for the support of the college of St. Paul, which was to have been located in the Bermudas, a college which he had conceived and won a charter for from the House of Commons. The college was never built, but Berkeley's stay in the United States influenced American academic life. Rent from the Rhode Island farm he occupied goes to support Berkeleian scholars at Yale University, and the famous Berkeleian Library at Yale was begun by a gift of about a thousand books that Berkeley sent from England. Berkeley also influenced Samuel Johnson, an important early American philosopher.

The following bibliography lists some secondary sources of interest to the student of Berkeley's philosophy.

Armstrong, D. M.: *Berkeley's Theory of Vision*, Melbourne, 1960.

Berkeley, George: *The Works of George Berkeley, Bishop of Cloyne*, T. E. Jessop and A. A. Luce (eds.), 8 vol., London, 1948–1956.

Bracken, H. F.: *The Early Reception of Berkeley's Immaterialism*, The Hague, 1959.

Grey, Denis: "The Solipsism of Bishop Berkeley," *Philosophical Quarterly*, vol. 2, pp. 338–349, 1952.

Hicks, G. D.: *Berkeley*, London, 1932.

Turbayne, C. M.: "Berkeley and Molyneux on Retinal Images," *The Journal of the History of Ideas*, vol. 16, pp. 339–355, 1955.

*Warnock, G. J.: *Berkeley*, Harmondsworth, 1953. (Pelican Paperbound.)

Van Steenburgh, E. W.: "Berkeley Revisited," *The Journal of Philosophy*, vol. 60, pp. 85–89, 1963.

A   From Berkeley's FIRST DIALOGUE

Hyl. Pardon me: the case of colours is very different. Can anything be plainer than that we see them on the objects?

Phil. The objects you speak of are, I suppose, corporeal Substances existing without the mind?

Hyl. They are.

Phil. And have true and real colours inhering in them?

Hyl. Each visible object hath that colour which we see in it.

Phil. How! is there anything visible but what we perceive by sight?

Hyl. There is not.

Phil. And, do we perceive anything by sense which we do not perceive immediately?

Hyl. How often must I be obliged to repeat the same thing? I tell you, we do not.

Phil. Have patience, good *Hylas;* and tell me once more, whether there is anything immediately perceived by the senses, except sensible qualities. I know you asserted there was not; but I would now be informed, whether you still persist in the same opinion.[1]

Hyl. I do.

Phil. Pray, is your corporeal substance either a sensible quality, or made up of sensible qualities?

Hyl. What a question that is! who ever thought it was?

Phil. My reason for asking was, because in saying, *each visible object hath that colour which we see in it,* you make visible objects to be corporeal substances; which implies either that corporeal substances are sensible qualities, or else that there is something beside sensible qualities perceived by sight: but, as this point was formerly agreed between us, and is still maintained by you, it is a clear consequence, that your corporeal substance is nothing distinct from sensible qualities.

Hyl. You may draw as many absurd consequences as you please, and endeavour to perplex the plainest things; but you shall never persuade me out of my senses. I clearly understand my own meaning.

Phil. I wish you would make me understand it too. But, since you are unwilling to have your notion of corporeal substance examined, I shall urge that point no farther. Only be pleased to let me know, whether the same colours which we see exist in external bodies, or some other.[2]

Hyl. The very same.

Phil. What! are then the beautiful red and purple we see on yonder clouds really in them? Or do you imagine they have in themselves any other form than that of a dark mist or vapour?

Hyl. I must own, *Philonous,* those colours are not really in the clouds as they seem to be at this distance. They are only apparent colours.

Phil. Apparent call you them? how shall we distinguish these apparent colours from real?

Hyl. Very easily. Those are to be thought apparent which, appearing only at a distance, vanish upon a nearer approach.

Phil. And those, I suppose, are to be thought real which are discovered by the most near and exact survey.

Hyl. Right.

Phil. Is the nearest and exactest survey made by the help of a microscope, or by the naked eye?

Hyl. By a microscope, doubtless.

Phil. But a microscope often discovers colours in an object different from those perceived by the unassisted sight. And, in case we had microscopes magnifying to any assigned degree, it is certain that no object whatsoever, viewed through them, would appear in the same colour which it exhibits to the naked eye.

Hyl. And what will you conclude from all this? You cannot argue that there are really and naturally no colours on objects: because by artificial managements they may be altered, or made to vanish.

Phil. I think it may evidently be concluded from your own concessions, that all the colours we see with our naked eyes are only apparent as those on the clouds, since they vanish upon a more close and accurate inspection which is afforded us by a microscope. Then, as to what you say by way of prevention: I ask you whether the real and natural state of an object is better discovered by a very sharp and piercing sight, or by one which is less sharp?

Hyl. By the former without doubt.

Phil. Is it not plain from *Dioptrics* that microscopes make the sight more penetrating, and represent objects as they would appear to the eye in case it were naturally endowed with a most exquisite sharpness? [3]

Hyl. It is.

Phil. Consequently the microscopical representation is to be thought that which best sets forth the real nature of the thing, or what it is in itself. The colours, therefore, by it perceived are more genuine and real than those perceived otherwise.

Hyl. I confess there is something in what you say.

Phil. Besides, it is not only possible but manifest, that there actually are animals whose eyes are by nature framed to perceive those things which by reason of their minuteness escape our sight. What think you of those inconceivably small animals perceived by glasses? must we suppose they are all stark blind? Or, in case they see, can it be imagined their sight hath not the same use in preserving their bodies from injuries, which appears in that of all other animals? And if it hath, is it not evident they must see particles less than their own bodies, which will present them with a far different view in each object from that which strikes our senses? Even our own eyes do not always represent objects to us after the same manner. In the *jaundice* every one knows that all things seem yellow. Is it not therefore highly probable those animals in whose eyes we discern a very different texture from that of ours, and whose bodies abound with different humours, do not see the same colours in every object that we do? From all which, should it not seem to follow that all colours are equally apparent, and that none of those which we perceive are really inherent in any outward object?

Hyl. It should.

Phil. The point will be past all doubt, if you consider that, in case colours were real properties or affections inherent in external bodies, they could admit of no alteration without some change wrought in the very bodies themselves: but, is it not evident from what hath been said that, upon the use of microscopes, upon a change happening in the humours of the eye, or a variation of distance, without any manner of real alteration in the thing itself, the colours of any object are either changed, or totally disappear? Nay, all other circumstances remaining the same, change but the situation of some objects, and they shall present different colours to the eye. The same thing happens upon viewing an object in various degrees of light. And what is more known than that the same bodies appear differently coloured by candle-light from what they do in the open day? Add to these the experiment of a prism which, separating the heterogeneous rays of light, alters the colour of any object, and will cause the whitest to appear of a deep blue or red to the naked eye. And now tell me whether you are still of opinion that every body hath its true real colour inhering in it; and, if you think it hath, I would fain know farther from you, what certain distance and position of the object, what peculiar texture and formation of the eye, what degree or kind of light is necessary for ascertaining that true colour, and distinguishing it from apparent ones.[4]

Hyl. I own myself entirely satisfied, that they are all equally apparent, and that there is no such thing as colour really inhering in external bodies, but that it is altogether in the light. And what confirms me in this opinion is that in proportion to the light colours are still more or less vivid; and if there be no light, then are there no colours perceived. Besides, allowing there are colours on external objects, yet, how is it possible for us to perceive them? For no external body affects the mind, unless it acts first on our organs of sense. But the only action of bodies is motion; and motion cannot be communicated otherwise than by impulse. A distant object therefore cannot act on the eye, nor consequently make itself or its properties perceivable to the soul. Whence it plainly follows that it is immediately some contiguous substance, which, operating on the eye, occasions a perception of colours: and such is light.

Phil. How! is light then a substance?

Hyl. I tell you, *Philonous,* external light is nothing but a thin fluid substance, whose minute particles being agitated with a brisk motion, and in various manners reflected from the different surfaces of outward objects to the eyes, communicate different motions to the optic nerves; which, being propagated to the brain, cause therein various impressions; and these are attended with the sensations of red, blue, yellow, &c.[5]

Phil. It seems then the light doth no more than shake the optic nerves.

Hyl. Nothing else.

Phil. And, consequent to each particular motion of the nerves, the mind is affected with a sensation, which is some particular colour.

Hyl. Right.

Phil. And these sensations have no existence without the mind.

Hyl. They have not.

Phil. How then do you affirm that colours are in the light; since by *light* you understand a corporeal substance external to the mind?

Hyl. Light and colours, as immediately perceived by us, I grant cannot exist without the mind. But, in themselves they are only the motions and configurations of certain insensible particles of matter.[6]

Phil. Colours then, in the vulgar sense, or taken for the immediate objects of sight, cannot agree to any but a perceiving substance.

Hyl. That is what I say.

Phil. Well then, since you give up the point as to those sensible qualities which are alone thought colours by all mankind beside, you may hold what you please with regard to those invisible ones of the philosophers. It is not my business to dispute about them; only I would advise you to bethink yourself, whether, considering the inquiry we are upon, it be prudent for you to affirm—*the red and blue which we see are not real colours, but certain unknown motions and figures, which no man ever did or can see, are truly so.* Are not these shocking notions, and are not they subject to as many ridiculous inferences, as those you were obliged to re-nounce before in the case of sounds?

Hyl. I frankly own, *Philonous*, that it is in vain to stand out any longer.[7] Colours, sounds, tastes, in a word all those termed *secondary qualities*, have certainly no existence without the mind. But, by this ac-knowledgment I must not be supposed to derogate anything from the reality of Matter or external objects; seeing it is no more than several philosophers maintain, who nevertheless are the farthest imaginable from denying Matter. For the clearer understanding of this, you must know sensible qualities are by philosophers divided into *primary* and *secondary*. The former are Extension, Figure, Solidity, Gravity, Motion, and Rest. And these they hold exist really in bodies. The latter are those above enumer-ated; or, briefly, all sensible qualities beside the Primary, which they assert are only so many sensations or ideas existing nowhere but in the mind. But all this, I doubt not, you are apprised of. For my part, I have been a long time sensible there was such an opinion current along phi-losophers, but was never thoroughly convinced of its truth until now.

Phil. You are still then of opinion that *extension* and *figures* are in-herent in external unthinking substances?

Hyl. I am.

Phil. But what if the same arguments which are brought against Secondary Qualities will hold good against these also?

Hyl. Why then I shall be obliged to think, they too exist only in the mind.

Phil. Is it your opinion the very figure and extension which you per-ceive by sense exist in the outward object or material substance?

Hyl. It is.

Phil. Have all other animals as good grounds to think the same of the figure and extension which they see and feel?

Hyl. Without doubt, if they have any thought at all.

Phil. Answer me, *Hylas.* Think you the senses were bestowed upon all animals for their preservation and well-being in life? or were they given to men alone for this end?

Hyl. I make no question but they have the same use in all other animals.

Phil. If so, is it not necessary they should be enabled by them to per-ceive their own limbs, and those bodies which are capable of harming them?

Hyl. Certainly.

Phil. A mite therefore must be supposed to see his own foot, and things equal or even less than it, as bodies of some considerable dimen-sion; though at the same time they appear to you scarce discernible, or at best as so many visible points?

Hyl. I cannot deny it.

Phil. And to creatures less than the mite they will seem yet larger?

Hyl. They will.

Phil. Insomuch that what you can hardly discern will to another extremely minute animal appear as some huge mountain?

Hyl. All this I grant.

Phil. Can one and the same thing be at the same time in itself of different dimensions?

Hyl. That were absurd to imagine.

Phil. But, from what you have laid down it follows that both the extension by you perceived, and that perceived by the mite itself, as likewise all those perceived by lesser animals, are each of them the true extension of the mite's foot; that is to say, by your own principles, you are led into an absurdity.

Hyl. There seems to be some difficulty in the point.

Phil. Again, have you not acknowledged that no real inherent property of any object can be changed without some change in the thing itself?

Hyl. I have.

Phil. But, as we approach to or recede from an object, the visible extension varies, being at one distance ten or a hundred times greater than at another. Doth it not therefore follow from hence likewise that it is not really inherent in the object?

Hyl. I own I am at a loss what to think.

Phil. Your judgment will soon be determined, if you will venture to think as freely concerning this quality as you have done concerning the rest. Was it not admitted as a good argument, that neither heat nor cold was in the water, because it seemed warm to one hand and cold to the other?

Hyl. It was.

Phil. Is it not the very same reasoning to conclude, there is no extension or figure in an object, because to one eye it shall seem little, smooth, and round, when at the same time it appears to the other, great, uneven, and angular?

Hyl. The very same. But does this latter fact ever happen?

Phil. You may at any time make the experiment, by looking with one eye bare, and with the other through a microscope.[8]

Hyl. I know not how to maintain it, and yet I am loath to give up *extension*, I see so many odd consequences following upon such a concession.

Phil. Odd, say you? After the concessions already made, I hope you will stick at nothing for its oddness. But, on the other hand, should it not seem very odd, if the general reasoning which includes all other sensible qualities did not also include extension? If it be allowed that no idea nor anything like an idea can exist in an unperceiving substance, then surely it follows that no figure or mode of extension, which we can either perceive or imagine, or have any idea of, can be really inherent in Matter; not to mention the peculiar difficulty there must be in conceiving a material substance, prior to and distinct from extension, to be the *substratum* of extension. Be the sensible quality what it will—figure, or sound, or colour; it seems alike impossible it should subsist in that which doth not perceive it.

Hyl. I give up the point for the present, reserving still a right to retract my opinion, in case I shall hereafter discover any false step in my progress to it.

Phil. That is a right you cannot be denied. Figures and extension being despatched, we proceed next to *motion*. Can a real motion in any external body be at the same time both very swift and very slow?

Hyl. It cannot.

Phil. Is not the motion of a body swift in a reciprocal proportion to the time it takes up in describing any given space? Thus a body that describes a mile in an hour moves three times faster than it would in case it described only a mile in three hours.

Hyl. I agree with you.

Phil. And is not time measured by the succession of ideas in our minds?

Hyl. It is.

Phil. And is it not possible ideas should succeed one another twice as fast in your mind as they do in mine, or in that of some spirit of another kind?

Hyl. I own it.

Phil. Consequently, the same body may to another seem to perform its motion over any space in half the time that it doth to you. And the same reasoning will hold as to any other proportion: that is to say, according to your principles (since the motions perceived are both really in the object) it is possible one and the same body shall be really moved the same way at once, both very swift and very slow. How is this consistent either with common sense, or with what you just now granted?

Hyl. I have nothing to say to it.

Phil. Then as for *solidity*; either you do not mean any sensible quality by that word, and so it is beside our inquiry: or if you do, it must be either hardness or resistance. But both the one and the other are plainly relative to our senses: it being evident that what seems hard to one animal may appear soft to another, who hath greater force and firmness of limbs. Nor is it less plain that the resistance I feel is not in the body.

Hyl. I own the very sensation of resistance, which is all you immediately perceive, is not in the *body*; but the cause of that sensation is.

Phil. But the causes of our sensations are not things immediately perceived, and therefore not sensible. This point I thought had been already determined.

Hyl. I own it was; but you will pardon me if I seem a little embarrassed: I know not how to quit my old notions.

Phil. To help you out, do but consider that if *extension* be once acknowledged to have no existence without the mind, the same must necessarily be granted of motion, solidity, and gravity—since they all evidently suppose extension. It is therefore superfluous to inquire particularly concerning each of them. In denying extension, you have denied them all to have any real existence.

Hyl. I wonder, Philonous, if what you say be true, why those philosophers who deny the Secondary Qualities any real existence, should yet attribute it to the Primary. If there is no difference between them, how can this be accounted for?

Phil. It is not my business to account for every opinion of the philosophers. But, among other reasons which may be assigned for this, it seems probable that pleasure and pain being rather annexed to the former than the latter may be one. Heat and cold, tastes and smells, have something more vividly pleasing or disagreeable than the ideas of extension, figure, and motion affect us with. And, it being too visibly absurd to hold that pain or pleasure can be in an unperceiving Substance, men are more easily weaned from believing the external existence of the Secondary than the Primary Qualities. You will be satisfied there is something in this, if you recollect the difference you made between an intense and more moderate degree of heat; allowing the one a real existence, while you denied it to the other.[9] But, after all, there is no rational ground for that distinction; for, surely an indifferent sensation is as truly *a sensation* as one more pleasing or painful; and consequently should not any more than they be supposed to exist in an unthinking subject.

Hyl. It is just come into my head, Philonous, that I have somewhere heard of a distinction between absolute and sensible extension. Now, though it be acknowledged that *great* and *small*, consisting merely in the relation which other extended beings have to the parts of our own bodies, do not really inhere in the Substances themselves; yet nothing obliges us to hold the same with regard to *absolute extension*, which is something abstracted from *great* and *small*, from this or that particular magnitude or figure. So likewise as to motion; *swift* and *slow* are altogether relative to the succession of ideas in our own minds. But, it doth not follow, because those modifications of motion exist not without the mind, that therefore absolute motion abstracted from them doth not.[10]

Phil. Pray what is it that distinguishes one motion, or one part of extension, from another? Is it not something sensible, as some degree of swiftness or slowness, some certain magnitude or figure peculiar to each?

Hyl. I think so.

Phil. These qualities, therefore, stripped of all sensible properties, are without all specific and numerical differences, as the schools call them.[11]

Hyl. They are.

Phil. That is to say, they are extension in general, and motion in general.

Hyl. Let it be so.

Phil. But it is a universally received maxim that *Everything which exists is particular*. How then can motion in general, or extension in general, exist in any corporeal Substance? [12]

Hyl. I will take time to solve your difficulty.

Phil. But I think the point may be speedily decided. Without doubt you can tell whether you are able to frame this or that idea. Now I am content to put our dispute on this issue. If you can frame in your thoughts a distinct abstract idea of motion or extension, divested of all those sensible modes, as swift and slow, great and small, round and square, and the like, which are acknowledged to exist only in the mind, I will then yield the point you contend for. But, if you cannot, it will be unreasonable on your side to insist any longer upon what you have no notion of.

Hyl. To confess ingenuously, I cannot.

Phil. Can you even separate the ideas of extension and motion from the ideas of all those qualities which they who make the distinction term *secondary*?

Hyl. What! is it not an easy matter to consider extension and motion by themselves, abstracted from all other sensible qualities? Pray how do the mathematicians treat of them?

Phil. I acknowledge, *Hylas*, is is not difficult to form general propositions and reasonings about those qualities, without mentioning any other; and, in this sense, to consider or treat of them abstractedly. But, how doth it follow that, because I can pronounce the word *motion* by itself, I can form the idea of it in my mind exclusive of body? Or, because theorems may be made of extension and figures, without any mention of *great* or *small*, or any other sensible mode or quality, that therefore it is possible such an abstract idea of extension, without any particular size or figure, or sensible quality, should be distinctly formed, and apprehended by the mind? Mathematicians treat of quantity, without regarding what other sensible qualities it is attended with, as being altogether indifferent to their demonstrations. But, when laying aside the words, they contemplate the bare ideas, I believe you will find, they are not the pure abstracted ideas of extension.

Hyl. But what say you to *pure intellect*? May not abstracted ideas be framed by that faculty?

Phil. Since I cannot frame abstract ideas at all, it is plain I cannot frame them by the help of *pure intellect;* whatsoever faculty you understand by those words. Besides, not to inquire into the nature of pure intellect and its spiritual objects, as *virtue, reason, God,* or the like, thus much seems manifest—that sensible things are only to be perceived by sense, or represented by the imagination. Figures, therefore, and extension, being originally perceived by sense, do not belong to pure intellect: but, for your farther satisfaction, try if you can frame the idea of any figure, abstracted from all particularities of size, or even from other sensible qualities.

Hyl. Let me think a little——I do not find that I can.

Phil. And can you think it possible that should really exist in nature which implies a repugnancy in its conception?

Hyl. By no means.

Phil. Since therefore it is impossible even for the mind to disunite the ideas of extension and motion from all other sensible qualities, doth it not follow, that where the one exist there necessarily the other exist likewise?

Hyl. It should seem so.

Phil. Consequently, the very same arguments which you admitted as conclusive against the Secondary Qualities are, without any farther application of force, against the Primary too. Besides, if you will trust your senses, is it not plain all sensible qualities coexist, or to them appear as being in the same place? Do they ever represent a motion, or figure, as being divested of all other visible and tangible qualities?

Hyl. You need say no more on this head. I am free to own, if there be no secret error or oversight in our proceedings hitherto, that all sensible qualities are alike to be denied existence without the mind.

B From Berkeley's *THIRD DIALOGUE*

Phil. Now, if you can prove that any philosopher hath explained the production of any one idea in our minds by the help of *Matter,* I shall for ever acquiesce, and look on all that hath been said against it as nothing; but, if you cannot, it is vain to urge the explication of phenomena. That a Being endowed with knowledge and will should produce or exhibit ideas is easily understood. But, that a Being which is utterly destitute of these faculties should be able to produce ideas, or in any sort to affect an intelligence, this I can never understand. This I say—though we had some positive conception of Matter, though we knew its qualities, and could comprehend its existence—would yet be so far from explaining things, that it is itself the most inexplicable thing in the world. And yet, for all this, it will not follow that philosophers have been doing nothing; for, by observing and reasoning upon the connexion of ideas, they discover the laws and methods of nature, which is a part of knowledge both useful and entertaining.

Hyl. After all, can it be supposed God would deceive all mankind? Do you imagine He would have induced the whole world to believe the being of Matter, if there was no such thing?

Phil. That every epidemical opinion arising from prejudice, or passion, or thoughtlessness may be imputed to God, as the Author of it, I believe you will not affirm. Whatsoever opinion we father on Him, it must be either because He has discovered it to us by supernatural revelation; or because it is so evident to our natural faculties, which were framed and given us by God, that it is impossible we should withhold our assent from it.[13] But where is the revelation? or where is the evidence that extorts the belief of Matter? Nay, how does it appear, that Matter, taken for something distinct from what we perceive by our senses, is thought to exist by all mankind; or, indeed, by any except a few philosophers, who do not know what they would be at? Your question supposes these points are clear; and, when you have cleared them, I shall think myself obliged to give you another answer. In the meantime let it suffice that I tell you, I do not suppose God has deceived mankind at all.

Hyl. But the novelty, *Philonous,* the novelty! There lies the danger. New notions should always be discountenanced; they unsettle men's minds, and nobody knows where they will end.

Phil. Why the rejecting a notion that hath no foundation, either in sense, or in reason, or in Divine authority, should be thought to unsettle the belief of such opinions as are grounded on all or any of these, I cannot imagine. That innovations in government and religion are dangerous, and ought to be discountenanced, I freely own.[14] But, is there the like reason why they should be discouraged in philosophy? The making anything known which was unknown before is an innovation in knowledge: and, if all such innovations had been forbidden, men would have made a notable progress in the arts and sciences.[15] But it is none of my business to plead for novelties and paradoxes. That the qualities we perceive are not on the objects: that we must not believe our senses: that we know nothing of the real nature of things, and can never be assured even of their existence: that real colours and sounds are nothing but certain unknown figures and motions: that motions are in themselves neither swift nor slow: that there are in bodies absolute extensions, without any particular magnitude or figure: that a thing stupid, thoughtless, and inactive, operates on a spirit: that the least particle of a body contains innumerable extended parts:— these are the novelties, these are the strange notions which shock the genuine uncorrupted judgment of all mankind; and being once admitted, embarrass the mind with endless doubts and difficulties. And it is against these and the like innovations I endeavour to vindicate Common Sense. It is true, in doing this, I may perhaps be obliged to use some *ambages,* and ways of speech not common.[16] But, if my notions are once thoroughly understood, that which is most singular in them will, in effect, be found to amount to no more than this:—that it is absolutely impossible, and a plain contradiction, to suppose any unthinking being should exist without being perceived by a mind. And, if this notion be singular, it is a shame it should be so at this time of day, and in a Christian country.

Hyl. As for the difficulties other opinions may be liable to, those are out of the question. It is your business to defend your own opinion. Can anything be plainer than that you are for changing all things into ideas?

You, I say, who are not ashamed to charge me with *scepticism*.[17] This is so plain, there is no denying it.

Phil. You mistake me. I am not for changing things into ideas, but rather ideas into things; since those immediate objects of perception, which, according to you, are only appearances of things, I take to be the real things themselves.

Hyl. Things! you may pretend what you please; but it is certain you leave us nothing but the empty forms of things, the outside only which strikes the senses.

Phil. What you call the empty forms and outside of things seem to me the very things themselves. Nor are they empty or incomplete, otherwise than upon your supposition—that Matter is an essential part of all corporeal things. We both, therefore, agree in this, that we perceive only sensible forms: but herein we differ, you will have them to be empty appearances, I real beings. In short, you do not trust your senses, I do.

Hyl. You say you believe your senses; and seem to applaud yourself that in this you agree with the vulgar. According to you, therefore, the true nature of a thing is discovered by the senses. If so, whence comes that disagreement? Why, is not the same figure, and other sensible qualities, perceived all manner of ways? And why should we use a microscope the better to discover the true nature of a body, if it were discoverable to the naked eye?[18]

Phil. Strictly speaking, *Hylas*, we do not see the same object that we feel; neither is the same object perceived by the microscope which was by the naked eye. But, in case every variation was thought sufficient to constitute a new kind or individual, the endless number or confusion of names would render language impracticable. Therefore, to avoid this as well as other inconveniences which are obvious upon a little thought, men combine together several ideas, apprehended by divers senses, or by the same sense at different times, or in different circumstances, but observed, however, to have some connexion in nature, either with respect to co-existence or succession—all which they refer to one name, and consider as one thing. Hence, it follows that when I examine by my other senses a thing I have seen, it is not in order to understand better the same object which I had perceived by sight—the object of one sense not being perceived by the other senses. And, when I look through a microscope, it is not that I may perceive more clearly what I perceived already with my bare eyes; the object perceived by the glass being quite different from the former. But, in both cases, my aim is only to know what ideas are connected together; and the more a man knows of the connexion of ideas, the more he is said to know of the nature of things. What, therefore, if our ideas are variable; what if our senses are not in all circumstances affected with the same appearances? It will not thence follow they are not to be trusted, or that they are inconsistent either with themselves or anything else; except it be with your preconceived notion of (I know not what) one single, unchanged, unperceivable, real nature, marked by each name: which prejudice seems to have taken its rise from not rightly understanding the common language of men, speaking of several distinct ideas as united into one thing by the mind. And, indeed, there is cause to suspect several erroneous conceits of the philosophers are owing to the same original: while they began to build their schemes not so much on notions as words, which were framed by the vulgar, merely for conveniency and dispatch in the common actions of life, without any regard to speculation.

Hyl. Methinks I apprehend your meaning.

Phil. It is your opinion the ideas we perceive by our senses are not real things, but images or copies of them. Our knowledge, therefore, is no farther real than as our ideas are the true representations of those originals. But, as these supposed originals are in themselves unknown, it is impossible to know how far our ideas resemble them; or whether they resemble them at all. We cannot, therefore, be sure we have any real knowledge. Farther, as our ideas are perpetually varied, without any change in the supposed real things, it necessarily follows they cannot all be true copies of them: or, if some are and others are not, it is impossible to distinguish the former from the latter.[19] And this plunges us yet deeper in uncertainty. Again, when we consider the point, we cannot conceive how any idea, or anything like an idea, should have an absolute existence out of a mind: nor consequently, according to you, how there should be any real thing in nature. The result of all which is that we are thrown into the most hopeless and abandoned Scepticism. Now, give me leave to ask you, First, Whether your referring ideas to certain absolutely existing unperceived substances, as their originals, be not the source of all this Scepticism? Secondly, whether you are informed, either by sense or reason, of the existence of those unknown originals? And, in case you are not, whether it be not absurd to suppose them? Thirdly, Whether, upon inquiry, you find there is anything distinctly conceived or meant by the *absolute* or *external existence of unperceiving substances*? Lastly, Whether, the premises considered, it be not the wisest way to follow nature, trust your senses, and, laying aside all anxious thought about unknown natures or substances, admit with the vulgar those for real things which are perceived by the senses?

Hyl. For the present, I have no inclination to the answering part. I would much rather see how you can get over what follows. Pray are not the objects perceived by the senses of one, likewise perceivable to others present? If there were a hundred more here, they would all see the garden, the trees, and flowers, as I see them. But they are not in the same manner affected with the ideas I frame in my imagination. Does not this make a difference between the former sort of objects and the latter?

Phil. I grant it does. Nor have I ever denied a difference between the objects of sense and those of imagination. But what would you infer from thence? You cannot say that sensible objects exist unperceived, because they are perceived by many.

Hyl. I own I can make nothing of that objection: but it hath led me into another. Is it not your opinion that by our senses we perceive only the ideas existing in our minds?

Phil. It is.

Hyl. But the same idea which is in my mind cannot be in yours, or in any other mind. Doth it not therefore follow, from your principles, that no two can see the same thing? And is not this highly absurd?

Phil. If the term *same* be taken in the vulgar acceptation, it is certain (and not at all repugnant to the principles I maintain) that different persons may perceive the same thing; or the same thing or idea exist in different minds. Words are of arbitrary imposition; and, since men are used to apply the word *same* where no distinction or variety is perceived, and I do not pretend to alter their perceptions, it follows that, as men have said before, *several saw the same thing,* so they may, upon like occasions, still continue to use the same phrase, without any deviation either from propriety of language, or the truth of things. But, if the term *same* be used in the acceptation of philosophers, who pretend to an abstracted notion of identity, then, according to their sundry definitions of this notion (for it is not yet agreed wherein that philosophic identity consists), it may or may not be possible for divers persons to perceive the same thing. But whether philosophers shall think fit to call a thing the *same* or no, is, I conceive, of small importance. Let us suppose several men together, all endued with the same faculties, and consequently affected in like sort by their senses, and who had yet never known the use of language; they would, without question, agree in their perceptions. Though perhaps, when they came to the use of speech, some regarding the uniformness of what was perceived, might call it the *same* thing: others, especially regarding the diversity of persons who perceived, might choose the denomination of *different* things. But who sees not that all the dispute is about a word? to wit, whether what is perceived by different persons may yet have the term *same* applied to it? Or, suppose a house, whose walls or outward shell remaining unaltered, the chambers are all pulled down, and new ones built in their place; and that you should call this the *same,* and I should say it was not the *same* house:—would we not, for all this, perfectly agree in our thoughts of the house, considered in itself? And would not all the difference consist in a sound? If you should say, We differ in our notions; for that you superadded to your idea of the house the simple abstracted idea of identity, whereas I did not; I would tell you, I know not what you mean by the *abstracted idea of identity;* and should desire you to look into your own thoughts, and be sure you understood yourself.[20] Why so silent, *Hylas?* Are you not yet satisfied men may dispute about identity and diversity, without any real difference in their thoughts and opinions, abstracted from names? Take this farther reflection with you—that whether Matter be allowed to exist or no, the case is exactly the same as to the point in hand. For, the Materialists themselves acknowledge what we immediately perceive by our senses to be our own ideas. Your difficulty, therefore, that no two see the same thing, makes equally against the Materialists and me.

Hyl. Ay, *Philonous,* But they suppose an external archetype, to which referring their several ideas they may truly be said to perceive the same thing.

Phil. And (not to mention your having discarded those archetypes) so may you suppose an external archetype on my principles;—*external,* I mean, to your own mind; though indeed it must be supposed to exist in that mind which comprehends all things; but then, this serves all the ends of *identity,* as well as if it existed out of a mind.[21] And I am sure you yourself will not say it is less intelligible.

Hyl. You have indeed clearly satisfied me—either that there is no difficulty at bottom in this point; or, if there be, that it makes equally against both opinions.

Phil. But that which makes equally against two contradictory opinions can be a proof against neither.

Hyl. I acknowledge it. But, after all, *Philonous,* when I consider the substance of what you advance against *Scepticism,* it amounts to no more than this:—We are sure that we really see, hear, feel; in a word, that we are affected with sensible impressions.

Phil. And how are we concerned any farther? I see this *cherry,* I feel it, I taste it: and I am sure *nothing* cannot be seen, or felt, or tasted: it is therefore real.[22] Take away the sensations of softness, moisture, redness, tartness, and you take away the *cherry.* Since it is not a being distinct from sensations; a *cherry,* I say, is nothing but a congeries of sensible impressions, or ideas perceived by various senses: which ideas are united into one thing (or have one name given them) by the mind;—because they are observed to attend each other. Thus, when the palate is affected with such a particular taste, the sight is affected with a red colour, the touch with roundness, softness, &c. Hence, when I see, and feel, and taste, in sundry certain manners, I am sure the *cherry* exists, or is real; its reality being in my opinion nothing abstracted from those sensations. But if, by the word *cherry,* you mean an unknown nature, distinct from all those sensible qualities, and by its *existence* something distinct from its being perceived; then, indeed, I own, neither you nor I, nor any one else, can be sure it exists.

Hyl. But, what would you say, *Philonous,* if I should bring the very same reasons against the existence of sensible things in a mind, which you have offered against their existing in a material *substratum?*

Phil. When I see your reasons, you shall hear what I have to say to them.

Hyl. Is the mind extended or unextended?

Phil. Unextended, without doubt.

Hyl. Do you say the things you perceive are in your mind?

Phil. They are.

Hyl. Again, have I not heard you speak of sensible impressions?

Phil. I believe you may.

Hyl. Explain to me now, O *Philonous!* how it is possible there should be room for all those trees and houses to exist in your mind. Can extended things be contained in that which is unextended? Or, are we to imagine impressions made on a thing void of all solidity? You cannot say objects are in your mind, as books in your study: or that things are imprinted on it, as the figure of a seal upon wax. In what sense, therefore, are we to understand those expressions? Explain me this if you can: and I shall then be able to answer all those queries you formerly put to me about my *substratum*.[23]

Phil. Look you, *Hylas*, when I speak of objects as existing in the mind, or imprinted on the senses, I would not be understood in the gross literal sense—as when bodies are said to exist in a place, or a seal to make an impression upon wax. My meaning is only that the mind comprehends or perceives them; and that it is affected from without, or by some being distinct from itself. This is my explication of your difficulty; and how it can serve to make your tenet of an unperceiving material *substratum* intelligble, I would fain know.

Hyl. Nay, if that be all, I confess I do not see what use can be made of it. But are you not guilty of some abuse of language in this?

Phil. None at all. It is no more than common custom, which you know is the rule of language, hath authorized: nothing being more usual, than for philosophers to speak of the immediate objects of the understanding as things existing in the mind. Nor is there anything in this but what is conformable to the general analogy of language; most part of the mental operations being signified by words borrowed from sensible things; as is plain in the terms *comprehend, reflect, discourse,* &c., which, being applied to the mind, must not be taken in their gross original sense.

NOTES

1   In reading Berkeley, it is necessary to pay close attention to the ambiguity involved in the use of certain English words. In the preceding lines, Philonous has used the word *immediately.* As it is used here, the Berkeleian position is tacitly granted by Hylas. There might be more difficulty in the argument for Philonous if Hylas were to insist that we do perceive things other than sensible qualities immediately, physical objects, for example.

2   That is, the same color as we see in it? The question is rhetorical, because Hylas has already said that he means the same color.

3   Dioptrics is the scientific study of the refraction of light.

4   A theory occasionally invoked in empiricist epistemology is the theory that the true qualities of objects can be sensed by a *standard* observer under *standard*

conditions. The problem with such a criterion is that unless the notion of a standard observer and standard conditions is to be arbitrary, from which the true qualities can hardly follow, some nonempiricistic rule must be invoked in order to determine what is standard. Hylas, however, goes on to admit that no such device as a *standard* observer in *standard* conditions can work.

5   It is hardly necessary to recapitulate scientific theories of Berkeley's time, one of which is alluded to here. The argument would seemingly apply under any explanation of how vision took place, where one aspect of the explanation involved light moving over some finite length of time from the object seen to the retina of the eye.

6   What is the meaning of *without* that Hylas intends? Notice that the phrase 'in themselves' is not clear, but Philonous takes this to mean that colors are to be identified with the motions of particles. The reader might notice that if Hylas's description of vision is accepted, it is difficult to locate the color of an object in the everyday sense as being *anywhere*, for an opponent can raise serious objections to every possibility. Berkeley avoids the difficulty by denying the existence of material objects, so that color does not have to be located either *in* the mind or *outside* of it. When one brings in the problem of the relationship of the mind to the brain, these questions prove to be extremely complicated.

7   Why does Hylas stop arguing? Apparently because he has identified colors with certain motions of matter, but these cannot be known by reasons of various arguments that he can now anticipate from Philonous. On the other hand, we do perceive colors.

8   As a matter of fact, persons who have astigmatism may see an object as having a different shape with each eye.

9   Earlier in the dialogue, Hylas has distinguished two kinds of heat, making greater heat identical with pain and lesser heat not necessarily identical with any sensation. Pain, obviously, is something perceived, so that greater heat must exist in a mind, according to Philonous. On the other hand, Hylas maintained that lesser heat could exist in material objects. Philonous's summary here is not entirely accurate, since his refutation of Hylas's view was not complete. In the next sentence, Hylas could mean that an indifferent sensation is *no* sensation, but Philonous might then argue that we could not *know* of such a sensation.

10   Here is an example of the ambiguous use of *without*. Does 'not without the mind' mean 'in the mind'? Or does the plausibility of this sentence rest on reading 'not without the mind' as meaning that without the reaction of some mind to its ideas, events could not move *swiftly* or *slowly*, but simply at whatever pace they moved. Usually the swiftness or slowness of events is related to what we are desiring at the time when the events are noticed. '*A* occurs without *B*.' can mean that *A* occurs spatially outside of *B*, or that *A* occurs when *B* does not, or even that *B* is not a cause of *A* in that *A* does not always follow *B*.

11   This remark is in reference to the traditional (Aristotelian) logic taught in the universities at Berkeley's time. Differences were required to explain how two objects could belong to different species within the same genus. A difference is consequently an appropriate property that the one object has that the other object does not have. If a property is abstracted from all sensible properties (there are no non-sensible properties for Philonous), then no difference can be

found between an object having the property and one that does not, so that Berkeley seems to be suggesting that abstraction is fruitless because we could not distinguish *different* abstract properties.

12   The basic tenet of nominalism, that only individuals or particulars exist, is simply assumed here without debate as a universally received maxim. In a live debate, Hylas might want to argue this. Still, the (scientific) view of matter which Hylas is representing is often taken to be consistent with this principle.

13   Notice the reference to supernatural revelation, not mentioned in earlier discussions of how we might know the existence of matter. Once again, this need not be a loophole that Hylas would want to explore if he represents scientific thought, since he has maintained that we can know matter through perception.

14   This incidental remark is a clue to Berkeley's religious and political conservatism.

15   What Berkeley appears to mean here seems to call for the addition of a *not* after *would*, although for some reason this emendation does not occur in any of Berkeley's revisions of the *Three Dialogues*.

16   *Ambages* are roundabout or circular ways.

17   Early in the first dialogue, Hylas and Philonous agreed to call a skeptic anyone who denied the reality of sensible things, meaning by sensible things those things immediately perceived by the senses. Hylas's doctrine of matter makes sensible things less intelligible (because of obscurities in this doctrine) than Philonous's view, according to Philonous. From this the charge of skepticism arises.

18   This is one of the best points allotted to Hylas in the dialogue. Note the circumspection with which Philonous replies, and the interesting point on which his reply depends, namely, that the object perceived through a microscope, for example, and the object of direct perception are never the same object. Hylas might have Philonous in difficulty if he were to explore the consequences of maintaining that the book one sees with the naked eye, and the book one sees when he puts his spectacles on are not the same object.

19   Is this point cogent? Could you argue that an unchanging object might have differing perspectives? Imagine a circle of people slowly walking around a statue, for example.

20   There is some question as to whether this argument is cogent. Philonous has distinguished between *sameness* and *identity*, but it would seem that his account of difficulties in the notion of identity leads us away from difficulties in sameness. If two people argue as to whether they see the same thing, how can the argument be resolved on empiricists' grounds?

21   The Mind in question is, of course, related to Berkeley's views about God.

22   Berkeley elsewhere claims to be able to distinguish hallucination from true perception in terms of the coherence of the sensations of the latter. At this point, however, it would seem that Berkeley is brushing over problems of hallucination.

23   Another good point for Hylas. Although Philonous protests that Hylas is taking him too literally (has he been guilty of taking Hylas too literally?) and denies the spatial suggestion of *in*, his positive point seems to be somewhat obscure.

In terms of the preceding argument, can he maintain that what he means is that the mind comprehends what is affected from without? Actually, he can because he supposes the affectation to be a consequence of mental substance, rather than material substance. Hume argues later that arguments against the existence of material substance could be supplemented by arguments against the existence of mental substance.

PART 5

Hume

(1711–1776)

The Association of Ideas

David Hume, like Berkeley, could not accept a rationalistic philosophy but accepted the view that an adequate philosophy would have to be built upon ordinary sense impressions. In accepting the empirical theory of the origins of knowledge, however, he drew conclusions more stringent than those which were drawn by Locke and Berkeley. Where Berkeley had taken empiricism to refute the existence of matter, or material substance, Hume took empiricism to be inconsistent with the existence of material *and* spiritual substances. For Hume, sense impressions do not yield knowledge of *any* kind of substance, which is sufficient warning that Hume will prove to be more skeptical than any of the philosophers that we have considered.

One fruitful way of looking at this skepticism is to observe that Hume believed that impressions could only give us probable knowledge, but that probable knowledge was a sufficient grounding (being the only grounding) for any significant knowledge that human beings might ordinarily be said to be capable of having. Thus Hume is the first important philosopher that we have considered to suppose that *certain* knowledge was not only a misleading goal for philosophy, but in fact an unobtainable goal. It is the position that *certain* knowledge is not possible that distinguishes modern empiricism and to some extent explains Hume's importance in the history of philosophy. The rationalistic philosophers have been right in holding that certain knowledge is not attainable through sense experience, but an adequate empiricistic counter to this must be, not that *parts* of sense experience are certain, but that we have *no* certain knowledge, so that the philosophical quest for certainty must end in failure. The problem for the empiricist thus becomes that of demonstrating that science does not require certain knowledge for its attainments. The severe difficulty facing such a program is provision of an empirical analysis of mathematical truth that can avoid Platonic objections that the certainty of mathematical truths which are required for scientific theorizing cannot be explained in terms of uncertain sense experiences.

Hume begins with a reformulation of the empiricistic account of ideas. He contends that everyone will, upon reflection, admit that there is an important qualitative difference between experiences at the time of their original occurrence, and at some time when they are either remembered or anticipated by the imagination. This difference is characterized as being one of *vividness*. An *impression*, which is after this point a technical term of Hume's philosophy, is similar to a Berkeleian idea in that it is the vivid and forceful mental occurrence that accompanies what might be called a present sensation. *Ideas*, in Hume's technical sense, are the result of the mind's analysis and combining of remembered impressions or parts thereof. Like Berkeley and Descartes, Hume takes the position that the powers of the human mind to form ideas are not unlimited but are bounded by the ability of the mind to analyze and combine whatever impressions it has had in the past. This position about the origin of ideas is taken by Hume to be obvious upon reflection, but he buttresses it with the empirical argument that wherever impressions of some sort are impossible to a person, the formation of ideas involving impressions of this sort is not possible. A congenitally blind man, for example, cannot form those ideas which are the result of analyzing and combining impressions of sight.

A Humean *impression* and a Berkeleian *idea* cannot be identified. One of Hume's major contributions to empiricism was to notice that simple sensations of sight, touch, hearing, etc., are obviously too meagre a basis on which to construct an adequate general theory of human knowledge. The simple fact is that all felt human emotion, as well as moral and aesthetic valuation, is completely unaccounted for in an empiricism which supposes that sensations are the result of sense-organ activity in terms of what is outside of the body. A feeling of anger, for example, is not analogous to a sight of blue in that the anger is clearly felt as my anger, but the blue as the blue of some object. Hume wished to include emotional impressions, as well as impressions of moral and aesthetic worth, as *basic* ingredients of empiricism, since there seems to be no way of obtaining an explanation of these experiences by the analysis and combination of sights, sounds, touches, etc. Consequently the kind of direct observation equivalent to an impression in Hume's sense is considerably more complicated than it appears to be in Berkeley's philosophy. For any philosopher who wishes to include the range of moral, emotional, and aesthetic experiences within an empiricistic account of human knowledge, Humean impressions will be a great advance over Berkeleian ideas. At the same time, there is a corresponding difficulty in that Hume should give an account of how we have impressions of this wider class, since a feeling of anger is not presumably seen with the eyes, heard with the ears, and so forth. Yet our understanding that we have these impressions is a straightforward consequence of an examination of our feelings. Ideas, on the other hand, must be understood because of the way in which we come to develop them. When we are unclear as to what the significance of an idea is, we can remove unclarity only by analyzing the idea into the impressions whose analysis and combination led to the formation of the idea. The basis for this is empirical, in the sense that Hume makes no claims as to the origins of impressions (we simply have them), but he claims that the distinction between ideas and impressions in terms of liveliness or vividness is presumably one that may be empirically verified.

To explain how various impressions are analyzed and combined to form an idea, Hume invokes the notion of association. Various impressions may be associated to form an idea, and various ideas may in turn be associated to form a complex idea. These associations must be explained, in Hume's philosophy, in terms that will permit a satisfactory account of the knowledge of common sense. The problem is to find some empiricistic account of association which will be comprehensive enough to explain why human beings seem to associate the same ideas, as witnessed by their success in communicating through language. Berkeley's account, as we have seen, resulted in the difficulty that there was no cogent explanation of the fact that general words stood for certain ideas but not for others. Hume's philosophy must tackle an analogous difficulty.

An explanation of the operation of association is given by Hume which utilizes the notions of resemblance, of contiguity, and of cause and effect. These he called natural relations between ideas. We shall consider resemblance in particular. The terminology 'natural relations between ideas' seems to suggest that *ideas* is being used here in a looser, more colloquial sense than the technical usage of *ideas* as opposed to *impressions,* since remarks made by Hume in his discussion indicate that impressions may resemble one another. At first sight it might be supposed that resemblance could be explained as the natural relation holding between any two things which had some parts in common. Thus, an object A consisting of the parts $a, b, c, d,$ and an object B consisting of the parts a, c, d, f might be said to resemble one another because they have the parts a, c, d in common. Throughout this discussion it will have to be assumed that the parts described are simple or ultimate in some sense, so that no part of one object is considered nonidentical with any part of the other, because the parts of one object are not analyzed finely enough. In terms of impressions, then, two experiences of objects would resemble one another if there were an impression as part of one experience identical (so far as can be remembered) with an impression which is part of the other. Even so, the account is obviously defective in that two objects A and B, consisting respectively of the parts a, b, c, d and e, f, g, h might be said to resemble one another in ways other than sharing parts. For example, the four parts of each may be arranged in some similar way, so that A and B resemble each other even though there is no part of A identical with any part of B. The four parts of each object, to make this perfectly clear, might be arranged as the corners of a square of similar size. Hume does not discuss this problem, perhaps because he holds that one would not be said to have an impression of a relation. One may see something he calls *red* but not something that he would call *on top of*. Hume does mention explicitly the fact that the simple ideas of blue and green resemble one another more than the simple ideas of blue and scarlet. If this is true, it cannot be because the impressions which give rise to the ideas of blue and green have identical parts more numerous than these in the impressions giving rise to the ideas of blue and scarlet. Exactly how Hume meant to explain this comparison of resemblances remains obscure.

It is interesting to note that even if resemblance could be defined in terms of the identity of common parts, there seems to be no way of construing identity in terms of resemblance. A theory of knowledge utilizing resemblance as a primitive or basic notion may not be able to account for the identity of objects, raising the interesting question of whether or not scientific theories may be constructed in terms of the resemblance of objects, without introducing a notion of the identity of objects as an additional primitive term.

An important feature of Hume's account is that he does not explain *why* ideas are associated, but attempts merely to *describe how* ideas are associated. By introspection, he discovers those ideas which are associated, and finds that they are in fact associated because they resemble one another or because they are related by contiguity or the cause-and-effect relationship. There is some apparent difficulty involved here in that at times objects are spoken of as resembling one another, and at other times ideas related to these objects by experience are said to resemble one another. As a result, the notion of resemblance does not help very much in the analysis of the association of ideas.

The fact that Hume explicitly rejects all explanations of *why* various ideas are in fact associated rather than others calls for some comment. To begin with, Hume has no explanation as to why, when a given idea occurs, some other idea is related to it by, for example, cause and effect, rather than by contiguity or resemblance. In other words, as a succession of ideas occurs to us, the sequence may be ordered by any one of the three natural relations, and it does not seem possible to predict, once an idea has occurred to us, which of the three natural relations will hold between it and the next idea which occurs to us. These associations are not logically necessary, but they are the result of custom or habit, according to Hume. The philosopher's job is to observe the associations and describe them: it cannot legitimately be to explain why they occur, because this is impossible.

The impossibility of this latter task is related to Hume's acceptance of scientific method as practiced by Newton. Newton took as his task not to explain *why* objects fall to the earth, etc., but to *describe how* they fell, that is, to give a formula describing the rate of their fall under specified conditions, the direction of their fall, and so forth. In an analogous fashion,

Hume took as his task not to explain *why* certain ideas are associated, but to describe how they are associated. The primitive, unexplained term *association* in Hume's theory of knowledge corresponds to the primitive, unexplained term *gravity* in Newton's theory of gravitation. How things fall is explained in terms of gravity, and how ideas are associated is explained in terms of association. Why things fall the way they do rather than some other way is not a significant problem for Newton, just as the problem of why ideas are associated the way they are rather than in other combinations is not a significant problem for Hume.

In taking this position, both Hume and Newton accepted views which have come to play an important role in contemporary empiricism. The basis of these views is sole reliance on observation, which comes to mean both ordinary experience *and* deliberate experimental observation as the test of the worth of any generalization. Metaphysics is simultaneously condemned. Hume's reason for this condemnation is precisely that metaphysical speculation is not subject to the check of observation, in that *any* observation would be compatible with most metaphysical theories.

We may see what an empiricist like Hume considers a metaphysical idea by discussion of the Humean reaction to the notion of substance. Hume argues that watching something change over a period of time is quite similar to watching something that does not change, in the sense that we see it throughout as one object. If, at the end of the change, we compare our memory of the object at the start with the object now, we see that the object may be quite different, as in Descartes's example of the piece of wax. To reconcile our contrary feelings that the object is the same and yet different, we invent or phantasize 'something unknown and invisible' which remains identical throughout the change. We call this substance. This tendency of the imagination to construct unobserved entities to explain sequences of impressions ought not to be accepted by philosophers because no experiment can demonstrate or refute the existence of substance or other metaphysical notions, since they are by their construction compatible with every observation. A metaphysical idea cannot be analyzed into impressions and is consequently either useless or meaningless. The point could be made in a more contemporary fashion by saying that since a metaphysical idea would have to be related to *every* impression, no way of *distinguishing* metaphysical ideas is possible. Consequently metaphysical ideas cannot serve as contributions to human knowledge. This feature of Hume's empiricism has proved very influential on contemporary empiricists, but as we shall see later, the Humean-Newtonian doctrine that any sound scientific generalization must *follow from* observation turned out to be entirely too restrictive.

Mathematical Truth and Skepticism

To this point, we have seen that impressions, as well as ideas derived from impressions, constitute the foundation for human knowledge in Hume's epistemology. But it is clear that we say that we know more than is legitimately entailed by our narrow range of impressions. Hume vacillates on the question of whether or not our impressions constitute knowledge. We have them, and they form the foundation of knowledge, but it is seemingly awkward to say either that they are certain or uncertain. What seems to be relatively certain or uncertain are the various opinions or judgments that are based on the impressions which we cannot doubt but which we do not *know* either.

The certainty of mathematics Hume takes cognizance of by holding that mathematical knowledge is really a special kind of comparison of the names of ideas which is undertaken by thought alone. When Hume says that mathematical knowledge is not dependent on what exists, he must be taken to mean that mathematical truths, being the mental comparison of ideas, cannot be subject to empirical check, since it is *ideas* which are being compared, and their relationships are not to be determined by scientific experiment. In another sense, of course, we would not have ideas without prior ordinary experience. All Hume's remarks on this topic are compact, and we learn little more than what has just been said, as well as that the nonempirical test of a mathematical truth is that its negation must result in contradiction; that is, we cannot consistently imagine its negation. If we imagine that the squares of the legs of a right triangle are not equal to the square of the hypotenuse, we can quickly find a contradiction in the system of which this statement is a theorem.

It is difficult to reconcile Hume's claims about the certainty of true mathematical statements with his obvious opinion that human knowledge is based solely on impressions. A reconciliation may be effected by drawing a distinction between significant and nonsignificant statements, and then claiming that *significant* statements (which make a nontrivial claim about our experiences) are never certain, while certain statements are never significant. In this way, statements of mathematics may be said to be nonsignificant in that their acquisition never increases our significant knowledge about the world, although it may enable us to organize this significant knowledge in some more convenient way. Then it could be claimed that mathematical knowledge is certain only in the sense that significant statements cannot controvert it. The Pythagorean theorem is true but not significant because we choose to apply the word *triangle* only to those ideas of which the Pythagorean theorem is true. If *triangle* is applied to something of which the Pythagorean theorem is not true, we take this as a discovery that the word *triangle* has been misapplied, and not as a proof that the theorem is false after all. Although this attempt at a reconciliation of Hume's remarks is compatible with what Hume says, there is no resolution of the status of mathematical truth in Hume's extant works, at least no clear resolution, and so we can take any such attempt at helping Hume out as but a charitable way of reading him to preserve his important empiricistic insight that certainty may not be required of scientific knowledge.

Hume's skepticism is a result of the fact that he limits certain knowledge in a rigorous sense to demonstrable mathematical truth. Whatever else we know, and this includes all our significant information, we know only probably. This second and more important kind of knowledge has been called *belief* by empiricists. Belief comprises probable opinion in experimental science, morality, political philosophy, and aesthetics. The application of association to impressions and ideas cannot result in certain knowledge. That two ideas are such that they resemble one another, or that they are contiguous, or that one is the cause of the other cannot be a necessary result of the nature of the ideas, but can only be some function of the way in which experience causes us to frame the ideas. This point assumes special significance in connection with cause and effect since cause and effect is the only relation of the three which could enable us to reason to existences and objects (to possible impressions) which we have not experienced. Resemblance and contiguity simply hold or do not hold between ideas that we already have. The relation of cause and effect, however, might enable us to say something about the unexperienced, thus enabling us to predict future events and otherwise discourse intelligibly about topics not entirely circumscribed by our meagre store of past experiences.

It is clear that we do assume cause-and-effect relationships, and it is also clear that they are used (as they were in the science of Hume's day) to predict the future and hence provide the basis for rational action. What Hume demonstrated is that reasoning involving cause and effect cannot be demonstrative; that is, the result of such reasoning is never a certain prediction, but only a probable one.

The argument that reasoning involving cause and effect is not demonstrative is based on two arguments. Experience with such reasonings indicates that they often fail. We can also see that such reasonings will fail by experimental introspection. Given some object, Hume argues that a man cannot determine any of its causes or effects with certainty. This seems a little strong, but it is clear that there are, say, effects which some objects in certain situations have that could not be guessed by inspection of the object in the lack of any more extended experience with it. Simple examples suffice to indicate that we cannot estimate with much accuracy the effects of some strange piece of apparatus under certain conditions. This argument to the probable nature of inferences of cause and effect is based on observation. Hume further argues that if cause-and-effect reasonings were demonstrative, then imagination of the negation of any correct statement of causal inference would be contradictory. We can, however, imagine two or more incompatible effects following from some given event or object taken as cause, so that reasoning from cause to effect violates the condition of contradiction placed on the negations of statements of demonstrable inference, which are certain. Given that something is X, the only way to investigate its effects is to observe X experimentally.

These arguments are not overwhelming in spite of their apparent plausibility. Part of their failure stems from the way in which we may be said to conceive the contradictory of a statement. Conception of a contradiction is at least implicitly a mark of the difference between the demonstrable truths of mathematics (whose contradictories are not conceivable) and the probable statements of the sciences. Nevertheless, it is possible to imagine the truth of either of a pair of contradictory statements in mathematics, unless the notion of 'conceiving a contradiction' is considerably sharpened. An example is *Fermat's Last Theorem* and its negation. Assuming again that we are dealing with plane triangles only, we can ask the following question: For $n \geqslant 3$, are there any three positive numbers x, y, and z which satisfy the relationship $x^n + y^n = z^n$? The negative answer to this question is called *Fermat's Last Theorem* among mathematicians, after the mathematician who advanced the claim. In spite of great effort, no one has been able to find a proof or disproof of *Fermat's Last Theorem*. Consequently, we might say that it is conceivable that either *Fermat's Last Theorem* or its negation may be a demonstrable truth of mathematics. Clearly not both can be true, but if one is true, then its negation is not obviously contradictory, or we would have a proof available as to which of the two is true. Consequently we cannot take the conceivability of contradiction in holding the negation of a claim X to be a test that X (if it is a mathematical statement) is a mathematical truth, since some mathematical truths will fail this test. Persons knowing little of mathematics may find it equally conceivable that either of two statements (for one of which there is a satisfactory proof that it is a mathematical truth) is a mathematical truth. And by the same token, scientists have reported that either of two effects might conceivably follow from some cause that is under experimental investigation. In order to make Hume's remarks effective, some further study of when a statement may be said to be contradictory is required.

Further, Hume's empirical proofs require some supplementation. Some arguments may be deductive in spite of the fact that the statements of the argument are about probabilities. Thus, it is a valid argument within the probability calculus to argue that if two independent events each have a probability of $\frac{1}{6}$, their joint occurrence has a probability of $\frac{1}{6}$ times $\frac{1}{6}$, or $\frac{1}{36}$. On the other hand, many philosophers have suggested that there may be legitimate nondeductive arguments (inductive arguments) holding between statements that are either true or false, in the sense that it is not known which value the statements have. For example, if I have observed 1,000,000 A's, and 998,567 of them have also been B's, I may argue that a new arbitrary A will be a B, assuming that I have no further information available that might influence the probabilities. Now, although the premises of such an argument may all be true while the conclusion is false, so that the argument is not deductively valid, one may also argue reasonably that the truth of the conclusion is more likely than the truth of its negation. If it is possible to construct an inductive logic, Hume's proof may be misleading. In other words, if either of two contradictory statements may both follow from some statement, this is still compatible with the possibility that the probability of the truth of one is much greater than the probability of the other. We may, however, take Hume to be arguing correctly that any analysis which *justifies* an assignment of probabilities cannot be based solely on our impressions.

Hume felt that there was no *certain* way of assigning probabilities. The acceptance of probabilities rests on psychological considerations, but we cannot know that these are reasonable. The occurrence of any event cannot establish a probability claim, since the occurrence of an event does not prove that the event is a probable or improbable event. We experience both.

Hume's skepticism is really his insistence that impressions cannot enable us to frame certain knowledge of the world. When this is coupled with the rejection of any rationalist methods, the result is that no empiricism based solely on impressions and immediate generalizations thereon can yield *any* certain knowledge. This is a strong claim which later empiricists have been forced to accept.

An interesting feature of this interpretation of Hume is that he does not seem to have considered himself a skeptic. While he felt that scientific practice could not be established on the basis of impressions alone without bringing in custom or habit, as we shall see in the next chapter, he seems to have developed his skeptical position in order to show that scientific methodology has no theoretical advantage over moral and political methodology. He apparently wished to become a Newton in the moral sciences (political theory, economics, and ethics) by using association and habit to demonstrate that moral questions might be as satisfactorily resolved as scientific questions. What his analysis accomplishes is that scientific methodology cannot be established on the basis of experience alone, contrary to the contention of some of the philosophers and to some of the implicit methodological assumptions of the scientists of his day.

The Cause-and-effect Relationship

Hume's analysis of the cause-and-effect relationship enables us to see how an analysis of an idea into impressions for the purposes of clarification is actually carried out. Throughout this discussion, Hume speaks of the constant conjunction of *objects*, which must be taken as a reference to what we ordinarily call objects, even though Hume's explicit consideration of what an object is does not involve a material substance anymore than Berkeley's consideration does. The analysis assumes that a relationship between cause and effect is intuitively known, and that in some sense this intuitive relationship is such that cause and effect are *necessarily* related. Thus, if we say that an event *a* is the cause of an event *b*, we would ordinarily say that *a must* be followed by *b* or is necessarily followed by *b*. Hume takes the analysis of this necessary connection to be an important problem.

Suppose that two events or objects thought to be in the causal relationship are examined. Hume speaks only of objects being in the causal relationship, but we often think of events as being in this relationship, and both shall be spoken of here, leaving open the question of how an object is to be distinguished from an event. It is immediately clear that the cause is taken to precede the effect and that the two are taken to be contiguous in space and time. The status of these two observations is quite different. That causes precede effects seems to be a trivial consequence of the way in which we define *cause* and *effect*, although this does not detract from what Hume says, since that is obviously true in virtue of our definitions. Contiguity proves more difficult to discuss. The fact that Hume uses this expression indicates that he was thinking about everyday occurrences, such as his examples of billiard balls striking one another. That cause and effect must be *separated* in space and time is surely the case, since this seems a necessary condition of our distinguishing *two* objects or events to be called, respectively, the cause and the effect. If they are definitely separated, the requirement of contiguity suggests that they are not to be separated by very much. Actually, although this view of the cause-and-effect relationship is perhaps true, it requires considerable augmentation to handle cases of causal laws in science. For one thing, it is not required in scientific cases that a cause be contiguous to one of its effects, but only that any cause and effect be related by a series of objects or events such that each object or event in this series be contiguous to the object or event preceding it and following it; and such that each event or object in the series is the effect of the object or event preceding it, and the cause of the object or event following it. In this way we may speak of *causal chains* connecting two events in the relationship of cause and effect which are not, considered in themselves, contiguous. Nevertheless, Hume's analysis could be extended if it were otherwise satisfactory to include such pairs of events.

A more serious question is that of relating two contiguous events. It is tempting to suppose that what we call cause and effect are simply two locations in some *continuous* causal chain. For Hume, the view that between any two instants of time or points in some body, another instant of time or another point in the body may be found, is excluded by his atomistic views of space and time. He would argue that we can have no *experience* of such a causal chain, which would involve experience of an infinite number of bodies or events, but that we can experience only disparate and finite sequences of bodies or events.

Contiguity and precedence of cause are all that we can determine of the causal relationship by examination of a single cause and effect. By considering several instances of cause and effect, a new feature comes into consideration. Let A-B, C-D, E-F, etc., be instances of cause and effect, such that A, C, and E resemble one another in some quality. Because of what we have said about identity, we cannot treat the sequences just mentioned as the same sequence of cause and effect. Still, we tend to regard objects which closely resemble one another as identical. Let us consider A, C, and E to be R-like objects in virtue of their resemblance, and B, D, and F to be S-like objects in virtue of their resemblance. To say that R-like objects cause S-like objects, we must have observed in every case that an R-like object is followed by an S-like object. Hume says that R-like objects, or simply R's (treating them as though they were identical in some respect) must be constantly conjoined with S-like objects, or S's. As a constant conjunction of R's and S's is repeated, Hume suggests that we come to expect that an S will follow an R, and finally that an S must follow an R. For Hume, the intuitive necessity that an effect must follow its cause is simply a result of the custom or habit that we acquire of expecting S's to follow R's when they have been uniformly noticed to do so in the past. This analysis accomplishes a grounding of the idea of the cause-and-effect relationship *in experience*.

After completing this analysis, Hume offers two distinct definitions of the relation of cause and effect. Defined as a philosophical relation, we may say that a cause is:

an object precedent and contiguous to another, and where all the objects resembling the former are placed in like relations of precedence and contiguity to those objects that resemble the latter.

On the other hand, as a natural relation, we may say that a cause is:

an object precedent and contiguous to another, and so united with it, that the idea of the one determines the mind to form the idea of the other, and the impression of the one to form a more lively idea of the other.

Why should Hume offer *two* definitions? An answer to this question may enable us to grasp the difference between a philosophical problem and a psychological problem. A natural relation is one which holds between ideas by virtue of their association. As we have seen, the natural relations are resemblance, contiguity in time and place, and causality. Natural relations are the relations of association which explain all unreflective belief. In analyzing a natural relation, we are discovering how people do, in fact, come to associate ideas. This question is not, strictly speaking, a philosophical question—but a question of psychology, or an empirical question. Hume's answer to these questions may not be an adequate account of how people do associate ideas (*if* they associate ideas, so that the general associationist account of knowledge is plausible), but even if it is false, its falsity does not mean that Hume's definition of the philosophical relation must also be rejected.

The first definition, in more contemporary terms, may be taken as an answer to the question "What do we mean by the words *cause, effect,* and *causal relationship*?". By Hume's theory of meaning, this should be traced solely to impressions and cannot incorporate *feelings* or *beliefs,* as the second definition does. This problem of meaning can be taken as a philosophical question. We might *mean* by a cause-effect relationship a constant union of various kinds of objects or events, but come to apply this relationship correctly in practice, not because of Hume's associationist account in terms of custom, but because of the *Intuition* of the rationalists or through some other means. Thus, it appears plausible that the question of what a word means can be separated in theory from the question of when we can apply a word correctly or know that the criteria giving its meaning are satisfied in some particular case. These problems of meaning are philosophical and are the result of reflection. A person has natural relationships between his ideas, and as a result may use and apply *cause, effect,* etc., correctly, even though he may be unaware of why the objects or events he calls *causes* can be grouped together. To return to a previous example, most of us can use the words *table, chair,* etc., without difficulty, at least well enough to communicate successfully to others, even though we would be unable to define *chair* in a philosophically adequate manner.

We can now see that a cause-and-effect relationship holds between *R*-like and *S*-like objects if and only if they are constantly conjoined; that is, a particular *R*-like object is always followed by a particular *S*-like object when they are contiguous in place and time, and this is taken to be what we mean by cause and effect. But we never experience *all* these constant conjunctions, or at least we cannot be sure that we have experienced all of them. Consequently the definition does not enable us to determine *which* of the constant unions we have observed in the past can be appropriately projected into the future as a causal relationship. It might be thought that Hume would argue that we must wait to see when the *feeling* arises to make a projection. But this is not so. The philosophical analysis of the cause-and-effect relationship enables us to determine rules (Hume cites eight), satisfaction of which we may take to lead to the custom or habit that the conjunction be projected as a cause-and-effect relationship. This projection is then at least partly justified because the projected cause-and-effect relationship can be shown to have properties which are given by the philosophical *analysis* of the relationship of cause and effect.

The first three of these rules are an immediate result of the earlier analysis, namely, that the cause and effect which is projected must be contiguous in space and time, that the cause must precede the effect, and that a constant conjunction must be observed between cause and effect. The rest of the rules provide the test of the occurrence of *resemblance* postulated in the definition to hold between the particular causes and the particular effects of any cause-and-effect relationship. Hume's fourth rule is that the same cause has the same effect and that an effect always arises from some one cause. An apparent exception to this could arise if some range of causes preceded the same effect, but Hume's fifth rule stipulates that this occurrence signals some common quality in the range of apparent causes which is the true cause of the effect. Similarly, if two apparently similar causes have different effects, this signals at least one quality in which the causes must differ. This is Hume's rule six. An example of the application of this rule would be two chemicals which might look alike, but behave quite differently. We can conclude that their behavior is *not* a function of their appearance. The seventh rule tells us that if some cause is increased or decreased, the effect will be increased or decreased accordingly; and the eighth rule is that if something thought to be a cause should occur, and the supposed effect not follow, the supposed cause may not be a *complete* cause. These eight rules enable one to design more effective tests of observed conjunctions in order to determine which may be validly projected. The relative sophistication of contemporary experimental design by comparison to these simple rules is an indication that Hume's rules are inadequate as they stand. Still, Hume has the historical merit of pointing out that the philosophical problem is not one of finding a necessary connection leading to *true* prediction of the future, but that of analyzing the successful predictions of the past in an effort to obtain rules that would enable our projections into the future to be more systematic and orderly than they might otherwise be.

Readings from Hume

The selection from Hume consists of sections II through IV and part of section V of Hume's *An Enquiry concerning Human Understanding.* Hume's *Enquiry* is readily available in reasonably priced editions, such as the version in *The English Philosophers from Bacon to Mill* (E. A. Burtt, editor) published by Random House, Inc. in *The Modern Library*. This edition is reprinted here. The *Enquiry concerning Human Understanding* is Hume's restatement in a somewhat more popular form of the first part of his *Treatise of Human Nature,* to which it should be compared. Hume was disappointed at the reception of the *Treatise* (1739) by the literary world, and he wrote the *Enquiry* (1748) to promote an interest in, and understanding of, the important ideas which had been proposed in the *Treatise.* This situation, the existence of a major epistemological work and an introduction to it in a somewhat less convoluted style, is not uncommon in the history of philosophy. A troubling question when this occurs is that of deciding whether or not any discrepancy between the two versions is due to a reconsideration of issues which should affect a reading of the major work, or whether it is due to a desire to keep less important issues and distinctions from distracting a reader of the introduction. These problems are most acute when the introductory or popular work was written after the supposed major work, as in the case of Hume.

In the *Treatise,* for example, Hume attempted to distinguish between arithmetic and geometry on the grounds that we had a perfect assurance of the truths of arithmetic, making them *certain,* while geometrical propositions failed of this precision and were *informative* about the world without being certain. In the *Enquiry,* on the other hand, Hume seems to have argued that geometrical *and* arithmetical propositions represent certain truths. Many later empiricists have supposed that Hume was confused about the distinction between pure and applied mathematics which has been considerably clarified since his time. With the use of this distinction, we may say that the inferences in pure Euclidean geometry are as certain

191

as they are in arithmetic, but that when we identify *light ray* with *straight line*, etc., to get an applied geometry, we turn pure geometrical assertions into assertions about the world which may well turn out to be false. These empiricists would then hold that Hume's position in the *Enquiry* was really the superior one, and the one that Hume's philosophical insight later led him to prefer, on the grounds that geometry and arithmetic should both be considered first as pure calculi, or formal systems. But it is possible to hold that Hume never made up his mind, or that he really preferred the version in the *Treatise* and tried to simplify his discussion of mathematics for the general reader when he came to write the *Enquiry*.

Hume has achieved a considerable reputation as a man of letters for contributions to literature other than his primarily philosophical works. He wrote a *History of England*, for example, that made him famous both in France and in England during his own lifetime. His philosophical reputation is so great among philosophers that it is sometimes a surprise for philosophers to discover that in England he may be better known as David Hume the historian, than as David Hume the philosopher.

The following secondary sources may prove useful to the reader of the *Enquiry* and the *Treatise*.

Aaron, R. I.: *The Theory of Universals*, Oxford, 1952.

Aschenbrenner, Karl: "Psychologism in Hume," *Philosophical Quarterly*, vol. 11, pp. 28–38, 1961.

*Basson, A. H.: *David Hume*, Harmondsworth, 1958. (Pelican Paperbound.)

Church, R. W.: *Hume's Theory of the Understanding*, London, 1935.

Flew, A. G. N.: *Hume's Philosophy of Belief: A Study of His Inquiry*, New York, 1961.

Passmore, John: *Hume's Intentions*, London, 1952.

Price, H. H.: *Hume's Theory of the External World*, Oxford, 1940.

Smith, N. K.: *The Philosophy of David Hume*, London, 1960.

Zabeeh, F.: *Hume: Precursor of Modern Empiricism*, The Hague, 1960.

From Hume's *ENQUIRY*

SECTION II   OF THE ORIGIN OF IDEAS

Everyone will readily allow that there is a considerable difference between the perceptions of the mind, when a man feels the pain of excessive heat, or the pleasure of moderate warmth, and when he afterwards recalls to his memory this sensation, or anticipates it by his imagination.[1] These faculties may mimic or copy the perceptions of the senses; but they never can entirely reach the force and vivacity of the original sentiment.[2] The utmost we say of them, even when they operate with greatest vigor, is, that they represent their object in so lively a manner, that we could *almost* say we feel or see it: But, except the mind be disordered by disease or madness, they never can arrive at such a pitch of vivacity, as to render these perceptions altogether undistinguishable. All the colors of poetry, however splendid, can never paint natural objects in such a manner as to make the description be taken for a real landscape. The most lively thought is still inferior to the dullest sensation.

We may observe a like distinction to run through all the other perceptions of the mind. A man in a fit of anger, is actuated in a very different manner from one who only thinks of that emotion. If you tell me, that any person is in love, I easily understand your meaning, and form a just conception of his situation; but never can mistake that conception for the real disorders and agitations of the passion. When we reflect on our past sentiments and affections, our thought is a faithful mirror, and copies its objects truly; but the colors which it employs are faint and dull, in comparison of those in which our original perceptions were clothed. It requires no nice discernment or metaphysical head to mark the distinction between them.³

Here therefore we may divide all the perceptions of the mind into two classes or species, which are distinguished by their different degrees of force and vivacity.⁴ The less forcible and lively are commonly denominated *thoughts* or *ideas*. The other species want a name in our language, and in most others; I suppose, because it was not requisite for any, but philosophical purposes, to rank them under a general term or appellation. Let us, therefore, use a little freedom, and call them *impressions*; employing that word in a sense different somewhat from the usual. By the term *impression*, then, I mean all our more lively perceptions, when we hear, or see, or feel, or love, or hate, or desire, or will. And impressions are distinguished from ideas, which are the less lively perceptions, of which we are conscious, when we reflect on any of those sensations or movements above mentioned.

Nothing, at first view, may seem more unbounded than the thought of man, which not only escapes all human power and authority, but is not even restrained within the limits of nature and reality. To form monsters, and join incongruous shapes and appearances, costs the imagination no more trouble than to conceive the most natural and familiar objects. And while the body is confined to one planet, along which it creeps with pain and difficulty; the thought can in an instant transport us into the most distant regions of the universe; or even beyond the universe, into the unbounded chaos, where nature is supposed to lie in total confusion. What never was seen, or heard of, may yet be conceived; nor is anything beyond the power of thought, except what implies an absolute contradiction.

But though our thought seems to possess this unbounded liberty, we shall find, upon a nearer examination, that it is really confined within very narrow limits, and that all this creative power of the mind amounts to no more than the faculty of compounding, transposing, augmenting, or diminishing the materials afforded us by the senses and experience.[5] When we think of a golden mountain, we only join two consistent ideas, *gold*, and *mountain*, with which we were formerly acquainted. A virtuous horse we can conceive; because, from our own feeling, we can conceive virtue; and this we may unite to the figure and shape of a horse, which is an animal familiar to us. In short, all the materials of thinking are derived either from our outward or inward sentiment: the mixture and composition of these belongs alone to the mind and will. Or, to express myself in philosophical language, all our ideas or more feeble perceptions are copies of our impressions or more lively ones.

To prove this, the two following arguments will, I hope, be sufficient. First, when we analyze our thoughts or ideas, however compounded or sublime, we always find that they resolve themselves into such simple ideas as were copied from a precedent feeling or sentiment. Even those ideas, which, at first view, seem the most wide of this origin, are found, upon a nearer scrutiny, to be derived from it. The idea of God, as meaning an infinitely intelligent, wise, and good Being, arises from reflecting on the operations of our own mind, and augmenting, without limit, those qualities of goodness and wisdom.[6] We may prosecute this inquiry to what length we please; where we shall always find, that every idea which we examine is copied from a similar impression.[7] Those who would assert that this position is not universally true nor without exception, have only one, and that an easy method of refuting it; by producing that idea, which, in their opinion, is not derived from this source. It will then be incumbent on us, if we would maintain our doctrine, to produce the impression, or lively perception, which corresponds to it.

Secondly. If it happen, from a defect of the organ, that a man is not susceptible of any species of sensation, we always find that he is as little susceptible of the correspondent ideas. A blind man can form no notion of colors; a deaf man of sounds. Restore either of them that sense in which he is deficient; by opening this new inlet for his sensations, you also open an inlet for the ideas; and he finds no difficulty in conceiving these objects. The case is the same, if the object, proper for exciting any sensation, has never been applied to the organ. A Laplander or Negro has no notion of the relish of wine. And though there are few or no instances of a like deficiency in the mind, where a person has never felt or is wholly incapable of a sentiment or passion that belongs to his species; yet we find the same observation to take place in a less degree. A man of mild manners can form no idea of inveterate revenge or cruelty; nor can a selfish heart easily conceive the heights of friendship and generosity. It is readily allowed, that other beings may possess many senses of which we can have no conception; because the ideas of them have never been introduced to us in the only manner by which an idea can have access to the mind, to wit, by the actual feeling and sensation.

There is, however, one contradictory phenomenon, which may prove that it is not absolutely impossible for ideas to arise, independent of their correspondent impressions. I believe it will readily be allowed, that the several distinct ideas of color, which enter by the eye, or those of sound, which are conveyed by the ear, are really different from each other; though, at the same time, resembling. Now if this be true of different colors, it must be no less so of the different shades of the same color; and each shade produces a distinct idea, independent of the rest. For if this should be denied, it is possible, by the continual gradation of shades, to run a color insensibly into what is most remote from it; and if you will not allow any of the means to be different, you cannot, without absurdity, deny the extremes to be the same. Suppose, therefore, a person to have enjoyed his sight for thirty years, and to have become perfectly acquainted with colors of all kinds except one particular shade of blue, for instance, which it never has been his fortune to meet with. Let all the different shades of that color, except that single one, be placed before him, descending gradually from the deepest to the lightest; it is plain that he will perceive a blank, where that shade is wanting, and will be sensible that there is a greater distance in that place between the contiguous colors than in any other. Now I ask, whether it be possible for him, from his own imagination, to supply this deficiency, and raise up to himself the idea of that particular shade, though it had never been conveyed to him by his senses? I believe there are few but will be of opinion that he can: and this may serve as a proof that the simple ideas are not always, in every instance, derived from the correspondent impressions; though this instance is so singular, that it is scarcely worth our observing, and does not merit that for it alone we should alter our general maxim.[8]

Here, therefore, is a proposition, which not only seems, in itself, simple and intelligible; but, if a proper use were made of it, might render every dispute equally intelligible, and banish all that jargon, which has so long taken possession of metaphysical reasonings, and drawn disgrace upon them. All ideas, especially abstract ones, are naturally faint and obscure: the mind has but a slender hold of them: they are apt to be confounded with other resembling ideas; and when we have often employed any term, though without a distinct meaning, we are apt to imagine it has a determinate idea annexed to it. On the contrary, all impressions, that is, all sensations, either outward or inward, are strong and vivid: the limits between them are more exactly determined: nor is it easy to fall into any error or mistake with regard to them. When we entertain, therefore, any suspicion that a philosophical term is employed without any meaning or idea (as is but too frequent), we need but inquire, *from what impressions is that supposed idea derived ?* And if it be impossible to assign any, this will serve to confirm our suspicion.[9] By bringing ideas into so clear a light we may reasonably hope to remove all dispute, which may arise, concerning their nature and reality.

SECTION III   OF THE ASSOCIATION OF IDEAS

It is evident that there is a principle of connection between the different thoughts or ideas of the mind, and that, in their appearance to the memory or imagination, they introduce each other with a certain degree of method and regularity. In our more serious thinking or discourse this is so observable that any particular thought, which breaks in upon the regular tract or chain of ideas, is immediately remarked and rejected. And even in our wildest and most wandering reveries, nay in our very dreams, we shall find, if we reflect, that the imagination ran not altogether at adventures, but that there was still a connection upheld among the different ideas, which succeeded each other. Were the loosest and freest conversation to be transcribed, there would immediately be observed something which connected it in all its transitions. Or where this is wanting, the person who broke the thread of discourse might still inform you, that there had secretly revolved in his mind a succession of thought, which had gradually led him from the subject of conversation. Among different languages, even where we cannot suspect the least connection or communication, it is found, that the words, expressive of ideas, the most compounded, do yet nearly correspond to each other: a certain proof that the simple ideas, comprehended in the compound ones, were bound together by some universal principle, which had an equal influence on all mankind.

Though it be too obvious to escape observation, that different ideas are connected together; I do not find that any philosopher has attempted to enumerate or class all the principles of association; a subject, however, that seems worthy of curiosity. To me, there appear to be only three principles of connection among ideas, namely, *resemblance, contiguity* in time or place, and *cause or effect.*

That these principles serve to connect ideas will not, I believe, be much doubted. A picture naturally leads our thoughts to the original:[10] the mention of one apartment in a building naturally introduces an inquiry or discourse concerning the others:[11] and if we think of a wound, we can scarcely forbear reflecting on the pain which follows it.[12] But that this enumeration is complete, and that there are no other principles of association except these, may be difficult to prove to the satisfaction of the reader, or even to a man's own satisfaction. All we can do, in such cases, is to run over several instances, and examine carefully the principle which binds the different thoughts to each other, never stopping till we render the principle as general as possible.[13] The more instances we examine, and the more care we employ, the more assurance shall we acquire, that the enumeration, which we form from the whole, is complete and entire.

SECTION IV   SCEPTICAL DOUBTS CONCERNING THE OPERATIONS OF THE UNDERSTANDING

PART I

All the objects of human reason or enquiry may naturally be divided into two kinds, to wit, *Relations of Ideas,* and *Matters of Fact.* Of the first kind are the sciences of Geometry, Algebra, and Arithmetic; and in short, every affirmation which is either intuitively or demonstratively certain. *That the square of the hypotenuse is equal to the square of the two sides,* is a proposition which expresses a relation between these figures. *That three times five is equal to the half of thirty,* expresses a relation between these numbers. Propositions of this kind are discoverable by the mere operation of thought, without dependence on what is anywhere existent in the universe. Though there never were a circle or triangle in nature, the truths demonstrated by Euclid would for ever retain their certainty and evidence.

Matters of fact, which are the second objects of human reason, are not ascertained in the same manner; nor is our evidence of their truth, however great, of a like nature with the foregoing. The contrary of every matter of fact is still possible; because it can never imply a contradiction, and is conceived by the mind with the same facility and distinctness, as if ever so conformable to reality. *That the sun will not rise tomorrow* is no less intelligible a proposition, and implies no more contradiction than the affirmation, *that it will rise.* We should in vain, therefore, attempt to demonstrate its falsehood. Were it demonstratively false, it would imply a contradiction and could never be distinctly conceived by the mind.

It may, therefore, be a subject worthy of curiosity, to enquire what is the nature of that evidence which assures us of any real existence and matter of fact, beyond the present testimony of our senses, or the records of our memory. This part of philosophy, it is observable, has been little cultivated, either by the ancients or moderns; and therefore our doubts and errors, in the prosecution of so important an enquiry, may be the more excusable; while we march through such difficult paths without any guide or direction. They may even prove useful, by exciting curiosity, and destroying that implicit faith and security, which is the bane of all reasoning and free enquiry. The discovery of defects in the common philosophy, if any such there be, will not, I presume, be a discouragement, but rather an excitement, as is usual, to attempt something more full and satisfactory than has yet been proposed to the public.

All reasonings concerning matter of fact seem to be founded on the relation of *Cause and Effect.* By means of that relation alone we can go beyond the evidence of our memory and senses. If you were to ask a man, why he believes any matter of fact, which is absent; for instance, that his friend is in the country, or in France; he would give you a reason; and this reason would be some other fact; as a letter received from him, or the knowledge of his former resolutions and promises. A man finding a watch or any other machine in a desert island, would conclude that there had once been men on that island. All our reasonings concerning fact are of the same nature. And here it is constantly supposed that there is a connexion between the present fact and that which is inferred from it. Were there nothing to bind them together, the inference would be entirely precarious. The hearing of an articulate voice and rational discourse in the dark assures us of the presence of some person: Why? because these are the effects of the human make and fabric, and closely connected with it. If we anatomize all the other reasonings of this nature, we shall find that they are founded on the relation of cause and effect, and that this relation is either near or remote, direct or collateral. Heat and light are collateral effects of fire, and the one effect may justly be inferred from the other.

If we would satisfy ourselves, therefore, concerning the nature of that evidence, which assures us of matters of fact, we must enquire how we arrive at the knowledge of cause and effect.

I shall venture to affirm, as a general proposition, which admits of no exception, that the knowledge of this relation is not, in any instance, attained by reasonings *a priori*; but arises entirely from experience, when we find that any particular objects are constantly conjoined with each other. Let an object be presented to a man of ever so strong natural reason and abilities; if that object be entirely new to him, he will not be able, by the most accurate examination of its sensible qualities, to discover any of its causes or effects.[14] Adam, though his rational faculties be supposed, at the very first, entirely perfect, could not have inferred from the fluidity and transparency of water that it would suffocate him, or from the light and wamth of fire that it would consume him. No object ever discovers, by the qualities which appear to the senses, either the causes which produced it, or the effects which arise from it; nor can our reason, unassisted by experience, ever draw any inference concerning real existence and matter of fact.

This proposition, that causes and effects are discoverable, *not by reason but by experience*, will readily be admitted with regard to such objects, as we remember to have once been altogether unknown to us; since we must be conscious of the utter inability, which we then lay under, of foretelling what would arise from them. Present two smooth pieces of marble to a man who has no tincture of natural philosophy; he will never discover that they will adhere together in such a manner as to require great force to separate them in a direct line, while they make so small a resistance to lateral pressure. Such events, as bear little analogy to the common course of nature, are also readily confessed to be known only by experience; nor does any man imagine that the explosion of gunpowder, or the attraction of a loadstone, could ever be discovered by arguments *a priori*. In like manner, when an effect is supposed to depend upon an intricate machinery or secret structure of parts, we make no difficulty in attributing all our knowledge of it to experience. Who will assert that he can give the ultimate reason, why milk or bread is proper nourishment for a man, not for a lion or a tiger?

But the same truth may not appear, at first sight, to have the same evidence with regard to events, which have become familiar to us from our first appearance in the world, which bear a close analogy to the whole course of nature, and which are supposed to depend on the simple quali- ties of objects, without any secret structure of parts. We are apt to imagine that we could discover these effects by the mere operation of our reason, without experience. We fancy, that were we brought on a sudden into this world, we could at first have inferred that one Billiard-ball would com- municate motion to another upon impulse; and that we needed not to have waited for the event, in order to pronounce with certainty concerning it. Such is the influence of custom, that, where it is strongest, it not only covers our natural ignorance, but even conceals itself, and seems not to take place, merely because it is found in the highest degree.

But to convince us that all the laws of nature, and all the operations of bodies without exception, are known only by experience, the following reflections may, perhaps, suffice. Were any object presented to us, and were we required to pronounce concerning the effect, which will result from it, without consulting past observation; after what manner, I beseech you, must the mind proceed in this operation? It must invent or imagine some event, which it ascribes to the object as its effect; and it is plain that this invention must be entirely arbitrary. The mind can never possibly find the effect in the supposed cause, by the most accurate scrutiny and obser- vation. For the effect is totally different from the cause, and consequently can never be discovered in it. Motion in the second Billiard-ball is a quite distinct event from motion in the first; nor is there anything in the one to suggest the smallest hint of the other. A stone or piece of metal raised into the air, and left without support, immediately falls: but to consider the matter *a priori*, is there anything we discover in this situation which can beget the idea of a downward, rather than an upward, or any other motion, in the stone or metal?

And as the first imagination or invention of a particular effect, in all natural operations, is arbitrary, where we consult not experience; so must we also esteem the supposed tie or connexion between the cause and effect, which binds them together, and renders it impossible that any other effect could result from the operation of that cause. When I see, for instance, a Billiard-ball moving in a straight line towards another; even suppose motion in the second ball should by accident be suggested to me, as the result of their contact or impulse; may I not conceive, that a hundred different events might as well follow from that cause? May not the first ball return in a straight line, or leap off from the second in any line or direction? All these suppositions are consistent and conceivable. Why then should we give preference to one, which is no more consistent or conceivable than the rest? All our reasonings *a priori* will never be able to show us any foundation for this preference.

In a word, then, every effect is a distinct event from its cause. It could not, therefore, be discovered in the cause, and the first invention or conception of it, *a priori*, must be entirely arbitrary. And even after it is suggested, the conjunction of it with the cause must appear equally arbitrary; since there are always many other effects, which, to reason, must seem fully as consistent and natural. In vain, therefore, should we pretend to determine any single event, or infer any cause or effect, without the assistance of observation and experience.

Hence we may discover the reason why no philosopher, who is rational and modest, has ever pretended to assign the ultimate cause of any natural operation, or to show distinctly the action of that power, which produces any single effect in the universe. It is confessed, that the utmost effort of human reason is to reduce the principles, productive of natural phenomena, to a greater simplicity, and to resolve the many particular effects into a few general causes, by means of reasonings from analogy, experience, and observation. But as to the causes of these general causes, we should in vain attempt their discovery; nor shall we ever be able to satisfy ourselves, by any particular explication of them. These ultimate springs and principles are totally shut up from human curiosity and enquiry. Elasticity, gravity, cohesion of parts, communication of motion by impulse; these are probably the ultimate causes and principles which we shall ever discover in nature; and we may esteem ourselves sufficiently happy, if, by accurate enquiry and reasoning, we can trace up the particular phenomena to, or near to, these general principles. The most perfect philosophy of the natural kind only staves off our ignorance a little longer: as perhaps the most perfect philosophy of the moral or metaphysical kind serves only to discover larger portions of it. Thus the observation of human blindness and weakness is the result of all philosophy, and meets us at every turn, in spite of our endeavors to elude or avoid it.

Nor is geometry, when taken into the assistance of natural philosophy, ever able to remedy this defect, or lead us into the knowledge of ultimate causes, by all that accuracy of reasoning for which it is so justly celebrated. Every part of mixed mathematics proceeds upon the supposition that certain laws are established by nature in her operations; and abstract reasonings are employed, either to assist experience in the discovery of these laws, or to determine their influence in particular instances, where it depends upon any precise degree of distance and quantity. Thus, it is a law of motion, discovered by experience, that the moment or force of any body in motion is in the compound ratio or proportion of its solid contents and its velocity; and consequently, that a small force may remove the greatest obstacle or raise the greatest weight, if, by any contrivance or machinery, we can increase the velocity of that force, so as to make it an overmatch for its antagonist.[15] Geometry assists us in the application of this law, by giving us the just dimensions of all the parts and figures which can enter into any species of machine; but still the discovery of the law itself is owing merely to experience, and all the abstract reasonings in the world could never lead us one step towards the knowledge of it. When we reason *a priori*, and consider merely any object or cause, as it appears to the mind, independent of all observation, it never could suggest to us the notion of any distinct object, such as its effect; much less, show us the inseparable and inviolable connexion between them. A man must be very sagacious who could discover by reasoning that crystal is the effect of heat, and ice of cold, without being previously acquainted with the operation of these qualities.

PART II

But we have not yet attained any tolerable satisfaction with regard to the question first proposed. Each solution still gives rise to a new question as difficult as the foregoing, and leads us on to farther enquiries. When it is asked, *What is the nature of all our reasonings concerning matter of fact?* the proper answer seems to be, that they are founded on the relation of cause and effect. When again it is asked, *What is the foundation of all our reasonings and conclusions concerning that relation?* it may be replied in one word, Experience. But if we still carry on our sifting humour, and ask, *What is the foundation of all conclusions from experience?* this implies a new question, which may be of more difficult solution and explication. Philosophers, that give themselves airs of superior wisdom and sufficiency, have a hard task when they encounter persons of inquisitive dispositions, who push them from every corner to which they retreat, and who are sure at last to bring them to some dangerous dilemma. The best expedient to prevent this confusion, is to be modest in our pretensions; and even to discover the difficulty ourselves before it is objected to us. By this means, we may make a kind of merit of our very ignorance.

I shall content myself, in this section, with an easy task, and shall pretend only to give a negative answer to the question here proposed.[16] I say then, that, even after we have experience of the operations of cause and effect, our conclusions from that experience are *not* founded on reasoning, or any process of the understanding. This answer we must endeavour both to explain and to defend.

It must certainly be allowed, that nature has kept us at a great distance from all her secrets, and has afforded us only the knowledge of a few superficial qualities of objects; while she conceals from us those powers and principles on which the influence of those objects entirely depends. Our senses inform us of the colour, weight, and consistence of bread; but neither sense nor reason can ever inform us of those qualities which fit it for the nourishment and support of a human body. Sight or feeling conveys an idea of the actual motion of bodies, but as to that wonderful force or power, which would carry on a moving body for ever in a continued change of place, and which bodies never lose but by communicating it to others; of this we cannot form the most distant conception. But notwithstanding this ignorance of natural powers and principles, we always presume, when we see like sensible qualities, that they have like secret powers, and expect that effects, similar to those which we have experienced, will follow from them. If a body of like colour and consistence with that bread, which we have formerly eaten, be presented to us, we make no scruple of repeating the experiment, and foresee, with certainty, like nourishment and support. Now this is a process of the mind or thought, of which I would willingly know the foundation. It is allowed on all hands that there is no known connexion between the sensible qualities and the secret powers; and consequently, that the mind is not led to form such a conclusion concerning their constant and regular conjunction, by anything which it knows of their nature. As to past *Experience*, it can be allowed to give *direct* and *certain* information of those precise objects only, and that precise period of time, which fell under its cognizance: but why this experience should be extended to future times, and to other objects, which for aught we know, may be only in appearance similar; this is the main question on which I would insist. The bread, which I formerly ate, nourished me; that is, a body of such sensible qualities was, at that time, endued with such secret powers: but does it follow, that other bread must also nourish me at another time, and that like sensible qualities must always be attended with like secret powers? The consequence seems nowise necessary. At least, it must be acknowledged that there is here a consequence drawn by the mind; that there is a certain step taken; a process of thought, and an inference, which wants to be explained. These two propositions are far from being the same, *I have found that such an object has always been attended with such an effect*, and *I foresee, that other objects, which are, in appearance, similar, will be attended with similar effects*. I shall allow, if you please, that the one proposition may justly be inferred from the other: I know, in fact, that it is always inferred. But if you insist that the inference is made by a chain of reasoning, I desire you to produce that chain of reasoning. The connexion between these propositions is not intuitive. There is required a medium, which may enable the mind to draw such an inference, if indeed it be drawn by reasoning and argument. What that medium is, I must confess, passes my comprehension; and it is incumbent on those to produce it, who assert that it really exists, and is the origin of all our conclusions concerning matter of fact.

This negative argument must certainly, in process of time, become altogether convincing, if many penetrating and able philosophers shall turn their enquiries this way and no one be ever able to discover any connecting proposition or intermediate step, which supports the understanding in this conclusion. But as the question is yet new, every reader may not trust so far to his own penetration, as to conclude, because an argument escapes his enquiry, that therefore it does not really exist. For this reason it may be requisite to venture upon a more difficult task; and enumerating all the branches of human knowledge, endeavour to show that none of them can afford such an argument.

All reasonings may be divided into two kinds, namely, demonstrative reasoning, or that concerning relations of ideas, and moral reasoning, or that concerning matter of fact and existence. That there are no demonstrative arguments in the case seems evident; since it implies no contradiction that the course of nature may change, and that an object, seemingly like those which we have experienced, may be attended with different or contrary effects. May I not clearly and distinctly conceive that a body, falling from the clouds, and which, in all other respects, resembles snow, has yet the taste of salt or feeling of fire? Is there any more intelligible proposition than to affirm, that all the trees will flourish in December and January, and decay in May and June? Now whatever is intelligible, and can be distinctly conceived, implies no contradiction, and can never be proved false by any demonstrative argument or abstract reasoning *a priori*.

If we be, therefore, engaged by arguments to put trust in past experience, and make it the standard of our future judgment, these arguments must be probable only, or such as regard matter of fact and real existence, according to the division above mentioned. But that there is no argument of this kind, must appear, if our explication of that species of reasoning be admitted as solid and satisfactory. We have said that all arguments concerning existence are founded on the relation of cause and effect; that our knowledge of that relation is derived entirely from experience; and that all our experimental conclusions proceed upon the supposition that the future will be conformable to the past. To endeavour, therefore, the proof of this last supposition by probable arguments, or arguments regarding existence, must be evidently going in a circle, and taking that for granted, which is the very point in question.

In reality, all arguments from experience are founded on the similarity which we discover among natural objects, and by which we are induced to expect effects similar to those which we have found to follow from such objects. And though none but a fool or madman will ever pretend to dispute the authority of experience, or to reject that great guide of human life, it may surely be allowed a philosopher to have so much curiosity at least as to examine the principle of human nature, which gives this mighty authority to experience, and makes us draw advantage from that similarity which nature has placed among different objects. From causes which appear *similar* we expect similar effects. This is the sum of all our experimental conclusions. Now it seems evident that, if this conclusion were formed by reason, it would be as perfect at first, and upon one instance, as after ever so long a course of experience. But the case is far otherwise. Nothing so like as eggs; yet no one, on account of this appearing similarity, expects the same taste and relish in all of them. It is only after a long course of uniform experiments in any kind, that we attain a firm reliance and security with regard to a particular event. Now where is that process of reasoning which, from one instance, draws a conclusion, so different from that which it infers from a hundred instances that are nowise different from that single one? This question I propose as much for the sake of information, as with an intention of raising difficulties. I cannot find, I cannot imagine any such reasoning. But I keep my mind still open to instruction, if any one will vouchsafe to bestow it on me.

Should it be said that, from a number of uniform experiments, we *infer* a connexion between the sensible qualities and the secret powers; this, I must confess, seems the same difficulty, couched in different terms. The question still recurs, on what process of argument this *inference* is founded? Where is the medium, the interposing ideas, which join propositions so very wide of each other? It is confessed that the colour, consistence, and other sensible qualities of bread appear not, of themselves, to have any connexion with the secret powers of nourishment and support. For otherwise we could infer these secret powers from the first appearance of these sensible qualities, without the aid of experience; contrary to the sentiment of all philosophers, and contrary to plain matter of fact. Here, then, is our natural state of ignorance with regard to the powers and influence of all objects. How is this remedied by experience? It only shows us a number of uniform effects, resulting from certain objects, and teaches us that those particular objects, at that particular time, were endowed with such powers and forces. When a new object, endowed with similar sensible qualities, is produced, we expect similar powers and forces, and look for a like effect. From a body of like colour and consistence with bread we expect like nourishment and support. But this surely is a step or progress of the mind, which wants to be explained. When a man says, *I have found, in all past instances, such sensible qualities conjoined with such secret powers:* And when he says, *Similar sensible qualities will always be conjoined with similar secret powers,* he is not guilty of a tautology, nor are these propositions in any respect the same. You say that the one proposition is an inference from the other. But you must confess that the inference is not intuitive; neither is it demonstrative: Of what nature is it, then? To say it is experimental, is begging the question. For all inferences from experience suppose, as their foundation, that the future will resemble the past, and that similar powers will be conjoined with similar sensible qualities. If there be any suspicion that the course of nature may change, and that the past may be no rule for the future, all experience becomes useless, and can give rise to no inference or conclusion. It is impossible, therefore that any arguments from experience can prove this resemblance of the past to the future; since all these arguments are founded on the supposition of that resemblance. Let the course of things be allowed hitherto ever so regular; that alone, without some new argument or inference, proves not that, for the future, it will continue so. In vain do you pretend to have learned the nature of bodies from your past experience. Their secret nature, and consequently all their effects and influence, may change, without any change in their sensible qualities. This happens sometimes, and with regard to some objects: Why may it not happen always and with regard to all objects? What logic, what process of argument secures you against this supposition? My practice, you say, refutes my doubts. But you mistake the purport of my question. As an agent, I am quite satisfied in the point; but as a philosopher, who has some share of curiosity, I will not say scepticism, I want to learn the foundation of this inference. No reading, no enquiry has yet been able to remove my difficulty, or give me satisfaction in a matter of such importance. Can I do better than propose the difficulty to the public, even though, perhaps, I have small hopes of obtaining a solution? We shall at least, by this means, be sensible of our ignorance, if we do not augment our knowledge.

I must confess that a man is guilty of unpardonable ignorance who concludes, because an argument has escaped his own investigation, that therefore it does not really exist. I must confess that, though all the learned, for several ages, should have employed themselves in fruitless search upon any subject, it may still, perhaps, be rash to conclude positively that the subject must, therefore, pass all human comprehension. Even though we examine all the sources of our knowledge, and conclude them unfit for such a subject, there may still remain a suspicion, that the enumeration is not complete, or the examination not accurate. But with regard to the present subject, there are some considerations which seem to remove all this accusation of arrogance or suspicion of mistake.

It is certain that the most ignorant and stupid peasants—nay infants, nay even brute beasts—improve by experience, and learn the qualities of natural objects, by observing the effects which result from them. When a child has felt the sensation of pain from touching the flame of a candle, he will be careful not to put his hand near any candle; but will expect a similar effect from a cause which is similar in its sensible qualities and appearance. If you assert, therefore, that the understanding of the child is led into this conclusion by any process of argument or ratiocination, I may justly require you to produce that argument; nor have you any pretence to refuse so equitable a demand. You cannot say that the argument is abstruse, and may possibly escape your enquiry; since you confess that it is obvious to the capacity of a mere infant. If you hesitate, therefore, a moment, or if, after reflection, you produce any intricate or profound argument, you, in a manner, give up the question, and confess that it is not reasoning which engages us to suppose the past resembling the future, and to expect similar

effects from causes which are, to appearance, similar. This is the proposition which I intended to enforce in the present section. If I be right, I pretend not to have made any mighty discovery. And if I be wrong, I must
acknowledge myself to be indeed a very backward scholar; since I cannot
now discover an argument which, it seems, was perfectly familiar to me
long before I was out of my cradle.

SECTION V   SCEPTICAL SOLUTION OF THESE DOUBTS

PART I

The passion for philosophy, like that for religion, seems liable to this
inconvenience, that, though it aims at the correction of our manners, and
extirpation of our vices, it may only serve, by imprudent management,
to foster a predominant inclination, and push the mind, with more determined resolution, towards that side which already *draws* too much, by the
bias and propensity of the natural temper. It is certain that, while we
aspire to the magnanimous firmness of the philosophic sage, and endeavour to confine our pleasures altogether within our own minds, we
may, at last, render our philosophy like that of Epictetus, and other *Stoics*,
only a more refined system of selfishness, and reason ourselves out of all
virtue as well as social enjoyment.[17] While we study with attention the
vanity of human life, and turn all our thoughts towards the empty and
transitory nature of riches and honours, we are, perhaps, all the while
flattering our natural indolence, which, hating the bustle of the world,
and drudgery of business, seeks a pretence of reason to give itself a full
and uncontrolled indulgence. There is, however, one species of philosophy
which seems little liable to this inconvenience, and that because it strikes
in with no disorderly passion of the human mind, nor can mingle itself with
any natural affection or propensity; and that is the Academic or Sceptical
philosophy. The academics always talk of doubt and suspense of judgment,
of danger in hasty determinations, of confining to very narrow bounds the
enquiries of the understanding, and of renouncing all speculations which
lie not within the limits of common life and practice. Nothing, therefore,
can be more contrary than such a philosophy to the supine indolence of the
mind, its rash arrogance, its lofty pretensions, and its superstitious credulity.
Every passion is mortified by it, except the love of truth; and that passion
never is, nor can be, carried to too high a degree. It is surprising, therefore,
that this philosophy, which, in almost every instance, must be harmless and
innocent, should be the subject of so much groundless reproach and ob-
loquy. But, perhaps, the very circumstance which renders it so innocent is
what chiefly exposes it to the public hatred and resentment. By flattering
no irregular passion, it gains few partizans: By opposing so many vices

and follies, it raises to itself abundance of enemies, who stigmatize it as libertine, profane, and irreligious.

Nor need we fear that this philosophy, while it endeavours to limit our enquiries to common life, should ever undermine the reasonings of common life, and carry its doubts so far as to destroy all action, as well as speculation. Nature will always maintain her rights, and prevail in the end over any abstract reasoning whatsoever. Though we should conclude, for instance, as in the foregoing section, that, in all reasonings from experience, there is a step taken by the mind which is not supported by any argument or process of the understanding; there is no danger that these reasonings, on which almost all knowledge depends, will ever be affected by such a discovery. If the mind be not engaged by argument to make this step, it must be induced by some other principle of equal weight and authority; and that principle will preserve its influence as long as human nature remains the same. What that principle is may well be worth the pains of enquiry.

Suppose a person, though endowed with the strongest faculties of reason and reflection, to be brought on a sudden into this world; he would, indeed, immediately observe a continual succession of objects, and one event following another; but he would not be able to discover anything farther. He would not, at first, by any reasoning, be able to reach the idea of cause and effect; since the particular powers, by which all natural operations are performed, never appear to the senses; nor is it reasonable to conclude, merely because one event, in one instance, precedes another, that therefore the one is the cause, the other the effect. Their conjunction may be arbitrary and casual. There may be no reason to infer the existence of one from the appearance of the other. And in a word, such a person, without more experience, could never employ his conjecture or reasoning concerning any matter of fact, or be assured of anything beyond what was immediately present to his memory and senses.

Suppose, again, that he has acquired more experience, and has lived so long in the world as to have observed familiar objects or events to be constantly conjoined together; what is the consequence of this experience? He immediately infers the existence of one object from the appearance of the other. Yet he has not, by all his experience, acquired any idea or knowledge of the secret power by which the one object produces the other; nor is it, by any process of reasoning, he is engaged to draw this inference. But still he finds himself determined to draw it: And though he should be convinced that his understanding has no part in the operation, he would nevertheless continue in the same course of thinking. There is some other principle which determines him to form such a conclusion.

This principle is Custom or Habit. For wherever the repetition of any particular act or operation produces a propensity to renew the same act or operation, without being impelled by any reasoning or process of the understanding, we always say, that this propensity is the effect of *Custom.* By employing that word, we pretend not to have given the ultimate reason of such a propensity. We only point out a principle of human nature, which is universally acknowledged, and which is well known by its effects. Perhaps we can push our enquiries no farther, or pretend to give the cause of this cause; but must rest contented with it as the ultimate principle, which we can assign, of all our conclusions from experience. It is sufficient satisfaction, that we can go so far, without repining at the narrowness of our faculties because they will carry us no farther. And it is certain we here advance a very intelligible proposition at least, if not a true one, when we assert that, after the constant conjunction of two objects—heat and flame, for instance, weight and solidity—we are determined by custom alone to expect the one from the appearance of the other. This hypothesis seems even the only one which explains the difficulty, why we draw, from a thousand instances, an inference which we are not able to draw from one instance, that is, in no respect, different from them.[18] Reason is incapable of any such variation. The conclusions which it draws from considering one circle are the same which it would form upon surveying all the circles in the universe. But no man, having seen only one body move after being impelled by another, could infer that every other body will move after a like impulse. All inferences from experience, therefore, are effects of custom, not of reasoning.[19]

Custom, then, is the great guide of human life. It is that principle alone which renders our experience useful to us, and makes us expect, for the future, a similar train of events with those which have appeared in the past. Without the influence of custom, we should be entirely ignorant of every matter of fact beyond what is immediately present to the memory and senses. We should never know how to adjust means to ends, or to employ our natural powers in the production of any effect. There would be an end at once of all action, as well as of the chief part of speculation.

But here it may be proper to remark, that though our conclusions from experience carry us beyond our memory and senses, and assure us of matters of fact which happened in the most distant places and most remote ages, yet some fact must always be present to the senses or memory, from which we may first proceed in drawing these conclusions. A man, who should find in a desert country the remains of pompous buildings, would conclude that the country had, in ancient times, been cultivated by civilized inhabitants; but did nothing of this nature occur to him, he could never form such an inference. We learn the events of former ages from history; but then we must peruse the volumes in which this instruction is maintained, and thence carry up our inferences from one testimony to another, till we arrive at the eyewitnesses and spectators of these distant events. In a word, if we proceed not upon some fact, present to the memory or senses, our reasonings would be merely hypothetical; and however the particular links might be connected with each other, the whole chain of inferences would have nothing to support it, nor could we ever, by its means, arrive at the knowledge of any real existence. If I ask why you believe any particular matter of fact, which you relate, you must tell me some reason; and this reason will be some other fact, connected with it. But as you cannot proceed after this manner, *in infinitum*, you must at last terminate in some fact, which is present to your memory or senses; or must allow that your belief is entirely without foundation.

What, then, is the conclusion of the whole matter? A simple one; though, it must be confessed, pretty remote from the common theories of philosophy. All belief of matter of fact or real existence is derived merely from some object, present to the memory or senses, and a customary conjunction between that and some other object. Or in other words; having found, in many instances, that any two kinds of objects—flame and heat, snow and cold—have always been conjoined together; if flame or snow be present anew to the senses, the mind is carried by custom to expect heat or cold, and to *believe* that such a quality does exist, and will discover itself upon a nearer approach. This belief is the necessary result of placing the mind in such circumstances. It is an operation of the soul, when we are so situated, as unavoidable as to feel the passion of love, when we receive benefits; or hatred, when we meet with injuries. All these operations are a species of natural instincts, which no reasoning or process of the thought and understanding is able either to produce or to prevent.

NOTES

1   This appeal to introspection seems to have been taken by the empiricists as a method of proof of their theories. Philonous, in Berkeley's *Dialogues*, challenged Hylas to frame an abstract idea. Hume is also constantly challenging the reader to introspect, for example, to understand differences in vividness between ideas and impressions. It may be asked whether these challenges by empiricists are entirely fair, since it is not clear how one could introspect and find the claims of the empiricists to be mistaken. An empiricist might always inform a recalcitrant introspector that he was not introspecting carefully enough. As a result, the introspective tests mentioned by Berkeley and Hume are not really convincing experiments. It is interesting to consider whether any mental image of any particular thing, no matter how familiar we might be with it in the ordinary sense, could be clear enough that we could answer all of the questions which might be asked about the particular thing by some philosophical adversary.

2   *Sentiment*, as used by Hume, might be translated into *feeling* or *awareness* in order to capture his meaning. The point is that Hume's *sentiment* is not as subjective as *sentiment* may be now in such contexts as "He expressed his sentiments about the book.".

3   *Nice* is a word which has received outrageous treatment in ordinary discourse, having come to be applied to almost everything which is at least mildly agree-

able. Hume's *nice* might be replaced as you read by *precise* or *discriminating*, either of which would be close to his meaning.

4   *Perception* has a multitude of philosophical uses. Here it occurs in the phrase 'perceptions of the mind', where it suggests whatever the mind is conscious of. By a kind of philosophical convention, the word *idea* is used to describe whatever is presented to the mind (This is true in Plato, Descartes, and Berkeley, as we have seen.), but Hume wants to make a crucial distinction between kinds of mental presentations in terms of vivacity. If the distinction is legitimate, how could Berkeley have maintained it?

5   Apparently, what Hume calls thought is what Descartes called imagination. See the discussion of imagination in the *First Meditation*.

6   The example of God seems a poor choice to illustrate Hume's point. Surely many theists would argue that the concept of God is a perfect illustration that not all ideas can be derived from sense experience, and Descartes explicitly took this view. Further, the notion of augmenting qualities without limit used by Hume in this sentence seems to be a stronger mental operation than empiricism can readily admit, even though Hume uses the word *augment* above in describing mental operations. We might legitimately request that Hume expand his explanation of augmentation.

7   That is, any idea that we have must be copied from impressions having qualities involved in the idea. The use of *copied* here seems much weaker than the *augmentation* allowed in the case of the idea of God.

8   This entire paragraph can be met only with astonishment. Hume has proposed a rule that ideas can always be resolved into impressions, a rule that he claims must *always* hold. Then he produces a counterexample, accepts it, but says that it is scarcely worth observing, and retains his general rule. What can we make of this? Perhaps Hume took the formation of the idea of this shade of blue to be such a small augmentation of impressions that it could be ignored, but this approach has severe consequences with respect to the purpose of his division of perceptions of the mind into two sharp classes. It might also be suggested that Hume should just change his mind on this point in order to preserve consistency, although it is awkward with respect to common sense. There are some grounds for supposing that Hume never became entirely clear in his own mind as to a distinction between using certain words correctly and being able to frame ideas corresponding to them. A blind man, for example, might not be able to have mental images of color (although even this does not seem logically impossible), even though he may be able to use color words like *red* correctly. Similarly, a person not acquainted with the missing shade of blue of the example might be able to say true things about it. Rationalists would explain this by means of abstract ideas which are not available to Hume. Perhaps Hume should distinguish between correct verbal behavior and the ability to frame images. But then a Humean rejoinder might be that correct verbal usage requires knowledge of syntactical regularities that could be stated only by inductive inference from observed language samples. On the other hand, these regularities might be syntactical *conventions*, but the topic is too difficult to treat here.

9   (The following footnote is Hume's.) It is probable that no more was meant by those, who denied innate ideas, than that all ideas were copies of our impres-

sions; though it must be confessed, that the terms, which they employed, were not chosen with such caution, nor so exactly defined, as to prevent all mistakes about their doctrine. For what is meant by *innate?* If innate be equivalent to natural, then all the perceptions and ideas of the mind must be allowed to be innate or natural, in whatever sense we take the latter word, whether in opposition to what is uncommon, artificial, or miraculous. If by innate be meant, contemporary to our birth, the dispute seems to be frivolous; nor is it worth while to inquire at what time thinking begins, whether before, at, or after our birth. Again, the word *idea,* seems to be commonly taken in a very loose sense, by Locke and others; as standing for any of our perceptions, our sensations and passions, as well as thoughts. Now in this sense, I should desire to know, what can be meant by asserting, that self-love, or resentment of injuries, or the passion between the sexes is not innate?

By admitting these terms, *impressions* and *ideas,* in the sense above explained, and understanding by *innate,* what is original or copied from no precedent perception, then we may assert that all our impressions are innate and our ideas not innate.

To be ingenuous, I must own it to be my opinion, that Locke was betrayed into this question by the schoolmen, who, making use of undefined terms, draw out their disputes to a tedious length, without ever touching the point in question. A like ambiguity and circumlocution seem to run through that philosopher's reasonings on this as well as most other subjects.

10   (The following footnote is Hume's.) Resemblance.

11   (The following footnote is Hume's.) Contiguity.

12   (The following footnote is Hume's.) Cause and effect.

13   (The following footnote is Hume's.) For instance, *contrast* or *contrariety* is also a connection among ideas but it may, perhaps, be considered as a mixture of *causation* and *resemblance.* Where two objects are contrary, the one destroys the other; that is, the cause of its annihilation and the idea of the annihilation of an object implies the idea of its former existence.

14   The defensibility of this claim is considerably helped by the locution 'entirely new to him'. It is not clear what an entirely new object would be, or even if one could be noticed, unless we define it as an object whose causes and effects we could not discover, making the claim true by definition. What Hume is concerned to establish, however, seems to follow from the *surprising* causes and effects we come to discern in some new objects of experience.

15   To the scientifically trained reader, Hume's remarks about force and momentum will not make good sense, since his description of the formulas is not quite right when read in terms of present-day scientific vocabulary. His underlying point, that laws of motion were discovered experimentally, is entirely sound. There is, however, a problem in his remark that the discovery of the law owes *merely* to experience (see the next sentence), since experiment *suggested* the laws, historically, but experiment (because of error) must be conceptually simplified and analyzed if its results are to be equivalent to consequences of the relevant law. Further, once a law is adopted, it is not treated simply as a generalization from experience. For these topics, see Norwood Russell Hanson's *Patterns of Discovery,* Cambridge, 1958, and R. B. Braithwaite's *Scientific Explanation,* Cambridge, 1955.

16   Why does Hume say that he will *pretend* only to give a negative answer? Because he later proposes that consideration of custom or habit will enable a solution of the problem.

17   Epictetus and the Stoics believed that involvement in the affairs of others, or too much desire in pursuit of our own ends, was certain to end in failure, frustration, and unhappiness. This followed from their view that events were completely determined, and hence one could only accept what would happen anyway. Consequently they counseled diminution of desire as much as possible, and contemplation of the determined universe as a philosophical goal and as a means of avoiding unhappiness. Hume points out that consistently following Stoical principles is a form of selfishness (in so far as avoidance of personal unhappiness is a goal), and a kind of behavior that removes all chance of moral action.

18   How may a thousand instances all be the same as some one instance? Although it seems a natural principle that our belief in some regularity should increase as observed instances of it increase, the number of observed instances is not, in some cases, as important as the differences between the instances. If some number of instances widely varying in spatio-temporal location and other features all confirm some regularity, we may believe the regularity to hold more strongly than some regularity whose confirming instances are greater in number, but much more similar in terms of spatio-temporal location, etc. These features of the confirmation of a regularity by consideration of instances of it are not adequately treated by Hume.

19   (The following footnote is Hume's.) Nothing is more useful than for writers, even, on *moral, political,* or *physical* subjects, to distinguish between *reason* and *experience,* and to suppose, that these species of argumentation are entirely different from one another. The former are taken for the mere result of our intellectual faculties, which, by considering *a priori* the nature of things, and examining the effects, that must follow from their operation, establish particular principles of science and philosophy. The latter are supposed to be derived entirely from sense and observation, by which we learn what has actually resulted from the operation of particular objects, and are thence able to infer, what will, for the future, result from them. Thus, for instance, the limitations and restraints of civil government, and a legal constitution, may be defended, either from *reason,* which reflecting on the great frailty and corruption of human nature, teaches, that no man can safely be trusted with unlimited authority; or from *experience* and history, which inform us of the enormous abuses, that ambition, in every age and country, has been found to make of so imprudent a confidence.

    The same distinction between reason and experience is maintained in all our deliberations concerning the conduct of life; while the experienced statesman, general, physician, or merchant is trusted and followed; and the unpracticed novice, with whatever natural talents endowed, neglected and despised. Though it be allowed, that reason may form very plausible conjectures with regard to the consequences of such a particular conduct in such particular circumstances; it is still supposed imperfect, without the assistance of experience, which is alone able to give stability and certainty to the maxims, derived from study and reflection.

    But notwithstanding that this distinction be thus universally received, both in the active and speculative scenes of life, I shall not scruple to pronounce, that it is, at bottom, erroneous, at least, superficial.

If we examine those arguments, which, in any of the sciences above mentioned, are supposed to be the mere effects of reasoning and reflection, they will be found to terminate, at last, in some general principle or conclusion, for which we can assign no reason but observation and experience. The only difference between them and those maxims, which are vulgarly esteemed the result of pure experience, is, that the former cannot be established without some process of thought, and some reflection on what we have observed, in order to distinguish its circumstances, and trace its consequences: Whereas in the latter, the experienced event is exactly and fully familiar to that which we infer as the result of any particular situation. The history of a Tiberius or a Nero makes us dread a like tyranny, were our monarchs freed from the restraints of laws and senates. But the observation of any fraud or cruelty in private life is sufficient, with the aid of a little thought, to give us the same apprehension; while it serves as an instance of the general corruption of human nature, and shows us the danger which we must incur by reposing an entire confidence in mankind. In both cases, it is experience which is the foundation of our inference and conclusion.

There is no man so young and unexperienced, as not to have formed, from observation, many general and just maxims concerning human affairs and the conduct of life; but it must be confessed, that, when a man comes to put these in practice, he will be extremely liable to error, till time and farther experience both enlarge these maxims, and teach him their proper use and application. In every situation or incident, there are many particular and seemingly minute circumstances, which the man of greatest talent is, at first, apt to overlook, though on them the justness of his conclusions, and consequently the prudence of his conduct, entirely depend. Not to mention, that, to a young beginner, the general observations and maxims occur not always on the proper occasions, nor can be immediately applied with due calmness and distinction. The truth is, an unexperienced reasoner could be no reasoner at all, were he absolutely unexperienced; and when we assign that character to anyone, we mean it only in a comparative sense, and suppose him possessed of experience, in a smaller and more imperfect degree.

PART 6

Kant

(1724–1804)

Kant's Synthesis

It is time to reflect momentarily on the status of rationalism and empiricism as they have been developed by the philosophers we have studied to this point. This is true because the history of philosophy indicates that the corrosive effects of Hume's empirical skepticism, as well as the limitations of rationalism in accounting for scientific statements that were obviously to be considered part of human knowledge, but which apparently lacked the *certainty* or *necessity* of rationalistic knowledge, resulted in a temporary impasse for philosophical epistemologists after the publication of Hume's *Treatise*. If scientific knowledge is to be plausibly justified, it is apparent that neither rationalism nor empiricism, as they have been characterized so far, can accomplish the task. Our simplified versions of the philosophers we have studied have concealed tensions and problems indicated in their writings which yield the suspicion that most of the great philosophers at least *suspected* that difficulties would force abandonment of either program if it was developed with uncompromising rigor. In fact, the writings of most philosophers contain elements of both rationalism and empiricism, although the major attempts to construct complete theories of knowledge before Kant had been along either of the two incompatible lines that have previously been indicated. By the eighteenth century, problems of philosophical epistemology, coupled with two centuries of accumulating scientific success *in spite of* no sound philosophical justification for the commonsense procedures adopted by most scientists, made it clear that a new approach to epistemology would have to be tried. The next two philosophers that we shall study, Kant and Peirce, represent modified rationalistic and empiricistic epistemologies, respectively, in that they attempted to adapt sound features of rationalism and empiricism to the problem of developing a theory of knowledge that would justify burgeoning scientific theory. Although the problem of developing such a theory of knowledge will not be pursued into contemporary issues, we may note that there is a severe contemporary problem in that scientists in such areas as nuclear physics and astrophysics are now dealing with objects and distances so small or so large, that the commonsense methodological rules of the theories of knowledge of the past have turned out to be decidedly inadequate. Extrapolations from observations of objects with which we can deal easily because of their sizes and distances to submicroscopic and intergalactic events have proved spectacular failures. In quantum physics, scientists themselves are concerned with their methodological inability to choose between conflicting interpretations of submicroscopic events. In astronomical theory, they are concerned with their inability to choose between steady-state and evolutionary theories of the universe. These controversies have led some scientists to realize that problems of justifying methodology are not simply a philosopher's pastime, in that normative methodological problems may be encountered in scientific theorizing at very crucial moments. To some extent, this has resulted in a *rapprochement* between philosophers concerned with justifying current scientific knowledge in terms of some epistemology, and those scientists concerned with improving their understanding of the ways in which methodology may be justified.

An obvious approach to the difficulty suggested above, that both rationalism and empiricism are inadequate, is to try to *combine* them. We might suppose that we could *synthesize* rationalism and empiricism by accepting a rationalistic epistemology to justify the mathematical knowledge required by science, and an empiricistic epistemology to explain scientific observations. Kant's importance to the history of philosophy was in seeing that a profoundly *new* methodology was required, not merely a combination of the two older ones. It is true that Kant speaks of his philosophy as a synthesis of rationalism and empiricism, but this does not indicate that scientific knowledge consists of bits and pieces each of which can be accounted for either in terms of pre-Kantian rationalism or of pre-Kantian empiricism. Kant's point is that all important instances of scientific knowledge are the result of observation *and* thought, empiricistic *and* rationalistic elements, *neither of which is intelligible without the other.* In a way, this may remind you of Aristotle's position, to which Kant owes some historical indebtedness. But where Aristotle took *experience* to be analyzable into material and formal aspects, and hence into empiricistic and rationalistic components, Kant took the different position that no observation could make *sense* or be *meaningful* unless prior thought not based on experience is presupposed. Instead of analyzing *primitive* experience into differing empiricistic and rationalistic components, Kant takes experience to be what it is because of the way we interpret it by means of the concepts that we bring to our experiences. Our experimental experiences do not simply exhibit order; they are orderly because we look for the order in them. We can *understand* them only by means of a prior conceptual framework which is built up out of a mental comprehension of order. We may take this conception of an interaction between experience and thought to be Kant's major contribution to epistemology. Kant's position is here taken to be a modified rationalism rather than a modified empiricism because he holds that the prior concepts we bring to experience may have the certainty and necessity that rationalists before him had attributed to what they called *knowledge*.

Kant's notion of an experience is considerably more complex than the notion of an experience which the empiricists before him had used. If we consider the illustration of two men standing in front of a painting, we have seen that there is a sense in which they can both be said to see_1 the same thing, but another sense in which they see_2 quite different things. Empiricism before Kant had a tendency to make sense perceptions like $seeing_1$ the foundation of human knowledge. This foundation was a kind of lowest common denominator of sense perception. The difficulty in this view was that the empiricist was then required to explain $seeing_2$ differences in terms of other sense experiences. As we have seen, this problem proves difficult in view of the commonsense observation that three people, A, B, and C, may be such that A and B see_2 something more similarly than A and C or B and C, even though the $seeing_1$ histories of A and C are more similar than the $seeing_1$ histories of A and B or B and C. This may be true if A and C are identical twins brought up in a similar environment while B is a stranger to both. The problem of accounting for differences in $seeing_2$ experiences proves refractory for empiricism. On the other hand, by making the foundation of scientific knowledge $seeing_2$ sense experiences and perceptions like it, Kant eliminates this difficulty while gaining the advantage of making his account fit our common observation that a trained observer and a tyro are said to be different because they *see* things differently. But these advantages are purchased at the cost of making perception a rationalistic experience that can no longer serve as an empirical primitive notion since perception now essentially involves, not just sense experience, but knowledge gained through judgment which is based on concepts developed prior to sense experiences.

To see how Kant took experience to be shaped by prior concepts, we may consider the problem of individuation. A general method for answering problems of individuation must enable us to tell in any case whether or not x and y (construed as two names or descriptions of objects) refer to the same individual object or not. Strictly speaking, it would appear that empiricism must hold that x and y refer to the same individual if and only if x and y may be analyzed as standing for the same tastes, colors, and so forth. According to Kant, this method is defective. Two objects might have all their empirically sensed properties so similar as to be indistinguishable, yet they might clearly be *different* objects because they occupied different spatial or temporal regions. Kant held that the two conditions, space and time, were necessary for individuating all objects of experience, and yet empiricists had never provided a way of directly experiencing a difference in space or in time. Since empiricists had provided no adequate justification for space and time as they are used in science (this seems largely true as an historical observation), and as many previous philosophers (some rationalists) had not included space and time as part of the complete description of objects, Kant's analysis of the importance of adequate concepts of space and time is a valuable insight. Kant's view is that space and time are not seen or heard like other empirical properties, and he holds that they are not abstracted from immediate sense experiences; he contends instead that immediate sense experience would be meaningless unless space and time are presupposed to be known in immediate sense experience. We do not see space or time, we see things in space and time. We could not, in fact, imagine what it would be like to see something that was not in space and time. This indicates that we must know space and time prior to experiencing objects in them.

Kant employs a distinction between the form and matter of experienced objects which is derived from the Aristotelian analysis. The matter of an object of experience is whatever appearances sense experience presents to the mind. The matter of an experience is thus its highly variable sensual content. Space and time, being present in every such experience in that we cannot experience or imagine objects without assigning them a location in space and time (Be careful! This means that although we may not imagine centaurs as living in some place and at some time, we cannot imagine a centaur as taking up *no* space or time.), are the *form* of sensed objects. Although any specified sense property may be *missing* in a given sense experience, *all* sense experiences have spatial and temporal properties. An observation of nothing but a uniform red field and an observation of nothing but a blue field would have the same spatial *form*, but different empirical content or matter.

Space is what Kant calls the form of outer intuitions, time the form of inner intuitions. *Intuition* is used here in a sense quite different than the sense suggested earlier in defining *rationalism*. *Intuition* was used in that connection to refer to the faculty invoked by rationalists to account for *certain* knowledge about non-sense-experienced objects. Kant uses *intuition* as almost synonymous with *sensation*, in that it suggests an immediate awareness of something. But it must also be observed that what Kant calls *empirical intuition* corresponds more strictly to *sensation*, since Kant held that we can have *pure intuitions* (immediate awarenesses) of the a priori particulars space and time.

Kantian space cannot be a concept abstracted from experience for a variety of reasons. Indeed, as we ordinarily say that we experience objects as outside us, Kant argues that this notion itself would not be possible unless a distinction between *outer* and *inner*, i.e., a *spatial* distinction, were itself presupposed. Kant further suggests that space cannot be abstracted from objects and the relations between objects because we can represent to ourselves space as empty of all objects. This argument appeals to introspection in that it holds that we can consistently conceive of empty space. It is correspondingly open to the usual arguments against introspective proof.

According to Kant, we know space by a *pure intuition* as a kind of object. Kant argues that space is a kind of object or particular on the grounds that there is only *one* space, and that when one speaks of diverse spaces, different parts of space is all that can be meant. Space is thus not a property of things but our manner of experiencing them. Similar arguments purport to show that time is presupposed in experience (in all experience, since temporal succession is perceived in inner experiences as well as outer), and that it is an object of pure intuition. We may then take space and time to be presupposed in perception. Kant's view that space and time are presupposed in perception needs modification in that some views that he took to be *indubitable* with respect to space and time as well as consequences of these views would have to be modified in the light of more recent mathematical and scientific views of space and time, particularly the theory of space-time of relativity, in which space and time are not so neatly separable as they are on the commonsense view.

A problem for Kantian epistemology is raised by consideration of Berkeley's point that a theory of knowledge must account for the knowledge of children who are able to know the relevant area of knowledge in that they can apparently use it. This raises some question as to what it may mean to say that space and time are presupposed in perception, since knowledge of space and time may not be held in any straightforward sense by many human beings who seem able to make accurate reports of their other perceptions. Kant replied to this by supposing that commonsense space and time underlie ordinary perceptions. The difficulty with this reply is that the necessity that Kant takes to characterize some judgments about space and time are not necessary for commonsense notions of space and time, since scientific research and theorizing occasionally change the nature of our commonsense conceptions about space and time. This is exactly what has happened since Kant, making the *necessity* of the propositions about Euclidean space, as they are characterized in Kant's philosophy, extremely dubious. In any current version of the Kantian system the various *spaces* considered by scientists would have to be allowed for by some revision of Kant's notion of *necessity* for geometrical propositions.

To this point, we have seen that what Kant calls sensibility or intuition he regards as a faculty of humans to apprehend particular objects as given in space and time. The matter of these apprehensions is given by empirical intuition of the sensible appearances of things. Sensibility, then, provides us with perceptions. But perceptions do not constitute knowledge. Even the pure intuition of space and time (which contains no sensible element) does not give us scientific knowledge. Knowledge arises when *judgments* about sense objects as given in space and time are made by the *understanding,* a distinct faculty of human beings, which provides knowledge through objects which are *thought,* by means of the concepts used to think them. To see what this means, we must examine Kant's analysis of *judgment,* which had great impact on the rationalistic philosophers who followed him.

The Synthetic A Priori

The central concept involved in grasping Kant's theory of judgment is his twofold classification of judgments into a priori–a posteriori and analytic-synthetic dichotomies. Any subject-predicate proposition asserted by someone which fits into these classifications may be considered a judgment, and all judgments may be analyzed in terms of these classifications.

Judgments are a priori if and only if they are absolutely independent of all experience. We have had examples of such judgments in the case of mathematical statements whose truth or falsity is independent of experience because these mathematical statements are not about experienced objects. The independence involved is logical independence. In order to make statements about truths of mathematics, we must have had enough experience to have mastered a language capable of handling these statements, but this is not what is in question. As we have seen in connection with Plato, no statement or set of statements about experienced objects can contradict a statement about mathematical objects. On the other hand, if a judgment may be contradicted by statements about experienced objects, that judgment is a posteriori. Kant gives necessary and sufficient conditions for a judgment to be a priori. If a judgment is thought as *necessary*, or if a judgment is thought as *universal,* then the judgment is a priori. The converse cases hold also. Now it is not clear what the distinction between *necessary* and *universal* is in this connection: they both seem to suggest, in qualifying an argument, that the judgment can have no exceptions. This criterion, it should be noted, is rationalistic in that its basis is whether or not exceptions to a judgment can be *thought.*

The other dichotomy of judgments involves a relationship between the subject and predicate of the judgment. Either the predicate is *contained* in the subject concept, or it is not. In the former case, the judgment is said to be analytic; otherwise it is said to be synthetic. There are a number of restatements of this definition in terms other than those of containment. We might say that if an analysis of the subject term of a judg-

223

ment can break it down into parts, one of which is the predicate, then the judgment is analytic, so that an analytic judgment has a relationship of identity holding between some part of the subject and the predicate. It should be remembered that "7 + 5 = 12" is explicitly cited as *synthetic,* not analytic, and that the requisite notion of identity is thus a problem for considerably greater analysis than Kant provides. The notion that seems to be at stake here is the notion of informativeness. A synthetic judgment is one that tells us something new, or informative, about the relationship between its subject and its predicate. An analytic judgment, since the relationship is always one of containment, is uninformative, save that it may enable us to note clearly that some such relationship is trivial, where we had mistakenly thought it to be of some informative importance.

The two dichotomies, if they are *distinct,* give rise to four possible forms of judgment: analytic a priori judgment, synthetic a priori judgment, analytic a posteriori judgment, and synthetic a posteriori judgment. No judgments would be considered analytic a posteriori judgments. An a posteriori judgment is dependent on experience, and hence gives us information, which an analytic judgment, being uninformative, does not. Synthetic a posteriori judgments are simply informative judgments about concepts derived from experienced objects which may be proved false by future experience. None of these judgments constitutes certain knowledge in the older rationalistic sense, since they rest upon experience and are to some extent problematic. On the other hand, the triviality of analytic a priori judgments, although they are certain, insures that they cannot give us knowledge, or add to what we already know. Knowledge, for Kant, consists primarily of synthetic a priori judgments, which are informative because they are synthetic, yet certain because they are a priori and cannot be contradicted by experience. The importance of synthetic a priori judgments in their role of principles of scientific and mathematical knowledge constitutes one of the claims upon which the adequacy of Kantian philosophy must be taken to rest.

What judgments are to be found among the synthetic a priori judgments? Synthetic a priori judgments are found in mathematics, natural science, legitimate metaphysics, and ethical theory, according to Kant's total philosophy, but only the first two cases concern us here. Except for certain analytic a priori statements of logic ($a = a$), Kant took all of the statements of mathematics to be synthetic a priori judgments. "7 + 5 = 12," for example, is both necessary (a priori) and yet synthetic, since Kant felt that the concept of putting seven and five together expressed by '7 + 5' was not equivalent to the concept of the number twelve. In addition, Kant took all of the principles on which he thought scientific laws to depend as synthetic a priori judgments, notably the statement of the causal principle "All alterations occur in accordance with the law of the connexion of cause and effect."

There are three traditional objections to Kant's definition and discussion of synthetic a priori judgments. To begin with, he does not *prove* that there are synthetic a priori judgments; he *assumes* that certain mathematical and scientific statments are both informative and necessary, and then proceeds to the problem of discussing how we come to form such judgments on the supposition that we do form them. By adopting such a procedure, Kant does not *refute* Humean skepticism; he simply begins by taking it to be a false or misleading basis for justifying those mathematical and scientific statements that common sense takes to be necessary. Kant takes Hume's failure to find this necessity in anything but custom a consequence of his incorrect epistemology. This objection to Kant, that he begins by assuming the existence of synthetic a priori knowledge, is not crushing since most philosophers take their epistemological question to be that of justifying what they initially take to constitute human knowledge. And a good case can be made that mathematical statements are not trivial. While "$7 + 5 = 12$" may strike us as so obvious as to be uninformative, so that Kant's position that it is synthetic seems mistaken, one can see that "$512,367 + 31,274 = 543,641$" is hardly obvious to the person who has not been trained in rapid addition.

The other philosophical objections are that the notion of containment used in defining analytic judgments is vague, and that Kant's dependence on the subject-predicate form of proposition led him astray. While both of these objections hold against Kant's formulations, the question is really one of whether these formulations might be improved so as to avoid these objections. Containment is vague because although we may speak of one box *containing* another and understand what this means, subjects and predicates or subject and predicate concepts are not physical objects to which this paradigm case of containment may apply. At the same time, the statement "If $a < b$, then $b > a$." is presumably *a priori*, and yet it does not have subject-predicate form. A great deal of effort has been expended by philosophers after Kant in an attempt to find some formulation of the a priori–a posteriori, analytic-synthetic dichotomies that is not open to objections of this kind.

There is, however, a further objection that deserves some close scrutiny. This objection is a variant of the historical argument against rationalism, namely, that Kant's assurance about the *necessity* of much of his scheme has been proved premature in the light of later scientific and mathematical developments. Kant believed that he had found a *complete* list of synthetic a priori judgments in the sense that he believed that all of the synthetic a priori judgments necessary for a justification of scientific knowledge could be deduced from his list. In view of the fact that Kant's list could be considered adequate for developing Newtonian physics, but not for contemporary nuclear physics or relativity theory, this belief is mistaken. Further, the Kantian position that Euclidean geometry is the only accurate description of space was proved wrong with the discovery of non-Euclidean geometries in the nineteenth century. Indeed, this is a special case of the remark made above, in that Newtonian physics is usually taken to presuppose a Euclidean geometry assigning space zero curvature, while relativity theory is usually taken to presuppose a Riemannian geometry assigning space positive curvature. The point of these remarks is that inability to conceive failure of universality cannot be taken by itself as a reliable index that some judgment is a priori, or synthetic a priori, if a criterion for being a synthetic judgment is added to it.

The supposition that there are synthetic a priori judgments, and that they constitute some kind of necessary knowledge, is reasonably distinctive of modified rationalism after Kant. Modified empiricists, as we shall see, take the position that the analytic-synthetic, a priori–a posteriori dichotomies divide all judgments or statements the same way, so that they are really two versions of the same principle of division. On this view, in connection with which the analytic-synthetic vocabulary is most often employed, synthetic statements are both informative and about the objects of experience. Analytic statements are then construed as statements which are immune to falsification by confrontation with true statements about experience. Analytic statements are adopted by convention to provide a convenient framework for organizing the information expressed in synthetic statements. Kant's classification of synthetic a priori judgments is then emptied into these two groups. The most important are the mathematical statements. They are interpreted by later empiricists as analytic. Most of the rest of the judgments that Kant took to be synthetic a priori are then declared to be either synthetic and hence not necessary, or meaningless, in which case they are dropped from the consideration of philosophers. In this connection, it should be noted that Kant did not create the analytic-synthetic distinction. There are foreshadowings of it in earlier philosophers, for example, in Hume's distinction between relations of ideas and matters of fact, even though Hume's treatment of this distinction construed as an insight into the analytic-synthetic distinction is quite cursory. Kant's importance to the history of philosophy was to attempt a rigorous treatment of the distinction, as well as to indicate a way in which it need not be construed as giving empiricists an impregnable position from which they could pass off the claims of the rationalists to certain knowledge as complete nonsense.

The Transcendental Deduction

From what has been said to this point, it should be obvious that Kant makes a good case for both intuition (sensibility) and understanding as contributing to our stock of knowledge, largely because of difficulties with the empiricist point of view. It may be nearly as obvious that the major difficulty in Kant's program is to provide a satisfactory account of how the intuition and the understanding influence one another.

Since synthetic a posteriori judgments are not necessary, the inter-action between intuition and the understanding must obviously be some way in which the active understanding operates upon the results of intui-tion. This operation is one of judgment. The understanding, by means of a priori concepts, is able to make judgments on the basis of the perceptions which intuition provides.

These judgments may be made clearer by considering the difference between perceptual judgments (or subjective empirical judgments) and objective empirical judgments. The difference between these two judg-ments is illustrated by the difference in force between "This shirt seems to be red." and "This shirt is red.". A perceptual judgment is a judgment which, if true, is true for some observer by virtue of some relation between intuitions which he has had. On the other hand, an objective empirical judgment is about some object, and it does not mention, either explicitly or implicitly, any special observer of this object. If an objective empirical judgment is true, it is true for everybody.

Kant does not question the existence of objective empirical judg-ments. We make them, and some of them must be true. After taking the existence of these judgments as an obvious fact, Kant takes his problem to be that of explaining the objectivity of these judgments. In other words, Kant takes the problem to be that of explaining where objective empirical judgments get their objective reference and general validity.

Assuming the legitimacy of objective empirical judgments has far-reaching consequences for Kant's epistemology. Since objective empirical judgments are about objects which have properties that one cannot experience, the assumption seems to generate a world of objects much like the assumption of a material world against which Berkeley had violently argued. But instead of taking the disastrous position (as Hylas did in the *Dialogues*) that these objects can be directly known or experienced, Kant takes a position compatible with Berkeley's strictures on this point by denying that we can have sensible knowledge of these things-in-themselves. Indeed, we may take Berkeley and Kant to agree that if there are material objects, they cannot be the objects of sense-experiential knowledge. But where Berkeley construed the notion of *material object* to be that of an *unperceived* object, and hence a contradictory notion, Kant construed *material object* to be something that, if it did exist, could not be known as it was through human perception because of the interaction between the human perceptual apparatus and the object perceived. Berkeley supposed any apparent order in the world could be accounted for by regular sequences of ideas. But Kant felt that there were more regular sequences in experience than Berkeley's theory could account for. Kant would agree with Berkeley's strictures against an assumption of material bodies on an epistemological basis of passively received ideas that are organized in fairly mechanical ways by the mind. But Kant further argues that this account of human nature is too poor; when an *active* mind is coupled with sense experience, however, we may rationally suppose that there may be legitimate grounds for the assertion of objective empirical judgments.

In a procedure reminiscent of certain analyses of Aristotle, Kant tries to list all the *forms* of objective empirical judgments. He felt, in fact, that he had produced a complete list. The *form* of an objective empirical judgment, say "This shirt is red.", constitutes such features as that it is affirmative, about a particular object, etc., and hence has the same form as the judgment "This book is blue.".

Suppose we take any particular objective empirical judgment and consider its form. We might also consider any perceptual judgment of the same form except that the words 'it seems to me' are added. For example, "This shirt is red." and "This shirt is red—it seems to me." might be the subject of comparison. In the second judgment, the words 'it seems to me' subtract somewhat from the force of "This shirt is red.". We might well ask exactly what is subtracted. In the subjective empirical judgment we are referring only to certain sense impressions—and suggesting that there might be an actual red shirt which accounts for them. The objective empirical judgment is that there is a shirt in which the property redness inheres. Kant supposes that the application of the a priori category of substance with qualities inhering constitutes the difference between a subjective empirical judgment and an objective empirical judgment. To each of the forms of objective empirical judgment, therefore, one may relate an a priori concept which Kant calls a category (in obvious reference to the Aristotelian term), the application of which accounts for the objective reference and general validity of the related judgment. When the category is not applied, only subjective empirical judgments can be made. One of these categories, incidentally, is cause and effect, and by its application Kant thought that he had avoided the subjectivism of Hume's analysis.

We may take our everyday use of objective empirical judgments to prove that they are in fact made. The Kantian analysis of the ground of such judgments in terms of the categories suggests that we do in fact apply the categories to our experiences in judgments. An obvious question, which Kant faces next, is whether or not the categories may be *legitimately* employed in this way. Kant's attempt to show that they may be legitimately employed is called the *Transcendental Deduction of the Pure Concepts of the Understanding.* 'The Pure Concepts of the Understanding' are simply the categories. *Transcendental* indicates that the use of the categories is to be justified for *every* area of human knowledge, not by means of sense experience, but by the means of showing that unless the Pure Concepts of the Understanding and their application is presupposed, sense experiences and the synthetic empirical judgments of science would not be possible. By a deduction, Kant means a justification, not a formally valid deductive argument.

Now the objects mentioned in an objective empirical judgment are not *generalizations* from experience, even though experience yields information about them. They are thus objects which are *thought*, and the real problem of the Transcendental Deduction may be taken to be that of showing that the applicability of the categories is a necessary condition of any objective experience of objects in so far as they are experienceable. Because of this the Transcendental Deduction contains considerable probing into the nature of thought, probing which at times becomes extremely complicated and somewhat obscure.

Suppose we take all the sense impressions available to us at any time. Some of these impressions we put together according to certain synthetic a priori rules in order to obtain an impression of an object. We may thus put together in terms of such a rule some color, a place, etc., and call it a shirt. The empiricists had held that we do this because certain impressions repeatedly occur together. But so many impressions are available to us that Kant supposes that we must have some way of unifying certain impressions independently of repeated association. It is clear that repeated association can lead us into error. If we had experienced only brown dogs up to a point, we might erroneously conclude that all dogs are brown. We do ascribe unity to groups of sense impressions and even to all our sense impressions (they are *our* sense impressions). This unity is an act of the understanding which synthesizes our impressions. That the unity of impressions must be due to the understanding follows from the passive character of sense intuition. We may call this unity *synthesis*, to signify that it is the synthetic connection of impressions into a unified representation which has been synthesized according to a rule of thought.

A unified manifold (field) of sense impressions suggests that a unified subject experiences it. The reason for this is that a unified manifold would otherwise exist which is not related to any understanding. But understanding is a necessary condition of unifying. Grasp by some understanding of a unified manifold of sense impressions is what Kant calls pure apperception, to contrast it with the contingent and uncertain self-awareness which may accompany some impressions, such as pain. This position reflects the general Kantian position of interdependence between mind and perception.

Knowledge of an object is then the consistent judgment that a category is applicable to the object synthesized out of various impressions. An unperceived object, for example, a unicorn, cannot be known because the empirical element is absent. The total argument shows that the knowledge of objects presupposes a unified understanding which employs categories to make objective judgments about synthesized impressions. Both the concepts (for the judgments) and the impressions (to be synthesized) must occur prior to knowledge. A full analysis of objective empirical judgments requires attention to some problems, of which we shall mention one. Kant's critique of the empiricistic view of the role of mind in knowledge is impressive, and at the very least it shows that some active or spontaneous mental activity seems to be required to explain the recognition of natural regularities. Still, it does not follow logically from this that the regularities are *manufactured* by this mental activity, which Kant comes close to accepting. Perhaps no reasonable alternative is available, but Kant's development is not entirely persuasive. An interesting problem for Kantian philosophy is that of explaining the similarity of categories which all minds develop. Some philosophers have attempted to explain this similarity in terms of physiological resemblances between human brains, but this seems to make the a priori concepts too arbitrary in that we could imagine that alternative physiological structures exist; but on the Kantian view we cannot imagine that alternative a priori concepts could exist. The Kantians, of course, are free to assume a similarity in the conceptual apparatus of different human beings, but non-Kantians who desire conversion may well ask for some account of it that is not explicitly available in Kant's treatment.

Readings from Kant

The obscurity of Kant's German prose is legendary. It may safely be said that of the seven philosophers discussed in this book, it is most difficult to support claims made for Kant's philosophy because of the fact that it is so difficult to find unambiguous texts supporting these claims. Even where this seems possible, it is not always possible to find texts that do not clash with texts that appear elsewhere.

As with Hume's *Treatise* and *Enquiry*, one is again confronted with a major epistemological work (the *Critique of Pure Reason*) and a more easily read introduction to it (the *Prolegomena to Any Future Metaphysics*). The interpretive situation discussed in connection with Hume's *Treatise* and *Enquiry* arises again because of the fact that the *Critique* (1781) was written before the *Prolegomena* (1783). But in this case there is a very important revision of the *Critique* which incorporates extensive changes over the first edition that appears four years after the publication of the *Prolegomena*. It thus seems possible to suppose that by comparing the two editions of the *Critique* with the *Prolegomena* we can ferret out Kant's *maturest* epistemological positions.

Unfortunately, it is not easy to *introduce* Kant through his maturest positions because of their difficulty. In many cases, the arguments of the *Prolegomena* are clear and convincing without being the arguments that Kant saw fit to accept as the foundation of his philosophy in the second edition of the *Critique*. For example, the distinction between subjective and objective empirical judgments which is discussed in the chapters on Kant and in the *Prolegomena* as an argument for the necessity of the application of the Pure Concepts of the Understanding to provide an epistemology adequate for justifying scientific knowledge is not presented as an explicit argument in the second edition of the *Critique*. Similarly, the arguments for the existence of things-in-themselves as material objects not known to us in perception as they really are, which are presented in the *Prolegomena*, do not occur in the Second Analogy of the second edition

231

of the *Critique*, where one might expect to find them. For these reasons, it is exceptionally difficult to select readings from Kant which are both introductory and yet representative of the epistemological reasoning that has made him such an important figure in the Western philosophical tradition.

The readings attempt to present a crucial early line of reasoning from the *Prolegomena* which is obviously one of the major *insights* into the critical philosophy that Kant formulated. In addition, they present some passages from the *second* edition of the *Critique of Pure Reason* which exhibit some of the Kantian positions that have already been discussed. Marginal notations such as 'B 9' in the selections from the *Critique* refer to the fact that the material in the text is the translation of the 9th paragraph of the second edition of the *Critique*. 'A 9' is used by scholars to refer to the ninth paragraph of the first edition.

Very little has been said in these notes about the editions of the works of the philosophers being considered. This information is not as important for the other six philosophers as it is for Kant. There are many fine editions of Plato's various dialogues, for example, and the student may be reasonably sure that recent editions that he finds in the library contain at least defensible translations from the Greek. This is not true for Kant's works. Because of the convolutions and obscurities of Kant's style, good English translations of his German that are philosophically defensible have not appeared until relatively recently, when the translations have been undertaken by men such as Professor Beck and Professor Kemp Smith, who have been able to make sound judgments of the philosophical importance and consistency of the translated material.

The Kant selections consist of the following passages:

A. Sections 17, 18, 19, and 20 of the Second Part of the Main Transcendental Problem from the *Prolegomena to Any Future Metaphysics*. From Immanuel Kant: *Prolegomena to Any Future Metaphysics*, translated by Lewis White Beck, copyright 1951 by the Liberal Arts Press, Inc., reprinted by permission of the Liberal Arts Press Division of the Bobbs-Merrill Company, Inc.

B. Sections I through V and part of VI of the Introduction to the second edition of the *Critique of Pure Reason*.

C. Section I of Chapter I of the Analytic of Concepts from the second edition of the *Critique of Pure Reason*.

D. Chapter II of the Analytic of Concepts from the second edition of the *Critique of Pure Reason*.

E. Part 22 of section 2 of the Deduction of the Pure Concepts of the Understanding from the second edition of the *Critique of Pure Reason*.

F. Parts 26 and 27 of section 2 of the Deduction of the Pure Concepts of the Understanding from the second edition of the *Critique of Pure Reason*.

Selections *B* through *F* are reprinted from Immanuel Kant's *Critique of Pure Reason*, translated by Norman Kemp Smith. Reprint rights have been given by kind permission of Macmillan and Company, Ltd., and St Martin's Press, Inc.

The secondary source material for Kant's philosophy is very extensive. There is, in fact, a journal (*Kant-Studien*) devoted exclusively to the study of Kant's philosophy. A few recent secondary sources which discuss in some detail the arguments of the *Critique of Pure Reason* and the *Prolegomena* are all that will be listed here.

Bird, Graham: *Kant's Theory of Knowledge*, New York, 1962.

Cassirer, H. W.: *Kant's First Critique*, London, 1954.

Ewing, A. C.: *A Short Commentary on Kant's Critique of Pure Reason*, Chicago, 1950.

*Körner, S.: *Kant*, Harmondsworth, 1955. (Pelican Paperbound.)

Paton, H. J.: *Kant's Metaphysic of Experience*, 2 vol., New York, 1936.

Smith, A. H.: *Kantian Studies*, Oxford, 1947.

Smith, N. K.: *A Commentary to Kant's 'Critique of Pure Reason,'* 2d ed., New York, 1962.

Weldon, T. D.: *Kant's Critique of Pure Reason*, 2d ed., Oxford, 1958.

Wolff, R. P.: *Kant's Theory of Mental Activity*, Cambridge, 1963.

A From the PROLEGOMENA

§ 17. The formal aspect of nature in this narrower sense is therefore the conformity to law of all the objects of experience and, so far as it is known *a priori*, their *necessary* conformity. But it has just been shown that the laws of nature can never be known *a priori* in objects so far as they are considered, not in reference to possible experience, but as things in themselves. And our inquiry here extends, not to things in themselves (the properties of which we pass by), but to things as objects of possible experience, and the complex of these is what we here properly designate as nature. And now I ask, when the possibility of knowledge of nature *a priori* is in question, whether it is better to arrange the problem thus: "How can we know *a priori* that things as objects of experience necessarily conform to law?" or thus: "How is it possible to know *a priori* the necessary conformity to law of experience itself as regards all its objects generally?"

Closely considered, the solution of the problem represented in either way amounts, with regard to the pure knowledge of nature (which is the point of the question at issue), entirely to the same thing. For the subjective laws, under which alone an empirical knowledge of things is possible, hold good of these things as objects of possible experience (not as things in themselves, which are not considered here). It is all the same whether I say: "A judgment of perception can never rank as experience without the law that, whenever an event is observed, it is always referred to some antecedent, which it follows according to a universal rule," or: "Everything of which experience teaches that it happens must have a cause."

It is, however, more suitable to choose the first formula. For we can a priori and prior to all given objects have a knowledge of those conditions on which alone experience of them is possible, but never of the laws to which things may in themselves be subject, without reference to possible experience. We cannot, therefore, study the nature of things a priori otherwise than by investigating the conditions and the universal (though subjective) laws, under which alone such a cognition as experience (as to mere form) is possible, and we determine accordingly the possibility of things as objects of experience. For if I should choose the second formula and seek the a priori conditions under which nature as an object of experience is possible, I might easily fall into error and fancy that I was speaking of nature as a thing in itself, and then move round in endless circles, in a vain search for laws concerning things of which nothing is given me.

Accordingly, we shall here be concerned with experience only and the universal conditions of its possibility, which are given a priori. Thence we shall define nature as the whole object of all possible experience. I think it will be understood that I here do not mean the rules of the observation of a nature that is already given, for these already presuppose experience. Thus I do not mean how (through experience) we can study the laws of nature, for these would not then be laws a priori and would yield us no pure science of nature; but [I mean to ask] how the conditions a priori of the possibility of experience are at the same time the sources from which all universal laws of nature must be derived.

§ 18. In the first place we must state that, while all judgments of experience are empirical (that is, have their ground in immediate sense-perception), all empirical judgments are not judgments of experience; but, besides the empirical, and in general besides what is given to the sensuous intuition, special concepts must yet be superadded—concepts which have their origin wholly a priori in the pure understanding, and under which every perception must be first of all subsumed and then by their means changed into experience.

Empirical judgments, so far as they have objective validity, are judgments of experience, but those which are only subjectively valid I name mere judgments of perception. The latter require no pure concept of the understanding, but only the logical connection of perception in a thinking subject. But the former always require, besides the representation of the sensuous intuition, special concepts originally begotten in the understanding, which make possible the objective validity of the judgment of experience.

All our judgments are at first merely judgments of perception; they hold good only for us (that is, for our subject) and we do not till afterward give them a new reference (to an object) and desire that they shall always hold good for us and in the same way for everybody else; for when a judgment agrees with an object, all judgments concerning the same object must likewise agree among themselves, and thus the objective validity of the judgment of experience signifies nothing else than its necessary universal validity. And conversely when we have ground for considering a judgment as necessarily having universal validity (which never depends upon perception, but upon the pure concept of the understanding under which the perception is subsumed), we must consider that it is objective also—that is, that it expresses not merely a reference of our perception to a subject, but a characteristic of the object. For there would be no reason for the judgments of other men necessarily agreeing with mine if it were not the unity of the object to which they all refer and with which they accord; hence they must all agree with one another.

§ 19. Therefore objective validity and necessary universality (for everybody) are equivalent terms, and though we do not know the object in itself, yet when we consider a judgment as universal, and hence necessary, we thereby understand it to have objective validity. By this judgment we know the object (though it remains unknown as it is in itself) by the universal and necessary connection of the given perceptions. As this is the case with all objects of sense, judgments of experience take their objective validity, not from the immediate knowledge of the object (which is impossible), but from the condition of universal validity of empirical judgments, which, as already said, never rests upon empirical or, in short, sensuous conditions, but upon a pure concept of the understanding. The object in itself always remains unknown; but when by the concept of the understanding the connection of the representations of the object, which it gives to our sensibility, is determined as universally valid, the object is determined by this relation, and the judgment is objective.

To illustrate the matter: when we say, "The room is warm, sugar sweet, and wormwood bitter," we have only subjectively valid judgments. I do not at all expect that I or any other person shall always find it as I now do; each of these sentences only expresses a relation of two sensations to the same subject, that is, myself, and that only in my present state of perception; consequently they are not valid of the object. Such are judgments of perception. Judgments of experience are of quite a different nature. What experience teaches me under certain circumstances, it must always teach me and everybody; and its validity is not limited to the subject nor to its state at a particular time. Hence I pronounce all such judgments objectively valid. For instance, when I say the air is elastic, this judgment is as yet a judgment of perception only; I do nothing but refer two of my sensations to each other. But if I would have it called a judgment of experience, I require this connection to stand under a condition which makes it universally valid. I desire therefore that I and everybody else should always connect necessarily the same perceptions under the same circumstances.

§ 20. We must consequently analyze experience in general in order to see what is contained in this product of the senses and of the under-standing, and how the judgment of experience itself is possible. The foundation is the intuition of which I become conscious, that is, percep-tion (*perceptio*), which pertains merely to the senses. But in the next place, there is judging (which belongs only to the understanding). But this judging may be twofold: first, I may merely compare perceptions and connect them in a consciousness of my particular state; or, secondly, I may connect them in consciousness in general. The former judgment is merely a judgment of perception, and hence is of subjective validity only; it is merely a con-nection of perceptions in my mental state, without reference to the object. Hence it does not, as is commonly imagined, suffice for experience that perceptions are compared and connected in consciousness through judg-ment; thence arises no universal validity and necessity by virtue of which alone consciousness can be objectively valid, that is, can be called ex-perience.

Quite another judgment therefore is required before perception can become experience. The given intuition must be subsumed under a concept which determines the form of judging in general relatively to the intuition, connects empirical consciousness of intuition in consciousness in general, and thereby procures universal validity for empirical judgments. A concept of this nature is a pure *a priori* concept of the understanding, which does nothing but determine for an intuition the general way in which it can be used for judgments. Let the concept be that of cause; then it determines the intuition which is subsumed under it, for example, that of air, relative to judging in general—namely, the concept of air in respect to its expan-sion serves in the relation of antecedent to consequent in a hypothetical judgment. The concept of cause accordingly is a pure concept of the under-standing, which is totally disparate from all possible perception and only serves to determine the representation subsumed under it, with respect to judging in general, and so to make a universally valid judgment possible.

Before, therefore, a judgment of perception can become a judgment of experience, it is requisite that the perception should be subsumed under some such concept of the understanding; for instance, air belongs under the concept of cause, which determines our judgment about it in respect to its expansion as hypothetical. Thereby the expansion of the air is repre-sented, not as merely belonging to the perception of the air in my present state or in several states of mine, or in the perceptual state of others, but as belonging to it necessarily. The judgment, "Air is elastic," becomes universally valid and a judgment of experience only because certain judgments precede it which subsume the intuition of air under the concept of cause and effect; and they thereby determine the perceptions, not merely with respect to one another in me, but with respect to the form of judging in general (which is here hypothetical), and in this way they render the empirical judgment universally valid.

If all our synthetical judgments are analyzed so far as they are objectively valid, it will be found that they never consist of mere intuitions connected only (as is commonly believed) by comparison into a judgment; but that they would be impossible were not a pure concept of the understanding superadded to the concepts abstracted from intuition, under which concept these latter are subsumed and in this manner only combined into an objectively valid judgment. Even the judgments of pure mathematics in their simplest axioms are not exempt from this condition. The principle, "A straight line is the shortest distance between two points," presupposes that the line is subsumed under the concept of magnitude, which certainly is no mere intuition, but has its seat in the understanding alone and serves to determine the intuition (of the line) with regard to the judgments which may be made about it, in respect to their quantity, that is, to plurality (as *judicia plurativa*). For under them it is understood that in a given intuition there is contained a plurality of homogeneous parts.

B   *From the CRITIQUE*

INTRODUCTION

1. THE DISTINCTION BETWEEN PURE AND EMPIRICAL KNOWLEDGE

B 1

There can be no doubt that all our knowledge begins with experience. For how should our faculty of knowledge be awakened into action did not objects affecting our senses partly of themselves produce representations, partly arouse the activity of our understanding to compare these representations, and, by combining or separating them, work up the raw material of the sensible impressions into that knowledge of objects which is entitled experience? In the order of time, therefore, we have no knowledge antecedent to experience, and with experience all our knowledge begins.

But though all our knowledge begins with experience, it does not follow that it all arises out of experience. For it may well be that even our empirical knowledge is made up of what we receive through impressions and of what our own faculty of knowledge (sensible impressions serving merely as the occasion) supplies from itself. If our faculty of knowledge makes any such addition, it may be that we are not in a position to distinguish it from the raw material, until with long practice of attention we have become skilled in separating it.

B 2

This, then, is a question which at least calls for closer examination, and does not allow of any off-hand answer:—whether there is any knowledge that is thus independent of experience and even of all impressions of the senses. Such knowledge is entitled a *priori*, and distinguished from the *empirical*, which has its sources a *posteriori*, that is, in experience.[1]

The expression 'a *priori*' does not, however, indicate with sufficient precision the full meaning of our question. For it has been customary to say, even of much knowledge that is derived from empirical sources, that we have it or are capable of having it *a priori*, meaning thereby that we do not derive it immediately from experience, but from a universal rule—a rule which is itself, however, borrowed by us from experience. Thus we would say of a man who undermined the foundations of his house, that he might have known *a priori* that it would fall, that is, that he need not have waited for the experience of its actual falling. But still he could not know this completely *a priori*. For he had first to learn through experience that bodies are heavy, and therefore fall when their supports are withdrawn.

B3   In what follows, therefore, we shall understand by *a priori* knowledge, not knowledge independent of this or that experience, but knowledge absolutely independent of all experience. Opposed to it is empirical knowledge, which is knowledge possible only *a posteriori*, that is, through experience. *A priori* modes of knowledge are entitled pure when there is no admixture of anything empirical. Thus, for instance, the proposition, 'every alteration has its cause', while an *a priori* proposition, is not a pure proposition, because alteration is a concept which can be derived only from experience.

2. WE ARE IN POSSESSION OF CERTAIN MODES OF *A PRIORI* KNOWLEDGE, AND EVEN THE COMMON UNDERSTANDING IS NEVER WITHOUT THEM

What we here require is a criterion by which to distinguish with certainty between pure and empirical knowledge. Experience teaches us that a thing is so and so, but not that it cannot be otherwise. First, then, if we have a proposition which in being thought is thought as *necessary*, it is an *a priori* judgment; and if, besides, it is not derived from any proposition except one which also has the validity of a necessary judgment, it is an absolutely *a priori* judgment.[2] Secondly, experience never confers on its judgments true or strict, but only assumed and comparative *universality*, through induction. We can properly only say, therefore, that, so far as we have hitherto observed, there is no exception to this or that rule. If, then,
B4   a judgment is thought with strict universality, that is, in such manner that no exception is allowed as possible, it is not derived from experience, but is valid absolutely *a priori*. Empirical universality is only an arbitrary extension of a validity holding in most cases to one which holds in all, for instance, in the proposition, 'all bodies are heavy'.[3] When, on the other hand, strict universality is essential to a judgment, this indicates a special source of knowledge, namely, a faculty of *a priori* knowledge. Necessity and strict universality are thus sure criteria of *a priori* knowledge, and are inseparable from one another. But since in the employment of these criteria the contingency of judgments is sometimes more easily shown than

their empirical limitation, or, as sometimes also happens, their unlimited universality can be more convincingly proved than their necessity, it is advisable to use the two criteria separately, each by itself being infallible.[4]

Now it is easy to show that there actually are in human knowledge judgments which are necessary and in the strictest sense universal, and which are therefore pure *a priori* judgments. If an example from the sciences be desired, we have only to look to any of the propositions of mathematics; if we seek an example from the understanding in its quite ordinary employment, the proposition, 'every alteration must have a cause', will serve our purpose. In the latter case, indeed, the very concept of a cause so manifestly contains the concept of a necessity of connection with an effect and of the strict universality of the rule, that the concept would be altogether lost if we attempted to derive it, as Hume has done, from a repeated association of that which happens with that which precedes, and from a custom of connecting representations, a custom originating in this repeated association, and constituting therefore a merely subjective necessity. Even without appealing to such examples, it is possible to show that pure *a priori* principles are indispensable for the possibility of experience, and so to prove their existence *a priori*. For whence could experience derive its certainty, if all the rules, according to which it proceeds, were always themselves empirical, and therefore contingent?[5] Such rules could hardly be regarded as first principles. At present, however, we may be content to have established the fact that our faculty of knowledge does have a pure employment, and to have shown what are the criteria of such an employment.

B5

Such *a priori* origin is manifest in certain concepts, no less than in judgments. If we remove from our empirical concept of a body, one by one, every feature in it which is [merely] empirical, the colour, the hardness or softness, the weight, even the impenetrability, there still remains the space which the body (now entirely vanished) occupied, and this cannot be removed. Again, if we remove from our empirical concept of any object, corporeal or incorporeal, all properties which experience has taught us, we yet cannot take away that property through which the object is thought as substance or as inhering in a substance (although this concept of substance is more determinate than that of an object in general).[6] Owing, therefore, to the necessity with which this concept of substance forces itself upon us, we have no option save to admit that it has its seat in our faculty of *a priori* knowledge.

B6

3. PHILOSOPHY STANDS IN NEED OF A SCIENCE WHICH SHALL DETERMINE THE POSSIBILITY, THE PRINCIPLES, AND THE EXTENT OF ALL *A PRIORI* KNOWLEDGE

But what is still more extraordinary than all the preceding is this, that certain modes of knowledge leave the field of all possible experiences and have the appearance of extending the scope of our judgments beyond all limits of experience, and this by means of concepts to which no corresponding object can ever be given in experience.

It is precisely by means of the latter modes of knowledge, in a realm beyond the world of the senses, where experience can yield neither guidance nor correction, that our reason carries on those enquiries which owing to their importance we consider to be far more excellent, and in their purpose far more lofty, than all that the understanding can learn in the field of appearances. Indeed we prefer to run every risk of error rather than desist from such urgent enquiries, on the ground of their dubious character, or from disdain and indifference. These unavoidable problems set by pure reason itself are *God, freedom,* and *immortality.* The science which, with all its preparations, is in its final intention directed solely to their solution is metaphysics; and its procedure is at first dogmatic, that is, it confidently sets itself to this task without any previous examination of the capacity or incapacity of reason for so great an undertaking.[7]

Now it does indeed seem natural that, as soon as we have left the ground of experience, we should, through careful enquiries, assure ourselves as to the foundations of any building that we propose to erect, not making use of any knowledge that we possess without first determining whence it has come, and not trusting to principles without knowing their origin. It is natural, that is to say, that the question should first be considered, how the understanding can arrive at all this knowledge *a priori,* and what extent, validity, and worth it may have. Nothing, indeed, could be more natural, if by the term 'natural' we signify what fittingly and reasonably ought to happen. But if we mean by 'natural' what ordinarily happens, then on the contrary nothing is more natural and more intelligible than the fact that this enquiry has been so long neglected. For one part of this knowledge, the mathematical, has long been of established reliability, and so gives rise to a favourable presumption as regards the other part, which may yet be of quite different nature. Besides, once we are outside the circle of experience, we can be sure of not being *contradicted* by experience.[8] The charm of extending our knowledge is so great that nothing short of encountering a direct contradiction can suffice to arrest us in our course; and this can be avoided, if we are careful in our fabrications — which none the less will still remain fabrications. Mathematics gives us a shining example of how far, independently of experience, we can progress in *a priori* knowledge. It does, indeed, occupy itself with objects and with knowledge solely in so far as they allow of being exhibited in intuition. But this circumstance is easily overlooked, since this intuition can itself be given *a priori,* and is therefore hardly to be distinguished from a bare and pure concept. Misled by such a proof of the power of reason, the demand for the extension of knowledge recognises no limits. The light dove, cleaving the air in her free flight, and feeling its resistance, might imagine that its flight would be still easier in empty space. It was thus that Plato left the world of the senses, as setting too narrow limits to the understanding, and ventured out beyond it on the wings of the ideas, in the empty space of the pure understanding. He did not observe that with all his efforts he made no advance—meeting no resistance that might, as it were, serve as a support upon which he could take a stand, to which he could apply his powers, and so set his understanding in motion. It is, indeed, the common fate of human reason to complete its speculative structures as speedily as may be, and only afterwards to enquire whether the foundations are reliable. All sorts of excuses will then be appealed to, in order to reassure us of their solidity, or rather indeed to enable us to dispense altogether with so late and so dangerous an enquiry. But what keeps us, during the actual building, free from all apprehension and suspicion, and flatters us with a seeming thoroughness, is this other circumstance, namely, that a great, perhaps the greatest, part of the business of our reason consists in analysis of the concepts which we already have of objects. This analysis supplies us with a considerable body of knowledge, which, while nothing but explanation or elucidation of what has already been thought in our concepts, though in a confused manner, is yet prized as being, at least as regards its form, new insight. But so far as the matter or content is concerned, there has been no extension of our previously possessed concepts, but only an analysis of them. Since this procedure yields real knowledge *a priori*, B 10 which progresses in an assured and useful fashion, reason is so far misled as surreptitiously to introduce, without itself being aware of so doing, assertions of an entirely different order, in which it attaches to given concepts others completely foreign to them, and moreover attaches them *a priori*. And yet it is not known how reason can be in position to do this. Such a question is never so much as thought of. I shall therefore at once proceed to deal with the difference between these two kinds of knowledge.

4. THE DISTINCTION BETWEEN ANALYTIC AND SYNTHETIC JUDGMENTS

In all judgments in which the relation of a subject to the predicate is thought (I take into consideration affirmative judgments only, the subsequent application to negative judgments being easily made), this relation is possible in two different ways.[9] Either the predicate B belongs to the subject A, as something which is (covertly) contained in this concept A; or B lies outside the concept A, although it does indeed stand in connection with it. In the one case I entitle the judgment analytic, in the other synthetic. Analytic judgments (affirmative) are therefore those in which the connection of the predicate with the subject is thought through identity; those in which this connection is thought without identity should be entitled synthetic. The former, as adding nothing through the predicate to the concept B 11 of the subject, but merely breaking it up into those constituent concepts that have all along been thought in it, although confusedly, can also be entitled explicative. The latter, on the other hand, add to the concept of the subject a predicate which has not been in any wise thought in it, and which no analysis could possibly extract from it; and they may therefore be entitled ampliative. If I say, for instance, 'All bodies are extended', this is an analytic judgment. For I do not require to go beyond the concept which I connect with 'body' in order to find extension as bound up with it. To meet with this predicate, I have merely to analyse the concept, that is, to become conscious to myself of the manifold which I always think in that concept. The judgment is therefore analytic. But when I say, 'All bodies are heavy', the predicate is something quite different from anything that I think in the mere concept of body in general; and the addition of such a predicate therefore yields a synthetic judgment.

Judgments of experience, as such, are one and all synthetic. For it would be absurd to found an analytic judgment on experience. Since, in framing the judgment, I must not go outside my concept, there is no need to appeal to the testimony of experience in its support. That a body is ex-
B 12   tended is a proposition that holds *a priori* and is not empirical. For, before appealing to experience, I have already in the concept of body all the conditions required for my judgment. I have only to extract from it, in accordance with the principle of contradiction, the required predicate, and in so doing can at the same time become conscious of the necessity of the judgment—and that is what experience could never have taught me. On the other hand, though I do not include in the concept of a body in general the predicate 'weight', none the less this concept indicates an object of experience through one of its parts, and I can add to that part other parts of this same experience, as in this way belonging together with the concept. From the start I can apprehend the concept of body analytically through the characters of extension, impenetrability, figure, etc., all of which are thought in the concept. Now, however, looking back on the experience from which I have derived this concept of body, and finding weight to be invariably connected with the above characters, I attach it as a predicate to the concept; and in doing so I attach it synthetically, and am therefore extending my knowledge. The possibility of the synthesis of the predicate 'weight' with the concept of 'body' thus rests upon experience. While the one concept is not contained in the other, they yet belong to one another, though only contingently, as parts of a whole, namely, of an experience which is itself a synthetic combination of intuitions.[10]

B 13   But in *a priori* synthetic judgments this help is entirely lacking. [I do not here have the advantage of looking around in the field of experience.] Upon what, then, am I to rely, when I seek to go beyond the concept A, and to know that another concept B is connected with it? Through what is the synthesis made possible? Let us take the proposition, 'Everything which happens has its cause'. In the concept of 'something which happens', I do indeed think an existence which is preceded by a time, etc., and from this

concept analytic judgments may be obtained. But the concept of a 'cause' lies entirely outside the other concept, and signifies something different from 'that which happens', and is not therefore in any way contained in this latter representation. How come I then to predicate of that which happens something quite different, and to apprehend that the concept of cause, though not contained in it, yet belongs, and indeed necessarily belongs, to it? What is here the unknown = X which gives support to the understanding when it believes that it can discover outside the concept A a predicate B foreign to this concept, which it yet at the same time considers to be connected with it? It cannot be experience, because the suggested principle has connected the second representation with the first, not only with greater universality, but also with the character of necessity, and therefore completely *a priori* and on the basis of mere concepts. Upon such synthetic, that is, ampliative principles, all our *a priori* speculative knowledge must ultimately rest; analytic judgments are very important, and indeed necessary, but only for obtaining that clearness in the concepts   B 14
which is requisite for such a sure and wide synthesis as will lead to a genuinely new addition to all previous knowledge.

5. IN ALL THEORETICAL SCIENCES OF REASON SYNTHETIC *A PRIORI* JUDGMENTS ARE CONTAINED AS PRINCIPLES

1. *All mathematical judgments, without exception, are synthetic.* This fact, though incontestably certain and in its consequences very important, has hitherto escaped the notice of those who are engaged in the analysis of human reason, and is, indeed, directly opposed to all their conjectures. For as it was found that all mathematical inferences proceed in accordance with the principle of contradiction (which the nature of all apodeictic certainty requires), it was supposed that the fundamental propositions of the science can themselves be known to be true through that principle. This is an erroneous view. For though a synthetic proposition can indeed be discerned in accordance with the principle of contradiction, this can only be if another synthetic proposition is presupposed, and if it can then be apprehended as following from this other proposition; it can never be so discerned in and by itself.

First of all, it has to be noted that mathematical propositions, strictly so called, are always judgments *a priori*, not empirical; because they carry with them necessity, which cannot be derived from experience. If this be   B 15
demurred to, I am willing to limit my statement to *pure* mathematics, the very concept of which implies that it does not contain empirical, but only pure *a priori* knowledge.

We might, indeed, at first suppose that the proposition 7 + 5 = 12 is a merely analytic proposition, and follows by the principle of contradiction from the concept of a sum of 7 and 5. But if we look more closely we

find that the concept of the sum of 7 and 5 contains nothing save the union of the two numbers into one, and in this no thought is being taken as to what that single number may be which combines both. The concept of 12 is by no means already thought in merely thinking this union of 7 and 5; and I may analyse my concept of such a possible sum as long as I please, still I shall never find the 12 in it. We have to go outside these concepts, and call in the aid of the intuition which corresponds to one of them, our five fingers, for instance, or, as Segner does in his *Arithmetic,* five points, adding to the concept of 7, unit by unit, the five given in intuition. For starting with the number 7, and for the concept of 5 calling in the aid of the fingers of my hand as intuition, I now add one by one to the number 7 the units
B 16   which I previously took together to form the number 5, and with the aid of that figure [the hand] see the number 12 come into being. That 5 should be added to 7, I have indeed already thought in the concept of a sum = 7 + 5, but not that this sum is equivalent to the number 12. Arithmetical propositions are therefore always synthetic. This is still more evident if we take larger numbers. For it is then obvious that, however we might turn and twist our concepts, we could never, by the mere analysis of them, and without the aid of intuition, discover what [the number is that] is the sum.

Just as little is any fundamental proposition of pure geometry analytic. That the straight line between two points is the shortest, is a synthetic proposition. For my concept of *straight* contains nothing of quantity, but only of quality. The concept of the shortest is wholly an addition, and cannot be derived, through any process of analysis, from the concept of the
B 17   straight line. Intuition, therefore, must here be called in; only by its aid is the synthesis possible. What here causes us commonly to believe that the predicate of such apodeictic judgments is already contained in our concept, and that the judgment is therefore analytic, is merely the ambiguous character of the terms used. We are required to join in thought a certain predicate to a given concept, and this necessity is inherent in the concepts themselves. But the question is not what we *ought* to join in thought to the given concept, but what we *actually* think in it, even if only obscurely; and it is then manifest that, while the predicate is indeed attached necessarily to the concept, it is so in virtue of an intuition which must be added to the concept, not as thought in the concept itself.

Some few fundamental propositions, presupposed by the geometrician, are, indeed, really analytic, and rest on the principle of contradiction. But, as identical propositions, they serve only as links in the chain of method and not as principles; for instance, $a = a$; the whole is equal to itself; or $(a+b)>a$, that is, the whole is greater than its part.[11] And even these propositions, though they are valid according to pure concepts, are only admitted in mathematics because they can be exhibited in intuition.

2. *Natural science (physics) contains* a priori *synthetic judgments as principles.* I need cite only two such judgments: that in all changes of the material world the quantity of matter remains unchanged; and that in all

communication of motion action and reaction must always be equal.[12] Both propositions, it is evident, are not only necessary, and therefore in their origin *a priori,* but also synthetic. For in the concept of matter I do not think its permanence, but only its presence in the space which it occupies. I go outside and beyond the concept of matter, joining to it *a priori* in thought something which I have not thought *in* it. The proposition is not, therefore, analytic, but synthetic, and yet is thought *a priori;* and so likewise are the other propositions of the pure part of natural science.

B 18

3. *Metaphysics,* even if we look upon it as having hitherto failed in all its endeavours, is yet, owing to the nature of human reason, a quite indispensable science, and *ought to contain* a priori *synthetic knowledge.* For its business is not merely to analyse concepts which we make for ourselves *a priori* of things, and thereby to clarify them analytically, but to extend our *a priori* knowledge. And for this purpose we must employ principles which add to the given concept something that was not contained in it, and through *a priori* synthetic judgments venture out so far that experience is quite unable to follow us, as, for instance, in the proposition, that the world must have a first beginning, and such like. Thus metaphysics consists, at least *in intention,* entirely of *a priori* synthetic propositions.

6. THE GENERAL PROBLEM OF PURE REASON

B 19

Much is already gained if we can bring a number of investigations under the formula of a single problem. For we not only lighten our own task, by defining it accurately, but make it easier for others, who would test our results, to judge whether or not we have succeeded in what we set out to do. Now the proper problem of pure reason is contained in the question: How are *a priori* synthetic judgments possible?

That metaphysics has hitherto remained in so vacillating a state of uncertainty and contradiction, is entirely due to the fact that this problem, and perhaps even the distinction between analytic and synthetic judgments, has never previously been considered. Upon the solution of this problem, or upon a sufficient proof that the possibility which it desires to have explained does in fact not exist at all, depends the success or failure of metaphysics. Among philosophers, David Hume came nearest to envisaging this problem, but still was very far from conceiving it with sufficient definiteness and universality. He occupied himself exclusively with the synthetic proposition regarding the connection of an effect with its cause (*principium causalitatis*), and he believed himself to have shown that such an *a priori* proposition is entirely impossible. If we accept his conclusions, then all that we call metaphysics is a mere delusion whereby we fancy ourselves to have rational insight into what, in actual fact, is borrowed solely from experience, and under the influence of custom has taken the illusory semblance of necessity. If he had envisaged our problem in all its universality, he would never have been guilty of this statement, so de-

B 20

structive of all pure philosophy. For he would then have recognised that, according to his own argument, pure mathematics, as certainly containing a *priori* synthetic propositions, would also not be possible; and from such an assertion his good sense would have saved him.

In the solution of the above problem, we are at the same time deciding as to the possibility of the employment of pure reason in establishing and developing all those sciences which contain a theoretical a *priori* knowledge of objects, and have therefore to answer the questions:

How is pure mathematics possible?
How is pure science of nature possible?

Since these sciences actually exist, it is quite proper to ask *how* they are possible; for that they must be possible is proved by the fact that they exist. But the poor progress which has hitherto been made in metaphysics, and the fact that no system yet propounded can, in view of the essential purpose of metaphysics, be said really to exist, leaves everyone sufficient ground for doubting as to its possibility.

B 21

C From the *CRITIQUE*

THE TRANSCENDENTAL CLUE TO THE DISCOVERY OF ALL PURE CONCEPTS OF THE UNDERSTANDING

Section 1   THE LOGICAL EMPLOYMENT OF THE UNDERSTANDING

The understanding has thus far been explained merely negatively, as a non-sensible faculty of knowledge. Now since without sensibility we cannot have any intuition, understanding cannot be a faculty of intuition. But besides intuition there is no other mode of knowledge except by means of concepts. The knowledge yielded by understanding, or at least by the human understanding, must therefore be by means of concepts, and so is not intuitive, but discursive.[13] Whereas all intuitions, as sensibile, rest on affections, concepts rest on functions. By 'function' I mean the unity of the act of bringing various representations under one common representation. Concepts are based on the spontaneity of thought, sensible intuitions on the receptivity of impressions. Now the only use which the understanding can make of these concepts is to judge by means of them. Since no representation, save when it is an intuition, is in immediate relation to an object, no concept is ever related to an object immediately, but to some other representation of it, be that other representation an intuition, or itself a concept.[14] Judgment is therefore the mediate knowledge of an object, that is, the representation of a representation of it. In every judgment there is a concept which holds of many representations, and among them of a given representation that is immediately related to an object. Thus in

B 93

the judgment, 'all bodies are divisible', the concept of the divisible applies to various other concepts, but is here applied in particular to the concept of body, and this concept again to certain appearances that present themselves to us. These objects, therefore, are mediately represented through the concept of divisibility. Accordingly, all judgments are functions of unity among our representations;[15] instead of an immediate representation, a *higher* representation, which comprises the immediate representation and various others, is used in knowing the object, and thereby much possible knowledge is collected into one. Now we can reduce all acts of the understanding to judgments, and the *understanding* may therefore be represented as a *faculty of judgment*. For, as stated above, the understanding is a faculty of thought. Thought is knowledge by means of concepts But concepts, as predicates of possible judgments, relate to some representation of a not *yet* determined object. Thus the concept of body means something, for instance, metal, which can be known by means of that concept. It is therefore a concept solely in virtue of its comprehending other representations, by means of which it can relate to objects. It is therefore the predicate of a possible judgment, for instance, 'every metal is a body'. The functions of the understanding can, therefore, be discovered if we can give an exhaustive statement of the functions of unity in judgments.

B 94

D *From the CRITIQUE*

ANALYTIC OF CONCEPTS
Chapter 2   THE DEDUCTION OF THE PURE CONCEPTS OF UNDERSTANDING

Section 1   § 13   THE PRINCIPLES OF ANY TRANSCENDENTAL DEDUCTION

Jurists, when speaking of rights and claims, distinguish in a legal action the question of right (*quid juris*) from the question of fact (*quid facti*); and they demand that both be proved. Proof of the former, which has to state the right or the legal claim, they entitle the *deduction*. Many empirical concepts are employed without question from anyone. Since experience is always available for the proof of their objective reality, we believe ourselves, even without a deduction, to be justified in appropriating to them a meaning, an ascribed significance. But there are also usurpatory concepts, such as *fortune, fate*, which, though allowed to circulate by almost universal indulgence, are yet from time to time challenged by the question: *quid juris*. This demand for a deduction involves us in considerable perplexity, no clear legal title, sufficient to justify their employment, being obtainable either from experience or from reason.[16]

B 117

Now among the manifold concepts which form the highly complicated web of human knowledge, there are some which are marked out for pure *a priori* employment, in complete independence of all experience; and their right to be so employed always demands a deduction. For since empirical proofs do not suffice to justify this kind of employment, we are faced by the problem how these concepts can relate to objects which they yet do not obtain from any experience. The explanation of the manner in which concepts can thus relate *a priori* to objects I entitle their transcendental deduction; and from it I distinguish empirical deduction, which shows the manner in which a concept is acquired through experience and through reflection upon experience, and which therefore concerns, not its legitimacy, but only its *de facto* mode of origination.[17]

B 118   We are already in possession of concepts which are of two quite different kinds, and which yet agree in that they relate to objects in a completely *a priori* manner, namely, the concepts of space and time as forms of sensibility, and the categories as concepts of understanding. To seek an empirical deduction of either of these types of concept would be labour entirely lost. For their distinguishing feature consists just in this, that they relate to their objects without having borrowed from experience anything that can serve in the representation of these objects. If, therefore, a deduction of such concepts is indispensable, it must in any case be transcendental.

We can, however, with regard to these concepts, as with regard to all knowledge, seek to discover in experience, if not the principle of their possibility, at least the occasioning causes of their production. The impressions of the senses supplying the first stimulus, the whole faculty of knowledge opens out to them, and experience is brought into existence. That experience contains two very dissimilar elements, namely, the *matter* of knowledge [obtained] from the senses, and a certain *form* for the ordering of this matter, [obtained] from the inner source of the pure intuition and thought which, on occasion of the sense-impressions, are first brought into action and yield concepts. Such an investigation of the first strivings of our faculty of knowledge, whereby it advances from particular percep-
B 119   tions to universal concepts, is undoubtedly of great service. We are indebted to the celebrated Locke for opening out this new line of enquiry. But a *deduction* of the pure *a priori* concepts can never be obtained in this manner; it is not to be looked for in any such direction. For in view of their subsequent employment, which has to be entirely independent of experience, they must be in a position to show a certificate of birth quite other than that of descent from experiences. Since this attempted physiological derivation concerns a *quaestio facti*, it cannot strictly be called deduction; and I shall therefore entitle it the explanation of the *possession* of pure knowledge.[18] Plainly the only deduction that can be given of this knowledge is one that is transcendental, not empirical. In respect to pure *a priori* concepts the latter type of deduction is an utterly useless enterprise which can be engaged in only by those who have failed to grasp the quite peculiar nature of these modes of knowledge.

But although it may be admitted that the only kind of deduction of pure *a priori* knowledge which is possible is on transcendental lines, it is not at once obvious that a deduction is indispensably necessary. We have already, by means of a transcendental deduction, traced the concepts of space and time to their sources, and have explained and determined their *a priori* objective validity. Geometry, however, proceeds with security in   B 120 knowledge that is completely *a priori,* and has no need to beseech philosophy for any certificate of the pure and legitimate descent of its fundamental concept of space. But the concept is employed in this science only in its reference to the outer sensible world—of the intuition of which space is the pure form—where all geometrical knowledge, grounded as it is in *a priori* intuition, possesses immediate evidence. The objects, so far as their form is concerned, are given, through the very knowledge of them, *a priori* in intuition. In the case of the *pure concepts of understanding,* it is quite otherwise; it is with them that the unavoidable demand for a transcendental deduction, not only of themselves, but also of the concept of space, first originates. For since they speak of objects through predicates not of intuition and sensibility but of pure *a priori* thought, they relate to objects universally, that is, apart from all conditions of sensibility. Also, not being grounded in experience, they cannot, in *a priori* intuition, exhibit any object such as might, prior to all experience, serve as ground for their synthesis. For these reasons, they arouse suspicion not merely in regard to the objective validity and the limits of their own employment, but owing to their tendency to employ the *concept of space* beyond the conditions of sensible intuition, that concept also they render ambiguous; and this, in-   B 121 deed, is why we have already found a transcendental deduction of it necessary. The reader must therefore be convinced of the unavoidable necessity of such a transcendental deduction before he has taken a single step in the field of pure reason. Otherwise he proceeds blindly, and after manifold wanderings must come back to the same ignorance from which he started. At the same time, if he is not to lament over obscurity in matters which are by their very nature deeply veiled, or to be too easily discouraged in the removal of obstacles, he must have a clear foreknowledge of the inevitable difficulty of the undertaking. For we must either completely surrender all claims to make judgments of pure reason in the most highly esteemed of all fields, that which transcends the limits of all possible experience, or else bring this critical enquiry to completion.

We have already been able with but little difficulty to explain how the concepts of space and time, although *a priori* modes of knowledge, must necessarily relate to objects, and how independently of all experience they make possible a synthetic knowledge of objects. For since only by means of such pure forms of sensibility can an object appear to us, and so be an object of empirical intuition, space and time are pure intuitions which contain *a priori* the condition of the possibility of objects as appear-   B 122 ances, and the synthesis which takes place in them has objective validity.

The categories of understanding, on the other hand, do not represent the conditions under which objects are given in intuition. Objects may, therefore, appear to us without their being under the necessity of being related to the functions of understanding; and understanding need not, therefore, contain their *a priori* conditions. Thus a difficulty such as we did not meet with in the field of sensibility is here presented, namely, how *subjective conditions of thought* can have *objective validity*, that is, can furnish conditions of the possibility of all knowledge of objects. For appearances can certainly be given in intuition independently of functions of the understanding. Let us take, for instance, the concept of cause, which signifies a special kind of synthesis, whereby upon something, A, there is posited something quite different, B, according to a rule. It is not manifest *a priori* why appearances should contain anything of this kind (experiences cannot be cited in its proof, for what has to be established is the objective validity of a concept that is *a priori*); and it is therefore *a priori* doubtful whether such a concept be not perhaps altogether empty, and have no object anywhere among appearances. That objects of sensible intuition must conform to the formal conditions of sensibility which lie *a priori* in the mind is evident, because otherwise they would not be objects for us. But that they must likewise conform to the conditions which the understanding requires for the synthetic unity of thought, is a conclusion the grounds of which are by no means so obvious. Appearances might very well be so constituted that the understanding should not find them to be in accordance with the conditions of its unity. Everything might be in such confusion that, for instance, in the series of appearances nothing presented itself which might yield a rule of synthesis and so answer to the concept of cause and effect. This concept would then be altogether empty, null, and meaningless. But since intuition stands in no need whatsoever of the functions of thought, appearances would none the less present objects to our intuition.

B 123

If we thought to escape these toilsome enquiries by saying that experience continually presents examples of such regularity among appearances and so affords abundant opportunity of abstracting the concept of cause, and at the same time of verifying the objective validity of such a concept, we should be overlooking the fact that the concept of cause can never arise in this manner. It must either be grounded completely *a priori* in the understanding, or must be entirely given up as a mere phantom of the brain. For this concept makes strict demand that something, A, should be such that something else, B, follows from it *necessarily and in accordance with an absolutely universal rule.* Appearances do indeed present cases from which a rule can be obtained according to which something usually happens, but they never prove the sequence to be *necessary.* To the synthesis of cause and effect there belongs a dignity which cannot be empirically expressed, namely, that the effect not only succeeds upon the

B 124

cause, but that it is posited *through* it and arises *out of* it. This strict universality of the rule is never a characteristic of empirical rules; they can acquire through inducton only comparative universality, that is, extensive applicability. If we were to treat pure concepts of understanding as merely empirical products, we should be making a complete change in [the manner of] their employment.

§ 14   TRANSITION TO THE TRANSCENDENTAL DEDUCTION OF THE CATEGORIES

There are only two possible ways in which synthetic representations and their objects can establish connection, obtain necessary relation to one another, and, as it were, meet one another. Either the object alone must make the representation possible, or the representation alone must make the object possible. In the former case, this relation is only empirical, and the representation is never possible *a priori*. This is true of appearances, as regards that [element] in them which belongs to sensation. In the latter case, representation in itself does not produce its object in so far as *existence* is concerned, for we are not here speaking of its causality by means of the will. None the less the representation is *a priori* determinant of the object, if it be the case that only through the representation is it possible to *know* anything *as an object*. Now there are two conditions under which alone the knowledge of an object is possible, first, *intuition*, through which it is given, though only as appearance; secondly, *concept*, through which an object is thought corresponding to this intuition. It is evident from the above that the first condition, namely, that under which alone objects can be intuited, does actually lie *a priori* in the mind as the formal ground of the objects. All appearances necessarily agree with this formal condition of sensibility, since only through it can they appear, that is, be empirically intuited and given. The question now arises whether *a priori* concepts do not also serve as antecedent conditions under which alone anything can be, if not intuited, yet thought as object in general. In that case all empirical knowledge of objects would necessarily conform to such concepts, because only as thus presupposing them is anything possible as *object of experience*. Now all experience does indeed contain, in addition to the intuition of the senses through which something is given, a *concept* of an object as being thereby given, that is to say, as appearing. Concepts of object in general thus underlie all empirical knowledge as its *a priori* conditions.[19] The objective validity of the categories as *a priori* concepts rests, therefore, on the fact that, so far as the form of thought is concerned, through them alone does experience become possible. They relate of necessity and *a priori* to objects of experience, for the reason that only by means of them can any object whatsoever of experience be thought.

The transcendental deduction of all *a priori* concepts has thus a principle according to which the whole enquiry must be directed, namely,

B 125

B 126

that they must be recognised as a *priori* conditions of the possibility of experience, whether of the intuition which is to be met with in it or of the thought. Concepts which yield the objective ground of the possibility of experience are for this very reason necessary. But the unfolding of the experience wherein they are encountered is not their deduction; it is only their illustration. For on any such exposition they would be merely accidental. Save through their original relation to possible experience, in which all objects of knowledge are found, their relation to any one object would be quite incomprehensible.

The illustrious Locke, failing to take account of these considerations, and meeting with pure concepts of the understanding in experience, deduced them also from experience, and yet proceeded so *inconsequently* that he attempted with their aid to obtain knowledge which far transcends all limits of experience. David Hume recognized that, in order to be able to do this, it was necessary that these concepts should have an *a priori* origin. But since he could not explain how it can be possible that the understanding must think concepts, which are not in themselves connected in the understanding, as being necessarily connected in the object, and since it never occurred to him that the understanding might itself, perhaps, through these concepts, be the author of the experience in which its objects are found, he was constrained to derive them from experience, namely, from a subjective necessity (that is, from *custom*), which arises from repeated association in experience, and which comes mistakenly to be regarded as objective. But from these premises he argued quite consistently. It is impossible, he declared, with these concepts and the principles to which they give rise, to pass beyond the limits of experience. Now this B 128 *empirical* derivation, in which both philosophers agree, cannot be reconciled with the scientific *a priori* knowledge which we do actually possess, namely, *pure mathematics* and *general science of nature*; and this fact therefore suffices to disprove such derivation.

While the former of these two illustrious men opened a wide door to *enthusiasm*—for if reason once be allowed such rights, it will no longer allow itself to be kept within bounds by vaguely defined recommendations of moderation—the other gave himself over entirely to *scepticism*, having, as he believed, discovered that what had hitherto been regarded as reason was but an all-prevalent illusion infecting our faculty of knowledge. We now propose to make trial whether it be not possible to find for human reason safe conduct between these two rocks, assigning to her determinate limits, and yet keeping open for her the whole field of her appropriate activities.

But first I shall introduce a word of explanation in regard to the categories. They are concepts of an object in general, by means of which the intuition of an object is regarded as determined in respect of one of the logical functions of judgment. Thus the function of the categorical judgment is that of the relation of subject to predicate; for example, 'All bodies

are divisible'. But as regards the merely logical employment of the understanding, it remains undetermined to which of the two concepts the function of the subject, and to which the function of predicate, is to be assigned.   B 129
For we can also say, 'Something divisible is a body'. But when the concept of body is brought under the category of substance, it is thereby determined that its empirical intuition in experience must always be considered as subject and never as mere predicate. Similarly with all the other categories.

E From the *CRITIQUE*

§ 22   THE CATEGORY HAS NO OTHER APPLICATION IN KNOWLEDGE THAN TO OBJECTS OF EXPERIENCE

To *think* an object and to *know* an object are thus by no means the same thing. Knowledge involves two factors: first, the concept, through which an object general is thought (the category); and secondly, the intuition, through which it is given. For if no intuition could be given corresponding to the concept, the concept would still indeed be a thought, so far as its form is concerned, but would be without any object, and no knowledge of anything would be possible by means of it. So far as I could know, there would be nothing, and could be nothing, to which my thought could be applied. Now, as the Aesthetic has shown, the only intuition possible to us is sensible; consequently, the thought of an object in general, by means of a pure concept of understanding, can become knowledge for us only in so far as the concept is related to objects of the senses. Sensible intuition   B 147
is either pure intuition (space and time) or empirical intuition of that which is immediately represented, through sensation, as actual in space and time. Through the determination of pure intuition we can acquire *a priori* knowledge of objects, as in mathematics, but only in regard to their form, as appearances; whether there can be things which must be intuited in this form, is still left undecided. Mathematical concepts are not, therefore, by themselves knowledge, except on the supposition that there are things which allow of being presented to us only in accordance with the form of that pure sensible intuition. Now *things in space and time* are given only in so far as they are perceptions (that is, representations accompanied by sensation)—therefore only through empirical representation. Consequently, the pure concepts of understanding, even when they are applied to *à priori* intuitions, as in mathematics, yield knowledge only in so far as these intuitions—and therefore indirectly by their means the pure concepts also—can be applied to empirical intuitions. Even, therefore, with the aid of [pure] intuition, the categories do not afford us any knowledge of things; they do so only through their possible application to *empirical intuition*. In other words, they serve only for the possibility of *empirical knowledge*, and such knowledge is what we entitle experience.

Our conclusion is therefore this: the categories, as yielding knowledge of
B 148   *things,* have no kind of application, save only in regard to things which
may be objects of possible experience.

F From the CRITIQUE

We have now to explain the possibility of knowing a *priori,* by means of
categories, whatever objects may *present themselves to our senses,* not
indeed in respect of the form of their intuition, but in respect of the laws
of their combination, and so, as it were, of prescribing laws to nature,
B 160   and even of making nature possible. For unless the categories discharged
this function, there could be no explaining why everything that can be
presented to our senses must be subject to laws which have their origin
a *priori* in the understanding alone.

First of all, I may draw attention to the fact that by *synthesis of
apprehension* I understand that combination of the manifold in an empirical intuition, whereby perception, that is, empirical consciousness of
the intuition (as appearance), is possible.

In the representations of space and time we have a *priori forms* of
outer and inner sensible intuition; and to these the synthesis of apprehension of the manifold of appearance must always conform, because in no
other way can the synthesis take place at all. But space and time are represented a *priori* not merely as *forms* of sensible intuition, but as themselves
intuitions which contain a manifold [of their own], and therefore are
represented with the determination of the *unity* of this manifold (*vide* the
B 161   Transcendental Aesthetic).[20] Thus *unity of the synthesis* of the manifold,
without or within us, and consequently also a *combination* to which everything that is to be represented as determined in space or in time must
conform, is given a *priori* as the condition of the synthesis of all *apprehension*—not indeed in, but with these intuitions. This synthetic unity can
be no other than the unity of the combination of the manifold of a given
intuition in general in an original consciousness, in accordance with the
categories, in so far as the combination is applied to our *sensible intuition.*
All synthesis, therefore, even that which renders perception possible, is
subject to the categories; and since experience is knowledge by means of
connected perceptions, the categories are conditions of the possibility of
experience, and are therefore valid a *priori* for all objects of experience.
B 162   When, for instance, by apprehension of the manifold of a house I
make the empirical intuition of it into a perception, the *necessary unity* of
space and of outer sensible intuition in general lies at the basis of my
apprehension, and I draw as it were the outline of the house in conformity
with this synthetic unity of the manifold in space. But if I abstract from the
form of space, this same synthetic unity has its seat in the understanding,
and is the category of the synthesis of the homogeneous in an intuition in

general, that is, the category of *quantity*. To this category, therefore, the synthesis of apprehension, that is to say, the perception, must completely conform.[21]

When, to take another example, I perceive the freezing of water, I apprehend two states, fluidity and solidity, and these as standing to one another in a relation of time. But in time, which I place at the basis of the appearance [in so far] as [it is] inner *intuition*, I necessarily represent to myself synthetic *unity* of the manifold, without which that relation of time could not be given in an intuition as being *determined* in respect of time-sequence. Now this synthetic unity, as a condition *a priori* under which I combine the manifold of an *intuition in general*, is—if I abstract from the constant form of *my* inner intuition, namely, time—the category of *cause*, by means of which, when I apply it to my sensibility, I determine *everything that happens* in accordance with the relation which it prescribes, and I do so *in time in general*. Thus my apprehension of such an event, and therefore the event itself, considered as a possible perception, is subject to the concept of the *relation* of *effects* and *causes,* and so in all other cases. B 163

Categories are concepts which prescribe laws *a priori* to appearances, and therefore to nature, the sum of all appearances (*natura materialiter spectata*). The question therefore arises, how it can be conceivable that nature should have to proceed in accordance with categories which yet are not derived from it, and do not model themselves upon its pattern; that is, how they can determine *a priori* the combination of the manifold of nature, while yet they are not derived from it. The solution of this seeming enigma is as follows.

That the *laws* of appearances in nature must agree with the understanding and its *a priori* form, that is, with its faculty of *combining* the manifold in general, is no more surprising than that the appearances themselves must agree with the form of a *priori* sensible intuition. For just as appearances do not exist in themselves but only relatively to the subject in which, so far as it has senses, they inhere, so the laws do not exist in the appearances but only relatively to this same being, so far as it has understanding. Things in themselves would necessarily, apart from any understanding that knows them, conform to laws of their own. But appearances are only representations of things which are unknown as regards what they may be in themselves. As mere representations, they are subject to no law of connection save that which the connecting faculty prescribes. Now it is imagination that connects the manifold of sensible intuition; and imagination is dependent for the unity of its intellectual synthesis upon the understanding, and for the manifoldness of its apprehension upon sensibility. All possible perception is thus dependent upon synthesis of apprehension, and this empirical synthesis in turn upon transcendental synthesis, and therefore upon the categories. Consequently, all possible perceptions, and therefore everything that can come to empirical consciousness, that is, all appearances of nature, must, so far as their connection is concerned, be B 165

B 164

subject to the categories. Nature, considered merely as nature in general, is dependent upon these categories as the original ground of its necessary conformity to law (*natura formaliter spectata*). Pure understanding is not, however, in a position, through mere categories, to prescribe to appearances any *a priori* laws other than those which are involved in a *nature in general*, that is, in the conformity to law of all appearances in space and time. Special laws, as concerning those appearances which are empirically determined, cannot in their specific character be *derived* from the categories, although they are one and all subject to them. To obtain any knowledge whatsoever of these special laws, we must resort to experience; but it is the *a priori* laws that alone can instruct us in regard to experience in general, and as to what it is that can be known as an object of experience.

§ 27   OUTCOME OF THIS DEDUCTION OF THE CONCEPTS OF UNDERSTANDING

We cannot think an object save through categories; we cannot *know* an object so thought save through intuitions corresponding to these concepts. Now all our intuitions are sensible; and this knowledge, in so far as its object is given, is empirical. But empirical knowledge is experience. *Consequently, there can be no a priori knowledge, except of objects of possible experience.*[22]

But although this knowledge is limited to objects of experience, it is not therefore all derived from experience. The pure intuitions [of receptivity] and the pure concepts of understanding are elements in knowledge, and both are found in us *a priori*. There are only two ways in which we can account for a *necessary* agreement of experience with the concepts of its objects: either experience makes these concepts possible or these concepts make experience possible. The former supposition does not hold in respect of the categories (nor of pure sensible intuition); for since they are *a priori* concepts, and therefore independent of experience, the ascription to them of an empirical origin would be a sort of *generatio aequivoca*. There remains, therefore, only the second supposition—a system, as it were, of the *epigenesis* of pure reason—namely, that the categories contain, on the side of the understanding, the grounds of the possibility of all experience in general. How they make experience possible, and what are the principles of the possibility of experience that they supply in their application to appearances, will be shown more fully in the following chapter on the transcendental employment of the faculty of judgment.

A middle course may be proposed between the two above mentioned, namely, that the categories are neither *self-thought* first principles *a priori* of our knowledge nor derived from experience, but subjective dispositions of thought, implanted in us from the first moment of our existence, and so ordered by our Creator that their employment is in com-

B 166

B 167

plete harmony with the laws of nature in accordance with which experience proceeds—a kind of *preformation-system* of pure reason. Apart, however, from the objection that on such an hypothesis we can set no limit to the assumption of predetermined dispositions to future judgments, there is this decisive objection against the suggested middle course, that the necessity of the categories, which belongs to their very conception, would then have to be sacrificed. The concept of cause, for instance, which expresses the necessity of an event under a presupposed condition, would be false if it rested only on an arbitrary subjective necessity, implanted in us, of connecting certain empirical representations according to the rule of causal relation. I would not then be able to say that the effect is connected with the cause in the object, that is to say, necessarily, but only that I am so constituted that I cannot think this representation otherwise than as thus connected. This is exactly what the sceptic most desires. For if this be the situation, all our insight, resting on the supposed objective validity of our judgments, is nothing but sheer illusion; nor would there be wanting people who would refuse to admit this subjective necessity, a necessity which can only be felt. Certainly a man cannot dispute with anyone regarding that which depends merely on the mode in which he is himself organised.

B 168

NOTES

1   It seems here that Kant makes pure knowledge (see the heading of this section) and a priori knowledge equivalent. At other times Kant distinguishes pure a priori knowledge from a priori knowledge which is not free from empirical elements, in other words, synthetic a priori knowledge. In this case, pure a priori knowledge is restricted to analytic a priori knowledge, as in the discussion immediately following. Apparently the difficulty is to be resolved by holding that a priori knowledge can be had about appropriate concepts derived partly from experience, in which case the knowledge may be said to be independent of experience.

2   The criterion of being *thought* as *necessary* is rationalistic.

3   This example seems puzzling, partly because of the use of the word *heavy*. If *are heavy* is replaced by *have weight*, then the statement may seem to be strictly universal, but then it is not an example of *empirical* universality. Consequently, *heavy* must be taken in some other sense. Other candidates, 'heavier than an equivalent volume of air', for example, run the risk of making the statement false (consider balloons filled with hydrogen as objects), so that the example is not very convincing.

4   One wishes that Kant had provided some examples of cases in which the one criterion could settle the a priori character of some judgment more quickly than the other. Since both criteria are criteria for the applicability of the same concept, and consequently when one is satisfied, the other must be also, it is not easy to understand what distinction Kant had in mind when he spoke of them as different criteria.

5   The two preceding sentences make interesting claims. One makes it an assumption of Kantian philosophy that some experiences are certain. This assumption is preceded by the claim that the a priori can be shown necessarily (a priori) to be indispensable for experience. As we can hardly doubt that we have experience, this purports to make the proof of a priori judgments indubitable.

6   Notice the distinction between (merely) empirical properties of an object, and concepts related to the concept of an object which experience has taught us. Some concepts taught by experience will not be directly experienced in any object.

7   In this context, *science* means broadly *branch of knowledge*. This section defines metaphysics as the study of certain specified problems, a definition that will be referred to later.

8   At several points in the discussion of Kant's philosophy, rationalistic elements are emphasized. This passage, which adumbrates the Kantian rejection of much of metaphysics on the grounds that it cannot be contradicted or controlled by experience, emphasizes the empirical element that experience should at least *potentially* be capable of conflicting with metaphysics, and should establish the fact that Kant's philosophy must be taken as a synthesis of the rationalisms and empiricisms which preceded his epistemological investigations.

9   The application to negative judgments requires some care. One cannot say that a negative analytic judgment holds if the predicate B is not contained in the subject concept A, since this would make negative analytic judgments synthetic. Presumably a negative analytic judgment is one in which the predicate complementary to B (*not-B*) is contained in the subject concept A.

10   Compare this passage with the passage connected with footnote 3. In footnote 3 it was deliberately suggested that "All bodies have weight." seemed *necessary*. Did it? Here Kant informs us that it is not necessary, indicating that the concept of body may not be a priori intelligible.

11   Here is an example indicating that Kant's intuition could not have the qualities of necessity which he supposed it to have. Contemporary mathematicians reject the general applicability of the rule that the whole is greater than any of its parts. The reasons for rejecting this rule derive from discoveries about the properties of infinite sets which were not made clear until after Kant's time. An exception to the rule based on the properties of infinite sets will be briefly sketched. Mathematicians say that two collections of things are of equal cardinality (intuitively, have the same number of things in them) when they may be placed in a one-to-one correspondence with each other. A one-to-one correspondence is a function which assigns each member of one collection a unique member of the other collection, and vice versa. Consider the set of all positive integers, $(1, 2, 3, 4, 5, \ldots)$, which can be called set A. From A, we could imagine ourselves removing all of the odd numbers, leaving the set of even numbers, $(2, 4, 6, 8, \ldots)$, which we could call set B. Intuitively, in view of the rule that the whole is greater than any of its parts, we would expect that A is larger than B, since B seems to have only some of the members of A. Yet a one-to-one correspondence may be established between A and B. If x is an arbitrary member of A, let $2x$ be the (unique) member of B correlated to x by the correspondence, and vice versa. By the rule discussed previously, A and B are in one-to-one correspondence and have the same cardinality, indicating

that the rule that a whole is greater than any of its parts does not *necessarily* hold in infinite collections.

12   Again, the first of these claims is now vitiated by the discovery of physicists that matter may be converted to energy. These critical comments show, not that Kantian philosophy needs to be rejected, but that the concept of a priori requires further analysis.

13   *Discursive* is *not* equivalent to *analytic*. *Discursive* is opposed to *intuitive*, and means *dealing with concepts*. Consequently, some discursive thought is synthetic a priori, and not analytic.

14   This sentence begins Kant's discussion of the relationship between concepts and objects. Since objects are not known directly or intuited directly, concepts must be related not to the object, but to its representation as a result of intuition, or to a concept of a kind of object formed by an intellectual synthesis which unifies a number of intuitions of similar objects.

15   The use of *function* here is puzzling. Kant means to say that a judgment is a unification of ideas. Apparently *function*, which is *defined* a few sentences later, indicates that a judgment unifies concepts in a manner analogous to the way in which diverse intuitions are unified into the concept of an object.

16   Clearly no legal title is available from experience. But the remark that it is not available from reason requires scrutiny. Reasoning will show us that these concepts are legitimate, but there is no prima facie case that they are, for the mere fact of reasoning does not show that we are reasoning *about* something. What is needed is a proof that these concepts can be applied in judgments about experience, particularly in judgments of objects not yet experienced.

17   Notice Kant's distinction between a transcendental and an empirical deduction. This distinction is similar to the distinction often made between the context of discovery and the context of justification of a theory in the philosophy of science. In rough terms, once a theory has been proposed, its acceptability may be judged (context of justification) without knowledge of how it came to be discovered (context of discovery). We may, for example, take a theory to be acceptable or unacceptable without knowing anything about the biography of the man who proposed it. Students sometimes suppose that the fact that we must acquire a language (through experience) in order to *express* our knowledge means that all knowledge is based on experience. But what is expressed (mathematical truth), for example, may well be true independently of our means of expressing it, indeed true if we never express it. Kant points out that the universality and necessity of a priori judgments means that the concepts employed cannot be *derived* from our limited experience, even though our experience may indicate that they can be successfully employed to develop knowledge.

18   Read *psychological* for *physiological*. Kant refers to an attempted empirical deduction from a history of someone's past experiences.

19   Notice that this is a succinct statement of Kant's crucial insight. We could not legitimately make judgments about *trees*, for example, based simply on sense experiences, since the stability, etc., of trees cannot *follow* from sense experience. Judgments about trees are based on the concept of a tree which results from the category of substance and accident as applied to certain of our sense experiences. Thus the category is an a priori condition of our being able to give

our sense experiences the significance that can result in human knowledge of a scientific kind.

20   (The following footnote is Kant's.) Space, represented as *object* (as we are required to do in geometry), contains more than mere form of intuition; it also contains *combination* of the manifold, given according to the form of sensibility, in an *intuitive* representation, so that the *form of intuition* gives only a manifold, the *formal intuition* gives unity of representation. In the Aesthetic I have treated this unity as belonging merely to sensibility, simply in order to emphasize that it precedes any concept, although, as a matter of fact, it presupposes a synthesis which does not belong to the senses but through which all concepts of space and time first become possible. For since by its means (in that the understanding determines the sensibility) space and time are first *given* as intuitions, the unity of this *a priori* intuition belongs to space and time, and not to the concept of the understanding.

21   (The following footnote is Kant's.) In this manner it is proved that the synthesis of apprehension, which is empirical, must necessarily be in conformity with the synthesis of apperception, which is intellectual and is contained in the category completely *a priori*. It is one and the same spontaneity, which in the one case, under the title of imagination, and in the other case, under the title of understanding, brings combination into the manifold of intuition.

22   (The following footnote is Kant's.) Lest my readers should stumble at the alarming evil consequences which may over-hastily be inferred from this statement, I may remind them that *for thought* the categories are not limited by the conditions of our sensible intuition, but have an unlimited field. It is only the *knowledge* of that which we think, the determining of the object, that requires intuition. In the absence of intuition, the thought of the object may still have its true and useful consequences, as regards the subject's *employment of reason*. The use of reason is not always directed to the determination of the object, that is, to knowledge, but also to the determination of the subject and of its volition —a use which cannot therefore be dealt with here.

PART 7

Peirce

(1839–1914)

Abductive Inference

We have seen that Kant's philosophy attempts to avoid difficulties in older forms of rationalism and empiricism by working out a synthesis or compromise incorporating the strong points of each. Now it should be noted that compromise solutions are not *necessarily* better than any of the solutions which they compromise among. If three doctors recommend, respectively, 50, 100, and 150 cubic centimeters of some drug to a patient afflicted with some disease, there is no way of proving that 100 cubic centimeters is the best amount to administer. Indeed, we can imagine cases in which one amount will cure, and the others will not, even though the curing amount is any one of the three. Nevertheless, at least one of Kant's insights in making a compromise, the insight that knowledge is not given in experience, but is at least partly a contribution of the knower in organizing his experiences, seems to be required for a theory of knowledge if awkward consequences of more traditional rationalism and empiricism are to be avoided. The details of Kant's epistemology indicate that the knower's contribution to knowledge is in some sense *necessary*, so that knowledge in Kant carries a distinctly rationalistic flavor in his compromise. It is clear that a more empiricistic compromise between traditional rationalism and empiricism will require a weakening of the knower's mental contribution to knowledge to a contribution which does not have the necessity of synthetic a priori judgments. Such a compromise, in which the knower's presuppositions determine partly what he comes to know without these presuppositions being necessary is represented by the philosophy known as pragmatism.

Pragmatism is the only major philosophical position in epistemology that has been developed largely by American philosophers. Except for some historical influences not equivalent to pragmatism in spirit, pragmatism is first formulated in the writings of the American philosopher Charles Peirce Unfortunately, the history of pragmatism is complicated by the fact that Peirce's formulation was adopted by William James and John Dewey, who influenced (one might almost say caused) the wide acceptance of pragmatism by empiricists, even though they seem to have misunderstood Peirce on some technical points. Pragmatism was formulated by Charles Peirce at one stage in his philosophical development, and this formulation was adapted into an empiricistic compromise in spite of the fact that Peirce himself was not nearly so empiricistic as the philosophers who called themselves pragmatists later. Thus, although we shall talk about Peirce, we shall also pay less attention to his actual views than we have to the views of previous philosophers that we have considered and pay correspondingly greater attention to the empiricistic compromise that develops out of his original work in epistemology.

Interestingly enough, Peirce's pragmatism developed out of Peirce's study of Kant's *Critique of Pure Reason* in response to slowly accumulating difficulties that Peirce found in Kant's treatment. Briefly, Peirce found major difficulties in the fact that Kant's table of the kinds of judgments made by the understanding was incomplete, and this seemed to Peirce to entail a complete revision of the categories. From this attempted revision Peirce's views about inference developed. This development led to the view that neither the results of observation nor the relationships of concepts could be considered certain and beyond revision, a key insight in the formulation of pragmatism.

The most important of Peirce's new logical views for the development of pragmatism was his contention that he had developed a new form of inference, which he called retroduction or abduction. This form of inference is now commonly called the method of hypothesis. Peirce contrasts abduction with induction. Induction is also of great importance for pragmatism, particularly when inductive inference is used to test the truth of a general statement. Suppose a statement says that three-fourths of all guinea pigs are white. Nothing about any particular guinea pig may be deduced from this statement, since a particular guinea pig's being white is compatible with this statement as well as a particular guinea pig's not being white. By contrast, if the statement said that all guinea pigs are white, then it can be deduced from that statement that any particular guinea pig is white. Consequently, a particular guinea pig's being black *refutes* the claim that all guinea pigs are white. The difficulty with induction, as Peirce clearly saw, is that *any* observations are compatible with the statement that three-fourths of all guinea pigs are white, since observation of fifty black ones may only indicate that a poor sample has been taken. We expect that the proportion of white guinea pigs among all guinea pigs will closely correspond to the proportion of white guinea pigs in a *fair* sample of guinea pigs, and Peirce takes a major problem of induction to be that of specifying rules for taking *fair* samples. This is an extremely complicated problem, which we shall leave at this point, noting only that Peirce's view of induction is similar to many modern views.

Abduction is quite different from either deduction or induction, and has the following form:

The surprising fact, *C,* is observed.
But if *A* were true, *C* would be a matter of course.
Hence, there is reason to suspect that *A* is true.

This argument is not a deduction since it does not claim that its conclusion *must* be true if its premises are true. On the other hand, it is not inductive since the statement referred to in the conclusion is not tested by sampling. The difference between abduction and induction is that the latter tells us that a statement, true in some observed cases, is likely to be true in unobserved cases, while the former allows us to conclude the likelihood of a fact totally unlike anything which is observed. Abduction allows us to explain things, and it allows us to infer *new* knowledge in a sense that is not possible through the use of deductive inference and possible in a very weakened sense in the use of inductive inference.

Peirce relates abduction to both induction and deduction. The hypothesis *A,* abductively inferred, must be such that *C* is deducible from it. (Here, since deduction holds between statements, it is meant that a statement describing *C* is deducible from some statement of *A.*) At the same time, *A* should be such that it may be inductively tested by *C* as well as by other facts.

In a way, abductive inference is the key to pragmatism. Although such inferences had been made before Peirce, the explicit analysis of them by Peirce as an integral part of scientific method allows the epistemological position of pragmatism to be formulated. By abductive inference we may accept hypotheses that are not known to be true, because they would, if true, explain some observed fact or range of facts. This fact, called *C* in the exhibited form of abductive inference, is characterized by pragmatists as a *surprising* fact. Presumably, an event or fact is surprising because we may have no current explanation for it, or because we were not expecting it in terms of the beliefs which we held at the time of its appearance.

Repeated application of abductive inference may led to continued revision of our hypotheses. For exmple, suppose that I accept a hypothesis, call it *A,* which I accepted in order to explain *C.* A new fact, *C',* may occur which is inexplicable in terms of *A.* At this point I may abductively infer a new hypothesis *A',* such that both *C* and *C'* are explained by it. In principle, I may imagine myself continuing to formulate new hypotheses *A', A'', A''',* etc., to explain any new surprising facts which occur. The formulation of each new hypothesis eliminates the surprising quality of the fact which it is invoked to explain, for the reason that after a hypothesis is abductively inferred to explain it, I psychologically tend to expect similar occurrences in the future.

Pragmatism is the extension of the possibility of revising hypotheses to all our knowledge. Pragmatists believe that all our important knowledge has the tentative status of a hypothesis, and that any part of it may require revision as a result of confrontation with experience. It is in this way that pragmatists feel that the rationalistic flavor of Kant's philosophy may be circumvented. Experience and understanding do influence one another. In some sense, however, experience is still primary in that none of the concepts brought by understanding to experience are necessary; indeed any of them may be revised when they conflict with experience, or when they fail to explain some experience, or even when they do not seem to be the most convenient explanation of some experience.

Pragmatism has some surprising consequences. To begin with, a pragmatist need not hold that we have any *certain* knowledge whatsoever. On the scheme of revising hypotheses, we only know that we are *improving* our hypotheses over a period of time, but never that we have one that will not be revised later. This view fits well with the history of science, in that it may explain the continual rejection and adoption of hypotheses in the history of science as a function of the way in which they explain or fail to explain scientific observation.

Further, this scheme of explaining improvement in understanding seems to entirely expunge human knowledge construed as certain information and to replace it by human *belief*. Many philosophers feel that some certainty is required if an epistemology is to be acceptable. The pragmatist avoids any requirement of certainty because of his novel view of man, a view in which the active powers of human understanding are secondary to man's goal-seeking behavior. A man, according to pragmatists, values beliefs only in so far as they are useful for attaining his goals. This rather novel view of man will be discussed in the next chapter.

There are two major and fairly obvious objections to pragmatism as it has been outlined. One objection is that while the pragmatic view seems to require that it is always possible to perform abductive inference in the face of surprising facts, this possibility cannot be explained solely on pragmatic grounds. This objection maintains that the view that abductive inference will always be possible is a rationalistic or mystical *belief* held as a fundamental tenet by the pragmatist, since it cannot itself be the conclusion of a deductive, abductive, or inductive inference about human experiences. Peirce himself recognized this and called the pragmatic belief that revision was always, in principle, possible a *hope*, although succeeding pragmatists have not always been so frank. It would seem that the pragmatist's best defense may be that this hope represents the smallest rationalistic segment possible in any compromise philosophy recognizing Kant's arguments for the inadequacy of traditional rationalism and traditional empiricism.

Another problem raised by pragmatism which is often cited as an objection is that more than one hypothesis may be abductively inferred anytime that a suitable C occurs. For example, two hypotheses A and A' may both be such that if they were true, C would be a matter of course.

Both of these hypotheses may also be compatible with our other past beliefs. The difficulty then is to choose between A and A', since it is clear that if they are *different* hypotheses, they could not both be *true* claims. Where more than two hypotheses are abductively inferred, the problem may be taken as comparing all possible pairs of such hypotheses, so that the problem of comparing *two* hypotheses is sufficient for raising the general objection to pragmatism. Pragmatism has trouble in framing a decision method for such a problem of choice, and we shall turn to this difficulty in the last chapter.

The Pragmatic Account of Ideas

The pragmatic dependence upon acceptable belief rather than certain knowledge for the consideration of epistemological problems may be illustrated by an example. Suppose one has as a problem to determine the temperature of some body of liquid. Ignoring the complication that the liquid may have no single temperature because it has different temperatures at different points, the problem is still quite indeterminate for a pragmatist. Traditional epistemologists would have supposed that there was such a property of the liquid as its temperature. Pragmatists would hold that such a property is somewhat vague until a *purpose* for discovering the temperature of the liquid is known, and they would hold that the liquid's temperature is always determined inexactly by measurement. On this latter point they are in agreement with rationalism. Pragmatists, however, would go on to hold that the temperature may be determined accurately enough for any given *purpose,* even though the temperature as determined by any measurement is not the precise temperature assigned to the liquid by older theories of knowledge. Thus, if the body of liquid is someone's bath, he is (normally) concerned to determine the temperature of the bath only to within several degrees. The big toe of his foot may well serve as an adequate gauge of the water's temperature for this purpose. If the body of liquid is being used to develop photographic film, determination of temperature may be more important, and chemical thermometers may be required to measure the temperature with sufficient accuracy to spell the difference between successful and unsuccessful development. Even greater accuracy may be required in sensitive chemical experiments, where special thermocouples may be required to measure temperatures. This indicates that we do not always need the most accurate estimate of the temperature which is possible or even the actual (theoretical) temperature, but only a determination *accurate enough* for a given purpose.

By extension, an acceptable answer to any question of fact is to be determined by reference to what is at stake in giving the answer. We need only consider answers that make a difference to us.

This account of human action seems well supported by observations of our behavior. Where an answer matters a great deal, we are likely to spend correspondingly greater time in obtaining it. As a result, pragmatists are able to view scientific method as an extension of common sense. In both cases, a common pattern of inquiry is adopted. Scientific inquiry is distinguished from ordinary inquiry largely by the importance with which its questions are treated, and the care with which the scientist formulates alternative hypotheses and accumulates observations to discriminate between them. Further, the scientist's inquiry is controlled to a greater extent by his self-conscious understanding of the pattern of inquiry.

By giving an account of abductive inference in terms of the psychological states which accompany it, this pattern of inquiry can be made reasonably explicit. The occurrence of an unexpected or unexplained event C is accompanied by doubt, in view of the fact that our previously accepted beliefs have broken down, and this doubt irritates thought into action. Thought's function is to find a belief or hypothesis A to account for the occurrence of C. Thought, of course, may provide more than one hypothesis that would explain C, so that some investigation may be required to choose a hypothesis that is acceptable. When an adequate hypothesis is found, belief is obtained again, and the organism is directed by the newly accepted beliefs or habits along with old beliefs and habits which are retained until fresh doubt occurs.

The essential importance of facts of an empirical kind in pragmatism is reflected in Peirce's description of fact as immediately known, while belief is mediately known and is abductively inferred from the facts. A belief is a habit of thought causing us to expect certain further events to occur, subject to continual revision. Now this account is not entirely clear until we understand in what way further events are expected.

This account must be distinguished, for example, from Humean induction. There, if A's have always been followed by B's, in an appropriate way, we may form the habit of expecting a B whenever an A occurs. Pragmatic belief is a much wider concept. Having found that my electric drill will make a suitable hole in ¼-inch steel plate for some immediate purpose, I may form the habit of expecting that the drill will perform suitably on later occasions. This situation is complicated. It is not possible, given this experience, to describe an event which I expect to be *invariably* followed by some other event. My habit or rule of action cannot be formulated as the rule "Always use an electric drill to make holes in ¼-inch steel plate.", or even as the directive "If you want to make holes in ¼-inch steel plate, an electric drill will do the job.". Instead, my habit may be formulated as the rule "If you should want to drill holes in ¼-inch steel plate, an electric drill is a good tool to try." When such a habit is reinforced by repeated success in drilling ¼-inch steel plate with an electric drill whenever the problem of providing holes in such plate arises, the habit becomes strengthened to a *belief*. My belief may be looked at as a disposition to act in a certain way, namely, to use an electric drill if faced with ¼-inch steel plate that I want to drill holes into.

This account of belief has the consequence of tying pragmatic inquiry very closely to purposes and ends, rather than to the disinterested search for certain knowledge characteristic of earlier philosophies. The account of pragmatists may be extended to provide an explanation of animal behavior, particularly as the pragmatists argue that beliefs may be followed and even formed without self-conscious thought about the fact that a belief is being followed or formulated. The difference between a dog, an ordinary person, and a scientist then becomes one of degree, centering about the critical self-awareness with which these three creatures formulate their beliefs and adhere to them.

Habit and belief, on this view, are different names for the same kind of rule of action, depending on the degree of entrenchment with which the rule is applied. An event conflicting with a habit would not be as surprising as an event conflicting with a belief. Another way to put this would be to say that beliefs are those rules of action that we would tend to preserve in the face of doubt, while habits are those rules of action that we would first revise or attempt to revise. Clearly one man's habit may be another man's belief, depending on the subjective order with which they have faced personal doubts and resolved them. This subjective element in pragmatism is thought by pragmatists to be entirely acceptable, since they feel that over long periods of time, the same rules of action will become beliefs for all interested human beings. This follows from their supposition that repeated confrontation with experience will cause defective habits to be rejected and similar or common beliefs to be retained.

There remains the particular case of our conceptions of objects. As might be expected, we do not know objects directly but know about them because we have beliefs about them, and these beliefs exhaust our conception of objects. To make our idea or conception of an object clear, we consider those practical effects it can conceivably have and *identify* our idea of the object with these effects. Peirce takes this definition to be an improvement upon the criteria of clearness and distinctness proposed by Descartes. He argues that it does little good to urge adoption of clear and distinct ideas, since we will in fact adopt ideas which appear clearly and distinctly to us. The problem is to decide when we are mistaking a seeming clearness and distinctness for true clearness and distinctness. This point reiterates our earlier objection to traditional rationalism, since it is in effect pointing out that if two people claim to have clear and distinct ideas which conflict, no satisfactory methodology for removing the conflict is available in the epistemological tradition of rationalism. By making an idea of an object coincident with our conception of its practical effects, however, a methodology seems to be provided, for conflicting ideas may then be resolved by studying which of the conflicting practical effects are found to obtain. If those of the one obtain, but not those of the other, the first idea is preferred as a conception of the object. In practice, it may happen that both ideas are defective, so that some new conception is called for as a synthesis of the initial ideas. Ideas are not absolutely clear and distinct for the pragmatists but relatively clear and distinct with respect to given ends.

An interesting feature of Peirce's account of the conception of an object is the way in which his account disposes of the controversy between rationalists and empiricists over the status of material objects. An empiricism which proposes to reduce our knowledge of an object to our experiences of it wreaks havoc with our intentions in speaking about an object, as we have seen. On the other hand, adoption of a rule specifying what is true of an object when it is not experienced involves a concession to rationalism. If belief is simply the practical effects of an object, then when that object is not being put to a practical test of its effects, we are simply not concerned about the object and may say anything that we like, because belief is not involved. To take Peirce's example, our experiences with a diamond indicate that, among other things, it will scratch most other solid objects. Our conception of a diamond then involves the practical effect that if we want to scratch glass, marble, or whatever, a diamond is a good tool for the purpose. Our disposition to use the diamond in these contexts exhausts our beliefs about it. When its practical effects are not being considered or tested, the diamond might be considered either hard or soft. Both views are compatible with our other beliefs, and neither can cause a genuine doubt. Peirce says that truth is not involved, and by this he means that supposition about a diamond's hardness which has no practical consequence is not a matter of belief. Since speculation about the diamond's hardness when it is not being tested or used has no practical consequences, we are free to invent any view about it that suits our convenience or aesthetic taste. It is not, in short, a genuine irritation or a genuine problem.

The Choice of Hypotheses

The material in the preceding chapters on Peirce should enable us to make clear two of the expressions commonly used in discussing various features of pragmatism: critical common-sensism and fallibilism. Both of these expressions apply primarily to Peirce's treatment of scientific inquiry. Critical common-sensism expresses the view that scientific inquiry is a self-aware and sophisticated version of commonsense inquiry. Fallibilism expresses the view that no statement of fact or hypothesis can be taken to be absolutely certain. For the pragmatist, all human beliefs confront experience simultaneously, and he is willing to reject any currently held belief in the face of some surprising fact, although he may well expect that certain beliefs will be more likely to be rejected than others.

Pragmatists make the synthetic a priori statements of Kant synthetic, except for many statements of mathematics, which are considered analytic. In theory, it would seem that pragmatists must treat all statements as synthetic, and many of them do. On the other hand, statements of logic and mathematics seem so immune to revision (we cannot imagine the surprising fact that would cause us to give them up) that many pragmatists in practice have insisted that these statements can safely be treated as analytic, or immune to revision. The pragmatic movement has not been entirely consistent on this issue, although modern empirical philosophers have spent much time *reducing* areas of uncertainty in logic and mathematics, and hence increasing the plausibility that these statements are conveniently considered to be analytic.

This reduction has been accomplished by the development of *formal* logic and *formal* systems. Formal logic, in this sense, is the restriction of inference to operations on symbols, which may be viewed as a kind of conservatism in logic. A valid deductive inference is one in which the premises could not be interpreted as true while the conclusion was interpreted as false. Descartes took this condition to be met when he could not *conceive* of the premises being true and the conclusion false. But the difficulty with conception is that simple inability to conceive the truth of the premises and the falsity of the conclusion may not *prove* the argument invalid but may only show that the powers of conceiving are weak. Further, some rules of procedure which have been accepted for a long time may turn out to be defective. For example, it was thought for thousands of years that everything could always be consistently divided into two large classes by means of any well-defined property. To the one class would belong everything having that property, and to the other class would belong everything not having that property. Thus, the concept that everything belonged either to the class **of red** things or to the class of things which are not red seemed to be perfectly straightforward. Nonetheless, it was discovered in the early twentieth century that this rule of procedure is defective. Suppose we consider everything, *including all classes.* Now we will define a class which we shall call W. The property of non-self-membership is used to define W. By way of background for this property, let *Troy* be some dog. Then Troy is a member of the class of all dogs, which we will designate as the class D. Now is D itself a member of D? Obviously not, since all members of the class D are dogs, and the class D is not itself a dog, but a collection of dogs. D is therefore not a member of itself. Let us define the class W mentioned above as the class of all things which are not members of themselves, and put everything else into the class $\widetilde{W}$ of things which are members of themselves. (You will probably not be able to think of an example of a member of $\widetilde{W}$, but this does not affect the validity of the argument.) What about the class W? Since it is something, it must be a member of W or of $\widetilde{W}$. But to say that W is a member of W is to say also that W is not a member of itself, or not a member of W, in view of the way in which W is defined. To avoid this contradiction, W must be taken as a member of $\widetilde{W}$, but this means that W is a member of itself, because if it were not, it would be a member of W. But we have already seen that if W is taken as a member of W, a contradiction results. Consequently, we conclude that W cannot be a member of either W or $\widetilde{W}$. This means that the general principle that all things may consistently be divided into two classes by any well-defined property is not a generally useful rule. Some philosophers have taken this to prove that the notion of a class is inherently contradictory, while others have supposed either that the class W cannot be consistently investigated, or that classes must be structured in infinitely many levels of generality, so that not everything can be considered at once.

The discovery of this defect in a previously accepted rule of procedure (which has far-reaching implications for mathematical systems), as well as other paradoxes in the accepted reasoning of the nineteenth century, led to the development of formal systems in which the rules of procedure are so restricted that they avoid paradox of this kind. Formal systems are such that the symbols of a formal system are not taken to have meaning but are treated quite objectively as *objects* which may be operated on by simple and unambiguous rules.

An example of a formal rule could be the following: "If *P* is a sentence and *Q* is a sentence, and *P and Q* represents their conjunction, then if *P and Q* is a premise in an argument, *P* may be asserted as the conclusion of the argument." This is a very cautious rule which is perfectly valid, as one can easily see by taking some examples of sentences in English. Let *P* be the sentence "John hit Mary." and *Q* be the sentence "Mary went to the hospital.". Now consider the following argument:

John hit Mary and Mary went to the hospital.
Therefore, Mary was hit by John.

This would normally be thought to be a valid argument, but it is not sanctioned by our formal rule, since to construe "John hit Mary." and "Mary was hit by John." as the *same* sentence, so that either expression can be substituted for *P*, is to smuggle in an assumption that these two sentences have the same meaning, which is nowhere expressed in the formal rule. Considered as *objects,* "John hit Mary." and "Mary was hit by John." are two *different* things. One of them has a 'J' as its leftmost part, and the other has an 'M'. This is sufficient to show that they are different, and that they cannot both replace *P* in one application of the cited rule. This illustrates the point of formal systems, which attempt to be so conservative in the rules that they allow that no unnoticed assumptions or unconscious presuppositions can be smuggled into an argument to affect its validity.

We may invent all the formal systems that we care to and interpret and use them in any way that is convenient. If they are interpreted in some way, and they lead to awkward consequences, we say not that the formal system is defective, but merely that it is not useful to interpret it in this fashion.

Modern empirical philosophers (including, of course, pragmatists) usually treat most mathematical statements in this fashion. Their answer to Kant would be that the statement "$7+5=12$" is a statement in a formal system used quite frequently which may be transformed into an obvious identity as follows: $7+5=12$, which is equivalent to $(1+1+1+1+1+1+1) + (1+1+1+1+1) = (1+1+1+1+1+1+1+1+1+1+1+1)$, is equivalent to the following identity using an associative law on the left hand side: $(1+1+1+1+1+1+1+1+1+1+1+1) = (1+1+1+1+1+1+1+1+1+1+1+1)$. If we interpret this statement such that what is taken to be seven objects is added to five objects and twelve objects do not result, we conclude that this formal system, arithmetic, is not conveniently applied to these objects. For example, if 7 cubic centimeters of water are added to 5 cubic centimeters of alcohol, 12 cubic centimeters of liquid do not result, but an amount of liquid somewhat less than 12 cubic centimeters. In the face of this fact, we do not reject the arithmetic statement "$7+5=12$" as false but conclude that it is not the right formal system for describing the addition of water to alcohol.

Thus it is possible to limit the analytic to statements which are posited to be true by virtue of their form. Notice that the combination of a formal system, and some interpretation of it, may lead to the rejection of both if some statement interpreted as true in the formal system under the interpretation is found in experience to be false. Then a new system *and* a new interpretation may have to be found. Although such an approach limits statements to analytic and synthetic statements, emptying Kant's synthetic a priori category of its content, it has the consequence that it is extremely difficult to find satisfactory rules for accepting or rejecting scientific hypotheses on the basis of observed fact.

To see this, consider the following diagram:

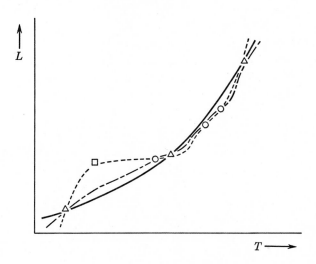

This diagram could represent the relationship between two observed properties *L* and *T* of some object, say the temperature and length of an iron bar, although we will take the diagram to represent the gathering of any scientific data and the fitting of those data to hypotheses. Let the symbols (△,○,□) in the diagram stand for observed facts, and the three lines (—, — - —, - -) stand for abducted hypotheses from the facts. A close study of this diagram will illustrate most of the problems associated with the acceptance or rejection of hypotheses on the basis of a pragmatic epistemology.

Suppose those facts represented by △ to be already accepted. Now let the theory represented by the line — be the result of an abductive inference, and let further facts be represented by ○ and □.

The basic problem is to avoid either one of two types of errors: we do not want to accept hypotheses that are false and we do not want to reject hypotheses which are true. Since hypotheses will never be conclusively shown to be true or false, we may revise this to say that we do not want to reject hypotheses that will have to be believed later, and we do not want to believe hypotheses that will have to be rejected later. Doubt forces us to accept some hypothesis. An interesting feature of pragmatism is that failure to choose between hypotheses is also taking an action and accepting a hypothesis whose risk must be evaluated along with the other alternatives. Once a genuine doubt assails us, some belief must be found to assuage our difficulty and make experience coherent, or we could consider ourselves *insane* in that we were not adjusting to empirical reality.

Fallibilism has several consequences for our diagram. Since an observation of fact will never be certain (because of the inherent error of observation), we can at best take our data points to be approximate. At the same time, since any of several abductive inferences may be possible from the data, we are faced with the difficulty of choosing from among many possible alternative hypotheses. In fact, through any number of finite points on a diagram like that above, an infinite number of distinct possible lines representing different hypotheses may be drawn. This is sufficient to indicate that the problem is complex: we are to choose some hypothesis from an infinite number of possibilities to fit data which are at best approximate. The pragmatic problem is to reduce this decision problem to manageable proportions.

What factors influence the decision? At least three have been commonly recognized in contemporary pragmatic thought: cost, simplicity, and evidential fit. The last is most familiar. We do not want to accept a hypothesis that conflicts with the data. Still, since the data are approximations, we could in principle accept any hypothesis on any data if we were willing to stretch the approximation involved sufficiently. Consider all the data represented by the symbols $\triangle$, $\bigcirc$, and $\square$ in the diagram. The datum represented by $\square$ is most troublesome. Intuitively, we might suppose that it was a mistake, and take the datum again, because it differs so widely from any reasonably smooth line passing through the other data. It is a difficult problem to decide how often a problematic datum must be verified before we are willing to accept it as true, and revise our hypotheses accordingly.

Simplicity is a characteristic of hypotheses which may seem to make them so intuitively acceptable if they are sufficiently simple that we would be willing to stretch the approximation of the data before decisively rejecting an intuitively simple hypothesis. If we ignore the datum represented by $\square$, both the hypothesis represented by — and the hypothesis represented by — — — might be said to satisfy the criterion of evidential fit. Nevertheless, most writers would agree that the hypothesis represented by — is *simpler* than the hypothesis represented by — — — . A satisfactory criterion of simplicity in this sense and an argument for using the criterion in the selection of hypotheses is still to be devised, although observation of successful scientific practice seems to indicate that some such factor may be important in the selection of hypotheses.

Cost is an interesting factor that has only recently been consciously explored. We might look at the cost of accepting a hypothesis as the amount of revision in our accepted beliefs which would be entailed by its adoption. The more our accepted beliefs conflict with a given hypothesis, the less likely we are to adopt it because the cost of its adoption is high. Where cost plays an important role, we may delay the adoption of a hypothesis until evidential fit can be very closely ascertained.

The point of this introduction of evidential weight, simplicity, and cost is that these factors do not seem to lead to any definite acceptance of certain hypotheses in certain situations. Indeed, by appropriately weighing these three factors, almost any decision might be pragmatically defended. Until pragmatism can explain some procedure for weighing evidential fit, simplicity, and cost in order to explain less intuitive applications of the criteria, the pragmatic account of scientific knowledge cannot be considered entirely adequate.

Readings from Peirce

The readings from Peirce are collected into three passages. Each of these is identified by its location in the *Collected Papers of Charles Sanders Peirce* through the use of the numbering system that is now used by Peirce scholars. For example, '5.189,' means that the reprinted passage may be found in volume 5 of the *Collected Papers* as the paragraph numbered 189.

A. This selection represents fragments 6.522–6.528, 5.189, 1.71–1.74, and 6.477 from the *Collected Papers*. These paragraphs were arranged in this fashion in a section called "Abduction and Induction" in Justus Buchler's collection of Peirce's writings called *Philosophical Writings of Peirce*, New York, 1955.

B. This selection is the first part of Peirce's essay "How to Make Our Ideas Clear," and is found as paragraphs 5.388–5.403 in the *Collected Papers*.

C. This selection consists of paragraphs 1.135–1.149 of the *Collected Papers*.

These paragraphs are reprinted here from the *Collected Papers of Charles Sanders Peirce*, edited by Charles Hartshorne and Paul Weiss. Reprinting rights have been given by kind permission of the Belknap Press of Harvard University Press.

Peirce spent much of his life in the employ of the U. S. Geodetic Survey doing experimental work on such problems as that of the density of the earth. Although his training and philosophical writings fitted him to an academic post, he found himself unable to hold such a post because of inability to get along with university administrators and professors. He was an exceedingly brilliant but eccentric man, and it is very difficult to obtain a sound biographical estimate of his personality. Pragmatism was really inaugurated as a philosophical movement by William James, and then later by John Dewey. James was quick to see the importance of Peirce's discoveries, but in characteristic fashion, Peirce quarreled with

278

James over events in which James seems to have been entirely considerate of Peirce. The events surrounding early American pragmatism and the personalities of Peirce and James make interesting intellectual history that the student should explore through some of the secondary sources which are now listed.

*Buchler, Justus: *Philosophical Writings of Peirce*, London, 1940. (Dover Paperbound.)

Feibleman, James: *An Introduction to Peirce's Philosophy Interpreted as a System*, London, 1960.

*Gallie, W. B.: *Peirce and Pragmatism*, Harmondsworth, 1952. (Pelican Paperbound.)

Goudge, T. A.: *The Thought of C. S. Peirce*, Toronto, 1950.

Murphey, M. G.: *The Development of Peirce's Philosophy*, Cambridge, 1961.

*Thompson, M.: *The Pragmatic Philosophy of C. S. Peirce*, Chicago, 1953. (University of Chicago Paperbound.)

Wiener, Philip, and Frederic Young: *Studies in the Philosophy of Charles Sanders Peirce*, Cambridge, 1952.

A   From the COLLECTED PAPERS OF CHARLES SANDERS PEIRCE

I

All our knowledge may be said to rest upon observed facts. It is true that there are psychological states which antecede our observing facts as such. Thus, it is a fact that I see an inkstand before me; but before I can say that I am obliged to have impressions of sense into which no idea of an inkstand, or of any separate object, or of an 'I', or of seeing, enter at all; and it is true that my judging that I see an inkstand before me is the product of mental operations upon these impressions of sense. But it is only when the cognition has become worked up into a proposition, or judgment of a fact, that I can exercise any direct control over the process; and it is idle to discuss the 'legitimacy' of that which cannot be controlled.[1] Observations of fact have, therefore, to be accepted as they occur.

But observed facts relate exclusively to the particular circumstances that happened to exist when they were observed. They do not relate to any future occasions upon which we may be in doubt how we ought to act. They, therefore, do not, in themselves, contain any practical knowledge.

Such knowledge must involve additions to the facts observed. The making of those additions is an operation which we can control; and it is evidently a process during which error is liable to creep in.

Any proposition added to observed facts, tending to make them applicable in any way to other circumstances than those under which they were observed, may be called a hypothesis. A hypothesis ought, at first, to be entertained interrogatively.[2] Thereupon, it ought to be tested by experiment so far as practicable. There are two distinct processes, both of which may be performed rightly or wrongly. We may go wrong and be wasting time in so much as entertaining a hypothesis, even as a question. That is a subject for criticism in every case. There are some hypotheses which are of such a nature that they never can be tested at all. Whether such hypotheses ought to be entertained at all, and if so in what sense, is a serious question; but it hardly concerns our present inquiry.[3] The hypotheses with which we shall have in this paper to deal are capable of being put to the test. How this is to be done is a question of extreme importance; but my intention is to consider it only in a very cursory manner, at present. There are, moreover, many hypotheses in regard to which knowledge already in our possession may, at once, quite justifiably either raise them to the rank of opinions, or even positive beliefs, or cause their immediate rejection. This also is a matter to be considered. But it is the first process, that of entertaining the question, which will here be of foremost importance.

Before we go further, let us get the points stated above quite clear. By a *hypothesis*, I mean, not merely a supposition about an observed object, as when I suppose that a man is a Catholic priest because that would explain his dress, expression of countenance, and bearing, but also any other supposed truth from which would result such facts as have been observed, as when van't Hoff, having remarked that the osmotic pressure of one percent solutions of a number of chemical substances was inversely proportional to their atomic weights, thought that perhaps the same relation would be found to exist between the same properties of any other chemical substance.[4] The first starting of a hypothesis and the entertaining of it, whether as a simple interrogation or with any degree of confidence, is an inferential step which I propose to call *abduction* (or *retroduction*). This will include a preference for any one hypothesis over others which would equally explain the facts, so long as this preference is not based upon any previous knowledge beating upon the truth of the hypotheses, nor on any testing of any of the hypotheses, after having admitted them on probation.[5] I call all such inference by the peculiar name, *abduction,* because its legitimacy depends upon altogether different principles from those of other kinds of inference.

Long before I first classed abduction as an inference it was recognized by logicians that the operation of adopting an explanatory hypothesis—which is just what abduction is—was subject to certain conditions. Namely, the hypothesis cannot be admitted, even as a hypothesis, unless it be supposed that it would account for the facts or some of them. The form of inference, therefore, is this:

> The surprising fact, C, is observed;
> But if A were true, C would be a matter of course,
> Hence, there is reason to suspect that A is true.

Thus, A cannot be abductively inferred, or if you prefer the expression, cannot be abductively conjectured until its entire content is already present in the premiss, "If A were true, C would be a matter of course."

The operation of testing a hypothesis by experiment, which consists in remarking that, if it is true, observations made under certain conditions ought to have certain results, and then causing those conditions to be fulfilled, and noting the results, and, if they are favourable, extending a certain confidence to the hypothesis, I call *induction*. For example, suppose that I have been led to surmise that among our coloured population there is a greater tendency toward female births than among our whites. I say, if that be so, the last census must show it.[6] I examine the last census report and find that, sure enough, there was a somewhat greater proportion of female births among coloured births than among white births in that census year. To accord a certain faith to my hypothesis on that account is legitimate. It is a strong induction. I have taken all the births of that year as a sample of all the births of years in general, so long as general conditions remain as they were then. It is a very large sample, quite unnecessarily so, were it not that the excess of the one ratio over the other is quite small. All induction whatever may be regarded as the inference that throughout a whole class a ratio will have about the same value that it has in a random sample of that class, provided the nature of the ratio for which the sample is to be examined is specified (or virtually specified) in advance of the examination. So long as the class sampled consists of units, and the ratio in question is a ratio between counts of occurrences, induction is a comparatively simple affair. But suppose we wish to test the hypothesis that a man is a Catholic priest, that is, has all the characters that are common to Catholic priests and peculiar to them. Now characters are not units, nor do they consist of units, nor can they be counted, in such a sense that one count is right and every other wrong. Characters have to be estimated according to their significance. The consequence is that there will be a certain element of guess-work in such an induction; so that I call it an *abductory induction*. I might say to myself, let me think of some other character that belongs to Catholic priests, beside those that I have remarked in this man, a character which I can ascertain whether he possesses or not. All Catholic priests are more or less familiar with Latin pronounced in the Italian manner. If, then, this man is a Catholic priest, and I make some remark in Latin which a person not accustomed to the Italian pronunciation would not at once understand, and I pronounce it in that way, then if that man is a Catholic priest he will be so surprised that he cannot but betray his understanding of it. I make such a remark; and I notice that he does understand it. But how much weight am I to attach to that test? After all, it does not touch an essential characteristic of a priest or even of a Catholic. It must be acknowledged that it is but a weak confirmation, and all the more so, because it is quite uncertain how much weight should be attached to it. Nevertheless, it does and ought to incline me to believe that the man is a Catholic priest. It is an induction, because it is a test of the hypothesis by means of a prediction, which has been verified. But it is only an abductory induction, because it was a sampling of the characters of priests to see what proportion of them this man possessed, when characters cannot be counted, nor even weighed, except by guess-work. It also partakes of the nature of abduction in involving an original suggestion; while typical induction has no originality in it, but only tests a suggestion already made.

In induction, it is not the fact predicted that in any degree necessitates the truth of the hypothesis or even renders it probable. It is the fact that it has been predicted successfully and that it is a haphazard specimen of all the predictions which might be based on the hypothesis and which constitute its practical truth. But it frequently happens that there are facts which, merely as facts, apart from the manner in which they have presented themselves, necessitate the truth, or the falsity, or the probability in some definite degree, of the hypothesis. For example, suppose the hypothesis to be that a man believes in the infallibility of the Pope. Then, if we ascertain in any way that he believes in the immaculate conception, in the confessional, and in prayers for the dead, or on the other hand that he disbelieves all or some of these things, either fact will be almost decisive of the truth or falsity of the proposition. Such inference is *deduction*. So if we ascertain that the man in question is a violent partisan in politics and in many other subjects. If, then, we find that he has given money toward a Catholic institution, we may fairly reason that such a man would not do that unless he believed in the Pope's infallibility. Or again, we might learn that he is one of five brothers whose opinions are identical on almost all subjects. If, then, we find that the other four believe in the Pope's infallibility or all disbelieve it, this will affect our confidence in the hypothesis. This consideration will be strengthened by our general experience that while different members of a large family usually differ about most subjects, yet it mostly happens that they are either all Catholics or all Protestants. Those are four different varieties of deductive considerations which may legitimately influence our belief in a hypothesis.

These distinctions are perfectly clear in principle, which is all that is necessary, although it might sometimes be a nice question to say to which class a given inference belongs. It is to be remarked that, in pure abduction, it can never be justifiable to accept the hypothesis otherwise than as an interrogation. But as long as that condition is observed, no positive falsity is to be feared; and therefore the whole question of what one out of a number of possible hypotheses ought to be entertained becomes purely a question of economy.[7]

II

Mill denies that there was any reasoning in Kepler's procedure.[8] He says it is merely a description of the facts. He seems to imagine that Kepler had all the places of Mars in space given him by Tycho's observations;

and that all he did was to generalize and so obtain a general expression for them. Even had that been all, it would certainly have been inference. Had Mill had even so much practical acquaintance with astronomy as to have practised discussions of the motions of double stars, he would have seen that. But so to characterize Kepler's work is to betray total ignorance of it. Mill certainly never read the *De Motu (Motibus) Stellae Martis,* which is not easy reading. The reason it is not easy is that it calls for the most vigorous exercise of all the powers of reasoning from beginning to end.

What Kepler had given was a large collection of observations of the apparent places of Mars at different times. He also knew that, in a general way, the Ptolemaic theory agrees with the appearances, although there were various difficulties in making it fit exactly. He was furthermore convinced that the hypothesis of Copernicus ought to be accepted. Now this hypothesis, as Copernicus himself understood its first outline, merely modifies the theory of Ptolemy so far as (to) impart to all the bodies of the solar system one common motion, just what is required to annul the mean motion of the sun. It would seem, therefore, at first sight, that it ought not to affect the appearances at all. If Mill had called the work of Copernicus mere description he would not have been *so very far* from the truth as he was. But Kepler did not understand the matter quite as Copernicus did. Because the sun was so near the centre of the system, and was of vast size (even Kepler knew its diameter must be at least fifteen times that of the earth), Kepler, looking at the matter dynamically, thought it must have something to do with causing the planets to move in their orbits. This retroduction, vague as it was, cost great intellectual labour, and was most important in its bearings upon all Kepler's work. Now Kepler remarked that the lines of apsides of the orbits of Mars and of the earth are not parallel; and he utilized various observations most ingeniously to infer that they probably intersected in the sun. Consequently, it must be supposed that a general description of the motion would be simpler when referred to the sun as a fixed point of reference than when referred to any other point. Thence it followed that the proper times at which to take the observations of Mars for determining its orbit were when it appeared just opposite the sun—the true sun—instead of when it was opposite the *mean* sun, as had been the practice. Carrying out this idea, he obtained a theory of Mars which satisfied the longitudes at all the oppositions observed by Tycho and himself, thirteen in number, to perfection. But unfortunately, it did not satisfy the latitudes at all and was totally irreconcilable with observations of Mars when far from opposition.

At each stage of his long investigation, Kepler has a theory which is approximately true, since it approximately satisfies the observations (that is, within 8′, which is less than any but Tycho's observations could decisively pronounce an error), and he proceeds to modify this theory, after the most careful and judicious reflection, in such a way as to render it more rational or closer to the observed fact. Thus, having found that the centre of the orbit bisects the eccentricity, he finds in this an indication of the falsity of the theory of the equant and substitutes, for this artificial device, the principle of the equable description of areas. Subsequently, finding that the planet moves faster at ninety degrees from its apsides than it ought to do, the question is whether this is owing to an error in the law of areas or to a compression of the orbit. He ingeniously proves that the latter is the case.

Thus, never modifying his theory capriciously, but always with a sound and rational motive for just the modification he makes, it follows that when he finally reaches a modification—of most striking simplicity and rationality—which exactly satisfies the observations, it stands upon a totally different logical footing from what it would if it had been struck out at random, or the reader knows not how, and had been found to satisfy the observation. Kepler shows his keen logical sense in detailing the whole process by which he finally arrived at the true orbit. This is the greatest piece of Retroductive reasoning ever performed.

III

Modern science has been builded after the model of Galileo, who founded it, on *il lume naturale*.[9] That truly inspired prophet had said that, of two hypotheses, the *simpler* is to be preferred; but I was formerly one of those who, in our dull self-conceit fancying ourselves more sly than he, twisted the maxim to mean the *logically* simpler, the one that adds the least to what has been observed, in spite of three obvious objections: first, that if so there was no support for any hypothesis; secondly, that by the same token we ought to content ourselves with simply formulating the special observations actually made; and thirdly, that every advance of science that further opens the truth to our view discloses a world of unexpected complications. It was not until long experience forced me to realize that subsequent discoveries were every time showing I had been wrong, while those who understood the maxim as Galileo had done, early unlocked the secret, that the scales fell from my eyes and my mind awoke to the broad and flaming daylight that it is the simpler Hypothesis in the sense of the more facile and natural, the one that instinct suggests, that must be preferred; for the reason that, unless man have a natural bent in accordance with nature's, he has no chance of understanding nature at all.[10]

B From the COLLECTED PAPERS OF CHARLES SANDERS PEIRCE

Whoever has looked into a modern treatise on logic of the common sort, will doubtless remember two distinctions between *clear* and *obscure* conceptions, and between *distinct* and *confused* conceptions.[11] They have lain in the books now for nigh two centuries, unimproved and unmodified, and are generally reckoned by logicians as among the gems of their doctrine.

A clear idea is defined as one which is so apprehended that it will be recognized wherever it is met with, and so that no other will be mistaken for it. If it fails of this clearness, it is said to be obscure.

This is rather a neat bit of philosophical terminology; yet, since it is clearness that they were defining, I wish the logicians had made their definition a little more plain. Never to fail to recognize an idea, and under no circumstances to mistake another for it, let it come in how recondite a form it may, would indeed imply such prodigious force and clearness of intellect as is seldom met with in this world. On the other hand, merely to have such an acquaintance with the idea as to have become familiar with it, and to have lost all hesitancy in recognizing it in ordinary cases, hardly seems to deserve the name of clearness of apprehension, since after all it only amounts to a subjective feeling of mastery which may be entirely mistaken. I take it, however, that when the logicians speak of "clearness," they mean nothing more than such a familiarity with an idea, since they regard the quality as but a small merit, which needs to be supplemented by another, which they call *distinctness*.

A distinct idea is defined as one which contains nothing which is not clear. This is technical language; by the *contents* of an idea logicians understand whatever is contained in its definition. So that an idea is *distinctly* apprehended, according to them, when we can give a precise definition of it, in abstract terms. Here the professional logicians leave the subject; and I would not have troubled the reader with what they have to say, if it were not such a striking example of how they have been slumbering through ages of intellectual activity, listlessly disregarding the enginery of modern thought, and never dreaming of applying its lessons to the improvement of logic.[12] It is easy to show that the doctrine that familiar use and abstract distinctness make the perfection of apprehension has its only true place in philosophies which have long been extinct; and it is now time to formulate the method of attaining to a more perfect clearness of thought, such as we see and admire in the thinkers of our own time.

When Descartes set about the reconstruction of philosophy, his first step was to (theoretically) permit scepticism and to discard the practice of the schoolmen of looking to authority as the ultimate source of truth. That done, he sought a more natural fountain of true principles, and professed to find it in the human mind; thus passing, in the directest way, from the method of authority to that of a priority, as described in my first paper.[13] Self-consciousness was to furnish us with our fundamental truths, and to decide what was agreeable to reason. But since, evidently, not all ideas are true, he was led to note, as the first condition of infallibility, that they must be clear. The distinction between an idea *seeming* clear and really being so, never occurred to him. Trusting to introspection, as he did, even for a knowledge of external things, why should he question its testimony in respect to the contents of our own minds? But then, I suppose, seeing men, who seemed to be quite clear and positive, holding opposite opinions upon fundamental principles, he was further led to say that clearness of ideas is not sufficient, but that they need also to be distinct, *i.e.*, to have nothing unclear about them.[14] What he probably meant by this (for he did not explain himself with precision) was, that they must sustain the test of dialectical examination; that they must not only seem clear at the outset, but that discussion must never be able to bring to light points of obscurity connected with them.

Such was the distinction of Descartes, and one sees that it was precisely on the level of his philosophy. It was somewhat developed by Leibnitz.[15] This great and singular genius was as remarkable for what he failed to see as for what he saw. That a piece of mechanism could not do work perpetually without being fed with power in some form, was a thing perfectly apparent to him; yet he did not understand that the machinery of the mind can only transform knowledge, but never originate it, unless it be fed with facts of observation.[16] He thus missed the most essential point of the Cartesian philosophy, which is, that to accept propositions which seem perfectly evident to us is a thing which, whether it be logical or illogical, we cannot help doing. Instead of regarding the matter in this way, he sought to reduce the first principles of science to formulas which cannot be denied without self-contradiction, and was apparently unaware of the great difference between his position and that of Descartes. So he reverted to the old formalities of logic, and, above all, abstract definitions played a great part in his philosophy. It was quite natural, therefore, that on observing that the method of Descartes labored under the difficulty that we may seem to ourselves to have clear apprehensions of ideas which in truth are very hazy, no better remedy occurred to him than to require an abstract definition of every important term. Accordingly, in adopting the distinction of *clear* and *distinct* notions, he described the latter quality as the clear apprehension of everything contained in the definition; and the books have ever since copied his words. There is no danger that his chimerical scheme will ever again be overvalued. Nothing new can ever be learned by analyzing definitions. Nevertheless, our existing beliefs can be set in order by this process, and order is an essential element of intellectual economy, as of every other. It may be acknowledged, therefore, that the books are right in making familiarity with a notion the first step towards clearness of apprehension, and the defining of it the second. But in omitting all mention of any higher perspicuity of thought, they simply mirror a philosophy which was exploded a hundred years ago. That much-admired "ornament of logic"—the doctrine of clearness and distinctness—may be pretty enough, but it is high time to relegate to our cabinet of curiosities the antique *bijou*, and to wear about us something better adapted to modern uses.

The very first lesson that we have a right to demand that logic teach us is, how to make our ideas clear; and a most important one it is, depreciated only by minds who stand in need of it. To know what we think, to be masters of our own meaning, will make a solid foundation for great and weighty thought. It is most easily learned by those whose ideas are meagre and restricted; and far happier they than such as wallow helplessly in a rich mud of conceptions. A nation, it is true, may, in the course of generations, overcome the disadvantage of an excessive wealth of language and its natural concomitant, a vast, unfathomable deep of ideas. We may see it in history, slowly perfecting its literary forms, sloughing at length its metaphysics, and, by virtue of the untirable patience which is often a compensation, attaining great excellence in every branch of mental acquirement. The page of history is not yet unrolled which is to tell us whether such a people will or will not in the long run prevail over one whose ideas (like the words of their language) are few, but which possesses a wonderful mastery over those which it has. For an individual, however, there can be no question that a few clear ideas are worth more than many confused ones. A young man would hardly be persuaded to sacrifice the greater part of his thoughts to save the rest; and the muddled head is the least apt to see the necessity of such a sacrifice. Him we can usually only commiserate, as a person with a congenital defect. Time will help him, but intellectual maturity with regard to clearness comes rather late, an unfortunate arrangement of Nature, inasmuch as clearness is of less use to a man settled in life, whose errors have in great measure had their effect, than it would be to one whose path lies before him. It is terrible to see how a single unclear idea, a single formula without meaning, lurking in a young man's head, will sometimes act like an obstruction of inert matter in an artery, hindering the nutrition of the brain, and condemning its victim to pine away in the fullness of his intellectual vigor and in the midst of intellectual plenty. Many a man has cherished for years as his hobby some vague shadow of an idea, too meaningless to be positively false; he has, nevertheless, passionately loved it, has made it his companion by day and by night, and has given to it his strength and his life, leaving all other occupations for its sake, and in short has lived with it and for it, until it has become, as it were, flesh of his flesh and bone of his bone; and then he has waked up some bright morning to find it gone, clean vanished away like the beautiful Melusina of the fable, and the essence of his life gone with it.[17] I have myself known such a man; and who can tell how many histories of circle-squarers, metaphysicians, astrologers, and what not, may not be told in the old German story?[18]

II

The principles set forth in the first of these papers lead, at once, to a method of reaching a clearness of thought of a far higher grade than the "distinctness" of the logicians. We have there found that the action of thought is excited by the irritation of doubt, and ceases when belief is attained; so that the production of belief is the sole function of thought. All these words, however, are too strong for my purpose. It is as if I had described the phenomena as they appear under a mental microscope. Doubt and Belief, as the words are commonly employed, relate to religious or other grave discussions. But here I use them to designate the starting of any question, no matter how small or how great, and the resolution of it. If, for instance, in a horse-car, I pull out my purse and find a five-cent nickel and five coppers, I decide, while my hand is going to the purse, in which way I will pay my fare. To call such a question Doubt, and my decision Belief, is certainly to use words very disproportionate to the occasion. To speak of such a doubt as causing an irritation which needs to be appeased, suggests a temper which is uncomfortable to the verge of insanity. Yet, looking at the matter minutely, it must be admitted that, if there is the least hesitation as to whether I shall pay the five coppers or the nickel (as there will be sure to be, unless I act from some previously contracted habit in the matter), though irritation is too strong a word, yet I am excited to such small mental activity as may be necessary to deciding how I shall act. Most frequently doubts arise from some indecision, however momentary, in our action. Sometimes it is not so. I have, for example, to wait in a railway-station, and to pass the time I read the advertisements on the walls, I compare the advantages of different trains and different routes which I never expect to take, merely fancying myself to be in a state of hesitancy, because I am bored with having nothing to trouble me. Feigned hesitancy, whether feigned for mere amusement or with a lofty purpose, plays a great part in the production of scientific inquiry. However the doubt may originate, it stimulates the mind to an activity which may be slight or energetic, calm or turbulent. Images pass rapidly through consciousness, one incessantly melting into another, until at last, when all is over—it may be in a fraction of a second, in an hour, or after long years—we find ourselves decided as to how we should act under such circumstances as those which occasioned our hesitation. In other words, we have attained belief.

In this process we observe two sorts of elements of consciousness, the distinction between which may best be made clear by means of an illustration. In a piece of music there are the separate notes, and there is the air. A single tone may be prolonged for an hour or a day, and it exists as perfectly in each second of that time as in the whole taken together; so that, as long as it is sounding, it might be present to a sense from which everything in the past was as completely absent as the future itself. But it is different with the air, the performance of which occupies a certain time, during the portions of which only portions of it are played. It consists in an orderliness in the succession of sounds which strike the ear at different times; and to perceive it there must be some continuity of consciousness which makes the events of a lapse of time present to us. We certainly only perceive the air by hearing the separate notes; yet we cannot be said to directly hear it, for we hear only what is present at the instant, and an orderliness of succession cannot exist in an instant. These two sorts of object, what we are *immediately* conscious of and what we are *mediately* conscious of, are found in all consciousness. Some elements (the sensations) are completely present at every instant so long as they last, while others (like thought) are actions having beginning, middle, and end, and consist in a congruence in the succession of sensations which flow through the mind.[19] They cannot be immediately present to us, but must cover some portion of the past or future. Thought is a thread of melody running through the succession of our sensations.

We may add that just as a piece of music may be written in parts, each part having its own air, so various systems of relationship of succession subsist together between the same sensations. These different systems are distinguished by having different motives, ideas, or functions. Thought is only one such system, for its sole motive, idea, and function, is to produce belief, and whatever does not concern that purpose belongs to some other system of relations. The action of thinking may incidentally have other results; it may serve to amuse us, for example, and among *dilletanti* it is not rare to find those who have so perverted thought to the purposes of pleasure that it seems to vex them to think that the questions upon which they delight to exercise it may ever get finally settled; and a positive discovery which takes a favorite subject out of the arena of literary debate is met with ill-concealed dislike. This disposition is the very debauchery of thought. But the soul and meaning of thought abstracted from the other elements which accompany it, though it may be voluntarily thwarted, can never be made to direct itself toward anything but the production of belief. Thought in action has for its only possible motive the attainment of thought at rest; and whatever does not refer to belief is no part of the thought itself.

And what, then, is belief? It is the demicadence which closes a musical phrase in the symphony of our intellectual life. We have seen that it has just three properties: First, it is something that we are aware of;[20] second, it appeases the irritation of doubt; and, third it involves the establishment in our nature of a rule of action, or, say, for short, a *habit*. As it appeases the irritation of doubt, which is the motive for thinking, thought relaxes, and comes to rest for a moment when belief is reached. But, since belief is a rule for action, the application of which involves further doubt and further thought, at the same time that it is a stopping-place, it is also a new starting-place for thought. That is why I have permitted myself to call it thought at rest, although thought is essentially an action. The *final* upshot of thinking is the exercise of volition, and of this thought no longer forms a part; but belief is only a stadium of mental action, an effect upon our nature due to thought, which will influence future thinking.

The essence of belief is the establishment of a habit, and different beliefs are distinguished by the different modes of action to which they give rise. If beliefs do not differ in this respect, if they appease the same doubt by producing the same rule of action, then no mere differences in the manner of consciousness of them can make them different beliefs, any more than playing a tune in different keys is playing different tunes. Imaginary distinctions are often drawn between beliefs which differ only in their mode of expression;—the wrangling which ensues is real enough, however. To believe that any objects are arranged as in Fig. 1, and to believe that they are arranged (as) in Fig. 2, are one and the same belief; yet it is conceivable that a man should assert one proposition and deny the other.[21] Such false distinctions do as much harm as the confusion of beliefs really different, and are among the pitfalls of which we ought

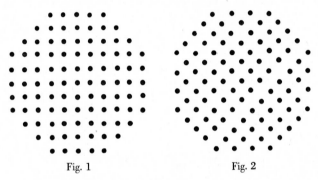

Fig. 1   Fig. 2

constantly to be aware, especially when we are upon metaphysica' ground. One singular deception of this sort, which often occurs, is to mistake the sensation produced by our own unclearness of thought for a character of the object we are thinking. Instead of perceiving that the obscurity is purely subjective, we fancy that we contemplate a quality of the object which is essentially mysterious; and if our conception be afterward presented to us in a clear form we do not recognize it as the same, owing to the absence of the feeling of unintelligibility. So long as this deception lasts, it obviously puts an impassable barrier in the way of perspicuous thinking; so that it equally interests the opponents of rational thought to perpetuate it, and its adherents to guard against it.

Another such deception is to mistake a mere difference in the grammatical construction of two words for a distinction between the ideas they express. In this pedantic age, when the general mob of writers attend so much more to words than to things, this error is common enough. When I just said that thought is an *action*, and that it consists in a *relation*, although a person performs an action but not a relation, which can only be the result of an action, yet there was no inconsistency in what I said, but only a grammatical vagueness.

From all these sophisms we shall be perfectly safe so long as we reflect that the whole function of thought is to produce habits of action; and that whatever there is connected with a thought, but irrelevant to its purpose, is accretion to it, but no part of it. If there be a unity among our sensations which has no reference to how we shall act on a given occasion, as when we listen to a piece of music, why, we do not call that thinking. To develop its meaning, we have, therefore, simply to determine what habits it produces, for what a thing means is simply what habits it involves. Now, the identity of a habit depends on how it might lead us to act, not merely under such circumstances as are likely to arise, but under such as might possibly occur, no matter how improbable they may be. What the habit is depends on *when* and *how* it causes us to act. As for the *when*, every stimulus to action is derived from perception; as for the *how*, every purpose of action is to produce some sensible result. Thus, we come down to what is tangible and conceivably practical, as the root of every real distinction of thought, no matter how subtle it may be; and there is no distinction of meaning so fine as to consist in anything but a possible difference of practice.

To see what this principle leads to, consider in the light of it such a doctrine as that of transubstantiation. The Protestant churches generally hold that the elements of the sacrament are flesh and blood only in a tropical sense; they nourish our souls as meat and the juice of it would our bodies.[22] But the Catholics maintain that they are literally just that; although they possess all the sensible qualities of wafer-cakes and diluted wine. But we can have no conception of wine except what may enter into a belief, either—

1. That this, that, or the other is wine; or,
2. That wine possesses certain properties.

Such beliefs are nothing but self-notifications that we should, upon occasion, act in regard to such things as we believe to be wine according to the qualities which we believe wine to possess. The occasion of such an action would be some sensible perception, the motive of it to produce some sensible result. Thus our action has exclusive reference to what affects the senses, our habit has the same bearing as our action, our belief the same as our habit, our conception the same as our belief; and we can consequently mean nothing by wine but what has certain effects, direct or indirect, upon our senses; and to talk of something as having all the sensible characters of wine, yet being in reality blood, is senseless jargon. Now, it is not my object to pursue the theological question; and having used it as a logical example I drop it, without caring to anticipate the theologian's reply. I only desire to point out how impossible it is that we should have an idea in our minds which relates to anything but conceived sensible effects of things. Our idea of anything *is* our idea of its sensible effects; and if we fancy that we have any other we deceive ourselves, and mistake a mere sensation accompanying the thought for a part of the thought itself. It is absurd to say that thought has any meaning unrelated to its only function. It is foolish for Catholics and Protestants to fancy themselves in disagreement about the elements of the sacrament, if they agree in regard to all their sensible effects, here or hereafter.

It appears, then, that the rule for attaining the third grade of clearness of apprehension is as follows: Consider what effects, which might conceivably have practical bearings, we conceive the object of our conception to have.[23] Then, our conception of these effects is the whole of our conception of the object.

III

Let us illustrate this rule by some examples; and, to begin with the simplest one possible, let us ask what we mean by calling a thing *hard*. Evidently that it will not be scratched by many other substances. The whole conception of this quality, as of every other, lies in its conceived effects. There is absolutely no difference between a hard thing and a soft thing so long as they are not brought to the test. Suppose, then, that a diamond could be crystallized in the midst of a cushion of soft cotton, and should remain there until it was finally burned up. Would it be false to say that that diamond was soft? This seems a foolish question, and would be so, in fact, except in the realm of logic. There such questions are often of the greatest utility as serving to bring logical principles into sharper relief than real discussions ever could. In studying logic we must not put them aside with hasty answers, but must consider them with attentive care, in order to make out the principles involved. We may, in the present case, modify our question, and ask what prevents us from saying that all hard bodies remain perfectly soft until they are touched, when their hardness increases with the pressure until they are scratched. Reflection will show that the reply is this: there would be no *falsity* in such modes of speech. They would involve a modification of our present usage of speech with regard to the words hard and soft, but not of their meanings. For they represent no fact to be different from what it is; only they involve arrangements of facts which would be exceedingly maladroit. This leads us to remark that the question of what would occur under circumstances which do not actually arise is not a question of fact, but only of the most perspicuous arrangement of them. For example, the question of free-will and fate in its simplest form, stripped of verbiage, is something like this: I have done something of which I am ashamed; could I, by an effort of the will, have resisted the temptation, and done otherwise? The philosophical reply is, that this is not a question of fact, but only of the arrangement of facts. Arranging them so as to exhibit what is particularly pertinent to my question— namely, that I ought to blame myself for having done wrong—it is perfectly true to say that, if I had willed to do otherwise than I did, I sho have done otherwise. On the other hand, arranging the fa⌐ so as to exhibit another important consideration, it is equally true that, when a temptation has once been allowed to work, it will, if it has a certain force, produce its effect, let me struggle how I may. There is no objection to a contradiction in what would result from a false supposition. The *reductio ad absurdum* consists in showing that contradictory results would follow from a hypothesis which is consequently judged to be false. Many questions are involved in the free-will discussion, and I am far from desiring to say that both sides are equally right. On the contrary, I am of opinion that one side denies important facts, and that the other does not. But what I do say is, that the above single question was the origin of the whole doubt; that, had it not been for this question, the controversy would never have arisen; and that this question is perfectly solved in the manner which I have indicated.

C From the COLLECTED PAPERS OF CHARLES SANDERS PEIRCE

Upon this first, and in one sense this sole, rule of reason, that in order to learn you must desire to learn, and in so desiring not be satisfied with what you already incline to think, there follows one corollary which itself deserves to be inscribed upon every wall of the city of philosophy:

Do not block the way of inquiry.

Although it is better to be methodical in our investigations, and to consider the economics of research, yet there is no positive sin against logic in *trying* any theory which may come into our heads, so long as it is adopted in such a sense as to permit the investigation to go on unimpeded and undiscouraged. On the other hand, to set up a philosophy which barricades the road of further advance toward the truth is the one unpardonable offence in reasoning, as it is also the one to which metaphysicians have in all ages shown themselves the most addicted.

Let me call your attention to four familiar shapes in which this venomous error assails our knowledge.

The first is the shape of the absolute assertion. That we can be sure of nothing in science is an ancient truth. The Academy taught it. Yet science has been infested with overconfident assertion, especially on the part of the third-rate and fourth-rate men, who have been more concerned with teaching than with learning, at all times. No doubt some of the geometries still teach as a self-evident truth the proposition that if two straight lines in one plane meet a third straight line so as to make the sum of the internal angles on the one side less than two right angles those two lines will meet on that side if sufficiently prolonged. Euclid, whose logic was more careful, only reckoned this proposition as a Postulate, or arbitrary Hypothesis. Yet even he places among his axioms the proposition that a part is less than its whole, and falls into several conflicts with our most modern geometry in consequence. But why need we stop to consider cases where some subtilty of thought is required to see that the assertion is not warranted when every book which applies philosophy to the conduct of life lays down as positive certainty propositions which it is quite as easy to doubt as to believe?

The second bar which philosophers often set up across the roadway of inquiry lies in maintaining that this, that, and the other never can be known. When Auguste Comte was pressed to specify any matter of positive fact to the knowledge of which no man could by any possibility attain, he instanced the knowledge of the chemical composition of the fixed stars; and you may see his answer set down in the *Philosophie Positive*.[24] But the ink was scarcely dry upon the printed page before the spectroscope was discovered and that which he had deemed absolutely unknowable was well on the way of getting ascertained. It is easy enough to mention a question the answer to which is not known to me today. But to aver that that answer will not be known tomorrow is somewhat risky; for oftentimes it is precisely the least expected truth which is turned up under the plowshare of research. And when it comes to positive assertion that the truth will never be found out, that, in the light of the history of our time, seems to me more hazardous than the venture of Andrée.[25]

The third philosophical stratagem for cutting off inquiry consists in maintaining that this, that, or the other element of science is basic, ultimate, independent of aught else, and utterly inexplicable—not so much from any defect in our knowing as because there is nothing beneath it to know. The only type of reasoning by which such a conclusion could possibly be reached is *retroduction*. Now nothing justifies a retroductive inference except its explanation of the facts. It is, however, no explanation at all of a fact to pronounce it *inexplicable*. That, therefore, is a conclusion which no reasoning can ever justify or excuse.

The last philosophical obstacle to the advance of knowledge which I intend to mention is the holding that this or that law or truth has found its last and perfect formulation—and especially that the ordinary and usual course of nature can never be broken through. "Stones do not fall from heaven," said Laplace, although they have been falling upon uninhabited ground every day from the earliest times.[26] But there is no kind of inference which can lend the slightest probability to any such absolute denial of an unusual phenomenon.

All positive reasoning is of the nature of judging the proportion of something in a whole collection by the proportion found in a sample. Accordingly, there are three things to which we can never hope to attain by reasoning, namely, absolute certainty, absolute exactitude, absolute universality. We cannot be absolutely certain that our conclusions are even approximately true; for the sample may be utterly unlike the unsampled part of the collection. We cannot pretend to be even probably exact; because the sample consists of but a finite number of instances and only admits special values of the proportion sought. Finally, even if we could ascertain with absolute certainty and exactness that the ratio of sinful men to all men was as 1 to 1; still among the infinite generations of men there would be room for any finite number of sinless men without violating the proportion.[27] The same is the case with a seven legged calf.

Now if exactitude, certitude, and universality are not to be attained by reasoning, there is certainly no other means by which they can be reached.

Somebody will suggest *revelation*. There are scientists and people influenced by science who laugh at revelation; and certainly science has taught us to look at testimony in such a light that the whole theological doctrine of the "Evidences" seems pretty weak.[28] However, I do not think it is philosophical to reject the possibility of a revelation. Still, granting that, I declare as a logician that revealed truths—that is, truths which have nothing in their favour but revelations made to a few individuals—constitute by far the most uncertain class of truths there are. There is here no question of universality; for revelation is itself sporadic and miraculous. There is no question of mathematical exactitude; for no revelation makes any pretension to that character. But it does pretend to be *certain;* and against that there are three conclusive objections. First, we never can be absolutely certain that any given deliverance really is inspired; for that can only be established by reasoning. We cannot even prove it with any very high degree of probability. Second, even if it is inspired, we cannot be sure, or nearly sure, that the statement is true. We know that one of the commandments was in one of the Bibles printed without a *not* in it. All inspired matter has been subject to human distortion or colouring. Besides we cannot penetrate the counsels of the most High, or lay down anything as a principle that would govern his conduct. We do not know his inscrutable purposes, nor can we comprehend his plans. We cannot tell but he might see fit to inspire his servants with errors. In the third place, a truth which rests on the authority of inspiration only is of a somewhat incomprehensible nature; and we can never be sure that we rightly comprehend it. As there is no way of evading these difficulties, I say that revelation, far from affording us any certainty, gives results less certain than other sources of information. This would be so even if revelation were much plainer than it is.

But, it will be said, you forget the laws which are known to us *a priori*, the axioms of geometry, the principles of logic, the maxims of *causality*, and the like. Those are absolutely certain, without exception and exact. To this I reply that it seems to me there is the most positive historic proof that innate truths are particularly uncertain and mixed up with error, and therefore *a fortiori* not without exception.[29] This historical proof is, of course, not infallible; but it is very strong. Therefore, I ask *how do you know* that *a priori* truth is certain, exceptionless, and exact? You cannot know it by *reasoning*. For that would be subject to uncertainty and inexactitude. Then, it must amount to this that you know it *a priori*; that is, you take *a priori* judgments at their own valuation, without criticism or credentials. That is barring the gate of inquiry.

Ah! but it will be said, you forget direct experience. Direct experience is neither certain nor uncertain, because it affirms nothing—it just *is*. There are delusions, hallucinations, dreams. But there is no mistake that such things really do appear, and direct experience means simply the appearance. It involves no error, because it testifies to nothing but its own appearance. For the same reason, it affords no certainty. It is not *exact*, because it leaves much vague; though it is not *inexact* either; that is, it has no false exactitude.

All this is true of direct experience at its first presentation. But when it comes up to be criticized it is past, itself, and is represented by *memory*. Now the deceptions and inexactitude of memory are proverbial.

. . . On the whole, then, we cannot in any way reach perfect certitude nor exactitude. We never can be absolutely sure of anything, nor can we with any probability ascertain the exact value of any measure or general ratio.

This is my conclusion, after many years study of the logic of science; and it is the conclusion which others, of very different cast of mind, have come to, likewise. I believe I may say there is no tenable opinion regarding human knowledge which does not legitimately lead to this corollary. Certainly there is nothing new in it; and many of the greatest minds of all time have held it for true.

Indeed, most everybody will admit it until he begins to see what is involved in the admission—and then most people will draw back. It will not be admitted by persons utterly incapable of philosophical reflection. It will not be fully admitted by masterful minds developed exclusively in the direction of action and accustomed to claim practical infallibility in matters of business. These men will admit the incurable fallibility of all opinions readily enough; only, they will always make exception of their own. The doctrine of fallibilism will also be denied by those who fear its consequences for science, for religion, and for morality. But I will take leave to say to these highly conservative gentlemen that however competent they may be to direct the affairs of a church or other corporation, they had better not try to manage science in that way. Conservatism—in the sense of a dread of consequences—is altogether out of place in science —which has on the contrary always been forwarded by radicals and radicalism, in the sense of the eagerness to carry consequences to their extremes. Not the radicalism that is cocksure, however, but the radicalism *that tries experiments*. Indeed, it is precisely among men animated by the spirit of science that the doctrine of fallibilism will find supporters.

Still, even such a man as that may well ask whether I propose to say that it is not quite certain that twice two are four—and that it is even not probably quite exact! But it would be quite misunderstanding the doctrine of fallibilism to suppose that it means that twice two is probably not exactly four. As I have already remarked, it is not my purpose to doubt that people can usually *count* with accuracy. Nor does fallibilism say that men cannot attain a sure knowledge of the creations of their own minds. It neither affirms nor denies that. It only says that people cannot attain absolute certainty concerning questions of fact. Numbers are merely a system of names devised by men for the purpose of counting. It is a matter of real fact to say that in a certain room there are two persons. It is a matter of fact to say that each person has two eyes. It is a matter of fact to say that there are four eyes in the room. But to say that *if* there are two persons and each person has two eyes there *will* be four eyes is not a statement of fact, but a statement about the system of numbers which is our own creation.

NOTES

1   In order to assess the claim made in the text chapters that Kant's synthesis between traditional empiricism and rationalism is primarily a rationalistic synthesis, and that Peirce's synthesis is empiricistic, this paragraph can be compared with similar remarks made by Kant. Where Kant said that knowledge *begins* with experience, Peirce says that knowledge *rests upon* experience. The difference is not unimportant. From the rest of this paragraph, we can see that Peirce is sensitive to the interplay of sense impressions and mental operations. But where Kant makes certain mental operations antecedent to *meaningful* experience, Peirce takes mental operations to *add* to what is observed or to judge the significance of what is observed. This allows observations to have a distinct character of their own, in some sense independent of our conceptual schemes, in that we cannot control what we observe by mental operations (although we can look to see what happens in some circumstances that particularly interest us). Kant and Peirce differ, not as Descartes and Hume, but in a much more subtle way that is worth thinking about.

2   That is, we should first ask ourselves what the consequences of adopting it are.

3   This remark conceals serious problems. From Peirce's immediately preceding remarks, one might suppose that a hypothesis which had no practical consequences could not be considered. To say that a hypothesis cannot be tested is not quite the same thing as to say that it has no practical consequences. Some hypotheses might be confirmed by any observation, and others might be so unclear that we could not determine what observations would confirm them. Two plausible broad rules of acceptance and rejection of hypotheses are possible. On the one hand, we might decide that we could accept only hypotheses that have not decisively *failed* an experimental test. On the other hand, we might decide to accept only those hypotheses that have been confirmed by some experiment which, if quite different results had been obtained, would have led to the rejection (by disconfirmation) of the hypothesis. The significance of the difference between these two rules is that all Kant's metaphysical hypotheses (such as the existence of God) would be *rejected* by the second rule

but accepted by the first rule. (Why?) Peirce, as well as other early pragmatists, wanted to accept the hypothesis of the existence of God, and hence he implicitly used a rule of acceptance more like the first rule just described. Later empiricists, who considered themselves more hardheaded (Peirce might argue that they were), wanted to reject all hypotheses that were not confirmed by an *experimentum crucis*, that is, an experimental test whose results would either disconfirm or strongly confirm the hypothesis for which it was designed. Many contemporary empiricists, wanting to accept some, but not all, of the hypotheses which are compatible with past experiment but which have not survived an *experimentum crucis* (there may not be one which can be readily performed), have tried to find some compromise rule between the two proposed above. The existence of God, construed as a hypothesis, would be taken by many theologians as having no *experimentum crucis* (It is compatible with any observation.), while other theologians have held that the *experimentum crucis* is to be performed after death, which is an example of an experiment that is not readily performed. Peirce restricts himself in the following passages to hypotheses for which a convenient *experimentum crucis* is available. It might also be noticed that rejection and acceptance of hypotheses is not an all-or-nothing operation for Peirce, since some are strongly held beliefs and others are only opinions or hunches. This calls for some complication of any extensive treatment of the issues raised in this footnote.

4   Van't Hoff was a contemporary of Peirce who first proposed some important generalizations about the laws of chemical solutions. His work is reviewed in most moderately technical surveys of chemical theory. The interesting point here is that van't Hoff's generalizations are inferences of the kind called *inductions* by many people and discussed earlier in the third chapter on Hume. Van't Hoff argued that because certain chemicals in solution had a certain property, all chemicals capable of being dissolved in the same circumstances would also exhibit this property. Because an inference of this sort is commonly called an induction, it is important to notice that Peirce calls it an abduction, reserving the use of *induction* for another purpose.

5   Unfortunately, Peirce does not discuss how one might legitimately prefer one hypothesis over another by abduction, where both hypotheses explain the facts.

6   There are some hidden problems in Peirce's example. One question is the formulation of the hypothesis as a *tendency*. It would be compatible with a tendency that the proportion of births in the populations be the same in any given census; consequently the *must* in the last sentence is too strong. (Anyone annoyed with the social implications of the example may substitute some other hypothesis about relative ratios in two populations.) All of these objections are saved by Peirce's formulation of an induction as essentially involving the hypothesis that random samples of a population will exhibit about the same statistics as the whole population. The difficulties in understanding what is meant by *random* and 'about the same' tend to make the formulation trivial. (Why?)

7   Compare this remark with footnote 5. Does the notion of economy solve the problem?

8   No exposition of Peirce's extended example from astronomy will be given

here. The interested reader may consult Norwood Russell Hanson's *Patterns of Discovery*, Cambridge, 1958 for a discussion of Kepler's reasoning from the standpoint of the philosophy of science. John Stuart Mill was an empiricist who lived after Hume, and who attempted a kind of total empiricism which made even mathematical statements empiricistic. What Peirce's example illustrates is what should be known independently of the example, that what Peirce calls abductive reasoning is an important aspect of scientific theorizing.

9   The *il lume naturale* is an expression equivalent to Descartes's *natural light*. See footnote 22 to the Descartes reading.

10   It is interesting to speculate on the relationship between simplicity, as it is discussed here, and the economy mentioned earlier (see footnote 7). Simplicity has always been cited since Copernicus as a criterion by which hypotheses of equal explanatory power can be discriminated. See the remarks on simplicity in Nelson Goodman's *The Structure of Appearance*, Cambridge, 1951 for clarification of a way in which economy and simplicity can be usefully distinguished.

11   The reader who does not think of Descartes at this point may turn to page 1 and start over.

12   This passage marks Peirce's correct observation that the philosophical methodology of his time was entirely inadequate to scientific inquiry.

13   The first paper referred to is one called "The Fixation of Belief," which was published before "How to Make Our Ideas Clear" in the *Popular Science Monthly* of 1878.

14   Several passages in this essay suggest that Peirce felt that a separate criterion for distinctness was unnecessary. Further, his own contribution is directed solely to the problem of making our ideas clear. Where he speaks of distinctness, as here, he either reduces distinctness to clearness, or *conjectures* what distinctness might mean. Clearly Peirce felt that his single rule for clearness was a considerable gain in simplicity for scientific inquiry, as well as in fruitfulness, by comparison to the older Cartesian doctrine of clearness *and* distinctness.

15   Leibnitz was a rationalistic philosopher who lived shortly after Descartes.

16   Leibnitz knew that a perpetual motion machine was impossible, because a moving machine requires work to be performed in order to sustain its motion, and no infinite source of energy to enable such continual work to be performed is available. Peirce suggests an analogy between a perpetual motion machine and the mind, which he argues cannot work perpetually without being fed information from the outside in the form of facts.

17   Melusina was the principal character of a story in which she was condemned to turn into a serpent every Saturday (for the day) from the waist down. She married a man named Raymond under the condition that he would not visit her on Saturday. When he broke this promise, Melusina disappeared.

18   A circle-squarer is someone who believes that he can, with ruler and compass (more properly, straightedge and compass, since no length can be measured under the stipulations of the problem), construct a square equal in area to an arbitrary circle. This problem, a live issue in Greek geometry, is now known to be impossible of solution, a fact which can be proved in an appropriate

algebraic system. In spite of this, many persons still propose solutions to the problem! A history of some of these attempts is found in Augustus DeMorgan's *Budget of Paradoxes.*

19   Whether sensations are completely present at every instant so long as they last raises the intriguing question of whether or not there is an instant at which they begin and an instant at which they end. Similar questions may be raised with respect to thought.

20   Are there unconscious beliefs? We must be aware of belief as it appeases the irritation of doubt, on Peirce's view. But a habit established by belief may be performed unconsciously until it breaks down in the face of some conflicting fact.

21   These two arrangements (Notice that Peirce takes the belief that the dots are arranged in such and such a way as his subject.) are similar, except for a rotation about their center. Any human purpose for which the one arrangement is suitable is also a purpose for which the other is suitable, *as long as they may both be freely manipulated.* This is Peirce's point, in that an apparent difference may be no real difference. Still, although Fig. 1 and Fig. 2 are identical except for their orientation, their orientation makes them different for purposes of communication in English. Peirce's example needs some amplification to take care of the significance (in some cases) of arrangement.

22   *Tropical* may mean *figurative.*

23   Peirce distinguishes three grades of clearness which are not to be thought of as degrees of the same concept. The first grade of clearness of an idea is familiarity with it, and the second grade of clearness is a satisfactory definition of it. These grades had been discussed before Peirce. The third grade of clearness is the significance of an idea with respect to its real consequences, or nonabstract consequences. It might be noted that the first two grades need not enable us to know whether two ideas can be distinguished.

24   Auguste Comte was a philosopher who maintained that metaphysical speculation (in Kant's sense) should be avoided and knowledge limited to the definite results of science. The example shows that Comte did not fare very well in his anticipations of future scientific thought.

25   Andrée attempted to fly over the polar regions in a balloon in the late nineteenth century, but he did not make it. It was a hazardous venture.

26   The striking fact about this example is that Laplace was one of the great mathematical astronomers.

27   Compare these remarks with the discussion in footnote 6.

28   William Paley wrote a book called *View of the Evidences of Christianity* in which he tried to ground Christian doctrine on natural science. Many of his arguments appear invalid.

29   This proof is simply that history records that many statements thought at one time to represent innate truths have proved false or misleading.

INDEX

A priori, 200–203, 212n.
  and a posteriori judgments, Kant on,
    223–226, 233, 234, 237–243, 249
Abstraction, 113, 149–154, 172n., 173n.,
  195
Accidental predication, 65–68, 72, 73, 85,
  92, 94
Actuality, 58
Adventitious ideas, 130, 135n.
Allegory of the cave, 46–50, 52n., 53n.,
  135
Apprehension, synthesis of, 254, 260n.
Aristotle, 3, 5, 54–98, 101, 102, 111, 133n.,
    135, 139, 145, 218, 220, 228
  on accidental predication, 65–73, 85,
    92, 94
  on the categories, 63–65, 77, 89, 90,
    96n.
  definition of knowledge, 57–62
  the development of his thought, 74, 75
  on essential predication, 66–73, 84, 85
  form and matter in, 58, 60, 89, 90, 97n.,
    111
  on knowledge, 57–62, 71–73
  on metaphysics, 61
  substance in, 58, 64, 68, 70, 71, 77, 87,
    88, 98n.
  views on sense experience, 71–73
Association, 179–181, 189, 196
Attribute, 65, 66, 82, 91, 96n.
  commensurately universal, 84–87, 96n.

Beck, L. W., 232
Belief, in empiricism, 183, 189, 209

Belief (cont.), pragmatist's notion of, 266,
    268–271
  (See also Opinion)
Berkeley, 135, 137–174, 177, 178, 187,
    209, 210n., 221, 228
  on abstract ideas, 149–154, 164, 165,
    169–171
  dialogue form in, 155
  on ideas, 148–151, 169–171
  on knowledge, 150, 151, 168, 169
  matter in, 147–151, 161, 165–167,
    173n., 228
  mind in, 150, 151, 159, 164, 165, 168,
    171
  nominalism of, 152–154
  phenomenalism of, 148
  on popular theories of knowledge, 143–
    148
  substance in, 159
  views on sense experience, 166

Categorical statements, 59
Categories, in Aristotle, 63–65, 77, 89, 90,
    96n.
  in Kant, 228–230, 251–257
Causation, 51n., 58, 81, 85, 142, 224, 229,
    245
  Hume's account of, 179, 180, 183, 184,
    187–190, 196–198, 200–209, 211n.
Certainty, 2, 14, 15, 19, 24, 57, 61, 67,
    101, 102, 104, 121, 122, 128, 177,
    182, 191, 263, 266
  Descartes on, 101–105
City-states, 13, 14

301